NIGERIA'S SOLDI]

MAX SIOLLUN

Nigeria's Soldiers of Fortune

The Abacha and Obasanjo Years

HURST & COMPANY, LONDON

First published in the United Kingdom in 2019 by
C. Hurst & Co. (Publishers) Ltd.,
41 Great Russell Street, London, WC1B 3PL
© Max Siollun, 2019
All rights reserved.
Printed in the United Kingdom by Bell & Bain Ltd, Glasgow

The right of Max Siollun to be identified as the author of
this publication is asserted by him in accordance with the
Copyright, Designs and Patents Act, 1988.

A Cataloguing-in-Publication data record for this book
is available from the British Library.

ISBN: 9781787382022

This book is printed using paper from registered sustainable
and managed sources.

www.hurstpublishers.com

For Jesse Isaiah, John and Rhoda

CONTENTS

CONTENTS

DEDICATION

I have often been asked why I did not include a biography of myself in my previous books. My response has always been that my books are about Nigerian history, not me. I have also been asked what motivates me to write. I will answer that question here for the first time.

I am in the unique position of being older than my own father. My father lived and died in the service of his country. Over ten thousand mourners speaking many different languages and of different faiths attended his funeral (in an era before it became 'fashionable' to hold large funerals). There is no good death, but for a young father with no known illness and not one single grey hair on his head to go to work in the service of his country, and never return, is particularly soul-destroying. Only one person out of the thousands at his funeral did not weep. That was me. As an infant I was too young to understand that I was attending my own father's funeral.

My father's habit of constantly writing in his diaries with exemplary attention to detail ensured that his memories did not die with him. He taught me the value of recording memories in writing. He was a meticulous note-taker and wrote in his diaries daily. Not just names and dates, but also emotional events (finding out about the death of a parent), from the joyous (writing about the day he got married and the day I was born), to the mundane (complaining in his diary about his newspaper not being delivered one day!). I have spent days, nights and years reading those diaries. While perusing them I feel like I am conversing with him. Through them he has inspired me, told me his innermost thoughts, given me advice, and even revealed surprises he was planning for his family which we did not know about. When family members cannot properly recollect a past family event, I often go to one of his diaries to verify what happened.

DEDICATION

Those who knew my father often comment on our remarkable physical resemblance which borders on me being his clone. I inherited his physical features, gait, voice, handwriting, mannerisms, and even birthmarks. Some years ago, someone tried to mock my physical resemblance to my father by referring to me as his 'replacement'. The attempted insult did not upset me one bit. My father had a strong idealistic streak, so I felt it was an honour to be referred to as his replacement. When a close friend of my father was presented with a copy of my first book, his first words were 'like father, like son'. I must have grown three feet taller that day. To me, there could be no higher compliment than to be likened to my dad.

My mother was an unwitting catalyst in my journey to historical writing. She wept constantly for several years after my father died, and in her grief would often 'see' him sitting at his desk working as was his habit when he returned home from the office. Despite her tears and sorrow, she preserved my father's diaries, documents and books locked in a trunk—waiting for the time when I would be mature enough to make use of them.

In her grief, she took one my father's diaries and continued writing where he stopped. She wrote viscerally day after day, in red ink. Messages to her dead husband, messages about her hopes and aspirations that her son would one day become like him and complete all the things he could not. I had become so accustomed to seeing her cry that I would usually sit motionless and watch tears roll down her cheeks. Then one day I stood up, walked over to her, and used my little hands to wipe the tears away from her face. She was so moved that she resolved that day to stop crying (at least in my presence). I have never revealed to anyone a word of what my mum wrote in that diary. I will make one exception for a passage that particularly resonated with me: 'Snatched by the cold hands of death without saying goodbye to his loved ones ... I know it isn't your fault because you wouldn't have for anything left me forever with our son who is your carbon copy. I pray that God who knows best will accept your soul wherever you are and grant you eternal rest.' Amen.

ACRONYMS

APP	All People's Party
AD	Alliance for Democracy
ADC	Aide de camp
CSO	Chief Security Officer
DMI	Directorate of Military Intelligence
GOC	General Officer Commanding
HRVIC	Human Rights Violations Investigation Commission
INEC	Independent National Electoral Commission
ING	Interim National Government
MOSOP	Movement for the Survival of the Ogoni People
NADECO	National Democratic Coalition
NALICON	National Liberation Council of Nigeria
NDA	Nigerian Defence Academy
NDSC	National Defence and Security Council
NIA	National Intelligence Agency
NMTC	Nigerian Military Training College
NPN	National Party of Nigeria
NRC	National Republican Convention
NSA	National Security Adviser
NTA	Nigerian Television Authority
OPEC	Organisation of Petroleum Exporting Countries
PDM	People's Democratic Movement
PDP	People's Democratic Party
SDP	Social Democratic Party
SSS	State Security Service

PREFACE

'Everything we hear is an opinion, not a fact. Everything we see is a perspective, not the truth.'

Marcus Aurelius

This book is a sequel to my previous works, *Oil, Politics, and Violence: Nigeria's Military Coup Culture (1966–1976)* and *Soldiers of Fortune: A History of Nigeria (1983–1993)*. It commences where the latter ended.

Nigeria matters. Professor John Paden's description of Nigeria as 'the most complicated country in the world' is not hyperbole. With over 300 ethnic groups and over 500 different languages spoken within its borders, it is akin to a modern-day Tower of Babel. It also appears to be a giant laboratory where global social questions may be tested. Can multi-ethnic, multi-religious countries coexist and succeed? Can a formerly colonised country become a global superpower? The answers to these questions in Nigeria can provide hope or despair elsewhere.

Trying to understand Nigeria can be a byzantine experience. It is a place where neighbourhood gossip and rumours are often regarded as more reliable purveyors of history and news than books, newspapers and other forms of information. Nigeria's leaders have contributed to this state of affairs. Only three of Nigeria's eight living heads of state, current and former, have bothered to write a biography. Given its leaders' refusal or reluctance to record their stewardship, or to promote the study of history in schools, Nigeria's history has frequently consisted of urban legends, personal beliefs and rival conspiracy theories that vary depending on the ethnicity, geographic origin or religion of the narrator. The breathtaking diversity of people and opinion in Nigeria makes it nearly impossible for a linear narrative of any event to emerge. The constantly contested nature of Nigeria's history does allow us, however, to examine its historical figures without portraying them as one-dimensional King Arthur-style heroes or as inveterate villains.

Throughout the peaks and troughs, twists and turns of Nigeria's history, there has rarely been a national hero. Instead there has been an institutional force that at different points in time acted as a national architect, as a catalyst for disunity, and as an armed special interest group with its own political agenda. Arguably, Nigeria's military has altered and influenced the country's development and history more than any other institution. The breathtaking cliff-edge decade covered by this book has incorrectly been dismissed as a dark age for Nigeria. It should instead be recognised as a transformational, watershed era. Nigerians have often tried to simplify or bury their history in order to escape the ghost of its dark and painful chapters. As a result the country's history is replete with well-known 'facts' that turn out to be false. To discover that what we once thought was true is in fact false is not a mistake. It is the acquisition of knowledge.

I must extend sincere thanks to Dr Suleiman Wali, Major-Generals Rabiu Aliyu and Ishola Williams, Major Aloysius Akpuaka, Lieutenant Boniface Ikejiofor, Kayode Ogundamisi, and several others who spared time to share their memories with me. My gratitude also goes to Professor Murray Last, Alex Thurston and Atta Barkindo for kindly making time to review and comment on some draft sections from this book, and to Jacqueline Farris, Marlene Maritz, Terver Malu, Kunle Ajibade, and Olufemi Anjorin for providing photos for this book.

LIST OF ILLUSTRATIONS

16. Left to right: President Obasanjo, Fidel Castro, Lt-General Gusau, in Cuba in 1999. Credit: Gusau Institute.
17. At the U.S. Oval Office in 2001, far left: President Obasanjo, far right: U.S. President George W.Bush. Credit: Gusau Institute.
18. At the Nigerian presidential villa in 2002, right: Former U.S. President Bill Clinton, second from right: President Obasanjo, centre: Obasanjo's wife Stella. Credit: Gusau Institute.
19. Lt-General Oladipo Diya. Credit: Independent Communication Network Limited.
20. Left to right: Commodore Ebitu Ukiwe (seated in white uniform), Brigadier-General Gusau (signing register), and Major-General Ibrahim Babangida (standing to right in green uniform) in 1986. Credit: Gusau Institute.
21. Lt-General Jeremiah Useni. Credit: Independent Communication Network Limited.
22. Shehu Musa Yar'Adua and his family (1990): left to right: Tukur, Ibrahim, Asyia, Buhari, Shehu Yar'Adua, Murtala, Binta Yar'Adua, Maryam, Ahmed, Aminu. Credit: Shehu Musa Yar'Adua Foundation.
23. President Babangida (right) and Major-General Aliyu Mohammed Gusau in 1989. Credit: Gusau Institute.
24. Lt-General Sani Abacha (middle, wearing sunglasses)—Abeokuta, July 18, 1990. Credit: Gusau Institute.

Map 1: Nigeria's States and Geo-Political Zones

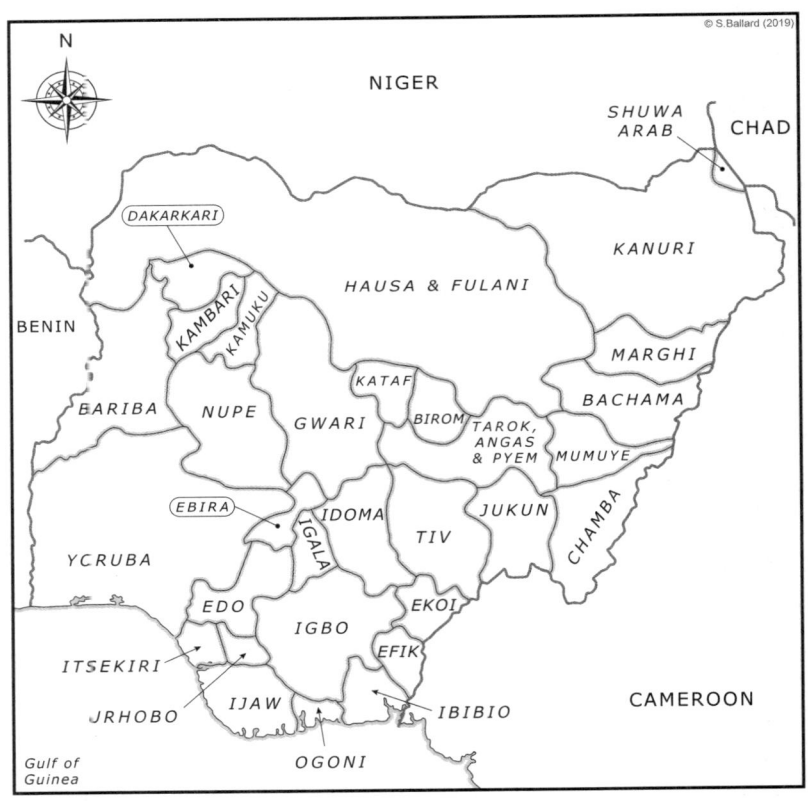

Map 2: Nigeria's Main Ethnic Groups

Map 3: Nigerian States That Have Adopted Sharia Law

CHILDREN OF ODUDUWA

Nigeria's military first seized power on January 15, 1966. The coup leaders described the takeover as a brief and temporary revolution to end corruption and ethnic rivalry. Over a quarter of a century and seven military governments later, the military was still in power. However, after 25 years of military rule, Nigeria was on the final lap of its marathon circular route back to democracy. Nigeria's military president, General Ibrahim Babangida, had promised to end his eight-year reign in power and return Nigeria to elected civilian rule on August 27, 1993. The return had already been postponed twice from 1990 to 1992, and yet again to June 12, 1993. By 1993 Nigeria was quasi-democratic and had elected governors and deputy governors in all 30 states, and elected senators and representatives in its two-chamber National Assembly. Only nine members of the government were serving military officers. The final outstanding step on Nigeria's road to democracy was to elect a civilian president. The question of who would become president reactivated old political networks and elevated the political fortunes of an entire region.

The Wild West

The Yoruba people of south-western Nigeria can simultaneously take credit for contributing to Nigeria's political sophistication and also the blame for acting as exporters of political instability. Political crises in Yorubaland have a habit of spilling over into other parts of the country. In 1962 the Action

Group party split when its leader, Obafemi Awolowo, tried to dismiss his deputy, Samuel Akintola. When the Western Region House of Assembly met to debate a motion of no confidence in Akintola, Yoruba members of parliament engaged in a chaotic fight inside the chambers during which they attacked each other with chairs, tables and even the speaker's ceremonial mace. Baton- and tear-gas-wielding police entered the chambers to restrain the fighting Assembly men. The political crisis in the Western Region descended into a state of near anarchy, which earned the region the nickname of the 'Wild West'. The federal government declared a state of emergency in the region in 1962, and deployed soldiers. These events, combined with Awolowo's imprisonment for treason, were contributory causes of two fratricidal military coups in 1966 during which Igbo and northern soldiers murdered each other. Somehow a political crisis in the south-west acted as a slippery slope that led to two military coups and a civil war in which the north and south-east were the main protagonists. In contrast, in 1993 the Yorubas were about to import a national political crisis, turning it into a local one, rather than exporting a regional crisis into other parts of the country.

Awoism

Since the 1960s, Yoruba politics have been dominated by a political orientation known as 'Awoism'. The phrase refers to the political philosophy of the late Yoruba political leader Obafemi Awolowo, who espoused policies he referred to as 'democratic socialism'. Its primary tenets were welfarism, free social services, and job creation. Awolowo loomed large over Yoruba politics for over forty years. He was an intensely intellectual man with great energy. In 1945 he co-founded and became the secretary of Egbe Omo Oduduwa (Society for the Descendants of Oduduwa). In Yoruba allegory, Oduduwa is the progenitor of Yoruba royal dynasties, and is revered as the father of the Yoruba people.

In 1951 Egbe Omo Oduduwa evolved into a political party called the Action Group, which was led by Awolowo. The Action Group developed the most clearly articulated and differentiated political ideology of any post-independence party in southern Nigeria. Awolowo had a ground-breaking term of office as the premier of Nigeria's Yoruba-dominated Western Region between 1955 and 1959. During this time, he introduced free education and free health care in his region, and established the first television station in Africa.

'My dear papa'

Awolowo exercised a hypnotic political hold on the Yoruba. Corruption allegations and a treason conviction for trying to overthrow the government in 1963 failed to taint his reputation among his people. Such tribulations instead enhanced his aura by giving him the appearance of a persecuted martyr. It was not only Yorubas that admired him. Some were sufficiently enamoured of him to commit murder for his sake. In January 1966, a group of Igbo army majors staged a violent coup, assassinated federal political leaders, and planned to break Awolowo out of prison and install him in the place of the men they killed. Leaders from other ethnic groups had the good sense to recognise how important he was to his people and also to publicly praise him. President Babangida marked Awolowo's 77th birthday in 1986 by sending him a flattering letter in which he greeted Awolowo with a salutation of 'My dear papa', and described him as 'the main issue in Nigerian politics during the last 35 years: The main political question has been whether you are with Chief Awolowo or against him.' However, one large prize eluded Awolowo throughout his illustrious life. Try as he might, he never became Nigeria's president. This failure to capture a position he felt he merited devastated him and his followers. When Awolowo died in 1987, prominent Nigerians queued up to eulogise him. The Igbo leader Chukwuemeka Ojukwu described him as 'the best president Nigeria never had'.

Awolowo's political ideology did not die with him. Many of those who benefited from his pioneering social welfare programmes continued to revere him. They referred to themselves as Omo Awolowo (Awolowo's children) or Awoists (disciples of Awolowo and his principles). Awolowo's ideas remain so deeply ingrained in the political consciousness of the Yoruba that being an Awoist is regarded by many Yorubas as the only legitimate apprenticeship prior to becoming a Yoruba politician on the national stage. Many Yoruba politicians mimicked Awolowo by wearing a red fez cap, round rimmed glasses, and even flashing the 'V' victory sign—all Awolowo's trademarks. Those who opposed Awolowo or who were not Awoists were often regarded as traitors to the Yoruba people. After the 1993 political crisis, the Awoists resuscitated the Yoruba cultural organisation Afenifere (literally, 'Society of those who love good for all') as a platform for Yoruba political solidarity. Afenifere was part political movement, part cultural organisation, and part personality cult. It started its meetings with incantations evoking Awolowo and his ideals. Its leadership and succession were gerontocratic. It was led by the veteran Awoist Michael Adekunle Ajasin, the former governor of Ondo State between 1979 and 1983, who was a member of Awolowo's Unity Party of Nigeria (UPN).

Throughout Nigeria's post-independence history the Yoruba had traditionally played second fiddle to whoever led Nigeria. After the military takeover in 1966, Yoruba military officers acted as deputies to the Igbo and northern military heads of state for the next decade (Brigadier Babafemi Ogundipe, Vice-Admiral Joseph Wey, Lt-General Olusegun Obasanjo). From 1979 until 1993, they were frozen out of leadership altogether. The Yoruba developed a tradition of being political 'silver medallists'.

Awolowo's death politically orphaned the Yoruba. He had served a dual role as the Yoruba leader and also as their political representative on the national stage. After his death Yoruba politics were dominated by two trends. Firstly, there was the search for another iconic, Moses-like leader to inherit Awolowo's dual role as ethnic leader and Yoruba representative on the federal stage. Secondly, a burning sense of injustice arose. The Yoruba developed a long persecution narrative that included events such as Awolowo's treason conviction, his failure to become president, and the military coup of 1983 which precluded the ruling National Party of Nigeria from fielding a southern presidential candidate in the next presidential election scheduled for 1987. Yorubas interpreted all these events as acts deliberately implemented to punish them, or block their aspirations for the political leadership of Nigeria which they deserved.

Babangida's promise to return Nigeria to democracy gave the Awoists a chance to once again challenge for political leadership and posthumously fulfil Awolowo's unfinished legacy. Three Awoists, Olu Falae, Ajibola 'Bola' Ige and Lateef Jakande, saw themselves as credible successors to Awolowo and potential presidential candidates. However, the Awoists' ambitions were dashed by the unpredictable machinations of Babangida's 'transition without end'[1] to democracy. In December 1992, Babangida banned 23 presidential aspirants (including the Awoists) from further participation in the transition programme. His decision virtually eliminated all Yoruba presidential candidates that met the Awoist criteria and allowed new contenders to emerge. One of them was his close friend Moshood Abiola.

Abiola was not an Awoist. Having kept out of politics since the early 1980s to consolidate his business empire, Abiola was enabled by the banning of so many presidential aspirants to emerge from the fringes to become a presidential candidate in 1993. Abiola was now the best hope for a Yoruba president.

However, the Awoists distrusted and disliked him. They regarded him as a traitor and northern stooge. He had refused to join Awolowo's political party even though he was Yoruba. Not only did he shun Awolowo's UPN party, but as a teenager he had instead joined firstly the rival National Council of Nigeria and the Cameroons (which was led by an Igbo), then later the National Party of Nigeria, which governed Nigeria between 1979 and 1983, and which many Yorubas viewed as the party of the northern establishment. The Abiola-owned *Concord Press* newspapers sometimes criticised Awolowo. To many Yorubas, criticism of Awolowo by a fellow Yoruba was the highest form of sacrilege. A Yoruba informed me that 'Abiola was one of the most hated individuals of the pro-democracy movement. He was seen as an imperialist who had been involved in plotting coups.'[2] Many Awoists never forgave Abiola for colluding with northerners to deny Awolowo the presidency. How could the Awoists support a man who had devoted much of his career to blocking the aspirations of their revered leader?

Abiola and Awolowo were not alike. Awolowo was trim, dapper and austere. In contrast, Abiola was a big bear of a man who towered over everyone, being well over six feet tall, with huge hands, a deep guttural voice and a flamboyance that made him appear larger than life. Awolowo was a socialist: Abiola was an ultra-capitalist billionaire who sat atop a vast corporate empire. Awolowo resigned from a military government lest he make himself a hypocrite by giving legitimacy to a dictatorship. Abiola, on the other hand, actively supported military rulers and made his fortune through his friendships and deals with them.

'Let us wait and see'

Moshood Kashimawo Olawale ('MKO') Abiola was born on August 24, 1937 to Salawu Adenekan Abiola (father) and Alhaja Suliat Wuraola Ayinke Abiola (mother) in the Gbagura area of Abeokuta in south-western Nigeria. He was the 23rd child of a 58-year-old father. All of his father's prior children had died in infancy; none lived for more than six months. His father named him Kashimawo ('let us wait and see'—if this one will live). He describes how he grew up poor, and had to wake up early at 3 am every day to walk four miles to collect and then sell firewood to support his family before going to school. He also formed and played in a music band with self-made instruments called the 'Kashimawo Orchestra'. The band accepted payment of 5 shillings per show or else food (a plate of rice or 12 balls of amala).

'My father sent me to come and read books and not to change my religion'

Despite being a Muslim, Abiola attended the Baptist Boys High School in Abeokuta (with the subsequent head of state General Obasanjo), read the Bible, and passed Christian religious studies exams. He declined to convert to Christianity because 'my father sent me to come and read books and not to change my religion'.[3] When Abiola was 12 years old, his mother predicted that her son would one day become very rich but 'unfortunately I will not live to see it'.[4] She died seven years later on December 10, 1956—the very day her son started his first job at Barclays Bank in Ibadan. Abiola moved to Glasgow, Scotland, in 1960 after obtaining a scholarship to study at the University of Glasgow. He and his first wife, Simbiat (née Atinuke), had their first two children, Kola and Deji, in Glasgow. Simbiat was from a wealthy family and later became the vice-chairperson of several of Abiola's companies.

The couple returned to Nigeria in the mid-1960s and Abiola worked briefly for Guinness as a commercial manager, but did not stay there long after his father forbade his son to work in a brewery. He then started a career as an accountant, and worked firstly at the Lagos University Teaching Hospital (LUTH) between 1966 and 1967. While working there he met and struck up a friendship with a young northern doctor called Dr Suleiman Wali. The two men's friendship would end tragically more than thirty years later. He then briefly worked for the international pharmaceutical company Pfizer before joining the telecommunications company International Telephone and Telegraph (ITT) in 1968 as its finance controller in Lagos. ITT changed his life. Although Abiola had returned to a country in the midst of civil war, the war presented him with an opportunity. The Nigerian military, then trying to quell a secessionist attempt by the Eastern Region, approached ITT to buy radio communications equipment. Abiola met and befriended several army officers while selling radio systems to the army. His relationship with two of those officers would define his life. One of them was a young captain who commanded the 44th Infantry Battalion (nicknamed 'The Rangers') during the civil war. His name was Ibrahim Babangida.

By 1969 ITT's Nigerian subsidiary was in serious financial trouble. Things got so bad that when Abiola wrote a cheque for £500 on behalf of the company, it bounced. To make matters worse, the Nigerian army owed ITT £3,500,000 (a huge sum of money in the 1960s) on a contract and had refused to pay for over three and a half years. A delegation of 12 senior ITT executives (including Abiola) visited the army colonel in charge of the contract to discuss the debt on April 4, 1969. For two or three successive days they sat and waited for the colonel each day from 7.30 am until 3.30 pm, when he finished work, but he refused to see them.

The following week Abiola decided to make his own attempt to get the debt paid. Knowing that army officers were notoriously early risers, he went to the colonel's office at 7 am. When the colonel arrived for work and walked towards his office with his swagger stick in hand, he found Abiola standing in front of his office door. The colonel ignored Abiola's greetings and tried to brush him aside by telling him, 'ITT man, leave this place!' However, Abiola stood his ground and replied, 'You are a debtor. You owe my company.'[5] An angry exchange of words ensued between the two men, and the colonel threatened to hit Abiola with his swagger stick. In another perhaps embellished account, Abiola claimed that the colonel reached for his pistol. The shouting match attracted the attention of the chief of staff (army), Brigadier Hassan Usman Katsina. Katsina called the two quarrelling men into his office and asked Abiola whether he knew the identity of the colonel with whom he nearly came to blows. Abiola replied by asking whether the colonel knew who he was. That response enraged the colonel even further.

'He was awesomely dreaded'

Unbeknown to Abiola, the young colonel was a fearsome character and a legend in the army. He was the army's inspector of signals. A senior member of the government said that the colonel:

> was more feared than the combined influence of all the twelve [state] Governors put together. He was awesomely dreaded by all that wore uniform at the time. He was extremely courageous and virtually a bulldozer on anything he set himself to prosecute rightly or wrongly ... [he] was the only officer in the Nigerian Army who could openly disagree with the Head of State and remind him that he was one of the people that sacrificed their lives to put him where he was.[6]

Abiola did not know any of this and still argued that the debt must be paid. However, the colonel blocked the payments and insisted that ITT had already made a 20% profit on the contract. The permanent secretary at the Ministry of Defence, Yusuf Gobir, mediated and, after more prolonged argument, the army agreed to pay what it owed. Abiola's recovery of the debt marked him out as a rising star in ITT. His near-suicidal courage in confronting the most intimidating officer in the entire Nigerian army also impressed the colonel.

'My white boss was misbehaving'

Abiola was ambitious, intelligent, had a sharp mind for making money, and could be ruthless. After recovering the debt, he demonstrated all of these attributes. Returning to the office with a cheque for the debt, Abiola found 'my white boss was misbehaving with the ladies and chasing them around, drunk probably'.[7] He got a photographer to take embarrassing photos of his boss cavorting about drunk, and showed the photos to senior management in London. Abiola successfully demanded that his boss should be fired, and that he should instead be appointed managing director of ITT's Nigerian office to replace him. As well as being paid a salary, Abiola asked ITT's senior management to grant him shares in ITT. When they refused, Abiola decided to resign and formed his own company called Radio Communications Nigeria Limited (RCNL). Just before departing, Abiola informed ITT that RCNL had secured a lucrative £30 million contract and that he would involve ITT in it if they sold half of ITT's shares to him. Abiola admitted, 'They sold the shares to me but the truth was that we [Radio Communications] had not landed any £30,000,000 contract. But it was too late for ITT to do anything about it.'[8] The shares became a gold mine. He bought his first plane in 1972, and took his elderly father for a 'test drive' (they flew together from Lagos to Kano). His father later died on July 9, 1978, aged 97.

In 1974 the federal Ministry of Communications invited telecom companies to bid for a contract to provide telephone exchanges throughout Nigeria. The director-general of communications, Theophilus Oluwole Akindele, and the federal commissioner for communications disagreed over the contract bidding process. The commissioner was the young army officer with whom Abiola had nearly come to blows five years earlier. By now he had been promoted to brigadier and in Abiola's words 'had become a close friend following the earlier misunderstanding'. The disagreement between the commissioner and director-general became public and was reported in national newspapers. The commissioner for communications won the power struggle, and the cabinet office sent Akindele on indefinite leave. In Akindele's absence the Ministry of Communications awarded ITT a contract worth $138.5 million to provide telephone exchanges in 38 locations throughout Nigeria that would handle 150,000 telephone lines (with the potential for more contracts worth over $1 billion).

'A politically powerful businessman named Alhaji Chief M.K.O. Abiola'

Abiola become stupendously wealthy (he claimed to be Africa's richest man) and had business interests in telecoms, shipping, banking and publishing, and even launched a football team called Abiola Babes, which played in the first division of Nigeria's professional football league. He became famous for his huge acts of generosity and philanthropy, and regularly donated vast amounts of money for the construction of schools and hospitals around the country. In 1990 alone he donated 1 million naira to every state university in Nigeria, and several millions more to federal universities. He also gave scholarships to thousands of students. By 1992 he had been awarded almost 200 chieftaincy and honorary titles by over 60 different communities across Nigeria. However, his wealth was not without controversy.

In 1980 the *Washington Post* published an article alleging that 'International Telephone and Telegraph Corp. has made questionable payments of millions of dollars beginning in 1975 and continuing into this year to gain huge telecommunications sales contracts in Nigeria, according to ITT sources'. The payments were made through ITT's subsidiary in Switzerland, where Swiss secrecy laws prevented US authorities from obtaining further records about the payments. The article also alleged that 'Central to the Nigerian payments is a politically powerful businessman named Alhaji Chief M.K.O. Abiola, who, sources say, has received large payments and has distributed some of the funds to Nigerian government officials'. By this time Abiola had become chairman of ITT's Nigerian subsidiary and was a member of the ruling National Party of Nigeria (NPN). ITT's general counsel, Howard J. Aibel, denied that ITT had done anything illegal:

> All of the top management, including our board of directors, are familiar with the arrangements with Chief Abiola. And they've been a matter of some scrutiny and concern. We're watching them. We pay him a lot of money. We've gotten a big benefit out of the arrangement. We think we have done a very honest and honorable job in supplying equipment in Nigeria and have brought real value to that country.[9]

When the *Washington Post* tried to interview Abiola, an ITT spokesman told them that Abiola would be occupied during the Muslim holy month of Ramadan. Furthermore, 'after Ramadan, Abiola said he would be too busy to answer questions.' The payments at issue started in 1975 (the same year that the army officer, who changed from being Abiola's enemy to his friend, became Nigeria's head of state). The officer's name was Murtala Muhammed.

Abiola's closeness to the military and his alleged shady deals with them were so well known that legendary Afro-beat musician Fela Anikulapo-Kuti released a 25-minute song entitled 'International Thief Thief', whose initial letters just happened to be the acronym of Abiola's company.

The Prodigal Son

Despite the controversy that followed him, Abiola was a greater political asset than the Awoists initially realised. He did something that Awolowo could never do: penetrate and gain political loyalty in the north. During the 1959 federal election campaign, Awolowo flew in a helicopter over northern cities and dropped political leaflets. Although Awolowo thought this was a brilliant publicity stunt and political coup, northerners were offended and perceived flying and overlooking emirs' palaces and residences, where Muslim women lived in seclusion, as utterly tactless violations of their privacy and culture. Abiola understood something that Awolowo never did: the north was not some backward enemy territory to be conquered and enlightened. Instead it was a powerful political constituency whose support was mandatory for anyone aspiring to political leadership of Nigeria. While Awolowo saw the north as a giant and sluggish 'gradual but sure brake on the fast-moving South ... and a dead weight on the country as a whole',[10] Abiola actively sought out friendships and alliances with northerners. Awolowo never became Nigeria's president partly because he never overcame the (real or imagined) perception in the north that he was an anti-northern tribalist. In contrast Abiola befriended northern emirs, businessmen and military officers. He was also the deputy leader of Nigeria's Supreme Council for Islamic Affairs.

The Awolowo Creed

To his credit Abiola realised that he was a political prodigal son in Yorubaland and tried to mend fences with the Awoists. Prior to contesting the presidential election in 1993, he sought their support for his campaign. The Awoists and Abiola crossed paths when the latter reached out and sought the support of the 83-year-old Awoist Adekunle Ajasin. Like most Awoists, the elderly Ajasin was sceptical about Abiola and regarded him as a stooge of the northern establishment. In March 1993, Abiola met Ajasin and other Awoists at Ajasin's house in Owo, Ondo State. The meeting took place in circumstances akin to a PhD viva examination. The Awoists asked Abiola to explain why he wanted to be president, and what policies he would implement if elected. After a thorough question-and-answer session, the Awoists were satisfied that Abiola's responses were 'Awoist in orientation'.[11] The Awoists reluctantly accepted that Abiola was their best hope for a Yoruba presidency. Significantly, Abiola also had the ears of the president. For the Awoists, it would have been utter madness to ignore the richest man in the continent who also happened to enjoy the luxury of being able to meet and speak with the president whenever he felt like it. Abiola was too good an opportunity to pass up. The political system that the military designed for the incoming civilian government reduced politics to a zero-sum game. Only two militarily created and financed parties, the Social Democratic Party (SDP) and the National Republican Convention (NRC), were eligible to contest the election. Abiola was the presidential candidate of the SDP. His even chance of becoming president was the best odds a Yoruba candidate had ever had. The Awoists endorsed Abiola, but asked him to accept the 'Awolowo Creed' (a list of Awolowo's and the Awoists' political ideals). Abiola's endorsement of the creed allowed the Awoists to conceptually reconcile themselves to their endorsement of a man they had been hostile to, on the basis that Abiola's political outlook had evolved to intertwine with theirs. That is the story of how the Awoists came to support a man they had previously distrusted.

Abiola won the landmark presidential election on June 12, 1993. His victory was so emphatic that he swept the polls in northern states such as Borno, Jigawa, Kaduna, Kano, Taraba and Yobe. Abiola even defeated his rival, Bashir Tofa, a Kanuri Muslim, in Tofa's home state of Kano. It was the first time in Nigeria's history that a southerner had won a presidential election. However, it being Nigeria, there had to be a twist in the tail.

2

STEPPING ASIDE

On June 23, 1993, Babangida shockingly annulled the presidential election results and declined to cede power to Abiola. The annulment engulfed Nigeria in its worst political crisis since the civil war and its consequences hung like a curse over Nigeria for the next five years. Yorubas interpreted the annulment as a deliberate act by the northern-led military government to prevent a southerner from becoming president.

A storm of protests, riots and strikes rocked Nigeria, especially in Lagos. Angry youths set up the obligatory burning barricades and hurled rocks at the police. They robbed and stoned or waved at passing cars (depending on their assessment of the political affiliation of the car's occupants). The intensity of the protests frightened markets, shops, banks and businesses into closing. In the absence of their proprietors, looters broke in and had a field day, stealing items such as cookers, fridges and televisions and carting them away in wheelbarrows and trolleys and on their heads. Fearing that pogroms would soon follow, thousands of the Igbo ethnic group fled from northern and southwestern Nigerian back to their homeland in the south-east. Igbos nicknamed the flight home '*Oso Abiola*' (Abiola escape).

'*What the hell is happening?*'

The circumstances of the annulment were opaque. It stunned not only the public, but also senior members of the government. Even the vice-president, Admiral Augustus Aikhomu, was caught off guard. When Aikhomu learned of the annulment, he phoned a senior security officer to exclaim, 'What the hell is happening?'[1] Even former military heads of state condemned the annulment. General Obasanjo held a forum at his farm in Ota, which was attended by another former military head of state, Major-General Muhammadu Buhari, who said, 'This military institution we know best has been desecrated, infiltrated and perverted ... our colleagues are messing up the country and nobody can deny it.'[2]

In late July, the National Defence and Security Council (NDSC) held a marathon meeting to debate the annulment and find a way out of the crisis. The meeting degenerated into a shouting match. Despite several days of discussion and hard bargaining, the key military stakeholders would not budge. They refused to accept Abiola as their president. Babangida said that NDSC members 'never saw him [Abiola] as somebody who is morally upright or fit ... and they didn't feel comfortable that this would be their commander-in-chief'.[3] Whether the annulment was Babangida's personal decision or something forced on him by other officers, he took the blame for it. Babangida had come to office eight years earlier with a reputation as an enlightened and benevolent dictator. His bonhomie and charisma were legendary. A government official who worked for Babangida was almost eulogistic in his praise of his personal qualities: 'All who have come in close contact with him acknowledge his disarming charm, his geniality and his warm friendliness. In him we see a man, agreeable, debonair and warm-hearted; a man modest in demeanour and humble in spirit, with a most winning smile and a most affable manner.'[4]

In the public perception, the annulment transformed Babangida from Nigeria's most enlightened military dictator into its most reviled. The tumultuous wave of protests and anti-military hostility placed severe pressure on Babangida to resign. Yet there was no word from him on whether he would keep his promise to leave power on August 27. Abiola too was feeling the pressure. After senior military officers advised him not to sleep at home and rumours spread that his life was in danger, Abiola flew to London on August 3. Although he said he travelled abroad to drum up international support and put pressure on the military, his journey bore the appearance of an escape. Travelling abroad when civil agitation against the military was at its most intense took the steam out of the struggle. It also played into the hands of civilian and military sceptics who doubted whether Abiola had the fortitude to be president.

No one knew whether Babangida would stay or go until he addressed the National Assembly on his birthday on August 17. Babangida 'offered as my personal sacrifice to voluntarily step aside as the President and commander in chief'. He had decided to jump rather than be pushed. However, he still refused to cede power to Abiola. He would instead hand over power to a civilian-led Interim National Government (ING) on August 27. However, he made no announcement about who would lead the ING, or about its other members or composition. Even the legal officers tasked with drafting the enabling legislation for the ING had no idea for whom they were drafting the governing instruments. Attorney-General Clement Akpamgbo, Professor Ben Nwabueze, retired Supreme Court judge Paul Nwokedi, Professor Oviagere, and the constitutional lawyer Dr (later Professor) Epiphany Azinge of the University of Benin got on with their task despite being kept in the dark. The legal officers drafted the ING's enabling legislation over five consecutive days without knowing for whom it would be promulgated. When they completed the text of the draft decree, they left a blank space for the name of the ING's leader to be inserted. The relevant part read: 'The head of the interim government shall be [*blank space*]'.

The military asked former head of state General Obasanjo to lead the ING but he declined. Yet Babangida continued with business as usual. He held a farewell military parade with his service chiefs on August 26. With only moments left before the end of his nearly eight-year reign, the entire nation was still in the dark about who would succeed him. Immediately after the farewell parade, Babangida returned to the council chambers inside the presidential villa to oversee the swearing-in ceremony of his successor. At 3 pm on August 26, government officials swarmed into the council chambers, which was filled to capacity. Although they knew they were about to witness the swearing in of the next head of state, most of the people inside the chambers had no idea who that person would be. Suddenly, the 57-year-old head of the Transitional Council, Ernest Shonekan, was called forward to be sworn in as head of the ING by Chief Justice Mohammed Bello. Shonekan swore in the other members of the ING on the following day.

Shonekan was, like Abiola, an Egba Yoruba from Abeokuta. He was a graduate of the Church Missionary Society Grammar School in Lagos, Nigeria's oldest secondary school. He had a degree in law from the University of London, and was also a graduate of Harvard Business School. Shonekan had a distinguished corporate career as a businessman and joined the legal department of the United Africa Company (UAC), which still exists today as Unilever. He rose to become UAC's deputy legal adviser, and later its chief executive. He headed the company at a time when it was the largest African-owned business in sub-Saharan Africa. After his successful business career, he entered politics in January 1993 when Babangida dissolved the federal cabinet and replaced it with a 31-member Transitional Council, which included only two serving military officers.[5] Babangida appointed Shonekan to head the Transitional Council, which was to oversee the transition from military to civilian rule. One of Shonekan's colleagues on the council described him as 'a simple, modest, unostentatious man of no exceptional ability yet one who always keeps his head as he weaves his way unobtrusively but shrewdly to his set objectives in life. He is, by any standard, a solid personality.'[6]

Shortly after Shonekan's swearing-in ceremony, Babangida moved out of the presidential villa and departed in a convoy with his family and belongings for his hilltop mansion in his home town of Minna in Niger State. He left without a farewell address to the military. It was a muted exit, a departure from the majestic and ostentatious ceremonies that usually accompanied Babangida's public appearances.

3

82 DAYS

The ING era is often treated as a mere punctuation mark in Nigeria's history. Glossing over the ING obscures key events that influenced subsequent controversies. Babangida's forced exit from power was a watershed. It was the first time in Nigeria's history that a military government had ceded power involuntarily by means other than a coup. For the first time since the commencement of military rule 27 years earlier, Nigerians challenged the military with mass civil disobedience and protests, and pressured the military into making concessions. Although the pro-democracy movement failed to achieve immediately its short-term goal of an Abiola presidency, the military's hurried replacement by a civilian government demonstrated that there were limits to the military's power and that civilians were not without influence.

The emergence of the unwieldy ING was testimony to Babangida's ingenious ability to manoeuvre his way out of one crisis after another with his head still attached to his body. It also once again demonstrated the extraordinary ability of the Nigerian state to absorb crises, and the propensity of its elite to take the country to the edge of a cliff, before pulling back at the last possible moment. The ING was a middle ground between the demands of the military and the pro-democracy opposition. It allowed the opposition to claim it had pushed the military out of power, while also giving the military a face-saving way out of power without acceding to the demands for an Abiola presidency.

The ING was to govern for only six months, during which time it was supposed to organise new elections (which Abiola was barred from contesting). However, Shonekan received a baptism of fire. One day after he was sworn in, oil workers walked off their installations, and air traffic and airport staff also went on strike. The strikes grounded flights and left thousands of passengers stranded around the country. The Murtala Muhammed airport in Lagos managed to stay open only with skeleton staff and drafted in air traffic controllers from the air force on an emergency basis. The Nigerian Labour Congress (NLC) and the National Union of Petroleum and National Gas Workers (NUPENG) also went on strike to protest against the establishment of the ING. The Campaign for Democracy (CD) called a three-day stay-at-home protest that shut down most of south-western Nigeria. The strikes and protests paralysed commercial activity in Lagos as shops, businesses and markets closed. Another grievance was the announcement on August 22 (four days before the ING was sworn in) that the government planned to introduce a new, expensive high-grade fuel. This measure was widely believed to be the first move towards removing the government subsidies which made Nigerian domestic petrol among the cheapest in the world. Fuel shortages caused lengthy queues and delays.

Shonekan inherited the animosity that had been directed at Babangida. Although the latter was no longer the head of state, the public and politicians viewed the ING as a puppet continuation of Babangida's government, rather than its replacement. Abiola's running mate, Babagana Kingibe, said that 'Leaving Shonekan in charge is like the military putting on a glove'.[1] Shonekan was a skilled and experienced executive with a successful corporate career. However, the cut-throat world of Nigerian politics was to be his greatest challenge. He correctly identified as a top priority the need to achieve rapprochement with those aggrieved over the June 12 election annulment. He conducted many consultations with political stakeholders and traditional leaders around the country, including visits to Benue, Edo, Kano and Sokoto states. He then sought to broaden his political base by pardoning exiled Nigerian politicians such as Richard Akinjide and Adisa Akinloye, who had been fugitives abroad since the military returned to power in 1984 and declared its intention to arrest them. He freed some journalists who had been arrested and detained by Babangida's government, and promised to ask the National Assembly to repeal repressive military decrees that restricted civilian and press freedom.[2] To address the lingering June 12 controversy he also established an eight-member panel of inquiry led by Justice Mamman Nasir, a former Federal Court of Appeal judge, to investigate the annulment of the June 12 election. He launched a media campaign that promoted the ING as 'a civilian government of national reconciliation', and announced that public enterprises such as the National Ports Authority, the Nigerian National Petroleum Corporation (NNPC) and the Nigerian Postal Service would be investigated for corruption. Seven senior NNPC officials were arrested on corruption charges.

'Curious but pregnant'

However, while Shonekan got down to business, the military also got down to theirs as if he did not exist. Although Decree 61 appointed Shonekan as the titular commander-in-chief of the armed forces, strangely Chief Justice Bello omitted Shonekan's designation as commander-in-chief when he swore him in as head of the ING. This was symptomatic of the military's indifference to Shonekan. Just before leaving power, Babangida had made a minor alteration that went unnoticed by most members of the public. A few days before Shonekan's inauguration Babangida amended the decree that created the ING by inserting a section that Professor Ben Nwabueze (one of the decree's draftsmen) described as 'curious but pregnant'.[3] Nwabueze insisted that this new section was not in the final draft that he and his colleagues had submitted to Babangida, and that it was mysteriously inserted after he had finalised the decree's text. The new section stipulated that if Shonekan's office became vacant by reason of his death or resignation, he would be replaced by the 'most senior minister'. However, the decree did not identify this 'most senior minister'. Only a few people noticed this strange amendment. The chief of training, operations and planning at Defence Headquarters, Major-General Ishola Williams, informed me that he and Vice-President Augustus Aikhomu objected to the amendment, but were overruled.[4]

The day before Babangida resigned (August 25), he met with the military service chiefs and dropped one of his characteristic bombshells. He announced that he would retire from the military, and would take all of them with him into retirement. However, Babangida omitted the minister of defence from the retirement list. Babangida claimed that this minister was exempted because the ING needed protection from being overthrown by radical and unpredictable junior officers. As Babangida put it, 'I thought the Interim National Government needed a very, very strong muscle so as to punch effectively.'[5] That 'strong muscle' was General Sani Abacha. Babangida added:

> '....we were not sure about what the younger officers were up to, so there was the need to back Shonekan's government with some degree of good military cover, so that his presence would be a deterrent: to ensure they don't get adventurous, so that Shonekon would have military backing to do whatever he wanted to do.'[6]

19

When Obasanjo discovered that Abacha would be left behind after Babangida's departure, he contacted his former deputy, Major-General Shehu Musa Yar'Adua, and urged him to resist. Yar'Adua was the political godfather of the SDP and had been instrumental in the negotiations to create the ING as a face-saving way for the military to leave government without having to hand over power to Abiola. However, Yar'Adua reluctantly yielded to Abacha's presence in the ING as he did not want to create another pretext for Babangida to remain in power.

Apart from a crippling political crisis and a furious electorate, Babangida left other 'parting gifts' for Shonekan. Before leaving power, Babangida appointed new heads of the army, navy and air force. All of the new appointees were his loyalists. Babangida appointed Lt-General Joshua Dogonyaro as the new chief of defence staff. Babangida wanted to appoint his childhood friend Major-General Abdulsalam Abubakar as chief of army staff but instead chose Lt-General Aliyu Mohammed Gusau after Abacha opposed Abubakar's candidacy. Both Dogonyaro and Gusau were fellow cadets in the Nigerian Defence Academy's first regular combatant course in 1967. Babangida also appointed Vice-Admiral Dan Preston Omatsola and Air Vice-Marshal Nsikak Eduok as the chief of naval staff and chief of air staff respectively.

August 1993 military redeployments

Post	Prior Holder	Replacement
Minister of Defence	General Sani Abacha	No change
Chief of Defence Staff	General Sani Abacha	Lt-General Joshua Dogonyaro
Deputy Chief of Defence Staff	Admiral Murtala Nyako	(*Post abolished*)
Chief of Army Staff	Lt-General Salihu Ibrahim	Lt-General Aliyu Mohammed Gusau
Chief of Naval Staff	Vice-Admiral Dan Preston Omatsola	Rear-Admiral Suleiman Saidu
Chief of Air Staff	Air Marshal Akin Dada	Air Vice-Marshal Nsikak Eduok

Rather than giving Shonekan 'military backing to do whatever he wanted to do', as Babangida claimed, Abacha's retention made Shonekan vulnerable. By late 1993 the army had factionalised into a group of rival conspiratorial cliques. The pro-Babangida clique were tagged the 'IBB boys'. Their rivals were a so-called 'Lagos group' of officers who were loyal to Abacha. The pro-Babangida and pro-Abacha groups had been wrestling each other for control of the army for three years. Dogonyaro and Gusau were in Babangida's camp and their appointments were chess moves in the rivalry between the two groups. Dogonyaro was an armoured corps officer who distinguished himself during a successful six-month tour of duty as the field commander of the Nigerian-led ECOMOG[7] peacekeeping mission in Liberia in 1990–1. He and Abacha had been long-time rivals, with the former opposing the multiple portfolios entrusted to Abacha (defence secretary, chief of defence staff, and chairman of the joint chiefs of staff). Dogonyaro had long canvassed for a separation of these portfolios and sometimes complained that he did not bargain well for himself in the aftermath of the coup that brought Babangida to power in 1985. Dogonyaro finally got his wish when Babangida divested Abacha of the chief of defence staff portfolio and granted it to Dogonyaro.

Like two prizefighters locked in a cage, it was obvious that Abacha and Dogonyaro would strike at each other once Babangida left the scene. It took exactly a week for one of them to strike the first blow. On September 3, Abacha used his position as secretary for defence to revoke Dogonyaro's appointment as chief of defence staff.[8] A terse statement from the Ministry of Defence claimed that Dogonyaro's appointment was routine, to 'reflect service interest and expediency'.[9] However, seasoned observers knew that it was part of the ongoing power struggle in the military. Abacha appointed Dogonyaro's contemporary from the NDA, Lt-General Diya (a Yoruba officer from the south-west), to replace him. Rather than accept demotion, Dogonyaro retired two weeks later (on September 18, 1993). In his retirement letter Dogonyaro said that 'the honourable secretary [Abacha] as an individual, was not prepared to work with me', and intriguingly added, 'I must also add that my decision is based on my firm conviction not to be party to any scheme or desire to perpetuate military rule under any guise.'[10] Abacha also revoked Babangida's appointment of Air Vice-Marshal Eduok as chief of air staff, and replaced him with Air Vice-Marshal Femi John Femi. Abacha seemed to have gained the upper hand in his struggle with the 'IBB boys' when he also summarily retired 17 officers who were key members of the Babangida regime, including Brigadier-Generals David Mark, Haliru Akilu, John Shagaya, Tunde Ogbeha,

Tunji Olurin and Raji Rasaki and Lt-Colonel Sambo Dasuki.[11] He made these changes without bothering to inform Shonekan.

'The veteran coup plotter was up to some game'

These redeployments caused press speculation that 'the veteran coup plotter was up to some game'.[12] When asked whether Abacha was removing other officers to pave the way for himself to assume political power, the director of defence information, Brigadier-General Fred Chijuka, replied: 'I have worked with him for the past 10 years ... I can vouch for him. He doesn't have the ambition of becoming head of state. I know his intention and capacity. He is not an ambitious man. He wants to remain at the background.'[13]

The military continued to initiate political moves without Shonekan's involvement. The chief of defence staff, Lt-General Oladipo Diya, set up a 'Moving the Nation Forward Committee' of officers from the army, navy and air force to review the political crisis and recommend a solution. The committee was led by the general officer commanding (GOC) 1 Mechanised Infantry Division in Kaduna, Brigadier-General Chris Alli. Its other members were Brigadier-Generals Ishaya Bamaiyi, Patrick Aziza, Ahmed Abdullahi and Bashir Magashi, Commodore Festus Porbeni, Air Commodore Magnus Johnson, and Colonel Lawan Gwadabe, who was its secretary. Some officers were not patient enough to wait for the committee's recommendation. Alli claimed that the commander of the armoured corps, Colonel Abubakar Umar, approached him, and asked for his support in deposing Shonekan and installing Abiola as president.[14]

'General Abacha can forever remain a hero or messiah in the country's annals'

The military had no shortage of civilian supporters urging them on to overthrow the ING. Support for a military intervention came even from elected civilian officials. A senior military officer alleged that 'the [civilian] state governors did not want Shonekan to succeed. They made Abacha's home their pilgrimage point and urged Abacha to take power.'[15] On October 19, the deputy governor of Osun State, Clement Adesuyi Haastrup, told the new GOC of 2 Division in Ibadan, Brigadier-General Godwin Abbe, to urge Abacha to intervene against the ING:

> so that, like the biblical Paul who is now a saint, General Abacha can forever remain a hero or messiah in the country's annals ... to General Abacha and other

military leaders, I say, this is your chance to prove your mettle. This is the time for you to make your own history. After June 12 election, there is no vacancy for leadership in the country but there is vacuum for a national hero or heroine.[16]

Even those who had made their reputation on the basis of an irrevocable opposition to military rule suddenly began advocating the military's displacement of the ING. At the November 3, 1993 launch of his book entitled *The June 12 Crisis*, the radical human rights lawyer Gani Fawehinmi, who had campaigned against military governments for several years, said that 'the military must intervene to stop this rot, to stop this war of Shonekan's government against the people'. He also called on 'all the progressives in and out of the military, to defend this country against the ING'.[17]

The fact that pro-democracy campaigners, civil rights activists and traditional rulers were openly canvassing for military intervention demonstrated the extent to which faith in democracy had eroded in Nigeria. By the 1990s military coups had become the most realistic and effective method of regime change.

'A reliable general is there'

Abiola also seemed to believe that the military could provide him with a solution. SDP member Abraham Babalola Borisade claimed that Abiola 'told the Yar'Adua group [of the SDP] that he had a friend within the hierarchy of the military that was defending his interests'.[18] According to Abiola, 'a reliable general [was] there' for him in the army. The identity of the 'reliable general' in whom Abiola put his faith became obvious on September 28 when he effusively praised one senior military officer in particular:

I have been talking to the military people. They are the people to talk to because the military caused this problem. But for people like Sani Abacha this country would have been plunged into bloodshed. I really commend General Sani Abacha because out of love for his country, he puts his common sense, experience, tact and intellect to ease out Babangida. I have no doubt that it is that common sense, that patriotism, that intellect that will ease out Babangida's surrogates too.[19]

Abiola kept in frequent contact with Abacha during his absence abroad and seemed to believe that he would return to a triumphant presidential inauguration if he cooperated with his 'reliable general'. He was further reassured when on his return to Nigeria, he found his military defenders 'were giving me presidential treatment'.[20] The plane that brought him back was directed to the presidential wing of the Murtala Muhammed International Airport in Lagos. Abiola admitted:

23

When I was abroad I was never in touch with Shonekan. It was Abacha and Diya who were in touch with me, and I was in touch with them. They gave me the impression that they were for democracy ... they gave me a red carpet treatment on arrival. They allowed the Air France plane that brought me to land at the presidential wing ... That night, I saw Abacha for about 4 hours. And we had very good discussions. I was expecting that when they had dealt with the so-called Babangida boys, he would put every other thing in place.[21]

MAD

On Monday, October 25, 1993 a group calling itself the Movement for the Advancement of Democracy (MAD) hijacked a Nigeria Airways airbus A310. The hijackers were teenagers named Kabir Adenuga, Kenny Rasaq-Lawal, Richard Ajibola Ogunderu and Benneth Oluwadaisi. They boarded an Abuja-bound plane in Lagos, and after it took off and reached an altitude of 30,000 feet, Ogunderu approached the cockpit with a replica gun and ordered the pilot to divert to Niamey, the capital of Nigeria's neighbour, Niger. Two of the other hijackers stayed in the main cabin to intimidate the passengers. They announced that they had hijacked the plane in protest at the June 12 election annulment, and gave Shonekan a 72-hour deadline to resign. They released 34 passengers but kept 159 others hostage on board.

Shonekan was abroad in Cyprus attending a Commonwealth Heads of Government meeting when the hijacking occurred. One source claims that when he repeatedly phoned Abacha for updates on the hijack, the latter refused to answer or return his calls. Abacha instead exclaimed, 'Does he think he is my boss?'[22] Strangely the Nigerian army did not get involved in the plane hijack involving its citizens. After a stand-off lasting a few days, gendarmes from Niger stormed the plane at night, rescued the passengers, and arrested the hijackers without bloodshed.[23]

Amidst the chaos, Abiola turned to the judiciary to try to validate his election victory. Although he was initially cynical about the prospect of Abiola as president, a young senator representing the Lagos West district had become one of Abiola's key allies. That senator was Bola Ahmed Tinubu. He became so close to Abiola, and was so aggrieved by the annulment, that earlier in 1993 he took his elderly mother, Alhaja Abibatu Mogaji, with him to a meeting in Abuja with Babangida to appeal for the annulment to be rescinded. His mother was the former president-general of the Association of Nigerian Market Women and Men, and had been active in mobilising strikes by traders. Although she was a Muslim, she removed her headscarf in Babangida's presence to plead with him to validate Abiola's election victory. Newspapers published an iconic photo of the grey-haired septuagenarian grandmother pleading with the younger president on Abiola's behalf. Although he and his mother's emotional appeals failed to persuade the military, Tinubu was undeterred. He turned to another branch of the state: the judiciary. Tinubu admitted that he 'engineered and proposed' a court case against the ING. He conscripted Professor Alfred Kasunmu to find a legal technicality with which to pick the ING apart. Kasunmu was a senior advocate of Nigeria, a highly esteemed former professor of law at the University of Lagos, and the former attorney-general of Lagos State. After digging through the legislation that created the ING, Kasunmu filed a court action on Abiola's behalf at the Lagos High Court on October 14, 1993, seeking a declaration that the ING was illegal. It was arguably the most significant court case in Nigeria for almost thirty years.

On Monday, November 8, Yoruba leaders held a two-hour meeting with Abacha at his home in Lagos to ascertain what he would do if the court judgment went in Abiola's favour. They urged him to intervene directly to remove the ING and install Abiola as president. The meeting concluded with Abacha neither accepting nor denying their request.

On Wednesday, November 10, 1993, the nation held its breath and waited for a court judgment which would have massive ramifications. The presiding judge was 52-year-old Justice Dolapo Akinsanya. She was the former director of civil litigation in Lagos State, and had been promoted to the Lagos State High Court bench three years earlier. Her younger sister, Modupe Onadeko, is a Harvard University-educated doctor of epidemiology at the University of Ibadan. Akinsanya and her family were not strangers to political trials and controversy. She was the eldest daughter of Professor Sanya Dojo Onabamiro, an esteemed biologist who worked at University College, Ibadan. Onabamiro was also the minister of education in the Western Region during the 1960s, as a member of the Action Group party. He was a key architect of the party's free education programme which it launched in 1955. He later became estranged from the party, and was one of two key prosecution witnesses during the Action Group leader Obafemi Awolowo's treason trial in 1962. Onabamiro gave evidence against Awolowo, alleging that he was a member of a so-called 'Tactical Committee' that Awolowo formed to plot the government's violent overthrow. He said that Awolowo instructed him and others, including Anthony Enahoro and Samuel Ikoku, in how to train men in weapons and munitions handling in Ghana, in preparation for overthrowing the federal government by force of arms.

Justice Akinsanya was under tremendous pressure. Her judgment would affect not only the political stability of the entire country, but her personal life too. Like both Shonekan and Abiola, she too was a Yoruba from Ogun State. She was also acquainted with the Shonekan family. Her husband and Shonekan were former classmates, and Shonekan's wife Margaret was the head prefect at Ibadan Grammar School when Akinsanya was a student there. Akinsanya prepared to deliver her judgment in a courtroom packed with lawyers and onlookers anxious to hear the outcome. The courtroom was so crowded that several of the lawyers had to stand throughout the proceedings as there were not enough seats for all of them.

The case revolved around a simple yet devastating technical error that Babangida made during his hurried exit from power (an error which his experienced legal advisers mysteriously failed to notice). In the midst of the confusion and crisis after the annulment, Babangida signed Decree 59 to officially end his eight-year-long reign with effect from August 26, 1993.[24] After signing Decree 59, Babangida also signed Decree 61[25] on August 26 to promulgate the ING and appoint Shonekan as its chairman. Unfortunately, by the time Babangida signed Decree 61, he had already ceased to be Nigeria's head of state by virtue of Decree 59, which stripped him of all executive powers as president. Babangida therefore had no power to enact Decree 61. By the time he signed the decree to create the ING, he had become a private citizen.

Justice Akinsanya ruled that Decree 61 (which created the ING) was illegal, and so consequently was the ING. Abiola's supporters were jubilant. This was not the first ruling that Akinsanya had made in Abiola's favour. Back in June, a shadowy organisation calling itself the Association for a Better Nigeria (ABN) had campaigned for an extension of military rule, and had filed a court action to stop the National Electoral Commission from releasing the June 12 election results. At the time, Akinsanya issued a judgment restraining the ABN from campaigning for an extension of military rule.[26]

'I am not in politics as a cowboy'

Akinsanya's judgment eroded the ING's credibility even further and raised the political temperature to boiling point. However, declaring the ING illegal was far easier than removing it from power. Shonekan's advisers argued that the court judgment was not binding, and decided to appeal against it; while Abiola's supporters urged him to unilaterally declare himself president and immediately form a government to replace the ING. However, Abiola instead wanted the ING to invite him to form a new government. He said, 'I am not in politics as a cowboy ... We must be very careful here. If you see a moving train, no matter how much you are in a hurry, you must move out of its way.'[27] When Abiola's advisers finally convinced him to declare himself president, he asked for his announcement to be delayed so that he could be sworn in with his vice-president, Babagana Kingibe. Like Abacha, Kingibe was a Kanuri Muslim from the north-east, and had extensive security contacts from his years in the Nigerian intelligence community. In Abiola's view, the electoral mandate belonged to both of them. The difficulty was that Kingibe could not be found.

While trying to locate Kingibe, news of the plan to declare Abiola president leaked to the military. Diya met with Tinubu and discouraged him from going through with the plan, and instead told him to let the military resolve the crisis. Tinubu claims that Diya told him: 'You've got the judiciary supporting you, you should now get the military backing. We are ready to back you.'[28] Abacha also contacted and briefed Abiola, Abiola's oldest son, Kola, and Tinubu, and persuaded them not to unilaterally declare Abiola as president until he had secured military backing for Abiola's leadership.

'You won't last four days'

Tinubu claimed that Abacha urged Abiola to wait for him to clear the 'land mines' surrounding the June 12 mandate, and promised him that it would take between three weeks and six months, after which he would install Abiola as president.[29] Abacha and Diya also informed Abiola that Colonel Abubakar Umar and several other officers were planning an anti-Abiola coup. Tinubu alleged:

> When Abiola met with Abacha, they told us that Col [Abubakar] Umar was planning to topple Abiola. They listed about 17 officers, including Joshua Dogonyaro[30] and the rest of them, who, they said, were involved in the coup plot. They told Abiola, 'You won't be able to stop them, you won't last four days.' They said they needed to get rid of these dangerous boys in the military. Abiola became a little jittery.[31]

Colonel Umar admitted planning a coup, but said that the coup's target was not Abiola. Rather, he sought to install Abiola as president.

The court judgment was good news not only for Abiola, but also for the military. It created a pretext for the military to once again take centre stage amidst the chaos. The day after the ING was declared illegal, the former minister of external affairs, Professor Bolaji Akinyemi, wrote a letter to Abacha in which he appealed to him to dissolve the ING, re-adopt the 1960 constitution, and form a transitional government based on the June 12 election.

In mid-November senior military officers criss-crossed the country and met with civil rights groups and traditional leaders to canvass support for a military resolution to the crisis. Diya told civil rights groups such as the Campaign for Democracy and the Civil Liberties Organisation that radical young officers were planning a violent coup, and that they had a list of 98 Nigerians (including members of civil rights groups) whom they would summarily execute during the coup.

On Friday, November 12, Abacha held a two-hour meeting with Yoruba traditional rulers at his house in Lagos. The traditional rulers tried to extract from Abacha his vision of a post-Shonekan government. However, Abacha maintained a tight poker face and declined to reveal whether he would revoke the June 12 election annulment and install Abiola as president.

Despite the uncertainty around him, Shonekan felt confident enough to move from his official residence at Akinola Aguda House in Abuja to the presidential villa. However, signs of his unpopularity emerged from time to time. University students stoned his convoy when he visited Port Harcourt on November 15 and the vehicles had to increase speed to escape the barrage. On his way back to Abuja, Shonekan took a different route to avoid the students. The ING compounded its unpopularity by enacting bizarre measures. It approved a 700% increase in the price of petrol from 70 kobo to 5 naira per litre. The ING was by then on life support.

Wednesday November 17 1993

On November 17, 1993 ING members arrived for a meeting with Shonekan at the presidential villa. However, they were kept waiting as Shonekan had to meet other unscheduled visitors. Abacha, Diya and Aliyu Mohammed Gusau, had also arrived and requested an urgent meeting with Shonekan. They did not come alone but arrived with heavily armed troops. An observer present at the villa described the armed detachment of soldiers accompanying the three generals as 'simply one of the most intimidating I had ever witnessed'.[32] Colonel Lawan Gwadabe, the former commander of the National Guard, was also present. Abacha, Diya and Gusau met with Shonekan in his office, in the company of the secretary to the ING, Alhaji Mustapha Umara. Shonekan may have been reassured by the presence of his good friend Gusau, who had been his squash partner for many years.

Senior military officers had frequently held briefings with Shonekan in the past. However, this time, the mood was very different. Abacha gave Shonekan an unflattering appraisal of the political situation. One publication claimed that he described Shonekan's government as 'weak, purposeless, and directionless'.[33] To add spice, the officers also informed Shonekan of the alleged plan by a group of radical junior officers to stage a bloody coup and execute several prominent Nigerians. Of course, there was no way of verifying this. After concluding his dire summary of the political situation, Abacha asked Shonekan if he was willing to resign. The officers did not take Shonekan's cooperation for granted. They had made contingency plans to deploy armoured tanks in Lagos and Abuja if he refused to go. One of the officers would then make a nationwide broadcast announcing the military's reassumption of power.

After the meeting concluded, Shonekan called his secretaries to his office at approximately 8 pm, and briefed them. Around 8.45 pm Shonekan's chief press secretary, Emma Agu, summoned the Nigerian Television Authority's (NTA) state house reporter, Muhammed Kudu Abubakar,[34] to record a speech by Shonekan. At 11 pm the NTA broadcast footage of Shonekan meeting with other members of the ING and reading a speech to announce his resignation. News of Shonekan's resignation had been broadcast on Radio Nigeria shortly before, at 10.30 pm, before its airing on the NTA. The announcement did not mention who would replace Shonekan. After he recording his speech, the senior officers offered Shonekan a lift but he declined, choosing instead to depart from Abuja and head south for Lagos late at night by road. He arrived in Lagos around 3 am.

It is not clear whether Shonekan voluntarily resigned, whether he was coerced into resigning, or whether what happened on the evening of November 17 was a military coup. A parallel can be drawn between the events of November 17, 1993 and January 16, 1966 after Nigeria's first military coup. On that Sunday evening in 1966, the GOC of the Nigerian army, Major-General Aguiyi-Ironsi, had (like Abacha 27 years later) arrived at the cabinet office to meet the civilian political leadership as part of a three-man security troika with the head of the navy, Commodore Joseph Wey, and the acting inspector-general of police, Alhaji Kam Selem. Like Abacha 27 years later, Aguiyi-Ironsi was also accompanied by several other intimidating armed soldiers who surrounded the premises. After giving a grim assessment of Nigeria's military and political predicament, Aguiyi-Ironsi 'requested' the federal council of ministers to resign and cede power to the military. Two ministers present at the meeting with Aguiyi-Ironsi later admitted that the ministers 'were too frightened and panicky to say "no" to Major-General J.T.U. Aguiyi-Ironsi … and this amidst the rattle and the whir of military engines in and around the cabinet premises on that awesome night'.[35] They 'voluntarily' resigned.

Shonekan's resignation 27 years later brought Nigeria full circle. Both incidents involved polite briefings by senior security officers to the civilian leadership, giving the civilians an opportunity to resign and save face. The conspicuous presence of soldiers at both resignations in 1966 and 1993 was meant as a reminder of the alternative scenario if the civilian government refused to resign. A senior officer later revealed that Shonekan 'was lucky to get off alive'.[36]

Shonekan's ING suffered death from a thousand cuts. Although its end was sudden, it had been under siege from its first day. It was detested in the southwest, the public treated it with disdain, pro-democracy campaigners protested against it, labour unions refused to work while it was in office, politicians incited the military to overthrow it, the military shunned and plotted against it, and the National Assembly refused to cooperate with it. It was all too much, and these forces combined to bring the ING tumbling down after only 82 days in office.

4

THE KHALIFA

1993 was a year of farce—even by Nigerian standards. It featured a presidential election that cost 15% of GDP, only to be retroactively declared void; the military displacement of a civilian government; and three different governments in three months. Now the military had another chance to end the chaos.

After shunting Shonekan aside, the military's attention turned to determining his successor without amplifying the crisis or provoking a backlash from the civilian populace or restive elements in the military. After Shonekan's resignation, Abacha, Diya and other senior officers flew down from Abuja to Lagos. Diya held a midnight press briefing at the air force mess on Kofo Abayomi Road in Victoria Island, Lagos. The following day Abacha summoned all military officers with the rank of brigadier-general upwards, and police officers with the rank of assistant inspector-general of police upwards, for a briefing at the defence headquarters in Dodan Barracks. After two and a half hours, Abacha departed without fielding questions from reporters, and headed for his official home at Flagstaff House on First Avenue in Ikoyi, Lagos, where he continued consultations with senior military officers and the inspector-general of police, Ibrahim Coomasie.

Senior officers later held another meeting at the Lagos guest house of Brigadier-General Bashir Magashi for the customary hard bargaining that follows military takeovers. The following officers attended the meeting: Abacha, Diya, Brigadier-General Chris Alli, Lt-Colonel Sambo Dasuki, Brigadier-Generals Ishaya Bamaiyi and Patrick Aziza, Major-General Tajudeen Olanrewaju, Air Commodore Magnus Johnson, Brigadier-General Ahmed Aboki Abdullahi, and Colonel Lawan Gwadabe.

'Tell your brother Diya that he will leave the Army in disgrace'

At the meeting they agreed to appoint Abacha as the new head of state, and Diya as Abacha's deputy and chief of general staff, Major-General Abdulsalam Abubakar as chief of defence staff, and Rear-Admiral Allison Madueke as chief of naval staff to succeed Rear-Admiral Saidu. Air Vice-Marshal Femi John Femi retained his position as chief of air staff. However, cracks in the facade of military unity appeared when Lt-General Gusau suddenly resigned from his position as chief of army staff, and retired without giving any public explanation. The GOC of 1 Mechanised Infantry Division, Brigadier-General Chris Alli, succeeded Gusau. However, Gusau made an ominous prediction about Diya. The two had been contemporaries at the Nigerian Defence Academy (NDA) and graduated together as cadets from the NDA's first regular combatant course in 1967. Gusau later told a mutual friend to 'Tell your brother Diya that he will leave the Army in disgrace'.[1/2] The chief of training, operations and planning at Defence Headquarters, Major-General Ishola Williams (another NDA classmate of Diya), was also unhappy. Williams was not a conformist in appearance or disposition. He unusually sported a beard and, despite serving in the military during 23 years of military rule, he had refused appointment to political posts. He told me that he refused to attend political meetings of the senior military leadership even when summoned to do so. He was known as:

> a thoroughbred professional who refused to suffer fools gladly. He was revered by his contemporaries and superiors alike and became the stormy petrel of every chief of army staff annual conference, where he regularly railed at the damage the military in politics was doing to the professional military, with all of his superior officers present.[3]

Williams abruptly resigned and refused to be involved with the new military takeover. He also enigmatically warned Diya that he 'wasn't going to last long'.[4] The fact that military rule was causing officers of the calibre of Gusau and Williams to resign prematurely out of frustration was a portent of what politics was doing to the military.

Apart from the military appointments, the meeting decided that the new 'provisional government should have a near complete civilian profile',[5] and that the states would be governed by new civilian administrators rather than military officers. (Neither promise was kept.) At 10.30 pm on November 18, Abacha made a nationwide broadcast. After confirming that he had succeeded Shonekan as head of state, he banned all political parties, proclaimed the immediate dissolution of the ING, the National Assembly, National Electoral

Commission and state houses of assembly in all 30 states of the country, and fired all 30 elected state governors. In their place, Abacha announced the establishment of a new Provisional Ruling Council (PRC) led by him (whose members are listed in the accompanying table). Instead of appointing civilian state administrators as he initially promised, Abacha chose military administrators to govern the states. The soldiers were once again in control.

Provisional Ruling Council, November 1993

Position	Name	State of Origin	Ethnicity	Religion
Head of State and Commander-in-Chief of the Nigerian Armed Forces	General Sani Abacha	Kano	Kanuri	Muslim
Chief of General Staff	Lt-General Donaldson Oladipo Diya	Ogun	Yoruba	Christian
Chief of Defence Staff	Major-General Abdulsalam Abubakar	Niger	Gwari	Muslim
Chief of Army Staff	Major-General Mohammed Christopher Alli	Kogi	Ebira[6]	Christian
Chief of Naval Staff	Rear-Admiral Allison Madueke	Anambra	Igbo	Christian
Chief of Air Staff	Air Vice-Marshal Femi John Femi	Kogi	Yoruba	Christian
Inspector-General of Police	Ibrahim Coomasie	Katsina	Fulani	Muslim
National Security Adviser	Ismaila Gwarzo	Kano	Hausa	Muslim

Attorney-General and Minister of Justice	Olu Onagoruwa	Ogun	Yoruba	Christian
Minister of External Affairs	Babagana Kingibe	Borno	Kanuri	Muslim
Minister of Internal Affairs	Alexander Uruemu Ibru	Delta	Urhobo	Christian

There were three strange features about the manner in which Abacha took over from Shonekan. Firstly, Abacha claimed to have succeeded Shonekan as the 'most senior minister' in accordance with Decree 61. However, that could not be so as a court had already invalidated Decree 61. Secondly, even if Decree 61 was still valid, the appropriate course was for Abacha to replace Shonekan as ING leader and for the ING to continue and supervise new elections as originally planned. Abacha's dissolution of the ING and of democratic structures made his assumption of power look like a coup. Thirdly, Abiola and his supporters did not object to Abacha's assumption of power.

Abiola visited Abacha shortly after the latter took power. Surprisingly, many Abiola supporters were jubilant were about the military's return. Some of them were heard triumphantly chanting 'MKO! MKO! Presido! Presido!' at the luxury Nicon Noga hotel in Abuja.[7] The day after Shonekan resigned, thousands of people in Ota, in Abiola's home state of Ogun, trooped out to celebrate the news of the ING's fall and sang solidarity songs. They staged a sit-down protest on a road at the Idiroko Junction to prevent politicians from fleeing to neighbouring Benin, as they had done when the military overthrew the previous civilian government in 1983. A Yoruba banker said, 'The real struggle in Nigeria is still to suppress the power of Babangida. Abacha is the only man strong enough to do the job ... and that is why we support this new regime.'[8] However, not everyone was enthusiastic about the return to military rule. The president of the Academic Staff Union of Universities, Professor Attahiru Jega of Bayero University, stated:

> The last 8 years of military rule under Babangida, in particular, have dragged this country into one of the worst kinds of economic and political crisis a developing country can experience. We have been made to experience an unimaginable degree of plunder and pillory, conditioned by fascism. Whatever seemingly logical and plausible reasons a band of military officers may use as an excuse to come

to power, cannot vitiate the undemocratic and fascistic essence and reality of military rule—a reality so nauseatingly fresh in our memory.[9]

'Shonekan was only picked up as a political courier'

Gani Fawehinmi described Abacha's replacement of Shonekan as 'an organised change of government' and added: 'The change of government, the present position of Abacha had long been organised by Babangida through decree 61 of 1993, section 4. Shonekan was only picked up as a political courier to give a breathing space so that Abacha would come in to give effect to section 4.'[10]

Others such as the former director-general of the Centre for Democratic Studies, Professor Omo Omoruyi, also alleged that there was a secret pact between Babangida and Abacha to rule Nigeria in succession to each other.[11] Although Babangida denied the existence of such a pact ('It is not true there was a pact or oath between us'), he admitted that 'Major-General Garba Duba, a very close friend of his [Abacha], once warned me that I should never allow Abacha to have the opportunity of being head of state'.[12]

Although this book is a historical account of a decade in the life of the nation, it would not be complete without an examination of the individuals who shaped the contours of that decade. In Nigeria's cut-throat Game of Thrones-style politics, one man stands out as the most intriguing. Abacha did not possess Balewa's eloquence, Azikiwe's charisma, Gowon's charm or Babangida's 'breathtaking wizardry in selling the past'.[13] Yet he was probably the most mesmerising protagonist of them all. Abacha had Pinochet's ruthlessness, Mobutu's kleptocratic streak, and the mystique of Putin. Abacha and his family were, and remain, intensely private. Even though he had spent a decade in the uppermost echelons of the government, he managed to maintain a veil of secrecy around himself by the time he became head of state in 1993. Nothing was known about the quiet, diminutive man (he stood approximately 5 feet 6 or 7 inches tall) who stared out without expression from behind dark sunglasses. That he wore dark glasses indoors and outdoors, day and night, added to his mystique and intimidating aura.

Babangida described Abacha as 'a man of very limited words. He doesn't talk a lot. You can't predict him.'[14] The media knew next to nothing about a man who had been de facto the second most powerful person in Nigeria for eight consecutive years. No one knew his hobbies, his favourite food or colour, who his friends were, or his temperament. So little was known about him that when he became head of state, media outlets could find nothing to publish other than a bland and mechanical one-paragraph recitation of the military command posts he held during his army career. Abacha did not grant interviews, allowed no leaks to the press, and limited his public statements to terse broadcasts during national near-death experiences like coups. Although Abacha's public pronouncements were rare, they always had great impact. His inaugural broadcast to the nation as head of state was his fourth pivotal public speech in a decade. His first was on December 31, 1983, when he announced the military's overthrow of President Shagari, and Shagari's replacement by Major-General Buhari. Twenty months later Abacha announced on August 27, 1935 that Babangida had overthrown and replaced Buhari. On April 22, 1990 Abacha rallied troops in Lagos to suppress a coup against his friend Babangida, then announced the coup's failure on a national broadcast.

Abacha was Nigeria's second head of state from the ancient northern city of Karo (the first being General Murtala Muhammed). He was born in Kano on September 20, 1943. Although Kano is traditionally a Hausa city, Abacha's father was a Kanuri. He attended the Gidan Makama Primary School and began his military training at the Nigerian Military Training College (NMTC) in Kaduna in 1962 along with Ibrahim Babangida, Mamman Vatsa, Sani Sami,[15] Sani Bello,[16] Garba Duba, Gado Nasko and Mohammed Magoro. Thereafter he proceeded to the Mons Officer Cadet School at Aldershot in the UK, and he was commissioned as a second lieutenant in 1964. In the early 1960s he met a young woman named Maryam Jiddah when he was a student at the Provincial Secondary School (now Rumfa College)[17] in Kano. At the time Maryam was a student at the Dala Girls Secondary School, also in Kano. They married in December 1965, and subsequently had ten children, seven sons and three daughters.[18]

After Nigeria's first military coup in January 1966, during which Igbo officers killed several northern military and political leaders, Abacha became, according to one of his Igbo colleagues, 'very unfriendly' and 'would barely exchange greetings' with Igbo officers.[19] This colleague informed me that Abacha 'took the coup badly'. Unsurprisingly, six months later in July 1966, Abacha was among the northern officers who staged a revenge coup against Igbo officers. Abacha fought for the federal army during the civil war between 1967 and 1970 as a member of the army's 2 Division. He remained out of the public limelight until December 31, 1983, at which time he was the commander of the strategic 9th Mechanised Brigade in Ikeja, Lagos State. On that day he teamed up with several of his decades-long military colleagues and friends such as Babangida, Buhari, Brigadier-Generals Ibrahim Bako and Jerry

Useni and Colonel Joshua Dogonyaro to overthrow President Shagari in a military coup.

After the coup, Abacha was appointed GOC of 2 Mechanised Division in Ibadan, and a member of the Supreme Military Council, which replaced Shagari's government. Just over a year and a half later, the military leadership split, and officers loyal to Babangida decided to overthrow Buhari. However, there was a sticking point: Abacha was loyal to Buhari. If Babangida could not obtain Abacha's support for the coup, it would fail and Babangida and the other officers in the plot would be executed. Babangida met Abacha to personally plead for his support in deposing Buhari. According to Babangida: 'Nobody could get him [Abacha] to be involved except me because of our relationship. If it were any other person, he would have gone to the side of Buhari. But when I sat him down, he said, "You are my chief, anything you want I will do." So the personal relationship also helped in trying to recruit people into this unholy alliance.'[20]

Abacha helped Babangida to overthrow Buhari on August 27, 1985. Babangida rewarded Abacha for his role in the coup by appointing him chief of army staff in his place when he became the new head of state. Although Babangida continually purged the army and retired his military chiefs throughout his eight years in power, Abacha always survived such purges. Babangida dissolved the entire Armed Forces Ruling Council (AFRC) on February 2, 1989, and reduced its reconstituted membership from 28 to 19; yet Abacha remained an AFRC member. On December 29, 1989 Babangida retired all of the military service chiefs, except of course Abacha. Not only did Abacha retain his post as chief of army staff but he gained a new portfolio as chairman of the Joint Chiefs of Staff.

Abacha survived Babangida's numerous purges because of his loyalty to him. Around 2 am on April 22, 1990, officers from the oil-producing areas of the south launched a violent coup attempt to depose Babangida. The plotters shelled Babangida's residence at Dodan Barracks in Lagos. The officer who led the assault was told to 'put his turret down and blow the place apart', and he undertook his mission as instructed: he blew the roof off Babangida's residence. The plotters searched for Abacha at his house, but could not find him as he was visiting a friend at a nearby guest house.[21] The mutineers then proceeded to shoot up the guest house in their search for him but could not find him as he was hiding in a bedroom concealed behind a panelled wall.[22] The shooting alerted his driver, who attempted to drive away, but he was shot and wounded by the mutineers. After the mutineers departed, Abacha sent for an armoured vehicle and troops to provide rein-forcing guards at the guest house. He then called his son Ibrahim, who picked him up in a civilian car and drove him to Flagstaff House, where he rendezvoused with Babangida and other key officers.

Abacha phoned key infantry, signals and military police installations and urged their commanders (including Colonels Raji Rasaki and Ishaya Bamaiyi) to counter-attack. The army's realisation that Abacha was still alive dramatically changed the vacillating soldiers' reaction to the coup. One soldier informed me that many soldiers immediately swung behind Abacha after concluding that hesitation in obeying Abacha's orders 'was not worth the risk'.[23] The mutineers surrendered after running out of ammunition following nearly twelve hours of fighting. Abacha announced the coup's failure in a characteristically terse nationwide broadcast, in which he casually referred to the mutineers as a 'national security nuisance'. Later that day Babangida addressed the nation to confirm his survival. He was especially grateful to Abacha, whom he referred to and praised by name. Abacha emerged from the April 1990 coup with his already formidable reputation greatly enhanced. Babangida promoted Abacha to a four-star general, thus making Abacha the first non-head of state ever to become a serving four-star general in Nigeria's history. Babangida also relin-quished his position as minister of defence to Abacha, who thus simultaneously served as minister of defence and chairman of the Joint Chiefs of Staff. The press dubbed him 'the Khalifa' (king in waiting).

After that April 1990 coup, Abacha behaved like a man aware that he was untouchable. When Lt-General Salihu Ibrahim succeeded Abacha as chief of army staff, Abacha refused to vacate Flagstaff House, even though it was meant to serve as the official residence of the incumbent chief of army staff. When Babangida moved Nigeria's capital from Lagos to Abuja in 1991, Abacha stayed behind in Lagos and did not move to Abuja to join Babangida. The Ministry of Defence (and Abacha) remained over 500 kilometres away from the new capital and seat of government. This led to the creation of two rival centres of military power, in Lagos and Abuja, led by Abacha and Babangida respectively. This was the beginning of Abacha's construction of his own political empire. He was bold enough to interfere with, and attempt to exercise operational control of, Babangida's personal security unit, the elite Brigade of Guards. He did so even though the brigade had its own commander who was not under Abacha's operational command, and who reported directly to Babangida. Even the all-powerful Babangida treated Abacha with kid gloves and never called him to order. Babangida tolerated Abacha's excesses because he 'may not be bright upstairs but he knows how to overthrow governments and overpower coup plotters. He saw to my coming to office in 1985 and to my protection in the many coups I faced.'[24]

Yet the Nigerian public were largely unaware of Abacha's antecedents. Two sentences from his inaugural speech stood out. He vowed that 'we will not settle anybody'. The fact that a head of state used a colloquial phrase such as 'settle' (which in Nigerian parlance means to bribe someone) demonstrated the extent to which settlement culture had seeped into Nigerian society. More ominously Abacha also warned that 'Any attempt to test our will shall be decisively dealt with'. He kept his word.

5

HE SAID SHE SAID

'If I had gone to the university for five hundred years, I would not have learnt what I've learnt in the last one year.'

Moshood Abiola

Abacha came to power in strange circumstances. His seizure of power was contrived by an alliance between military officers, pro-democracy groups and traditional rulers. Bizarrely, Abiola was an accomplice to the military takeover. Before taking power, Abacha and Diya met and gave Abiola, Tinubu, Yoruba traditional leaders and pro-democracy groups prior notice of the military takeover. However, all parties left with substantially different interpretations of what they had discussed and agreed on with each other. The military were convinced that they had secured the consent of pro-democracy groups and traditional leaders for another military government, whereas the civilian groups believed that Abacha's only job was to take whatever measures were necessary to declare Abiola as president. Although they tried to keep their cooperation secret, a drip-feed of information leaked out from both sides. The events of the days immediately prior to and after Abacha's assumption of power demonstrated the extraordinary level of collaboration between Abacha, Abiola and the civilian pro-democracy campaigners. Diya claimed that 'We made wide consultations. With a lot of people; pro-democracy activists. Nobody, not one person said he did not support Abacha.'[1]

Sunday November 21 1993—Abiola's house: Ikeja, Lagos

Four days after Abacha took power, Abiola, his SDP supporters and other loyalists met at his house in Lagos to formulate their response to the new regime. Abacha and Diya offered ministerial posts in the new government to Abiola's supporters. These offers of government participation divided Abiola's supporters. Abiola claimed that some of his followers argued that they should 'cooperate' with Abacha or risk losing out to his political rivals who would not hesitate to join his government. Abiola said that 'the Kingibes and Jakandes were of the opinion that if we refused to cooperate, the Yar'Adua group would cooperate with the junta and their people would become ministers and make money'.[2] Kingibe later summarised the outcome of that meeting in a letter to Abiola:

> following the collapse of the interim government on November 17th, 1993, all of us for democracy and for the restoration of June 12 election even during your [Abiola] long sojourn abroad met on November 21, 1993 in your house. We considered what should be our reaction to the new development. *The overwhelming majority decided that we should cooperate with and participate if invited into the new government.* There were a few vocally expressed dissenting views, including your [Abiola] own. However, you [Abiola] yourself summed up the conclusion of the meeting by saying that anyone who wanted to may participate in the government if invited.[3]

Monday November 22 1993—Abacha's house, Lagos

The next day Abiola and Abacha met at Abacha's home in Lagos. National television broadcast footage of the two men warmly embracing and smiling. Abiola brought some of his supporters, including Kingibe, Jakande and Bola Tinubu. Neither Abacha nor Abiola revealed what they had discussed at this meeting, or its outcome. Abiola's heavily publicised presence at Abacha's house conferred legitimacy on the latter's assumption of power, and gave the impression that Abiola consented to it. After this meeting, the normally bombastic and talkative Abiola maintained an uncharacteristic public silence and refused to condemn the military assumption of power, which had dissolved his party and the democratically elected institutions necessary for him to govern as president. What was behind Abiola's benign disposition towards another military leader who had taken power without uttering a single word about Abiola's electoral mandate?

It seems that Abiola reached some form of 'armistice' agreement with the new military government. After the meeting at Abiola's house, his supporters relayed their decision to participate in Abacha's government to the 'Awoists'. One of Abiola's Awoist supporters was Adekunle Michael Ajasin, who claimed that he was:

> informed that Chief Abiola had struck a deal with Abacha such that within six months of Abacha in power, Abiola would be sworn in. The period of Abacha was to be used to prepare the grounds by placating those opposed to Abiola, recalling the electoral commission to complete its aborted job on the June 12 election, and preparing for the installation of the winner of the election, that is, Chief MKO Abiola.[4]

Diya corroborated Ajasin's statement and admitted that the initial objective of the military's return to power was to engineer an Abiola presidency. Diya later said: 'The objective then was to validate it [Abiola's election victory]. That is the truth. But we had a sort of divided opinion. Some queried if we could validate it straight away like that or if we could try to correct the system and then validate it thereafter.'[5]

'He virtually begged me to accept the offer'

Abiola seemed to believe that the fastest route to becoming president was not via a civilian uprising against the military, but by relying on backdoor deals with the military. Abiola was so confident that Abacha would cede power to him that he submitted to Abacha the names of his allies whom he wanted to be appointed as government ministers. One of the ministers that Abiola nominated was Olu Onagoruwa, a prominent civil rights lawyer who had campaigned against military rule for several years. Onagoruwa claimed that Abiola phoned him two days after Abacha dissolved the ING and:

> virtually begged me to accept the offer of the post of attorney-general and minister of justice. This would give him rest of mind and would form part of his strategy for regaining his victory at the presidential polls of June 12th ... 'Have you been given any definite promise?' I asked him. Abiola replied, 'Everything has been well arranged. I am very positive about this', he said ... I said to him, 'If this is your position, I will come home and take up the appointment.'[6]

The ministers whom Abiola nominated were to be his ears and eyes in the government. Abiola's nominees agreed to join the cabinet on the understanding that they would resign if Abacha reneged on his promise to Abiola. Solomon Lar and other SDP members also phoned Abacha to submit a list of ministers whom they wanted in the government.[7]

Tuesday November 23 1993—'the coming of Chief Abiola was a foregone conclusion under the new plan'

Ajasin also said that he was 'assured by emissaries of the new helmsman that the coming of Chief Abiola was a foregone conclusion under the new plan'.[8] Ajasin nominated Mrs Mobolaji Osomo as a minister in the new government. Other Abiola supporters (apart from Onagoruwa and Osomo) and SDP members decided to accept ministerial appointments in Abacha's government. These included Abiola's vice-presidential running mate, Babagana Kingibe; the coordinator of Abiola's presidential campaign, Dr Jonathan Zwingina; the former governor of Lagos State, Lateef Jakande; Ebenezer Babatope; the former governor of Anambra State, Jim Nwobodo; Jerry Gana; the former Senate president, Iyorchia Ayu; the former governor of Kano State, Abubakar Rimi; and the former governor of Plateau State, Solomon Lar. With so many SDP members joining the government, Abacha's cabinet bore the appearance of an Abiola committee led by Abacha.

Incredibly, pro-democracy leaders took the risk of accepting the dissolution of all democratically elected structures in the country in exchange for ministerial posts in an unelected military government. Many Nigerians were astonished by the presence of Abiola's supporters and so-called pro-democracy leaders in a military government. This seriously eroded the credibility of the pro-democracy movement, and Nigerians began to view civilian and military leaders as part of the same unreliable and interchangeable elite group. A Campaign for Democracy activist said that when he saw the names of civilians who joined the new military government, 'It was the biggest shock of my life. We took risks in the name of democracy. Hundreds were killed by the National Guards. Hundreds were detained by the SSS [State Security Service] and police. Then, our so-called pro-democracy leaders joined the military to terminate democracy. I still cannot believe it.'[9]

The intellectual figures whom Abacha assembled in his cabinet gave him credibility at a time of uncertainty. The president of the Civil Liberties Organisation, Olisa Agbakoba, said, 'Whether we like it or not Abacha stole a major coup by bringing into his government all these people—Jakande, Babatope, Onagoruwa, who would lend him credibility and legitimacy.'[10] For the remainder of 1993 Abiola faded into the background, and refrained from criticising Abacha, and the pro-democracy tumult subsided. Everyone adopted a wait-and-see approach to Abacha, who, strangely, ran the government from Nigeria's former capital city of Lagos, and had not bothered to move into the presidential villa at Abuja. He did not move to Abuja until February 1994. For the first five months of Abacha's tenure, Abiola barely said a word in public or raised a finger against the government. He had either given up his fight for the presidency or was quietly content with Abacha's rule. Then, all hell broke loose.

'The Abacha Coup: Our Original Plan'

Everything was quiet until *Newswatch* magazine published an explosive interview with Brigadier-General David Mark in its April 11, 1994 edition. Mark had been one of the most powerful officers in the Babangida government, but Abacha retired him shortly after Babangida's reign ended. Mark was a member of perhaps the most politicised cohort in the history of the Nigerian army: the third regular combatant course of the Nigerian Defence Academy (NDA). The graduating cadets of 'Course Three', as they were known, produced more members of military governments than any other cadet cohort in the history of the Nigerian army.

A brief biography of Mark is necessary to contextualise the importance attached to his published interview and to the power he held and continued to hold for several years. He was an Idoma from Benue State in the middle belt. Mark was intellectually sophisticated and intense. A military colleague described him as 'an immensely amiable and focused officer with unusual political attitudes and an inclination consistent with the prevailing habits of his cohorts of the 3rd Nigerian Defence Academy Regular Course'.[11] After graduating from the NDA in 1970, he enlisted in the strategically important signal corps. He served under the long-time inspector of signals, Brigadier Murtala Muhammed, who later became head of state in 1975. A signals officer who worked with Mark informed me that he was 'the most feared officer in signals'.[12] In 1976, Mark was appointed the chairman of the abandoned property implementation committee in Port Harcourt which adjudicated in so-called cases of 'abandoned properties' from which their Igbo owners fled during the civil war, only to find them occupied by members of other ethnic groups who refused to vacate when their Igbo owners returned after the war concluded.

The technical expertise of signals officers and their ability to disrupt or sever telecommunications networks make them key strategic assets during coups. Mark was a participant in the 1983 and 1985 coups that brought Buhari and Babangida, respectively, to power. After the 1985 coup, Babangida appointed Mark as the military governor of Babangida's home state of Niger, and later as the minister of communications. During his time at the ministry he became a friend and business associate of Abiola. At the time the June 12 election annulment occurred, Mark was serving as the director of strategic studies at the National War College in Abuja.[13] Ironically he was then delivering lectures on the role of the military in a democratic society.

'It was a coup against democracy'

Mark blew the lid off intra-military intrigues in an explosive, no-holds barred interview which was published under the title 'The Abacha Coup: Our Original Plan'.[14] Mark contradicted Diya's public statement that 'our stay will be brief'.[15] Instead he alleged that Abacha had a secret plan to rule until the end of the 20th century: 'The hidden agenda is for the regime to end on a historic note on the 31st December 1999.' Alarmingly, Mark added that Abacha and Diya had briefed pro-democracy campaigners and traditional rulers in advance and secured their consent for a return to military rule:

> He [Diya] eventually assured us that after an extensive consultation with Gani [Fawehinmi], Beko, [Femi] Falana, Onagoruwa, the CLO, CD, the elders, the Obas, and the leaders of thought they agreed to support a total military regime for no less than five years ... after Diya consulted with the Yoruba leaders of thought, they unanimously and unequivocally agreed to forgo June 12 and instead opted for a military government.

'Federal appointments are not designed as a compensation for the civil war'

Mark also claimed that the military agreed to appoint two vice-presidents, one a civilian who would be in charge of the federal ministries, and the other a military chief of general staff who would be responsible for the administration of states. Alex Ekwueme, an Igbo, was nominated as the civilian vice-president, Diya as chief of general staff, and Lt-General Aliyu Mohammed as minister of defence. However, that plan failed when, according to Mark, Diya 'went berserk' and objected to Ekwueme on the ground that 'federal appointments are not designed as a compensation for the civil war', and Abacha refused to surrender the defence portfolio.

Mark added:

> Abacha's regime qualifies for a space in the Guinness Book of Records as the greatest betrayal of the century. It is a betrayal of the military officers involved,

it is a betrayal of the CD and CLO people and it is a betrayal of the hope and aspirations of Nigerians. It is a betrayal of democracy. It was not a coup against the ING but as it turned out was a coup against democracy, supported and nourished by politicians who behaved like chameleons. Surprisingly it was Abiola's close associates who were urging Abacha to take over. They dined with Abiola in the afternoon but in the night urged Abacha to seize power and forget June 12. I never believed that human beings could be so treacherous, unprincipled, and shameless.

Mark's interview damaged the credibility of major players across the political spectrum: the military, elected politicians, pro-democracy campaigners, and even Yoruba traditional rulers. If true, his allegations portrayed all of them as being in a venal alliance. The interview sent shock waves across the political landscape.

'This man is a do-nothing head of state'

The shocking revelations in Mark's interview with *Newswatch* reactivated the opposition, which suddenly realised that Abacha spoke rarely and that his government was merely treading water. Gani Fawehinmi declared, 'This man is a do-nothing head of state.' He added: 'I don't see any difference between Babangida and Abacha. The only difference I see is that Babangida could be seen to be doing something negative ... He's [Abacha's] negatively stationary. Babangida was negatively moving into disaster. Abacha is stationary but negatively digging a hole for the demise of the Nigerian people. There is no difference between the two of them.'[16]

The government reacted to contain the turbulence arising from Mark's interview. After *Newswatch* published the interview, the State Security Service (SSS) arrested its editors Dan Agbese, Ray Ekpu and Yakubu Mohammed on April 7. The SSS demanded to see copies of *Newswatch*'s next edition, and raided Agbese's house on Monday April 11, in the process ransacking every one of the seven bedrooms, and took away several documents.

Although the government had set up a National Constitutional Conference Commission in line with Abacha's promise to establish a conference to discuss Nigeria's future constitution, not much had happened on this front and at least six members of the commission threatened to resign unless the government briefed them. It was only then that the government hurriedly took steps in mid-April 1994 to prepare for the constitutional conference. In response, Celestine Owodiong, a history lecturer, sarcastically asked, 'Does it mean that the military government was not working on any programme between November 17th 1993 and April 15th 1994?'[17] Despite these preparatory steps, the government did not establish the conference for another two and a half months. However, the government's silence, combined with Mark's revelations had roused the opposition to greater vigilance. It also ruptured the collaboration between the military and Yoruba political groups. The government's honeymoon period had ended.

6

CONFRONTATION

By April 1994 the nudge-nudge, wink-wink understandings between civilian politicians, pro-democracy groups and the military had broken down. The civilian opposition had to face the consequences of their naivety. Rulers do not easily give up power; rather, power must be snatched away from them. Abiola's supporters had also demonstrated the usual Nigerian civilian weakness of falling into every trap that the military set for them. The politicians now realised belatedly that they had made a mistake by not maintaining a united front in support of the June 12 election or the ING. Had they called Babangida's bluff and allowed the ING to stabilise and conduct free elections, the military would have had no pretext to force out the ING and resume military rule.

Six months had passed and Abacha had not made any announcement regarding the fate of the annulled June 12 election. A frustrated Tinubu met Diya and demanded explanations. Tinubu claimed he told Diya, 'This is my last visit to you ... if you are not in this government to actualise June 12, you have betrayed us, you have betrayed the masses of Nigeria and you will not come back the same.' When Diya asked Tinubu whether this statement was a declaration of war, Tinubu replied by telling him to interpret it as he pleased.[1]

On May 15, 1994 a group of veteran politicians, Awoists and pro-democracy groups formed an umbrella organisation called the National Democratic Coalition (NADECO). It was the nearly 70-year-old Anthony Enahoro who proposed NADECO's formation to Ajasin at a meeting of Afenifere,[2] which accepted the idea. Although he was not a Yoruba, Enahoro (an Esan) was a veteran Awoist politician from the pre-independence era who had proposed the successful motion which eventually led to Nigeria's independence in 1960. He had also been charged with treason alongside Awolowo in 1962. He then fled to the United Kingdom, but the British government repatriated him to face trial in Nigeria. He was convicted alongside Awolowo and imprisoned, but was released by the military government in 1967. Like Enahoro, many of the Awoists in NADECO had been former members of the Action Group. NADECO's 70-year-old deputy leader, Abraham Adesanya, was one of Awolowo's defence lawyers at his treason trial in 1962. He was also the first person to visit Awolowo and commiserate with him on July 10, 1963 after Awolowo's first son died. Several retired military officers such as the former chief of defence staff Lt-General Julius Akinrinade, Major-General Olufemi Olutoye and Air Commodore Dan Suleiman also joined NADECO. The organisation's aim was to end military rule immediately and campaign for Abiola to become president.

Abiola wanted to be president but could not make up his mind whether confrontation, compromise or back-door deals were the best way of achieving that objective. At first Abiola insisted on the validation of the June 12 election results. Then, according to NADECO's Ajasin, he changed his mind and opted to accept fresh elections during which he would sponsor another candidate, Lateef Jakande, who would resign and allow Abiola to contest the presidency. Abiola then changed his mind again, and went back to seeking validation of the annulled election result. NADECO members were frustrated by Abiola's vacillation and decided to take a more confrontational stand against the military. They urged Abiola to be resolute, stay the course, and fight for his mandate. NADECO gave Abacha's government a 15-day deadline (expiring on May 31, 1994) to resign and install Abiola as president. NADECO's backing seemed to reinvigorate Abiola, and he too changed his attitude and became more hostile to the military. He appeared more resolute than before.

Abiola's renewed agitation for the presidency emboldened the politicians. The former Senate president Ameh Ebute issued a statement reconvening the Senate, which Abacha had dissolved six months earlier. Within a few days more than 300 members of the House of Representatives reconvened in Lagos and issued a statement supporting Ebute's position. State legislatures in Delta, Kano, Lagos and Katsina States also reconvened. Several other political groupings mobilised as well, including the Eastern Mandate Union, the National Unity Organisation of Nigeria (NUON) led by General Obasanjo, the

Democratic Alternative, Muslim Rights Concern, and the National Association of Sea Dogs.

'Let the heavens fall'

At a Nigerian Institute of International Affairs event in Lagos in June, Abiola whipped up the audience by rhetorically asking them, 'Are you ready for my presidency?' The audience chanted 'yes' back at him. When someone asked 'when?' he replied, 'I will be sworn in on the first anniversary of the election ... and then let the heavens fall.'[3] The government did not take Abiola seriously. Diya said that 'Abiola is just joking. He doesn't mean it. I know him very well. He is my good friend. I know he can't do it. I think all those things he is saying are mere threats.'[4]

As NADECO's May 31 deadline approached, NADECO member Bola Tinubu vowed that if Abacha failed to call on Abiola to form a new government before the end of the month, 'the lovers of democracy in the country will not hesitate to make this country ungovernable for the present administration.'[5] NADECO's confrontational stance put the government on red alert. The chief of army staff, Major-General Chris Alli, ordered aggressive surveillance at military barracks and at locations in or near military units. He also ordered civilians to be expelled from all military barracks. The director of defence information, Brigadier-General Fred Chijuka, subtly warned Abiola by telling reporters that 'government knows what to do' if he carried out his threat. The inspector-general of police, Ibrahim Coomasie, released a strongly worded statement in which he described NADECO as an 'illegal organisation', and warned: '...any person, whether a politician or a retired military officer or a pro-democracy crusader who thinks he is in a position to install another government is advised in his own interests to tread with caution as security agencies are prepared to act decisively on such matters.'[6] He added that there would be 'grave consequences' for 'these treasonable acts'.

'There will be confrontation with the military'

Yet Tinubu continued to insist that 'Abacha must resign. Enough is enough of the military.' When asked what would happen if the government did not resign by May 31, Tinubu replied, 'Confrontation. There will be confrontation with the military.'[7]

The government then started cracking down on opposition groups. Security forces arrested Ebute and charged him with treason. Next, they raided

Obasanjo's farm in Ota on June 4, 1994, to prevent the inauguration of NUON. In the space of one week, 30 NADECO members were arrested or asked to submit to interrogation, including Ajasin, Enahoro, Bola Ige, Christian Onoh, Jonah Jang and Dan Suleiman. As security forces started rounding up pro-democracy activists, Abiola became more defiant. He dared security forces to 'come and arrest me. I will be sworn in as president of Nigeria.' He added, 'They have no business arresting those they are arresting. If they want anything, let them come for me. No bastard can do that.'[8] But the security forces did not respond to Abiola's challenge, and left him alone. The most the police did was to place Abiola's house and business premises under 24-hour surveillance.

As more and more politicians and pro-democracy campaigners fell into the security forces' dragnet, Tinubu went into hiding. However, he continued to grant interviews to local and foreign media from his hiding places while security forces hunted for him. Tinubu claimed that he was receiving threatening phone calls from unknown persons. One of the callers warned him, 'We know that you are meeting. You must stop that meeting or we will deal with you appropriately.' His house in Victoria Island, Lagos, was petrol-bombed. After accepting that his life was in danger and Nigeria was no longer safe for him, he disguised himself by dressing like a northerner with a turban and *babanriga*. After bidding farewell to Abiola's wife Kudirat (who initially did not recognise Tinubu in his disguise), he fled into exile after a motorbike escape in the early hours of the morning across Nigeria's border into the neighbouring Benin Republic. NADECO opened their own underground railroad of sorts by creating secret escape routes through which their members fled into exile to avoid the security forces.

'I don't think he is the Messiah Nigeria is looking for'

Support for Abiola's renewed claim for the presidency was not unanimous among Yorubas. Former head of state General Obasanjo, who had attended the Baptist Boys High School with Abiola, was not an Abiola fan. Obasanjo said of Abiola: 'I know him very well, much more than all of you. He was my classmate but I don't think he is the Messiah Nigeria is looking for.'[9] Obasanjo's comment caused the Abeokuta (Abiola's home town) brains trust to join the debate. Abeokuta is something of an artistic, intellectual and political hub in Nigeria. Most countries, let alone one town, would be proud to boast of the eminent personalities that have emerged from Abeokuta. The town's famous citizens include Africa's first Nobel Prize laureate, Professor Wole Soyinka, former head of state General Obasanjo and Ernest Shonekan, Fela Anikulapo-Kuti and his brother Beko Ransome-Kuti, the chairman of the opposition Campaign for Democracy. Abiola replied to Obasanjo by saying:

he [Obasanjo] claimed he was my classmate. It is a lie! He was a year my junior in school. All these petty elements should go and sit down. Let him go to his ward and contest an election to see how many votes he can get ... Let him produce a member of his family whose life he has improved.[10]

Soyinka also replied to Obasanjo:

This Nigeria had stopped looking for a messiah light eons ago and all she seeks is a good manager. The Nigeria I know does not care if such an individual is a cross-eyed hunchback, knock-kneed womaniser, or homosexual, atheist, animist, Muslim, or Christian born again ... The Nigeria I know lays only one condition on credentials of such a hybrid. He or she must be democratically elected.[11]

'Have you shown the same respect for us?'

Yoruba traditional rulers also made various contradictory pronouncements about Abiola. Following a meeting between Babangida and traditional rulers on July 2, 1993, the foremost Yoruba traditional ruler, the Ooni of Ife, Okunade Sijuwade, had threatened that Yorubas would secede if Abiola was not declared president. Less than one month after Abacha seized power in November 1993, the same Oba Sijuwade, who had threatened to pull his people out of Nigeria, led 18 of the Yoruba obas to Dodan Barracks on a courtesy visit to Abacha and commended him for 'pre-empting and forestalling the imminent state of war and disintegration' in Nigeria. The oba of Lagos, Adeyinka Oyekan, also wrote a letter to Abacha telling him: 'It is by the grace of Allah that as a crowning of all your achievements, you should become head of state and commander-in-chief.'[12]

Such Yoruba flip-flopping continued into 1994. NADECO had called for a boycott of the ward elections for delegates to be elected to the constitutional conference. On May 19, 1994 Yoruba traditional rulers met in the palace of the Awujale of Ijebu, Sikiru Adetona, at Ijebu-Ode. The Yoruba traditional rulers supported NADECO's call to boycott the constitutional conference elections. However, three days later another group of Yoruba traditional rulers met in Ibadan, with Diya, the military administrator of Ogun State, Lt-Colonel Daniel Akintonde, and the former military governor of the Western Region, Major-General Robert Adeyinka Adebayo. At the meeting, the Alake of Egbaland, Oyebade Lipede, scolded Diya: 'You are our son. We see how your fellow northerners worship their emirs. Have you shown the same respect for us?' After Diya assured them that the annulled June 12 election would be discussed at the constitutional conference, this group of traditional rulers told the public to ignore the earlier May 19 statement calling for a boycott. Conflicting messages from the Yoruba traditional leaders caused tragicomic consequences for Yoruba candidates for the constitutional conference. Olu Falae was elected as a delegate to the conference in his Akure Local Government Area of Ondo State. However, after being declared winner, Falae refused to accept victory or his place as a delegate to the conference.

'We wish him good luck'

The Yorubas' lack of cohesion also disappointed others who felt let down by the south-west and were reluctant to throw their weight behind a cause whose leaders could not get their house in order. They recalled that Abiola had warmly embraced Abacha on national television just six months earlier. How could people risk their lives in a struggle against a man with whom Abiola was in alliance so recently? After the experience of 1993 many people from other parts of Nigeria sat on the fence to see the depth of Abiola's conviction before taking risks on his behalf again. A former majority leader in the dissolved Delta State House of Assembly, Aneke Ifemeni, said, 'We want to see Abiola's seriousness before we can support him. We wish him good luck and hope he can stand by his words.'[13] Many in the military also did not believe that the politicians and pro-democracy campaigners were sincere. Diya claimed:

> Some of those now openly opposing Abacha's administration urged him to intervene to save the nation from disintegration. Chief MKO Abiola himself gave advice on the formation of a cabinet of men of 'timber and calibre' to gain public acceptance. He even nominated some people to ministerial appointment. Again, he wrote to congratulate General Sani Abacha as the head of state, commander in chief of the armed forces of the Federal Republic of Nigeria and crowned it by taking a photograph with him as his recognised head of state. Having done all these, you can appreciate the surprise of this administration when Chief Abiola turned around to distance himself openly from the Abacha administration and threatened to declare himself president of this country.[14]

Abiola was doing all the right things but at the wrong time. He failed to grasp that momentum is not an automatic device that he could control and switch on and off at will at a time and place of his choosing. Political momentum was with him in mid-late 1993, but instead of riding its wave, he allowed it to dissipate, then tried to reactivate it twelve months later. In 1994, Abiola belatedly did what he should have done in 1993: confront the military, galvanise public opinion, and try to make the country ungovernable for the military. In contrast, what he did in 1993—go abroad and seek international support—was more appropriate for 1994. By the time he woke up in 1994, the venom and heat of the opposition to military rule had substantially cooled. He was retroactively trying to resuscitate a pro-democracy movement that had lost steam in the ensuing eleven months. He wrote to US Vice-President Al Gore on June 3 to inform him of his intention to form a government on or before June 12. In the letter Abiola requested US support for his government, and urged the US to sustain the visa ban it imposed on Nigerian government officials, and to pressure the Nigerian government to refrain from arresting pro-democracy campaigners. His letter was unlikely to make much headway in the US as Western countries usually support governments, not individuals. This is especially the case with individuals who are opposition figures.

Abacha ignored NADECO's May 31 deadline. Both sides waited to see what the other would do. The military anticipated some form of organised protest or resistance on June 12, 1994—the first anniversary of the annulled election. Diya admitted, 'There was apprehension as all waited to see what NADECO would do beyond the terminal date of the ultimatum. Perhaps there was going to be an insurrection or some other form of active resistance to the government.'[15] Abacha and Abiola were finally going to face off. The nation waited for either man to make the first move, like a crowd waiting to see which of two Wild West gunslingers would draw their weapon first.

7

ENOUGH IS ENOUGH

The Epetedo Declaration

The government anticipated that Abiola would make a move on June 12, the first anniversary of the annulled election. A large crowd converged in the Lagos working-class neighbourhood of Epetedo on the afternoon of June 11, after rumours started swirling around that someone very important would visit later that day. Around 5 pm Abiola caught the government off guard by making a sudden appearance in Epetedo. He addressed several thousand jubilant residents in the pouring rain near the Eleganza Sports Complex. He told the crowd: 'Today, people of Nigeria, I join you in saying enough is enough! We have endured 24 years of military rule in our 35 years of Independence.' In this famous speech, which his supporters later branded 'the Epetedo declaration', Abiola declared:

> Our patience has come to an end. As of now, from this moment, a new government of national unity is in power throughout the length and breadth of the federal republic of Nigeria, led by me, Bashorun M.K.O. Abiola, as president and commander-in-chief ... I call upon the usurper, General Sani Abacha, to announce his resignation forthwith, together with the rest of his illegal ruling council.

Abiola held the Nigerian coat of arms aloft as his supporters cheered him on. Abiola also appointed retired Air Commodore Dan Suleiman, a Bachama Christian from Adamawa State in the north, as the vice-president of his 'government of national unity'. The police immediately declared Abiola a wanted person and surrounded his house after he returned home. In an escape that has never been fully explained till this day, Abiola somehow managed to leave his house and abscond without the armed police officers stationed outside noticing. Popular accounts claimed that Abiola evaded the police by disguising himself as a woman. The chances of a man as large and proud as Abiola convincingly disguising himself as a woman are extremely slim. A far more likely explanation is that Abiola had moles and sympathisers in the police. Assistant Commissioner of Police Kehinde Oyenuga (a Yoruba) was a close friend of Abiola's aide Prince Ademola Adeniji-Adele, and NADECO member Wahab Dosunmu is his wife's uncle. Oyenuga claims that when Abiola made the Epetedo declaration, he deliberately ordered police patrol vehicles away from Epetedo to prevent his arrest.[1]

'Chief Abiola's situation became precarious'

It is difficult to decipher what Abiola and NADECO hoped to achieve with the presidential declaration. Both the declaration and the ultimatum to the government seemed like spontaneous measures without deep preparation, a plan B or international support. There was no daring escape plan or human shield of protesters. Abiola's and NADECO's primary tactic seemed to consist of telling the government precisely what they planned to do in advance. They appeared to think that uttering words and threats would somehow catapult Abiola into the presidential villa. NADECO's leader, Michael Ajasin, later said:

> We had reckoned that the proclamation would shake the military and possibly attract the backing of some of its top officers ... But for various reasons that we later discovered, these military sympathisers could not do anything to assist Chief Abiola. With neither military backing nor territorial control Chief Abiola's situation became precarious, leading to his decision to go into hiding.[2]

Abiola went into hiding and was not seen or heard from for the next twelve days. Neither was Abacha. Abiola emerged from hiding on Wednesday, June 22, after allegedly hiding at the house of Wahab Dosunmu in Lagos (according to Dele Mumodu).[3] He addressed a rally at the Abebe playing ground in the Surulere area of Lagos, accompanied by NADECO members such as Suleiman, Cornelius Adebayo, Wahab Dosunmu and Olabiyi Durojaiye. The event was part political rally, part religious revival. It featured brass bands, trumpets, dancing, and a crowd chanting political songs and 'MKO! MKO!' Abiola said that he had been 'consulting' with members of his government of national unity during his twelve days of silence. He announced the first major policy measure of his new government by declaring that 'with immediate effect education throughout Nigeria will be made available to all children free of fees, levies, or any imposition to give equality of opportunity to all our children regardless of the circumstances of their parents'. After addressing the rally, Abiola climbed into a black Toyota Land Cruiser owned by Prince Ademola Adeniji-Adele, and proceeded in a slow convoy with *okadas* (motorcycle taxis) accompanying him as unofficial outriders all the way to his neighbourhood in the Ikeja area of Lagos. Despite knowing that the police were looking for him, he naively went back home. When he arrived, he found the police already there waiting for him. Depending on whom one asks, either two, five or six hundred policemen came to arrest Abiola. Whatever the number, a great many armed police moved in and surrounded his house. Given the large crowd that accompanied him, the police wisely kept their distance. A bloodbath would have ensued had they tried to apprehend him in full view of the crowd. The police barricaded Abiola and his family inside his house, and refused to allow anyone to leave or enter. NADECO planned to protect Abiola by using thousands of sympathisers to form a human shield around the dwelling. However, after eating and drinking, the crowd of supporters began to disperse and go home.

'Why are they letting you talk on the phone to the BBC?'

Around 10.30 pm the police positioned three armoured vehicles at the gates of Abiola's house. His wife Kudirat (who spoke Hausa fluently) went outside and in Hausa, asked them what they wanted. They told her they had a warrant for Abiola's arrest. Kudirat flew into a rage, started arguing with them, and asked why they had to send so many officers to arrest one man. She said that if they had to arrest Abiola, she would allow only five or six of them inside the house. After a stand-off, four to six senior police officers entered Abiola's home, and went upstairs into his living room, where they informed him that they had orders to arrest him. The police led Abiola away at about 1 am on June 23, 1994. Assistant Commissioner of Police Oyenuga confirmed that Abiola had surrendered and that the police did not have to storm his house in order to arrest him.[4/5] Abiola preferred to hand himself over to Oyenuga, whom he trusted to protect him from being manhandled or mistreated by other officers.

Abiola was in fact comfortable enough to place a phone call to the BBC while being arrested. The world was treated to a tragicomic radio broadcast during which Abiola described his arrest live on air to the BBC journalist Robin Denselow while he was being led away by the police ('Yes, I am being arrested'). In a chaotic and noisy 'interview' while police, supporters and bystanders jostled and shouted in the background, Abiola cheerily reassured the concerned Denselow, 'Don't worry yourself, my friend,' and made an analogy with Mandela's experience. He said arrest and imprisonment was one of the 'qualifications' required for leadership 'in this part of the world'. When the puzzled Denselow asked him, 'Why are they letting you talk on the phone to the BBC while they are in the middle of arresting you?', the ever witty Abiola replied, 'They have come to arrest me, not to arrest my mouth!' and laughed. Abiola may have been relaxed because he did not believe the police would detain him for long. His doctor, Ore Falomo, said that Abiola 'thought it would be a matter of two, three weeks' before his release.[6] Abiola was so casual about his arrest that he told Denselow: 'Please let me go. I am delaying them!' Abiola then got into a car with his wife Kudirat and Oyenuga and continued speaking on the phone to the BBC. Denselow even cheekily asked whether he could speak to the police officer in the car with them before ominously concluding his interview by saying, 'You still say you're the president of Nigeria but it is not much good if you're going to be in jail.'

When Kudirat tried to stay with her husband, the police aggressively separated the couple, and pushed her away. Six police officers held Kudirat and pinned her down while they took Abiola away. As she struggled and refused to be parted from her husband, her covering fell off in the melee. She continued fighting with them as they placed Abiola in the back seat of a waiting Peugeot 504. Several officers sat on either side of him on the back seat. After they took him away, Kudirat became more enraged and spat at the police officers. Abiola was driven to the airport and made to board a plane to Gashua in Yobe State in the north-east.

Trade unions reacted swiftly to Abiola's arrest. The secretary-general of the Nigerian Union of Petroleum and Natural Gas Workers (NUPENG), Frank Ovie Kokori (an Urhobo from Delta State in the south), was a good friend of Kingibe, and a former member of the SDP. He also knew Abiola and Yar'Adua. NUPENG called an indefinite strike on July 4, and was soon joined by the Petroleum and Natural Gas Senior Staff Association (PENGASSAN) and the Nigerian Labour Congress (NLC). The NLC chairman, Paschal Bafyau, had formed a political party in the late 1980s, the Labour Party, and was also a former member of the SDP. The trade unions demanded the unconditional release of Abiola and other political detainees, the dropping of all charges against them, the release of the June 12, 1993 election results, and the installation of the election winner as president. They also demanded that the government should immediately reopen the *Concord* and *Punch*, newspapers which the government had closed. NUPENG and PENGASSAN[7] defiantly remained on strike for seven weeks and crippled the country's economic and social life, especially in the south-west. The government came under serious pressure as a result. A government delegation led by Diya entered negotiations with the workers' unions. It included the military service chiefs, the minister of petroleum, Don Etiebet, the minister of labour and productivity, Brigadier Samuel Ogbemudia, and the minister of internal affairs, Alex Ibru. The unions' delegation included NLC chairman Bafyau, his deputy, Adams Oshiomole, and Frank Ovie Kokori of NUPENG.

'The most important case in Nigeria'

The police's treatment of Abiola heightened his standing with his fellow Yorubas. When the police brought him to court in a 'Black Maria', newspapers published an iconic black-and-white photo of Abiola climbing down from the back, which evoked memories of Awolowo doing the same during his treason trial in 1962.

The federal government arraigned Abiola on charges of treasonable felony. The presiding judge, Justice Abdullahi Mustapha, described his trial as 'the most important case in Nigeria'. Mustapha was, like former President Babangida, an alumnus of Government College, Bida, in Niger State. Despite the seriousness of the case, the judge displayed some humour. When Abiola's lawyer, Alao Aka-Bashorun, insisted on reading out the names of all 60 of Abiola's defence lawyers, Mustapha jocularly retorted that he would allow him to do so as long as the names reflected a federal character and cut across religious barriers. People inside the court chuckled at the remark. While Aka-Bashorun read the names, Mustapha joked with Aka-Bashorun and assigned states of origin to the individuals.

Abiola's lawyers complained that their client had been injured after falling down in the back of the van while it was being driven at high speed. Justice Mustapha ordered the police to stop the practice of bringing Abiola to court in a Black Maria, and then adjourned the trial. Then something strange happened. The court suddenly resumed sitting only two days after the judge announced that he had adjourned the trial for two weeks. The government flew Justice Abdullahi Mustapha from Benin to Abuja specifically to preside over a bail application for Abiola. An Ibadan-based lawyer, Ajibola Olanipekun, who had been procured by the Ibadan politician Lamidi Adedibu, filed the bail motion, supposedly on behalf of one of Abiola's children with the name of Adenike. Strangely, neither Abiola nor his chief lawyer, Godwin Olusegun Kolawole ('GOK') Ajayi, was present at the proceedings, and Abiola's family (other than 'Adenike') were unaware of the bail application. Even though Abiola and Ajayi were absent, NLC officials, including its president, Paschal Bafyau, were in court. Oddly, the government's lawyer, Dairo Amupitan, did not object to the bail application. When two of Abiola's lawyers protested to Justice Mustapha that they did not have Abiola's or Ajayi's consent for the bail application, and that Abiola did not have a child named Adenike, Mustapha ignored them and, at 5.40 pm on August 5, 1994, granted bail to Abiola. The only conditions attached to his bail were that Abiola could not do anything to undermine the peace, stability and unity of the country, address political rallies, or travel abroad without the court's consent. Despite barring Abiola from travelling abroad without permission, Justice Mustapha did not order Abiola's passport to be impounded. Why would he order Abiola not to travel abroad, but then fail to take the one additional step that would ensure compliance with his order? The judge had granted freedom to a man who did not ask for it, and without the knowledge of his chief lawyers or family. In a bizarre reversal of normal processes, this may have been the first time in Nigeria's history that the prosecution in a criminal trial decided to grant bail to a defendant, while the defendant's lawyers objected. It was utterly strange.

Unbeknown to Abiola, the bail application by 'Abiola's children' was orchestrated between the NLC and Abiola's sympathisers in the government in an attempt to get Abiola out of detention in a face-saving manner for the government and Abiola himself. Abiola's sympathisers in the government, led by Diya and supported by the chiefs of the army, navy and air force staff, respectively Major-General Alli, Rear-Admiral Madueke and Air Vice-Marshal Femi, planned and assisted Abiola's release. Diya had colluded with Bafyau and the NLC to organise the bail application and assembled Yoruba ministers, the minister of labour and productivity Brigadier Ogbemudia (retired), and the union leaders to meet and appeal to Abacha to release Abiola. On Wednesday, July 27, 1994, Yoruba ministers in the government such as Babatope, Onagoruwa, Wole Oyelese and (Mrs) Mobolaji Osomo also met with Abacha (with Diya's consent and support) for nearly two hours and pleaded with him to release Abiola, as did Ghana's President Jerry Rawlings. Abacha agreed. So far so good.

Diya's plan was for the inspector-general of police, Ibrahim Coomasie, to release Abiola, who would then board a plane that Diya had placed on standby at the Abuja airport, ostensibly to convey him to Lagos. Diya also planned for the minister of internal affairs, Alex Ibru, to accompany Abiola to the airport, and en route inform him that the plane would take him not to Lagos, but instead into exile abroad. In addition, Femi procured an air force jet to escort Abiola's plane once it took off from Abuja.

Two days after Justice Mustapha approved bail for Abiola (Sunday, August 7, 1994), NLC leaders arrived at the office of the commissioner of police for the Federal Capital Territory in preparation for receiving Abiola upon his release. Meanwhile, Babatope and Ibru met with Diya at his residence and remained on tenterhooks, hoping their plan would succeed.

However, the plan developed two hitches. Firstly, Coomasie suddenly went AWOL and could not be found to order Abiola's release. So Diya and Alli turned to the commissioner of police for the Federal Capital Territory. He in turn said he could not order Abiola's release without approval from his boss, Coomasie. An enraged Diya threatened to arrest the commissioner if he did not procure Abiola immediately. Secondly, Abiola was unsure whether he should accept bail. He instead sent a handwritten note to Attorney-General Onagoruwa stating:

> I was shown the copy of the court order by the court bailiffs in the office of the DC [Deputy Commissioner of Police] at Abuja Police Headquarters on Monday 8th August, 1994 at 8:12 p.m. The order relates to the conditions of bail stipulated by Justice A. Mustapha on 5/8/94. I will need to consult my legal representative, Chief G.O.K. Ajayi, SAN, before I can make up my mind as to what action to take on the court order. Thank you. (Signed) MKO Abiola[8]

With Abiola prevaricating, Diya asked Oba Adedapo Tejuoso to speak to him, and prevail upon him, stressing the importance of accepting bail as his life was in danger.

'NADECO leaders that should be held responsible'

Abiola made a terrible decision. He rejected bail for himself and instead opted to remain in detention. His rejection of bail which the government and senior military officers had so carefully engineered for him was mystifying. He failed to realise that he could cause far more trouble for the government as a free man rather than as a detainee. Once detained, he had no bargaining chips, and the only thing he could negotiate was his personal freedom. So why did

Abiola reject bail despite the tremendous risks that senior civilian and military officers in the government took for him? It seems that NADECO leaders and one of his wives advised him to reject bail unless it was unconditional and unless it allowed him to continue pursuing his presidential claim.

The minister of transport, Ebenezer Babatope, later claimed:

> Abacha agreed and everything was being done to facilitate Abiola's early release. The then Chief of General Staff, Lt-General Oladipo Diya, even sent an executive jet to Benin to go and bring the judge, who was to handle the matter. But what eventually happened, NADECO leaders told Abiola not to accept the bail offered him. So, Abacha had no blame over the continued incarceration of Abiola, it was NADECO leaders that should be held responsible.[9]

It seemed that Abiola and his advisers wanted Abiola to go from prison to president in one leap. Even Nelson Mandela (to whom they rather immodestly compared Abiola) had to wait for some years after his release from prison before becoming South Africa's president.

Abiola's oldest son, Kola, was so enraged that NADECO and his father's legal team rejected bail for his father that he tried to terminate Ajayi's appointment as chief counsel to Abiola, and replace him with the legendary constitutional lawyer Rotimi Williams. This caused a rift between him and his stepmother, Kudirat, who wanted to retain Ajayi. Williams applied to the court to replace Ajayi. Kudirat's insistence that Ajayi remain her husband's lead lawyer caused confusion for the court, which could not decide whether to take instructions from Abiola's wife or his son.

Neither the government nor the trial judges wanted Abiola's trial to continue. The government was on shaky legal ground because the section of the criminal code which they charged Abiola for violating dealt with the office of an elected president. Abacha was not an elected president and, as a military ruler, had no fixed term of office. A lengthy trial would open a Pandora's box with a lengthy legal examination of the legality of Abacha's government. No court was likely to convict Abiola for usurping an office to which he had been elected, and which Abacha had no constitutional basis to hold. It also raised the spectre that if Abiola was acquitted, his lawyers would file a court motion to declare the military government illegal, just as the military had done to the INC. Shortly after granting bail to Abiola in August, Justice Mustapha asked the chief judge of the Federal High Court to recuse him from presiding over Abiola's trial and to transfer the case to another judge. Mustapha made a courtroom address withdrawing himself from the case, after which people in the gallery burst into loud applause. Finding another judge to replace Mustapha became a tortuous affair. Two more judges withdrew from adjudicating Abiola's trial. Most judges in the country did not want to be involved in an essentially political case that pitted a presidential election winner against a military head of state.

Ironically, Abiola indirectly provided the government and the judges with a pretext to halt his trial but keep him in detention. In 1992 the Abiola-owned *Weekend Concord* newspaper published an exposé alleging that nine Supreme Court judges had compromised their integrity and neutrality by accepting gifts of Mercedes-Benz cars from former President Babangida.[10] Eight of the judges subsequently sued the *Concord* for libel. This severely complicated Abiola's prospects of freedom as the judges' libel suit was still pending when Abiola went on trial for treason. In November 1994 a court once again granted bail to Abiola. However, the government decided to appeal against the bail order to the Supreme Court. Abiola's lawyers argued that judges who were suing one of Abiola's businesses could not be expected also to preside over his trial. They asked the judges to recuse themselves owing to conflict of interest. This was a tactical error by Abiola's legal team. The recusal of eight of the eleven justices meant that the Supreme Court could not form a quorum to hear the appeal regarding bail for Abiola. The only way to form a quorum was to appoint more justices to the Supreme Court. The authority to do so resided with the head of state. Chief Justice Muhammadu Lawal Uwais[11] appealed to Abacha to make the appointments. Uwais recalled:

> We were working so hard, our number was depleted ... nearly every one of us was sitting every week. We had judgments to write and so on, it wasn't easy, and he deliberately refused. I approached him [Abacha] on a number of occasions, explaining that we were being overworked; we needed more justices and he will just listen, nothing will happen, for the simple reason, he didn't want Abiola's appeal to be heard.[12]

'I just don't want this man around'

Abiola's legal team had once again played right into Abacha's hands. The disqualification of most Supreme Court judges, and Abacha's refusal to appoint new ones, effectively meant the adjournment of Abiola's trial indefinitely. With Abiola's trial caught in the inertia of legal technicalities, the government had to find another way to continue detaining him. The attorney-general claimed that Abacha remarked, 'I just don't want this man [Abiola] around.'[13] Abacha converted the terms of Abiola's detention and instead detained him under the notorious Decree 2, which empowered the government to detain without charge or trial, anyone it considered a security risk. Under Decree 2 Abiola would not be allowed to make any further bail applications, nor would he be tried by a civilian court. Detention orders under Decree 2 required the consent and signature of the chief of general staff, Diya. When Diya refused to sign Abiola's detention order, Decree 2 was amended to empower the inspector-general of police to authorise Abiola's continued detention, which he did.

Abiola's commercial and family life suffered while he was in detention. He ordered all of his children abroad who had not yet commenced university to return to Nigeria in order to conserve money. His detention also generated bitter squabbling in his family, with different members of the family insisting on representation by different lawyers or arguing over his business and financial assets. It moreover caused a rift between the Yoruba political elites in the government and those in the opposition. On August 15, NADECO held a meeting at Ajasin's house with Yoruba ministers in Abacha's government (Babatope, Osomo, Onagoruwa, Jakande and Oyelese) and asked them all to resign if Abiola was not unconditionally released immediately. The ministers refused to resign, instead arguing that they needed to remain in the government in order to give Yorubas a voice within it.

'Enough is now enough'

Meanwhile the labour union strike had entered its sixth week and become the longest strike in Nigeria's history. For three days at the height of the crisis, Abacha was incommunicado and senior officers could not reach him for advice on how to respond to a labour union strike that was crippling the economy. They were simply told that he was feeling ill, was confined to bed on medical advice, and would not be able to speak to anyone. When Abacha eventually re-emerged, he came out with all guns blazing. Abacha made a 30-minute-long nationwide televised broadcast on August 17. Members of the opposition who had expected him to announce concessions or Abiola's release were disappointed. He absolved himself of blame for the June 12 annulment by stating: 'The elections were aborted by a previous government which was replaced by another government before this administration came into being and that June 12 was the culminating point of several anti-democratic injustices. It is instructive to emphasise that this administration did not instigate the problems associated with the annulled election.' He somewhat disingenuously neglected to mention that he was the common denominator in all three of Nigeria's most recent governments to which he referred. He was the second most powerful person in the government that annulled the election, the most senior minister in the government that followed, and the head of the third government after the election. He described the strike by labour unions as 'economic sabotage which carries severe penalties under our laws'. He warned:

> this administration would not stand by and watch the wilful destruction of the economic life of the country. Nations have been known to go to war on the mere threat to their economic interest. Government has remained silent not because it was weak to act. Our deliberate silence was to give erring unions time to do some rethinking and retrace their steps. Unfortunately it is obvious that this is not the case. Enough is now enough.

Ironically Abacha voiced the same phrase, 'enough is enough', that Abiola had used when he declared himself president a month earlier. Abacha dissolved the national executive boards of the striking trade unions, fired their executives, and appointed new sole administrators to replace them. Abacha named former Benue State deputy governor Ason Bur as the NLC's sole administrator, former NLC secretary-general Lasisi Osunde as PENGASSAN's sole administrator, and Ahmed Jalingo for NUPENG. Policemen took over the unions' headquarters and sealed off their premises. The government ordered all retired former NNPC workers and other oil workers to return to work in their state of residence, in order to replace the strikers. The government also arrested leaders of the striking trade unions, including Kokori, and sent them to prison.

Abacha touched a raw nerve when he said that 'the crisis ought to be a national one in which no ethnic group should seek any undue prominence' — an obvious reference to Yorubas, who viewed the annulment as being directed at them. Many June 12 supporters outside the south-west resented the way the south-west Yorubanised the annulment by portraying it as an injustice against the Yoruba rather than an injustice against Nigerian democracy. The Igbo politician Chuba Okadigbo said that 'he [Abiola] was surrounded by his tribesmen who were even more confused themselves ... They tribalised him, put a barrier around, cut him off.'[14]

'He accused me of planning to release Chief Abiola'

Abiola's decision to reject bail ended the careers of several people. Abacha went into bunker mode and no longer trusted some of his senior officers. When Alli and Madueke arrived for a Provisional Ruling Council (PRC) meeting on August 24, 1994, Abacha took them aside for separate briefings.

Diya attended Alli's briefing with Abacha and sat on one side of the table next to Alli, while Abacha sat on the other side. Abacha got straight down to business in his characteristically terse manner. In Alli's words, 'he accused me of planning to release Chief Abiola from detention, telling service officers that funds were short in coming and accused me of positioning my men in strategic positions. In addition, he said that I was carrying out some postings of officers without his knowledge.'[15]

Abacha summarily retired Alli, and then Madueke that same day. The retirement of these two ended Igbo involvement in the upper echelons of the PRC. Madueke was Igbo and, although Alli is an Ebira from Kogi State, he grew up in the Igbo town of Onitsha and speaks fluent Igbo. Both men had been close friends since their childhood when they attended Our Lady's High School in Onitsha in the early to mid-1960s. To replace Alli and Madueke, Abacha appointed Major-General Alwali Kazir and Rear-Admiral Mike Akhigbe respectively.

'Abubakar was the most sincere and straightforward'

The chief of defence staff, Major-General Abubakar, had been walking a tightrope. Abacha distrusted him because of his closeness to Babangida and viewed him as the latter's mole inside the government. However, Abubakar had the good sense to keep his head down and avoid giving Abacha an excuse to get rid of him. Abiola's aide, Bola Tinubu, said:

> out of all the military generals I met through Abiola while he was lobbying for the restoration of his mandate, Abubakar was the most sincere and straightforward. He pointedly told Abiola that no military officer would want to help him real se his mandate, unless the military general wanted to get himself into trouble. While other generals we had met lied, Abubakar was different. He simply said: 'Look, I am a professional soldier and I want to retire a general. I don't want to be involved in politics. I cannot help you. I don't want to be involved.'[16]

NADECO's ultimatum and Abiola's presidential declaration seemed to be turning points that hardened Abacha's resolve. According to Diya, 'Abacha became a totally changed man.'[17] In September 1994 he dismissed all civilians from the PRC, and enlarged its membership from 11 to 25, all of whom were now military or police officers. He also fired the minister of justice, Olu Onagoruwa, who later said: 'When the ultimatum of 31st May 1994 was given to the government by NADECO, Abacha went into an irredeemable rage. He trusted nobody anymore, including his senior soldiers. General Diya was no longer trusted. This distrust spilled over to civilian members of the government and marked the isolation and decline of General Abacha's regime.'[18] Abacha dropped all pretence that his government was a civilian-military hybrid. He had gone into full military government mode.

8

THE 'PHANTOM COUP'

Even with Abiola in detention, Abacha had other powerful enemies who were roaming free. The 1994 constitutional conference unwittingly set in motion a chain of events that threatened the lives of several military officers and members of the opposition. Yar'Adua had been elected as a conference delegate. He was a political heavyweight: wealthy, a great political strategist, who still harboured ambitions of becoming president. He was from a Fulani royal family, who were Nigeria's equivalent of the Kennedys—a wealthy political oligarchy. He held the traditional title of Tafidan Katsina.[1] His father, Musa Yar'Adua, was the former minister for Lagos and also the Mutawallen Katsina (the custodian of the treasury of the Katsina Emirate Council). He was also a nephew of the former military governor of the Northern Region and chief of staff (army), Major-General Hassan Usman Katsina. As a young man Yar'Adua had been a maverick. He attended the Katsina Provincial Secondary School. One of his classmates there (who also lived in the same dormitory) was the future head of state Major-General Muhammadu Buhari. Yar'Adua was not a great student. It is said that although he was a class prefect he would often sneak out to smoke cigarettes.

After finishing school, Yar'Adua and Buhari enrolled at the Nigerian Military Training College (NMTC) in 1962. One of their contemporaries was Ibrahim Bako, who was later shot dead while trying to arrest President Shagari during the December 1983 military coup that brought Buhari to power. After attending the NMTC, Yar'Adua was admitted to the elite Sandhurst Royal Military Academy in England. Military enrolment did not improve Yar'Adua's poor academic application. His tactics and map-reading tutor at Sandhurst, Captain Alexander, called Yar'Adua's written work 'appalling' and thought that 'the only conclusion is that he is idle'.[2] Yar'Adua fought during the civil war as a member of the federal army's 2 Division, commanded by Colonel Murtala Muhammed. Some senior officers wanted Muhammed to be court-martialled after he disobeyed orders from Supreme Headquarters during a botched river crossing that led to the loss of over a thousand of his men and millions of pounds' worth of military equipment. However, any plans for a court martial were dropped after Yar'Adua and other some officers threatened to mutiny if Muhammed was punished.

Yar'Adua was a ringleader in two coup plots. During the July 1966 counter-coup, he was tasked with primary responsibility in the south-east. His mission was to apprehend or eliminate the military governor of the Eastern Region, Lt-Colonel Ojukwu. Just as Yar'Adua and his colleagues (including Lieutenant Muhammadu Jega, currently the emir of Gwandu) were preparing to strike, their battalion commander, Lt-Colonel David 'Baba' Ogunewe, found them in the early hours of the morning already awake, dressed in battle attire, and ready to commence the coup in Enugu. A tense and angry exchange between Ogunewe and the northern soldiers then followed. Remarkably, Ogunewe somehow managed to 'talk down' the northern soldiers, avoid bloodshed, and convinced them to hand the armoury keys to him.

'In case anything goes wrong, this is goodbye'

Nine years later, Yar'Adua was at it again. He was one of six colonels, including Buhari and Babangida, who planned and staged a coup against General Gowon on July 29, 1975. Yar'Adua's job was to persuade other officers to join the plot. He duly recruited Lt-Colonels Babangida and MD Jega, and Major Aliyu Mohammed Gusau. Yar'Adua also had the job of visiting Brigadier Murtala Muhammed at his house to inform him that he would become the head of state if the coup succeeded. The night before the coup, Yar'Adua moved his wife Binta and their children to the home of his cousin MT Usman. Around 7 pm, Yar'Adua stepped outside with Usman and bluntly told him, 'Tonight we are going to take [over] the government. So in case anything goes wrong, this is goodbye.'[3] Usman was so shocked and frightened by the news that he could not sleep that night. Usman, his wife, Yar'Adua's wife, and the entire household stayed awake all night praying and awaiting news of the coup's success. This duly came the following morning when the

Brigade of Guards commander, Colonel Joseph Garba, announced the regime change. The new regime led by Brigadier Murtala Muhammed appointed Yar'Adua as the federal commissioner for transport. However, Muhammed lasted only six months. On February 13, 1976 soldiers from minority ethnic groups in the middle belt ambushed Muhammed's car and assassinated him during a failed coup attempt. The majority of the army remained loyal, rallied behind the chief of army staff, Lt-General Theophilus Danjuma, and suppressed the coup. Muhammed's deputy, Lt-General Olusegun Obasanjo, succeeded him as head of state. With Obasanjo and Danjuma at the top of the new regime, the coup's net effect was to place the two most high-profile positions in the government in the hands of Christians. To assuage the feelings of the Muslim north, it was important to place a Muslim Hausa or Fulani in a highly visible position. Danjuma identified two leading contenders: the former boyhood classmates Buhari and Yar'Adua, both of whom were Fulani Muslims from the north-west.

'He was a very inflexible person'

According to Danjuma's assessment of the two candidates, Buhari

> is one of the most upright army officers that the Nigerian army has produced—very clean, a very strict officer. Unfortunately for him ... I observed that he was a very inflexible person ... I observed that he was too rigid, he was too inflexible to hold a political post. If you are in politics, you must be flexible; you must compromise from time to time. In politics, they call it pragmatism. But in the military, if you are pragmatic, it is regarded as a weakness. I said no, not Buhari. Shehu, I didn't know him well except that I knew that, of all the officers of his rank, he was the most politicised. So, sending a politicised army officer to a political post, I thought, was a good thing. That was how I named Shehu the next Chief of Staff [Supreme Headquarters].[4]

Lt-Colonel Yar'Adua was duly promoted to the rank of brigadier over several senior officers in order to make him Obasanjo's deputy. He was later promoted again to major-general and retired with Obasanjo when the military ceded power to an elected civilian government in 1979. Thereafter he became a successful businessman with interests in various industries including agriculture, banking, media and shipping. He also remained active in politics and vied for the presidential nomination of the SDP.

By 1994, the chain-smoking Yar'Adua was no longer a scheming young army officer, but had become an influential and sophisticated political player with contacts all around the country. His political protégés include Atiku Abubakar, former police officer Tony Anenih and Yomi Edu. Yar'Adua also had a personal history with Abacha. During the civil war both men fought as members of the army's 2 Division under Colonel Murtala Muhammed. When Yar'Adua went to Pakistan in 1974 to attend a ten-month course at the Command and Staff College in Quetta, he sold his Mercedes 280 coupé to Abacha. There was also a complex family dynamic between them. Abacha was not his wife Maryam's first husband. Her first husband was Yar'Adua's father-in-law, Shehu Usman, the Sarkin Musa (district head) of Funtua district in Katsina. Usman was the father of Yar'Adua's wife Binta.[5] Maryam was briefly married to Usman for one or two years, before divorcing him and later marrying Abacha in 1965.

'Our stay will be brief'

After Abacha became head of state, Yar'Adua consistently demanded that he should make clear how long he intended to stay in power. Abacha revealed little beyond a vague statement from his deputy, Diya, that 'our stay will be brief'.[6] On June 27, 1994 Abacha established a National Constitutional Conference to design a new constitution for Nigeria. The conference was expected to be little more than a glorified talking shop to keep the politicians busy, distracted and well fed while Abacha consolidated himself in power. A conference member complained that 'since we came, no senior government official ever showed any interest in what we are doing here'. Another member described their daily routine as 'sleep, wake up, eat, attend brief meeting, and cocktails, eat and sleep'.[7] The plan seemed to be working, until proceedings became unexpectedly lively. The conference was empowered to determine General Abacha's tenure. Barnabas Gemade led a 30-member political transition committee. In December 1994, the Gemade committee recommended a further two-year tenure for the military, which would extend military rule until December 31, 1997. However, Yar'Adua was determined to use the conference as a platform to push the military out of power as soon as possible.

His supporters went to work. On December 6, 1994, another conference member, Sule Odoma, a medical doctor of Igala ethnicity, proposed a motion rejecting the December 1997 exit date for the military. The conference supported him, vetoed the Gemade committee's recommendation, and instead passed a motion calling on the military to leave office no later than January 1, 1996. This motion rattled the government. Yar'Adua had played his best card.

Now it was the government's turn to respond. The following day, the government ordered members of the conference transition committee to return the official cars issued to them for 'servicing'. Senior government officials also met with the conference chairman, Adolphus Karibi-Whyte, and lobbied conference delegates to revoke the motion.

'I will get him, including that Obasanjo'

In his memoirs, Abacha's first chief of army staff, Major-General Chris Alli, claimed that on one occasion while he and Abacha discussed Yar'Adua, 'Abacha snapped his fingers and swore, I will get him, including that Obasanjo.'[8] Yar'Adua had attracted the attention of the security forces before. The State Security Service arrested him in early 1994, then released him. Now he had given them another reason to take renewed interest in him. The government intensified its pressure on conference members by suddenly adjourning the conference. At 1 am on March 9, 1995, eight armed security officers, including the commissioner of police for the Federal Capital Territory, surrounded Yar'Adua's residence in Apo conference village in Abuja. The security men had a warrant signed by the inspector-general of police, Ibrahim Coomasie, and arrested Yar'Adua for 'acts prejudicial to state security' and for worsening 'the economic adversity of the state'. The officers flew Yar'Adua south to Lagos and detained him at the Kirikiri Maximum Security Prison, Nigeria's most notorious gaol.

The conference reconvened in April without Yar'Adua. Some conference delegates suddenly changed their minds about the January 1996 handover date. Conference delegate Tony Anenih and 35 others tabled a new motion stating that the January 1, 1996 terminal date for military rule 'is not realistic'. Justice Karibi-Whyte initially resisted reopening the issue as it had already been determined. However, the conference 'vacated' its earlier January 1, 1996 motion, and on April 25, 1995 passed a new, unanimous motion allowing the military to determine how long it would remain in power. By doing so, the conference violated its own rule of not reopening issues that had already been decided. Several conference members loyal to Yar'Adua, and other prominent members such as Alex Ekwueme, did not attend the session where this motion was passed. Rather than framing the parameters of what Abacha's government could and could not do, the conference ended up consolidating the government's power and giving it carte blanche to do as it pleased. Abacha had made good on his promise to 'get' Yar'Adua. One down, one to go.

Since leaving power, former head of state General Obasanjo had been in the habit of criticising all of his successors: Shagari, Buhari, Babangida, Shonekan, and now Abacha. President Shagari was so irritated by Obasanjo's criticisms that he asked the secretary to the government, Shehu Musa, to visit Obasanjo in his home town of Ota and 'find out why he has been making embarrassing public statements against the administration.'[9] Shagari alleged that 'some public statements by General Obasanjo severely criticising the [Shagari] administration seemed to point to at least a tacit incitement of the military against the government.'[10] He also pointed out that military officers frequently visited Obasanjo's home before the 1983 coup that deposed Shagari. According to Babangida (who was described as 'the moving spirit'[11] of that 1983 coup), the coup leaders asked Obasanjo to lead the new military government, but Obasanjo declined because 'he said it would destroy his integrity, that he handed over to Shagari and that it is not right for him to get involved. But he [Obasanjo] said he was not stopping us from going ahead with the plot.'[12]

After Abacha seized power in 1993, he met Obasanjo and asked for his advice on how long the military should stay in power. Obasanjo replied, 'You have no business being there not to talk about how long you can stay.'[13] By 1994 Obasanjo's rhetoric against Abacha had become more critical. In a televised edition of the BBC news programme *Newsnight*, he also accused the Abacha government of 'spending money like a drunken sailor' and asked, 'Where is all the money going?'

While other critics were sent to prison to reassess their views, nothing happened to Obasanjo. His larger-than-life status made him seemingly untouchable. Obasanjo was not like the others who had been arrested and imprisoned. He was no Johnny Just Come (or 'JJC' as Nigerians call them). Obasanjo's life story is like a guide to post-independence Nigerian history. He was either a direct participant in or a witness to virtually all seminal post-independence historical events. As an army officer he served in the colonial Nigerian army when it was still controlled by the British, and remained in the army when Britain transferred command to Nigerian officers in 1965. He served in the first African-led UN peacekeeping mission in the Congo, and his best friend, Chukwuma Kaduna Nzeogwu, was one of the ringleaders of Nigeria's first military coup on January 15, 1966. He was a former head of state, the first military ruler to hand over power to an elected civilian government, and a victorious civil war hero who obtained the military surrender that preserved the Nigerian union. He nearly became United Nations secretary-general, and also made a diplomatic breakthrough which led to Nelson Mandela being released after decades in prison. He also had extensive local and international contacts. However, Abacha was unlike the other heads of state that Obasanjo had criticised: Abacha was not interested in being popular and had no fear of, or respect for, big-name reputations.

Power, or the perception that one has it, can impair a person's reasoning and scramble their radar for sensing danger. Obasanjo was abroad, attending a United Nations conference in Denmark, when his friend Yar'Adua was arrested. Yar'Adua's arrest convinced Obasanjo's Nigerian and foreign friends that he would be next. Several of them, including the US ambassador to Nigeria, Walter Carrington, warned him not to return to Nigeria. Carrington offered Obasanjo asylum in America but Obasanjo rejected the offer, countering that he had not committed any crime and thus had no reason to remain abroad. Obasanjo did not fall into a trap. Rather, having walked past the trap, he turned around and deliberately dived into it.

In an act of spectacular hubris, Obasanjo returned to Nigeria on March 13. Security officers seized his passport upon his arrival at the Murtala Muhammed airport in Lagos, then arrested him the next day. He was detained at the Zone 2 headquarters of the Nigerian police at Onikan in Lagos, then was later moved to the police headquarters in Moloney Street. Obasanjo's good friend, former US President Jimmy Carter, travelled to Nigeria on his behalf and met Abacha on March 20 to appeal for Obasanjo's release. Abacha found it difficult to ignore a revered former US president and compromised. He authorised Obasanjo's release from detention and instead kept him under house arrest at his farm in Ota from March 22. He remained under house arrest for the next two months (without being told why he was detained) until June 14 when armed soldiers took him from his farmhouse to the army officers' mess in Milverton Road in Ikoyi, Lagos.

In February 1995, a few weeks before Obasanjo was arrested, the prolific Nigerian rumour mill claimed that there had been an attempted coup against Abacha and that the government was secretly arresting suspects. The rumours became so strong that on March 7, the director of defence information, Brigadier-General Chijuka, publicly denied the arrests and dismissed them as 'destabilising rumours'.

Publish and Be Damned

The young and glamorous Christine 'Chris' Anyanwu was the editor-in-chief of an avant-garde weekly news magazine called *The Sunday Magazine* (*TSM*).

As a female editor in a male-dominated industry, Anyanwu was an anomaly. *TSM* had a reputation for publishing exposés about the government. After a quiet news year, *TSM* got an unexpected break. One of its employees, Ifeoma Ifejika, was dating an officer in the army's directorate of legal services. Ifeoma saw her boyfriend being arrested and narrated the story of what happened to her *TSM* colleagues. The public did not know that as well as Ifeoma's boyfriend several other officers had also been secretly arrested. The government did not announce the arrests or even tell the arrested men why they were being detained: they were in fact suspected of being involved in a coup plot. *TSM* journalists wanted to take advantage of their access to the information and treat the arrests as a major news scoop. They decided to publish an article about the coup and increased their print run in anticipation of a blockbuster edition of the magazine. However, the Directorate of Military Intelligence (DMI) knew of *TSM*'s plans and telephoned Anyanwu to order her to kill the story. She refused and published the story, and even included an editorial column mentioning the DMI's attempts to intimidate her into aborting the story.

Only three days after the director of defence information had denied the arrests or the existence of a coup plot, the chief of defence staff, Major-General Abdulsalam Abubakar, confirmed that the government had indeed foiled a coup and that some officers had been arrested. However, Abubakar did not disclose their identities. The government's denial followed by its confirmation made the public sceptical. When the coup rumours first started, the director of military intelligence, Major-General Abdullahi Sarki Mukhtar, had investigated but found no evidence of a plot. Mukhtar was from the corps of military police and had a law degree. Mukhtar's conclusion led Abacha to reshuffle the intelligence network. He reassigned Mukhtar, then appointed Brigadier-General Ibrahim Sabo, an infantry officer with no background in military intelligence, to replace him. He also appointed Air Vice-Marshal Idi Musa as the chief of defence intelligence. The new intelligence team dug for evidence of a coup more feverishly than their predecessors and secretly arrested several more officers without public announcement.

'This will definitely give you many enemies'

The government set up a Special Investigation Panel (SIP) led by Brigadier-General Felix Mujakperuo to investigate the coup allegations.[14] Mujakperuo was an Urhobo from Delta State and had won the sword of honour for being the best cadet from his graduating class in 1971 (the fifth regular course of the Nigerian Defence Academy). He had a master's degree in military law from the Judge Advocate General's Legal Center and School in the US.[15] Mujakperuo knew coup intrigues well and had prior investigative experience. He had served in the corps of military police, and was also a member of a previous SIP that had investigated a prior coup in 1986, as a result of which eleven officers were executed. Mujakperuo later described his job as chairman of the SIP as 'one of the dirtiest' roles given him. He added: 'You come across your friends and find yourself determining a matter affecting their lives without having any power to help them out. This will definitely give you many enemies.'[16]

The suspects dreaded facing the SIP's interrogation team. The feared, pipe-smoking Colonel Frank Omenka was the head of the security group at the Directorate of Military Intelligence. He was intelligent, multilingual, and a ruthless interrogator with a large bag of physical and psychological tools that he used on detainees to extract information. In 1995, forensic evidence was like science fiction in Nigeria. Hence, without it, security forces often relied on confessions as a primary method of evidence gathering. To facilitate the rapid extraction of confessions they often resorted to torture. Lt-Colonel Martin Azuka Igwe was the commander of the 11 Field Engineer Regiment. When he was arrested, he denied being part of a coup plot and so his interrogators applied physical pressure to try to get him to confess: 'They tied my hands and legs behind me altogether and then put a pipe through my elbow, raised me up and I was suspended like a chicken in barbecue. Then they were asking me questions, hitting me, abusing me and saying that I must accept to have planned a coup. The chief torturers were Lieutenant-Colonel Frank Omenka and Hassan Zakari Biu.'[17]

'if your wife is beautiful, in the next one week, someone else would be screwing her'

Igwe claimed that Omenka taunted him by waving a file in his face and saying, 'This file contains all the evidence I need to tie you to a firing squad, and if your wife is beautiful, in the next one week someone else would be screwing her.'[18] Other defendants reported similar torture. Colonel Gabriel Ajayi had openly advocated the validation of the June 12, 1993 election results. He was arrested and later said:

> My torture was so severe, gruesome, intense and deadly as they wanted me to own up to an imaginary coup that I was not involved in. I was brutalised, demeaned, dehumanised, humiliated, pulverised, tied up, tied down, chained to

the wall, chained to the ceiling, abused, tied up like a barbecue ram, turned upside down and insulted. They wanted me to confess and make a statement for an offence I did not commit.[19]

Colonel Lawan Gwadabe was tortured so badly that he lost consciousness, and could not walk for several weeks thereafter. Another favoured form of torture was to tie several suspects together semi-naked, leave them outside in the open overnight next to hidden microphones and listen in to their conversations to find out whether they would reveal any incriminating information. Other suspects also encountered tough interrogation at the hands of Omenka, Colonel Kolawole John Olu, Lt-Colonel Mahmud Santuraki (Babangida's former intelligence officer), and assistant commissioner of police Hassan Zakari Biu.

The SIP claimed to have found evidence of three different but overlapping coup plots, one allegedly headed by Colonels Gwadabe and Bello-Fadile, a second led by Major Akinloye Akinyemi, and a third led by Yar'Adua. It recommended a trial.

The Trial

On June 5, 1995, the chief of defence staff, Major-General Abubakar, established a Special Military Tribunal to try the suspects. The government did not name those involved but there was great speculation that Yar'Adua and Obasanjo were among them. Brigadier-General Patrick Aziza, an Urhobo from Delta State, led the tribunal. Aziza was the third officer from the Niger Delta to lead a military coup tribunal (after Major-Generals John Obada and Charles Ndiomu in 1976 and 1986 respectively). The other tribunal members, and the lawyers representing the prosecution and defendants, are listed in the accompanying table.

Special Military Tribunal, 1995

Special Military Tribunal	Prosecution Lawyers	Defence Lawyers
Brigadier Patrick Aziza (chairman)	Colonel O Shuaibu	Brigadier Idada Ikponwen
Colonel Yakubu Abubakar	Lt-Colonel Dave Ike	Major Patrick Ake
Colonel TN Abdul	Major DB Dakar	Navy Commander LM Fabiyi

Colonel David Ndefo Major M Abdulrahman

Lt-Colonel LA Adeoye

Navy Captain Francis E
Agbiti

Group Captain I
Abdulraman

Judge Advocate:

Lt-Colonel Mohammed
Maina

Waiting list:

Colonel R Elebor

Colonel Abel FK Akale

Lt-Colonel AY Achubor

The trial took place in the conference room of the Lagos Garrison Command on Kofo Abayomi Street, Victoria Island, Lagos. The tribunal was supposed to commence proceedings at 11 am on June 5, but in typical Nigerian fashion it did not start for another six hours. There was an element of tragicomedy when Aziza noticed that Captain Usman Sudik Abdulyekeen ('USA') Suleiman, who was among the suspects, was not present. Suleiman was the former ADC to the former military governor of Kaduna State, Colonel Abubakar Umar. Aziza asked out loud, 'Where is Captain Suleiman?' Despite speculation that Suleiman had been tortured to death, the SIP had actually cleared him of involvement in the coup. Suleiman was nowhere to be seen because, despite his being cleared, someone had deemed it fit to continue detaining him without charge or trial for eleven months in an underground cell with his hands and legs chained.

Aziza called each defendant's name and asked if they had an objection to the inclusion of any tribunal member. Obasanjo, who was the most senior officer ever to be tried for coup plotting, objected to being tried by a junior officer like Aziza. Trial by an officer of at least equal rank was standard procedure in court martials. As a four-star general, the only officer of equivalent rank in the whole of Nigeria was Abacha himself. Obasanjo's objection was predictably denied. Nonetheless, in strange deference to military norms Aziza referred to Obasanjo and Yar'Adua as 'Sir' each time he addressed them, even though he held the power of life and death over both of them.

The Key Suspects

The corps of army legal services attracted the attention of intelligence agencies when some of its members were overheard criticising military rule and advocating a return to civilian governance. The department was due to hold its annual military law seminar in Enugu in 1995. Military intelligence found this a great opportunity to infiltrate the department and place its members under surveillance. They sent several beautiful young women to the seminar with recording devices to attend a party organised by the seminar participants.

Colonel Ralph Sixtus Babatunde ('RSB') Bello-Fadile was an erudite Yoruba officer and the director of army legal services. He had five degrees, including a PhD in international law, and two master's degrees in criminal law and military justice. He had been advocating the military's resignation from government and its replacement by a civilian interim government. This displeased the powers that be. Being charged for coup plotting was a strange reversal for him. In 1990 he had been the judge advocate tasked with providing legal advice to members of the Special Military Tribunal during the trial of officers who attempted a coup against Babangida that year.

Colonel Roland Emokpae was the assistant director of army legal services at 82 Division in Enugu. He was Bello-Fadile's deputy, and the two officers had been contemporaries at the Nigerian Defence Academy. Emokpae hosted the 1995 annual military law seminar in Enugu, shortly after which he was posted out of the army legal services department and sent to the corps of military police in Lagos as the new deputy provost marshal. He was known for being outspoken. He also harboured a long residual grievance against Abacha whom he blamed for revoking his admission to study criminal justice at the University of Nebraska in 1980, and instead replacing him with another officer whom Abacha favoured.

Colonel Lawan Gwadabe was the commander of 23 Brigade in Yola in Adamawa State in the north-east. He had been a strategically placed officer in the previous military regime led by Babangida. He played a key role in the coup that brought Babangida to power and participated in the operation to arrest Babangida's predecessor, Buhari, and take him into custody. Babangida later appointed Gwadabe as military governor of Niger State, Babangida's home state. A senior colleague described him as 'a well coordinated, brash, affable, and brilliant but politicised officer who was firmly ensconced in General Babangida's bandwagon. He, like most from their clique, had no measurable regard for General Sani Abacha, both from the moral and professional standpoints.'[20] After Babangida's retirement he became the principal staff officer to Abacha but did not last long in that role. Abacha posted him to Gambia where he became the interim chief of staff of the Gambian army. However, during his tour of duty there, Gambian soldiers staged a military coup and overthrew the government of President Sir Dawda Jawara. Gwadabe returned to Nigeria after the coup and was posted to Yola. The GOC of 3 Armoured Division, Brigadier-General Tajudeen Olanrewaju, summoned him to a meeting ostensibly about the incursion of Cameroonian gendarmes into Nigerian territory. When Gwadabe arrived, he did not see Olanrewaju but was instead arrested.

Major Akinloye Akinyemi was a difficult man to kill. By 1995, 117 people had been executed by firing squad in Nigeria after being convicted of coup plotting. Yet Akinyemi was the only Nigerian to be tried for coup plotting twice and still live to tell the tale. In 1987 Akinyemi was quietly arrested, and a military tribunal chaired by Brigadier Oladipo Diya tried him for allegedly planning a coup against Babangida. The government made no public announcement about this coup plot, perhaps because Akinyemi's brother, Professor Bolaji Akinyemi, was a senior government minister at the time. The tribunal found him not guilty of treason but convicted him of a lesser offence. He was again tried for coup plotting in 1990, but survived. In 1995 he was arrested for coup plotting for the third time. By this stage his brother Bolaji had become a member of NADECO.

The Case for the Prosecution

The alleged coup plots were bewildering and opaque. The intricate details that the prosecution presented about the three overlapping plots are summarised below.

Plot One: Yar'Adua

Yar'Adua was charged with conspiracy to commit treason, concealment of treason, illegal possession of firearms, and stealing. The prosecution alleged that Yar'Adua instigated another plot by inciting Babangida's former ADC, Lt-Colonel Sambo Dasuki, who had been a key member of the Babangida government, and who was also the son of the sultan of Sokoto, Ibrahim Dasuki. Although Sambo Dasuki had moved to Washington DC, the SIP alleged that he sponsored Bello-Fadile to travel around Nigeria to recruit more officers into the plot. Dasuki in turn supposedly recruited Bello-Fadile and Lt-Colonels Bulus, Usman and MA Ajayi. The government declared Dasuki a suspect in the coup and a wanted fugitive from justice.

Plot Two: Gwadabe and Bello-Fadile

After being interrogated, Bello-Fadile alleged that, at the behest of Dasuki, he met Yar'Adua to obtain funds for a coup. According to the prosecution, Dasuki also asked Bello-Fadile to recruit Gwadabe. Bello-Fadile allegedly met with Gwadabe at Bonny Camp, Lagos, in early 1994. At that meeting it was said that Gwadabe and Bello-Fadile hatched a plot, and Gwadabe decided to contribute money towards it. Bello-Fadile also claimed that some Americans had provided him with a detailed layout of the presidential villa, which they would storm using former presidential bodyguards. The prosecution alleged that they recruited Colonels Gabriel Ajayi, Roland Emokpae and Emmanuel Ndubueze and Lt-Colonels Igwe, Obalisa, Olowokun and Mapaiyeda to assist them. The plot was finalised on February 15, 1995, during the army's annual legal seminar. The plan was to assassinate Abacha using snipers or explosives on March 1, 1995 at the Sallah praying ground. They would then arrest all the army GOCs, and eliminate all officers of the rank of brigadier-general and above. After displacing Abacha, they planned to use retired senior army officers to gain credibility for the new regime, then discard them as soon as their regime stabilised.

Plot Three: Major Akinyemi

Major Akinyemi's plot was supposedly the most elaborate. The prosecution alleged that in order to start a guerrilla war, Akinyemi planned to create a paramilitary group in Lagos by setting up a bogus security company. Strangely, this was exactly the same method that the 1990 coup plotters had used to recruit armed men for their coup, in which Akinyemi was a co-accused. It would have been incredibly naive of Akinyemi to attempt another coup using exactly the same method, which had been foiled five years earlier. Nonetheless, the prosecution claimed that Akinyemi had divided the country into seven sectors: Lagos, Ibadan, Enugu, Benin, Jos, Abuja and Port Harcourt. His armed recruits would then dress in white robes during the day to avoid detection, before striking their targets.

The Case for the Defence

The defendants pleaded not guilty, and denied plotting or knowing anything about the plan. Bello-Fadile sought to retract his confessions in which he had implicated Yar'Adua, Obasanjo and others. He claimed they were obtained under duress after he had been severely tortured. Yar'Adua admitted that he had met Colonel Bello-Fadile twice in the lobby of the Hilton Hotel. He said that at their first meeting, they discussed the work of a judicial panel in which Bello-Fadile was involved, but he could not remember what they had talked about at the second meeting. When security officers searched Yar'Adua's house in Kaduna, they found an old sub-machine gun which he had used during the civil war. He claimed that he kept the gun for sentimental reasons. However, prosecutors charged him with illegal possession of the gun, and also alleged that Yar'Adua and 150 of his supporters met in Lagos at the end of February 1995 to finalise arrangements for the plot. Yar'Adua denied having been in Lagos in February. He said that as it was Ramadan, he had not left the north.

Investigators also claimed that Bello-Fadile visited Obasanjo at his farm in the first week of February 1995, and informed him about the coup. During the Special Investigation Panel's investigation, Obasanjo asked Bello-Fadile to tell him exactly where on his farm they had met. Bello-Fadile claimed it was in his office. Obasanjo said this was not true as he had not received guests in his office for over two years. His driver corroborated this and told investigators that he had not seen Obasanjo meet guests in his office for years. An air force officer also testified on Obasanjo's behalf that Bello-Fadile could not have met Obasanjo in Ota during the first week of February as Bello-Fadile was in Abuja on February 1 and 2, and Obasanjo was abroad from February 2 until February 9. According to Obasanjo, investigators had provided Bello-Fadile with a sketch of his farm and, after torturing him, tutored him so he could claim to have met Obasanjo at locations on the farm to which he had never actually been.

For failing to report the alleged visits from Bello-Fadile, Obasanjo was charged with concealment of treason (a crime invented under Obasanjo's watch in 1976). After the failed 1976 coup, investigators discovered that many of those they wanted to prosecute had not physically taken part in the coup. Rather, they had heard rumours about a possible coup but failed to report them to the authorities. To get around this inconvenient hurdle, the government, then led by Obasanjo, enacted Decree 8 of 1976: the Treason and Other Offences (Special Military Tribunal) Decree. This created a new crime referred to as 'concealment of treason' (failing to disclose knowledge of a coup). Abacha's agents did not tire of reminding Obasanjo that he was the architect of his own misfortune since it was his government that had introduced the crime of concealment of treason into Nigerian law. There was a further allegation against Obasanjo, that he visited the detained Abiola in November 1994, and afterwards wrote a letter to Abacha stating that if anything happened to Abiola in detention, Abacha would be regarded as a murderer. The Special Investigation Panel produced a copy of the letter as evidence against Obasanjo.

The Verdict

On Friday, July 14, 1995 Brigadier-General Chijuka publicly announced that the tribunal had tried 51 people. Of these, seven defendants were acquitted. An eighth unnamed person was also acquitted but his case was referred for further consideration. Three accused were not present at the trial—Dasuki, Lt-Colonel Anthony Nyiam and Great Ogboru—and were declared suspects who would be arrested on sight.[21] The tribunal convicted the remaining 40 people of various offences. Although Chijuka did not reveal the names of the 40 or their sentences, many believed that Yar'Adua and Obasanjo were among them. However, the coup controversy did not end there. Since the defendants had no right to appeal against their sentences to civilian courts, only the Provisional Ruling Council could alter the sentences.

Accessories after the Fact

The government was not satisfied with capturing Obasanjo, Yar'Adua and other officers. It extended its prosecution to journalists and human rights activists whom it accused of being 'accessories after the fact of treason'. Gwadabe, one of those on death row, had a link to *TSM*, which placed its editor Chris Anyanwu in trouble. He had donated $1,200 to *TSM* five years earlier when the magazine was founded. Gwadabe's financial contribution led investigators to claim that he was a shareholder or investor in *TSM* and had been leaking classified information to the magazine. They accused *TSM* of publishing false stories regarding the coup plot. The State Security Service arrested and interrogated Anyanwu. She claimed that during one of the interrogations, police officer Hassan Zakari Biu slapped her and used his finger to gouge and injure her eye while she was handcuffed. Other journalists who published articles about the coup, such as Kunle Ajibade (a journalist with *The News* magazine), Ben Charles-Obi (editor of *Weekend Classique* magazine) and George Mbah (assistant editor of *Tell* magazine), were also arrested and placed on trial by Aziza's tribunal. Anyanwu, Ajibade, Charles-Obi and Mbah were convicted of being accessories after the fact of treason and sentenced to life imprisonment.[22]

Rebecca 'Becky' Ikpe[23] was an accountant with the Nigeria Deposit Insurance Corporation, a regulatory agency in the banking sector. She was a Tiv from Upu-Otukpo in Benue State, and was Bello-Fadile's sister-in-law (her sister was his wife). Bello-Fadile asked Navy Commander Fabiyi, one of the defence lawyers, to pass on a box containing his defence legal notes to Ikpe. Fabiyi was the director of the navy's legal services department. He and Bello-Fadile were from the same town of Kabba in Kogi State in the middle belt. As instructed, Fabiyi passed on the box to Ikpe. However, Bello-Fadile had smuggled a note inside the box which asked Ikpe to relay information about the defendants' plight to human rights groups and activists whose names he listed, including the chairman of the Campaign for Democracy, Beko Ransome-Kuti. Ransome-Kuti was a medical doctor but had given up his medical practice to devote himself to the pro-democracy struggle. He was arrested so frequently by the security forces that his daughters kept a bag permanently packed for him, ready for his next arrest and detention. Beko was not the type to pass up an opportunity to expose government excesses. He duly faxed details of the note from Bello-Fadile to other human rights organisations, which in turn sent it to organisations abroad. Security forces traced the faxes to Beko, and arrested him and other human rights activists, claiming that they had faxed the documents abroad in order to blackmail the government. After being arrested, Gwadabe also sent a message to his relative Sanusi Mato to spread news of his arrest to his friends and associates. Mato did as he was instructed and also contacted and met Anyanwu. The tribunal tried Ikpe, Beko and Mato, convicted them of being accessories after the fact of treason, and sentenced them to life imprisonment.

Three weeks after the main trials had finished, the defence lawyer Fabiyi was himself arrested as an accessory after the fact. Fabiyi had defended Gwadabe's former ADC, Akin Olowokere, who had since become the paymaster of Abacha's bodyguards. Prosecutors accused Olowokere of leaking details regarding Abacha's timetable to the coup plotters. The tribunal sentenced Fabiyi to death after a hearing that he claimed lasted less than ten minutes.

Although the authorities had not announced the names of those on trial or the sentences, news of the coup plots and trials leaked out. Local and foreign media were demanding explanations from the Nigerian government and were not convinced that there was really a coup. Nigerian media termed the affair a 'phantom coup', an imaginary plot cooked up by the government as a convenient way of eliminating its rivals. The fact that those convicted were a motley crew of retired generals, civil society campaigners, journalists and reporters, all of whom just happened to be government opponents, deepened the scepticism. Even a senior Directorate of Military Intelligence officer, Colonel Steve Idehenre, later expressed his doubts about the veracity of the coup charges. He said:

> General Yar'Adua was not involved in the phantom coup just as ... Obasanjo were [sic] not involved. General Mukhtar who was at the DMI then discovered that both Yar'Adua and Obasanjo were set up so he did not recommend their prosecution, which caused his transfer. The transfer of Mukhtar gave way to General Sabo who had no previous intelligence training to take over the position of head of DMI.[24]

As rumours that Yar'Adua had been sentenced to death and Obasanjo to life imprisonment gripped the national and international media, foreign countries sent a wave of appeals for the death sentences to be commuted and for those convicted to be released. Presidents Mandela of South Africa, Clinton of the US, Mugabe of Zimbabwe and Biya of Cameroon, the ECOWAS chairman President Jerry Rawlings of Ghana, the United Nations, Britain, France, Germany and the Vatican (among many others) sent appeals and emissaries to Abacha, to urge clemency.

'An irony of fate'

The appeals also split the military. Officers sent competing petitions, some for the sentences to be commuted, and others for them to be carried out. When Abacha visited Sokoto State on Tuesday, August 1, 1995, the state's military administrator, Colonel Yakubu Mu'azu, who was Abacha's former military assistant, urged him publicly in the presence of Ibrahim Dasuki, the sultan of Sokoto, whose son was a suspect in the coup, to ignore the pleas for clemency. A few days later the military administrator of Ogun State, Lt-Colonel Daniel Akintonde, who was Diya's former ADC, called for clemency. The sharp difference in views between Abacha's former military assistant and Diya's former ADC was itself emblematic of the growing rift between Abacha and Diya. Middle-belt officers were another important constituency. Many of them rejected clemency for those convicted, and argued that the 1976 and 1986 coups, in which middle-belt officers had been swiftly executed, had set precedents for the treatment of convicted coup plotters. They further argued that the appeals for clemency were evidence of double standards simply because most of the 1995 accused were from majority ethnic groups, unlike those in the 1976 and 1986 plots. Middle-belt officers doubtless remembered that Obasanjo was the head of the government that had approved the execution of their kinsmen in 1976. The military administrator of Ondo, Colonel Ahmed Usman, said on the same day that Mu'azu made his statement: 'There is no sound moral basis whatsoever in this barrage of appeals. Those now caught up in this coup plot were the originators of the decree under which they have now been convicted. It is an irony of fate that it is those who signed the decree into law that the world is now clamouring for clemency for.'[25] Usman is from Kogi State in the middle belt (as were two of those convicted, Colonels Bello-Fadile and Oloruntoba). Dissent within the military about the fate of the convicted men became so clamorous that Defence Headquarters and General Staff Headquarters ordered all military administrators to stop speaking publicly on the issue.

'You should not be here'

As the pro- and anti-execution arguments went back and forth, the convicted men remained nervously on death row, unsure of what would happen to them. Some of them sent final instructions to their spouses and children. Yar'Adua feared that he would be executed at any moment. Three days after his death sentence, he sent a copy of his will and a notebook with instructions to his political protégé, Atiku Abubakar. The psychological uncertainty got the better of some of the convicted men, who succumbed to depression or illness. The Christians and Muslims among them constantly read their Bibles and Korans, and formed impromptu prayer groups. As a former head of state, Obasanjo was spared some of the indignities inflicted on the others: he was not chained and had his own cell. He and Yar'Adua were sources of inspiration and leadership to the other convicts. A publication claimed that the chief of defence staff, Major-General Abubakar, was the only serving army officer who had the courage to visit Obasanjo in prison. Abubakar apparently did so in order to commiserate with Obasanjo and to dissociate himself from any involvement in his incarceration.[26] Obasanjo's long-time friends and former military colleagues Lt-General Danjuma and Major-General Joseph Garba also visited him. Danjuma had been chief of army staff and Garba the federal commissioner for external affairs when Obasanjo was head of state. Danjuma was known for being stern and unemotional. When he saw his former boss humiliated and imprisoned with armed robbers and murderers, he shed tears and told him, 'You should not be here.'[27] Garba also wept when he saw Obasanjo. Unable to speak or stop his tears, Garba simply shook his head.

On July 22, the prisoners were terrified by the booming sounds of gunfire inside the Kirikiri prison as soldiers executed a large number of death-row inmates by firing squad non-stop for ninety minutes. These were 43 armed robbers, whose execution the government had approved. The executions were the government's attempt to demonstrate strength in response to international pressure, and to intimidate the coup prisoners by suggesting that they might be next.

The government was still determined to win the propaganda war and to show that the plotters were guilty. It aired a 50-minute documentary programme about the Special Military Tribunal proceedings on the state-owned Nigerian Television Authority. The heavily edited programme featured excerpts from the trial, including clips of Bello-Fadile reading his testimony. One of the clips showed him thanking the tribunal for its 'patience' and the 'special concessions' given to him, and commending it for reinforcing his 'belief in the rule of law'. It also showed other suspects and defendants mechanically reading statements that incriminated Yar'Adua and Obasanjo as well as still photos (with no audio) of Obasanjo's response to the allegations.

On October 1, 1995 Abacha addressed the nation. The coup prisoners would not be released but none of them would be executed either. Those that were sentenced to death had their sentences commuted to life or 25 imprisonment. Those sentenced to life imprisonment had their sentences reduced to 15 years. The journalists convicted of being accessories after the fact also had their sentences reduced to 15 years. It was the first time in Nigeria's history that death sentences for coup plotting had been revoked.

The convicts were relieved to be spared but still maintained that they were unjustly imprisoned for a bogus coup. Given the personal acrimony between the prisoners and their captors, and their different definitions of a coup, we may never discover whether they had really planned a coup against Abacha in 1995. The concept of exactly what constitutes a coup enlarged during the Babangida era, and grew even more during the Abacha era. In terms of the Babagida–Abacha paradigm, criticism of and opposition to the government were elevated to the status of a coup attempt. It is likely that on this basis the government and some of its investigators subjectively believed there was a coup attempt in 1995. Five years after the alleged coup, SIP chairman Mujakperuo said, 'Based on the evidence before me, I recommended Generals Obasanjo and Yar'Adua for trial because there was a coup in the making ... and with the evidence before my panel, they were coup plotters in March 1995.'[28]

However, some of the prosecutions seemed vindictive. When investigators could not obtain evidence of plotting by a suspect, they often charged defendants with other totally unrelated offences. For example, some officers were prosecuted and tried by the tribunal for illegal possession of firearms, which, in some cases, were their own personal service pistols. The tribunal convicted Shehu Sani, the Kaduna coordinator of the Campaign for Democracy, of operating an illegal organisation and for being an accessory after the fact of treason. Illegal possession of firearms and operating an illegal organisation were strange crimes to try before a secret military tribunal. Nonetheless, the nature of the trials had broader ramifications. The liberal application of the crime of 'concealment of treason' encouraged a culture of informing in the army. In addition to performing their professional duties, military personnel were also expected to be informants against their colleagues. What is more, the challenges that Abacha faced in two successive years—Abiola's presidential declaration in 1994 and the alleged coup in 1995—elevated his sense of insecurity to the point of paranoia. After the 1995 coup, security became his primary preoccupation.

9

THE OGONI THIRTEEN

The facts of Nigeria's oil industry are well known and stark. Between 1970 and 1995, Nigeria earned over $200 billion from oil exports. A spike in global oil prices during the 1970s sent the government's income sky-rocketing. The 1970s 'oil boom' brought unprecedented riches to Nigeria that had not been dreamt of at independence. Nigeria's earnings from crude oil exports rose by over 500% between 1970 and 1974. The oil boom massively increased Nigeria's wealth, and created a nouveau riche with an insatiable appetite for foreign luxury goods. Although the new-found oil wealth created and enriched a small coterie of overnight millionaires, it failed to become a vector for mass economic growth and mobility. Nigeria became a wealthy country full of poor people. Nigeria's per capita income barely changed during the 25 years between 1970 and 1995. The people who live in the oil-producing areas, the so-called 'Niger Delta', pay a steep price to sustain Nigeria's riches. More than 40,000 oil spills have occurred since oil was first commercially drilled in Nigeria in 1956 at Oloibiri in present-day Bayelsa State. The ubiquitously quoted statistic is that 70% of Nigeria's foreign exchange earnings come from oil exports. The statistic hardly ever quoted is that 80% of Nigeria's oil is obtained from only four of the country's 36 states—Akwa Ibom, Bayelsa, Delta and Rivers states, all of which are in the Niger Delta. That four states bore the overwhelming financial burden of the remaining 32 states and the federal capital made conflict virtually certain. Despite providing the vast majority of Nigeria's wealth, the oil-producing states remained among the poorest and least developed regions in Nigeria.

Apart from frequent oil spills, oil companies engage in a peculiar practice termed 'flaring'. Natural gas is a by-product of oil extraction. Rather than capturing and selling the gas as they do in other countries, international oil companies operating in Nigeria burn the gas in the open air. These flames burn 24 hours a day, seven days a week, all year round. One particular flame in the Niger Delta has been witnessed by the author for decades from miles away, and has been burning for over fifty years. Flaring produces other hazardous side effects. It causes acid rain which contaminates rivers and farmland. In an area where farming and fishing are the primary traditional sources of livelihood, the effect is particularly deleterious.

The government had many chances to address the injustices of the country's oil industry, but either ignored them or ruthlessly suppressed agitation in the Delta. In February 1966 a maverick Ijaw former police officer, Isaac Adaka Boro, who had been fired for going AWOL from duty, led a group called the Niger Delta Volunteer Force (NDVF) in declaring the oil-producing Niger Delta area an independent republic. Nigeria's first military government led by Aguiyi-Ironsi responded to the declaration by arresting and trying Boro and his NDVF colleagues, and sentencing them to death.[1]

The Ogoni People

The Ogoni are an ethnic group located in a densely populated pocket in south-east Nigeria. By the early 1990s the Ogoni numbered approximately 500,000. The Ogoni comprise six clans: the Babbe, Eleme, Gokana, Ken-Khana, Nyo-Khana and Tai. This small ethnic group, which represented less than 1% of Nigeria's population, mounted a spirited protest and publicity campaign that brought their plight, and the injustices of Nigeria's oil industry, not only to the doorstep of the Nigerian government, but also into the conscience and living rooms of people around the globe.

As the biggest oil company operating in Nigeria, the Anglo-Dutch oil company Shell was a major target of residents of the oil-producing communities. By 1990 Shell operated more than a thousand oil wells in Nigeria linked by 1,700 km of pipelines. Ninety-six of those oil wells were located in Ogoniland, which was criss-crossed by pipelines laid by Shell and other oil companies. Ogonis estimated that 900 million barrels of oil had been extracted from their lands, and had earned US$30 billion in revenues for the Nigerian government. Although oil from their land made the Nigerian government rich, and was used to develop other parts of Nigeria, Ogoni-land suffered from institutional underdevelopment, pollution, unemployment, poverty and lack of education.

MOSOP

In January 1990, the Ogonis launched an organisation called the Movement for the Survival of the Ogoni People (MOSOP) as an umbrella movement for Ogoni emancipation. They also drafted an Ogoni 'Bill of Rights' that demanded political and economic autonomy for the Ogoni, royalties for the oil extracted from Ogoni lands, and compensation for environmental damage caused by oil drilling. MOSOP issued the Bill of Rights on August 26, 1990 at Bori, the traditional capital of Ogoni-land, and it was signed by 30 prominent Ogonis, including the heads of five of the six Ogoni clans.[2] MOSOP sent a copy of the Bill of Rights to the federal government, and also a 'demand notice' to oil companies telling them to leave Ogoni-land if they were unwilling to pay compensation for the environmental devastation caused by their oil exploration. MOSOP also flew an Ogoni flag and adopted *Aaboo Aaboo pa Ogoni* ('Rise up, rise up, Ogoni') as the Ogoni 'national anthem'.

MOSOP's president, Garrick Barilee Leton, was a biochemist and former government official who had previously served as commissioner for health in Rivers State and as federal commissioner for education. Its vice-president, Edward Kobani,[3] was also a former government commissioner, and the national publicity secretary of the SDP. The group's publicity secretary was a childhood friend of Kobani, Kenule ('Ken') Saro-Wiwa. Kobani and Saro-Wiwa had known each other for over thirty years. It was Kobani who coined the name Movement for the Survival of the Ogoni People, and Saro-Wiwa who was instrumental in drafting the Bill of Rights, which he described as 'the bible of the movement'. Although he was not MOSOP's official leader, Saro-Wiwa was its star player.

Kenule Beeson Saro-Wiwa

MOSOP and Saro-Wiwa are so closely intertwined that it is impossible to discuss one without the other. The movement's evolution largely followed the trajectory of Saro-Wiwa's life. Saro-Wiwa claimed that while he was working in his study one night in late 1989, he received a spiritual calling to dedicate himself to uplifting and promoting the cause of the Ogoni people.

Saro-Wiwa was a diminutive, pipe-smoking man, standing only 5 feet 2 inches tall, and with a Napoleon complex to boot. He carried two enormous chips on his narrow shoulders: one due to the teasing he received about his height, and the second a result of being the victim of ethnic chauvinism. As a student he attended Government College Umuahia, an elite school in Igboland. As the only Ogoni in a school of 300 students, most of whom were Igbo, Saro-Wiwa soon learned to fight his own battles. While there he was subjected to taunting by Igbo classmates and reminded of the Ogonis' supposedly inferior status. The mistreatment that Saro-Wiwa and other Ogonis suffered at the hands of their Igbo neighbours reinforced their resolve to strengthen and defend Ogoni identity and cohesion.

A civil war erupted when the Igbo-dominated Eastern Region seceded from Nigeria in 1967 and declared itself an independent republic known as Biafra. Ogoni-land was included in the territory that the Biafrans carved out for their new state. When the Nigerian government used force to retrieve its territory, civil war erupted. Saro-Wiwa made no secret of where his loyalties lay. He bitterly opposed Biafra and supported the federal government. He did not wish to substitute minority subject status in Nigeria for minority subject status in a new Igbo-dominated country. He later published a memoir of his experiences during the war entitled *On a Darkling Plain*. The book included lacerating criticism of the Nigerian and Biafran leaders. However, his scorn for the Igbo leaders of Biafra burned even more intensely in the book. Igbos did not forget this, and regarded him as a saboteur of their cause.

Saro-Wiwa had not always opposed the oil companies. As a young man he had applied (unsuccessfully) for a job with Shell. The federal government appointed him as the administrator of Bonny Island on November 11, 1968, at the age of just 26. He later became commissioner for works, land and transport, before moving to the education ministry in 1969 as the first commissioner for education in Rivers State. He used this post to address the educational underdevelopment of Ogonis. By the mid-1950s, only one Ogoni had ever attended university.[4] Saro-Wiwa granted educational scholarships to hundreds of Ogoni youths, thereby creating a new school and university-educated Ogoni class that respected him and owed him fierce loyalty.

His involvement in government led to his meeting and forming friendships in the 1960s and 1970s with senior army officers such as Colonels Obasanjo and Danjuma. Saro-Wiwa's military friends included a quiet army officer named Sani Abacha, who lived next door to him on Nzimiro Street in Port Harcourt. The two men were close enough for their children to become playmates. Ken's son Ken Jr became good friends with Abacha's eldest son, Ibrahim.

Saro-Wiwa was most famous as a satirical journalist, playwright and screenwriter. He wrote for a massively popular Nigerian television programme called *Basi and Company*, which drew audiences of 30 million viewers. His presence in MOSOP was a huge boost for the group: his celebrity status and local and international contacts helped the group to disseminate its message far and wide.

Ogoni Day

MOSOP's zenith came in January 1993 when it organised an enormous 'Ogoni Day' rally attended by 300,000 people. Mobilising 60% of the Ogoni population for this rally was a staggering achievement. At the rally MOSOP leaders including Saro-Wiwa led chants of 'No to Shell' and demanded that the company leave Ogoni-land. Saro-Wiwa declared Shell 'persona non grata in Ogoni-land', and told the crowd, 'I do not want any blood spilt. Not of an Ogoni man. Not of any strangers amongst us. We are going to demand our rights peacefully, non-violently, and we shall win!' Saro-Wiwa was so proud of the Ogoni Day rally that he declared that he would have died a happy man had he died that day.

To bind every Ogoni to the cause, MOSOP also established a One Naira Ogoni Survival Fund (ONOSUF), to which every Ogoni man, woman and child was asked to make a symbolic contribution of one naira. MOSOP mounted an extremely successful PR campaign to bring the Ogonis' plight to the attention of the international community. Its consistent and singular narrative of a small oppressed minority group being crushed under the combined weight of greedy exploitative international oil companies, especially Shell, and a ruthless and unsympathetic military government, resonated with international audiences. MOSOP presented their grievances to the United Nations, and collaborated with foreign production companies to produce the documentary films *Delta Force* and *The Drilling Fields*. The scenes of environmental degradation and violence in these films shocked international audiences and garnered sympathy for Ogonis overseas. MOSOP's campaign was well timed as it coincided with increasing global awareness of, and sensitivity to, environmental issues.

The Ogonis' demands and protests threatened to block the arteries that kept oil flowing—the lifeblood of Nigeria's government. By demanding autonomy and control of natural resources on their land, the Ogoni were indirectly asking the government to surrender some of its powers to a small ethnic group that constituted a tiny part of Nigeria's population. The federal government could not ignore MOSOP's demands since they posed uncomfortable questions about the nature and existence of the Nigerian federation. MOSOP's successful publicity machine gained the federal government's attention. On two occasions in 1993 the federal government invited Saro-Wiwa and MOSOP leaders for talks in the capital, Abuja. Ogoni leaders, including Saro-Wiwa, Kobani, Leton, Albert Badey and Dr Bennett Birabi,[5] met first with the inspector-general of police, Aliyu Atta, in January 1993. Then on May 7, 1993 they held meetings in Abuja with the national security adviser, Lt-General Aliyu Mohammed Gusau,[6] the director of military intelligence, Brigadier Haliru Akilu, and the secretary to the federal government, Aliyu Mohammed. At both meetings the government asked the Ogoni delegation to summarise their grievances and demands in a memorandum, provide a list of unemployed Ogoni youths, and submit a comparative analysis of the treatment of oil-producing areas in different parts of the world.[7] In the meantime the security officers ominously cautioned that MOSOP should desist from confrontational activities. The year 1993 was a tense time. The military was preparing for a landmark presidential election to return the country to democracy, intra-military tensions were high, and the last thing it needed was disturbance in the oil sector.

MOSOP may have been impressed that the government granted them an audience with such a high-powered delegation. However, the fact that the government representatives for these meetings were leaders of the security and intelligence agencies should have signalled to MOSOP that the government perceived it as a security risk, and that MOSOP was now swimming in the dangerous shark tank of federal politics. The presence of Lt-General Mohammed and Akilu at the second meeting virtually ensured that head of state General Babangida's ears and eyes were in the room even if he was not physically present. Babangida had finely tuned antennae for detecting subversion, and he surrounded himself with men of like mind. Akilu and Mohammed were two of his closest military confidants going back several decades. Mohammed was then the longest-serving military intelligence officer in the army, and had known Babangida for almost thirty years. He was the godfather of Nigeria's modern intelligence network. Akilu's job was to sniff out signs of rebellion against Babangida. Akilu had well-honed military credentials. During the Maitatsine religious riots of the early 1980s, Akilu (then a major) was the commanding officer of 146 Infantry Battalion. His troops, together with soldiers from 202 Armoured Battalion, conducted a brutal and bloody suppression of the riots that involved using tanks and firing artillery in heavily populated city centres to subdue and kill over five thousand members of the Maitatsine sect.

In October 1986 a trail-blazing investigative journalist, Dele Giwa, was called in for questioning by intelligence officers working for Akilu. Giwa had been working on articles regarding the inner intrigues and controversies of members of the military government. The next day, Akilu phoned Giwa's house, spoke to his wife, and asked for Giwa's address and a physical description of his home. On the following day unidentified men dropped off a parcel bomb at Giwa's house which killed him in his study. Giwa's family accused Akilu of organising his murder. Akilu denied responsibility and persuasively argued that if he wanted Giwa dead, he 'wouldn't have been stupid enough to phone [Giwa's] wife two times and keep telling her that I am the one phoning'.[8]

Mohammed and Akilu were hard, grizzled men, experts in security, not environmental matters. Their primary objective was security and order. For MOSOP's campaign to have even the slightest chance of success, it was absolutely vital for it to remain peaceful. Unfortunately MOSOP's youths did not hear the message.

The MOSOP Civil War

The emotionally charged atmosphere in Ogoni-land presented both an opportunity and a danger. MOSOP's incessant highlighting of grievances committed against the Ogoni, coupled with its success at bringing the Ogoni cause to the attention of the federal government and the international community, created a sense of empowerment and inflated expectations of radical change in Ogoni-land. The younger MOSOP generation had unrealistic notions of what MOSOP could achieve. They disseminated fantastic tales of how every Ogoni would be paid $1 million and would live in luxury without having to work after the Ogonis received billions of naira in compensation from Shell and the government.

'You don't have radical grandpas'

MOSOP was also torn by ideological differences. The rift took on the appearance of an inter-generational conflict that pitted the younger MOSOP generation loyal to Saro-Wiwa against the older generation loyal to Leton and Kobani. Saro-Wiwa courted the youths' support because 'you don't have radical grandpas'.[9] Young Ogonis became increasingly confrontational in their demands made of oil companies and the federal government. They favoured proactive opposition against the government. The older generation feared that MOSOP was being radicalised, and worried about the youths' restless and near-mutinous agitation. Leton and Kobani felt the Ogoni were far more likely to achieve their aims through negotiation than by confrontation.

Although it is difficult to navigate through the swamp of accusations and counter-accusations decades after the fact (obscured as they are by emotion and grievance), there were four main areas of discord within MOSOP. The first was the objectives and leadership of other organisations that existed under the MOSOP umbrella. These included the National Youth Council of Ogoni People (NYCOP), the Federation of Ogoni Women's Associations (FOWA), the Ogoni Teachers Union (OTU), the Conference of Ogoni Traditional Rulers (COTRA), the Council of Ogoni Churches (COC), the National Union of Ogoni Students (NUOS), Ogoni Students Union (OSU), Ogoni Central Union (OCU) and the Council of Ogoni Professionals (COP). While Saro-Wiwa argued that incorporating these organisations into MOSOP would show the group's broad-based grassroots nature, Leton and Kobani accused Saro-Wiwa of using these subsidiary organisations, with their alphabet soup of acronyms, to pack MOSOP's executive ranks with his loyalists, and dilute the power of his opponents. An incident in 1993 exposed the internal rifts and bitterness within MOSOP.

The Willbros Incident

On April 30, 1993 Ogoni farmers in the village of Biara protested against an American sub-contracting company appointed by Shell named Willbros, and accused it of destroying their newly planted crops to make way for the construction of an oil pipeline, refusing to pay them compensation, and failing to conduct an environmental impact assessment of their project as stipulated by Nigerian law. When Willbros called for security to tackle the protesters, soldiers shot and killed one of the protesters, and wounded eleven others, including a mother of five, Karalolo Kogbara, whose left arm had to be amputated.

As Saro-Wiwa was abroad in May 1993, other MOSOP leaders agreed to a deal with Willbros for the company to pay compensation to those killed and wounded during the protests. When Saro-Wiwa learned of the deal, he repudiated it, and claimed that in his absence the other MOSOP leaders had sold out the Ogoni cause for a paltry sum of money. This led to some Ogonis accusing those who negotiated the deal of betraying their people in exchange for bribes from international oil companies.

Secondly, federal politics in far-away Abuja widened the rift between MOSOP's leadership triumvirate. Saro-Wiwa argued that Ogonis should boycott the June 12, 1993 presidential election, Nigeria's first presidential election after a decade of military dictatorship. Saro-Wiwa felt that participating in the election would legitimise a constitutional order which denied the Ogoni control of the natural resources extracted from their land. In contrast Leton and Kobani argued that the Ogonis should participate in the election and vote for a candidate—Moshood Abiola of the SDP—from whom they could extract a commitment to address the Ogonis' grievances. Leton and Kobani had joined the SDP in 1993 in violation of a MOSOP convention that its officers could not simultaneously hold posts in MOSOP and in partisan federal political groups. Leton was also later appointed director of Abiola's campaign organisation. The following year Saro-Wiwa himself flouted the same MOSOP convention when he stood for election to the National Constitutional Conference.

'A private army of storm troopers'

MOSOP elders were enraged when, without consultation with or approval from their steering committee, Saro-Wiwa unilaterally declared during a televised interview with CNN that Ogonis would boycott the June 12, 1993 election. On June 2, 1993 MOSOP's steering committee held a stormy meeting at the house of its president, Garrick Leton, in Port Harcourt. The boycott issue was so passionately debated and divisive that MOSOP vice-president Kobani put the motion to a vote. MOSOP voted in favour of a boycott by 11 votes to 6. However, Leton and Kobani accused Saro-Wiwa of contriving the vote by inviting NYCOP members to the meeting and allowing them to vote even though they had no right to do so. The next day Leton, Kobani, Albert Badey, TN Nwieke and other Ogoni elders visited Saro-Wiwa at his house and asked him to rescind the boycott or mitigate its impact by leaving each Ogoni person to decide whether or not to vote as a matter of individual choice. Saro-Wiwa refused. Leton and Kobani resigned from MOSOP in protest. In his resignation letter, Kobani described NYCOP as 'a private army of storm-troopers bent on insulting, intimidating and marginalising the top leadership of the Ogoni nationality in MOSOP'.[10]

Under Saro-Wiwa's influence, MOSOP members boycotted the ill-fated June 12, 1993 elections. The boycott was enforced as much as it was observed.

NYCOP youths 'policed' the boycott by barricading roads to block election officers from delivering election materials, and by intimidating voters into staying away from the polling booths. They threatened to burn the home of anyone who came out to vote. In retaliation for Saro-Wiwa's arrest and harassment by security forces, NYCOP members attacked and burned police stations, raided their armouries, and looted shops. A group of eleven prominent Ogonis apologised for, and dissociated themselves from, the violence and clashes with police. The apology was printed in a national newspaper. To Saro-Wiwa and the youth, the apology was evidence of the older leaders' quisling status. Angry youths attacked and burned the houses of several Ogoni leaders, and forced them to flee. To those attacked, the attacks were evidence that Saro-Wiwa was using NYCOP as his personal gang of enforcers.

Vultures

Following Leton's and Kobani's resignations, Saro-Wiwa became the new MOSOP president and Ledum Mitee, a lawyer, its new vice-president. NYCOP members who were loyal to Saro-Wiwa depicted Leton and Kobani as traitors to the Ogoni cause. In local parlance they were termed 'vultures'—those who collaborated with the Ogonis' enemies to betray and prey upon their own people. The term 'vulture' became a dangerous epithet with which to be associated. It came to represent the worst form of treachery to the Ogoni cause, and those to whom it was applied faced violence or even death. The leadership rift in MOSOP and the accusations and counter-accusations of betrayal and collusion with the government created an intense atmosphere of suspicion and witch-hunting.

In response to rising insecurity, Ogoni villagers formed vigilante groups of youths, often including NYCOP members. These groups saw themselves as guardians of their community. Exhilarated by the power of being unofficial police, they 'investigated' crimes as varied as theft and witchcraft. Ogoni youths became increasingly rebellious and, in some instances, extorted money from villagers. They also embarked on 'witch-hunting' expeditions to expose and execute villagers who allegedly engaged in sorcery. Conveniently, an accusation of being a witch could sometimes be refuted only by paying money to the youths. The youths also procured the services of herbalists who provided them with magic charms that made them 'invulnerable', such as amulets sown into the skin and potions which intoxicated and made the youth reckless and unpredictable, as much as they made them feel invincible. Leton later claimed that NYCOP members conducted secret trials during which Saro-Wiwa's opponents were 'sentenced to death' and their properties burned. Saro-Wiwa exchanged hostile correspondence with Badey and Kobani. In a withering letter Saro-Wiwa told Kobani: 'Edward, I will rebuke you as the *Mene Kpamagbara* of Bodo—your chief. When are you going to take responsibility for your own failures? I cannot stop you from envying my achievements. I invite you to copy my ways and you will find that which you desire most: the Ken Saro-Wiwa image. Good advice and it is free.'[11]

In addition to the intra-group struggles, MOSOP's relationship with the federal government and oil companies soured further. Security forces arrested Saro-Wiwa a number of times in 1993 and confiscated his passport in June 1993 in order to prevent him from travelling to Vienna to attend a UN World Conference on Human Rights. In July 1993 he and two other MOSOP members were arrested and charged with sedition.

Yet Saro-Wiwa still believed he could extract concessions from the government, especially when Abacha became head of state. Saro-Wiwa's lawyer, Barry Kumbe, said, 'It's true that Ken initially welcomed the Abacha coup.'[12] Relations between Abacha and Saro-Wiwa were cordial enough for Abacha to apologise to Saro-Wiwa after his passport was seized by security agents, and to order it to be returned. Saro-Wiwa had also asked Abacha to send the army into Ogoni-land to protect Ogonis from attacks by their neighbours such as the Andonis. Saro-Wiwa walked straight into a trap that gave the government the pretext to do what it had always wanted to: impose a military crackdown on Ogoni-land.

'Wasting operations'

The military appointed Major Paul Okuntimo to command a State Internal Security Task Force. On May 12, 1994 Okuntimo sent a memorandum—'Rivers State Internal Security Operations: Law and Order in Ogoni'—to the military administrator of Rivers State, Lt-Colonel Dauda Musa Komo, in which he outlined plans for a severe escalation of military activity. The memorandum noted: 'Shell operations still impossible unless ruthless military operations are undertaken for smooth economic activities to commence.' Okuntimo recommended 'wasting operations'[13] against MOSOP 'coupled with psychological tactics', restrictions on unauthorised visitors (especially those from Europe) to Ogoni-land, surveillance of Ogoni leaders considered a security risk, and direct supervision by the Rivers State military administrator to avoid interference from other superior officers.

Okuntimo rigorously implemented his security plan. Soldiers under his command flooded into Ogoni-land and turned it into a closed military zone sealed off from the outside world. NYCOP, who regarded themselves as the guardians of Ogoni-land, responded to the soldiers as an army of occupation to be resisted, and unwisely confronted them. The army arrested, killed or maimed hundreds of Ogonis. Several Ogoni women claimed that soldiers killed their children or husbands, then gang-raped them. Shell was deeply implicated in the affair after it provided finances to pay the soldiers on the mission.

At a filmed press conference, Okuntimo mockingly related how he had cowed the Ogoni civilian population, and boasted of knowing over two hundred ways to kill a human being. While holding a microphone in one hand, and wildly gesticulating with the other, he took the audience through the repertoire of devices he employed to tame Ogoni-land, speaking in a booming, excited voice:

> The first three days of the operation I operated in the night. Nobody knew where I was coming from. What I will just do is that I will take some detachments of soldiers. They will just stay at the four corners of the town. They ... have automatic rifles that sound death. If you hear the sound you will freeze. And then I will equally choose about twenty [soldiers] and give them ... grenades, explosives—very hard ones. So we shall surround the town at night ... The machine gun with five hundred rounds will open up. When four or five like that open up and we are throwing grenades and they are making 'eekpuwaa'! ... and they know I am around, what do you think the people are going to do? And we have already put roadblocks on the main road, we don't want anybody to start running ... so the option we made was that we should drive all these boys, all these people into the bush with nothing except the pants and the wrapper they are using that night.[14]

Things were about to get worse.

The Ogoni Four

On May 21, 1994 Saro-Wiwa and Mitee were travelling in separate cars to a series of rallies near Giokoo when police at the Kpopie junction stopped them and told them to turn back. Mitee recalled:

> I was driving in front and the police who were escorting us told us to stop ... We stopped and I came out of the car and the police told me that we couldn't go any further. They said they had taken a decision that Ken had to turn back. They said I had to go one way, and Ken another. They wanted to separate us. So I only walked to Ken's vehicle and he wound down his window. He said, 'What is hap-

pening?' I said, 'These people say you can't go any further' and all that, and he said, 'Okay'. He told the driver to turn around. I said, 'I'll go home and pick up my things and I'll meet you.' He said, 'All right, join me in the office.' And that was it.[15]

A crowd of their supporters congregated around their cars, and the two conferred before complying with the police order. The government claimed that before departing, Saro-Wiwa spoke to some of his supporters in an Ogoni dialect and told them to 'deal with' the 'vultures' in Giokoo who were on the government's payroll, and who were colluding with the government to obstruct him.[16]

As Saro-Wiwa departed, less than one mile away, the *gbenemene* or traditional chief of Gokana, James Pago Bagia, was preparing to host an important meeting at his palace in Giokoo. One of the meeting's purposes was to arrange a reception for two prominent Ogonis from Gokana who had been appointed to the Rivers State government, Barinem Kiobel and Mene Gbaragba. Kobel had recently been appointed as the commissioner for commerce and industry, and Gbaragba the chairman of the Gokana Caretaker Committee in Gokana Local Government Area.

Dozens of the Ogoni elite attended the meeting. The attendees included Chief Samuel Orage, a former commissioner for health in the Rivers State government; his younger brother, Chief Theophilus P Orage, secretary to the Gokana Council of Chiefs; Albert Tombari Badey, a former secretary to the Rivers State government; Edward Kobani and his younger brother, Mohammed; and Chief Francis S Kpai. Bagia did not realise that his palace would become a crime scene later that day.

Chief Obadiah Nalelo, chairman of the Gokana Council of Chiefs and Elders, declared the meeting open at some time between 11 and 11.30 am. Edward Kobani was the first person to address the meeting, followed by Badey. As Badey spoke, a NYCOP member named Theophilus Ntoo arrived at the palace on a motorcycle. Ntoo informed the crowd milling around that the police had blocked Saro-Wiwa's attempt to address a rally in the town, and that some Ogoni 'vultures' were behind the police's action. He also alleged that Saro-Wiwa told Ogoni youths that the 'vultures' were meeting at the palace to share money given to them by the government and Shell, and should be dealt with. Mohammed Kobani or David Keenom came out of the meeting hall and remonstrated with Ntoo. In the intense atmosphere prevailing, Ntoo's appearance had an incendiary effect on the crowd.

Ntoo left, but a few minutes later a mob of several hundred or several thousand people (depending on who is asked) chanting war songs and wielding macheres, bottles, knives, stones and clubs descended on the palace. Some had travelled there on foot, others by motorcycle. Precisely how hundreds of teenagers and young men knew where and when the meeting was taking place, and assembled so quickly, is a matter of speculation. The brutality of what happened next needs to be described in detail as it provides a context for subsequent events during the following eighteen months.

A member of the crowd, Kpuinen Bera, allegedly shouted '*E-sho-be*' (a war cry) and encouraged the others to attack the chiefs. The mob besieged the meeting hall and brutally assaulted Chief Kpai, Nalelo, Badey and the Orage brothers with fists, knives, clubs and broken bottles. They beat Kpai unconscious and seriously wounded Theophilus Orage's right eye. Perhaps thinking that Kpai was dead, the mob turned their attention away long enough for Mohammed Kobani and others to drag him back inside the hall. Some of the injured men retreated into a corner of the hall, but the attackers pursued them inside and continued beating them. A young woman was among the attackers.

The mob then destroyed vehicles, vandalised the premises and hacked Badey to death. They then turned their attention to Edward Kobani. His younger brother, Mohammed Kobani, was wounded while trying to defend him. Edward was hit with a rake that fractured his skull. The mob dragged his corpse out onto the palace veranda and mutilated it in an unspeakable manner.

Kpai and Badey managed to escape and tried to flee in a taxi but were prevented from doing so by the pursuing crowd. They also tried to shelter in a Methodist church but were stopped once again. A woman took pity on Kpai and Badey after seeing their bloodied and dishevelled state and allowed them into her house. When the attackers threatened to kill her unless she handed the men over, the woman had to give them up. The crowd stripped both men, beat them again, and dragged them around. Badey, an asthmatic, tried to use his inhaler but the crowd, mistaking it for a device that he could use to call for help, snatched it away and beat him to death.

Although some people fled, a crowd of several hundred or a few thousand still remained. They took TP Orage's corpse away in a wheelbarrow, and those of Badey, Kobani and Samuel Orage were removed in a white Volkswagen belonging to Nalelo, before being set ablaze until they were burned beyond recognition.[17]

News of the violence began to spread. After hearing that her father had been attacked, Theophilus Orage's daughter went to the *gbenemene*'s palace by motorcycle taxi. When she arrived, the motorcycle was unable to get near because of the crowd. However, the mob recognised her and attacked her. Although she was badly beaten, she and her siblings managed to escape on motorcycles while being pursued.

Some people who escaped reported the mayhem to police officers at Kpopie Junction and the Bori police station. The police officers at both locations informed them that in the absence of their commanding officer, they could not mobilise as they did not have orders to do so.

After seeing that his brother had been killed, Mohammed Kobani ran behind Bagia's house and took refuge in the Gberesako shrine—the shrine of the Ogoni Spirit—a location considered sacrosanct. Chief Kpai and Bagia joined him and hid with him in the shrine. Although the Ogonis are nominally Christians, they still hold to pre-Christian animist beliefs. While the attackers were willing to commit murder, they considered killing someone inside the shrine a sacrilege that would bring curses on them, their families and future descendants. They urged Bagia, who as the *gbenemene* was regarded as the custodian of the shrine, to pour a libation to allow them to remove Kobani from the shrine so they could kill him. Bagia refused their request and entered the shrine. Several angry youths set fire to his palace and three cars belonging to Badey, Orage and Kobani.

Some gruesome claims were later made. Leton alleged that Theophilus Orage was cooked and eaten by his murderers: 'They cooked and ate him... I am ashamed to be an Ogoni. In fact I no longer consider myself an Ogoni.'[18]

After several hours of violence, the mob finally dispersed around 5 or 6 pm after hearing gunshots from approaching soldiers.

'Our great-grandchildren will hear it. They will hear it'

A number of features made these attacks particularly shocking and horrific. Firstly, the age of the attackers and the age of the victims. The murderers were youths and those they killed were supposedly their revered elders and leaders. In most Nigerian communities it is considered sacrilege to argue publicly with one's elders, let alone strike them. Secondly, the attack took place at the residence of an Ogoni traditional leader, a symbol of traditional authority in Ogoni society. The youths murdered elders and leaders in their community, in public, at the premises of a traditional leader, and close to a shrine considered spiritually sacred. This triple desecration demonstrated the extent to which authority and respect had broken down among Ogoni youths, and how older leaders had lost control to what had essentially become a youth rebellion. One

Ogoni remarked, 'The whole of Ogoni-land was there; more than 1,000 men were there when this man [Kobani] was arrested and executed by these youths. How come nobody raised a finger in his defence? Yet he was a chief, a prime minister of Ogoni-land, hacked to death in front of his kinsmen. This sad history will continue to be told and our great-grandchildren will hear it. They will hear it.'

The four murder victims were influential, wealthy and well connected. All of them were also founder members of MOSOP. Given their prominence, the government would not let the murders go unavenged. Security forces arrested Saro-Wiwa, Mitee and Kiobel the next morning, and accused them of inciting the mob to murder the victims. Kiobel's arrest was strange since the meeting at which the murders occurred had been called in his honour. He did not have an obvious motive to kill men who had organised a reception to pay him respect. An additional irony was that two of the victims, the Orage brothers, were brothers-in-law of Saro-Wiwa, while the other two, Badey and Kobani, had been his close friends.[19] Samuel Orage's wife Elizabeth was the older sister of Saro-Wiwa's first wife, Maria. Theophilus Orage was the older brother of Saro-Wiwa's father-in-law.

The murders sent shock waves through Ogoni-land. The victims' families were traumatised. Mohammed Kobani, for one, was angry that press coverage of the mayhem focused on the arrest of Saro-Wiwa, and not on the fact that four people had been murdered. He said, 'Is it not ridiculous that the press ignored the murder of prominent sons of Ogoni? Instead, it is Ken that is making the headline.'[20]

'Ogoni is bleeding'

On Sunday, May 23, 1994, Lt-Colonel Komo addressed a filmed press conference. Komo was well connected in the military. Like the GOC of the Lagos Garrison Command, Brigadier-General Ishaya Bamaiyi, Komo was from the Christian-minority but militarily significant Zuru ethnic group in the northeast.[21] At the press conference Komo had with him a bag containing the charred bones and remains of the victims. He invited the journalists to inspect the bag's contents. Although no one had been charged with the murders, and the investigation and trial had not commenced, Komo already felt he knew who was responsible. He said: 'Ogoni is bleeding ... and not [because of] federal troops ... but by the irresponsible and reckless thuggery of the MOSOP element ... which must stop immediately.' He appealed to the press not to allow themselves to be used as propaganda tools 'by a dictator like Ken Saro-Wiwa'. Komo promised that 'whoever is involved, no matter how highly placed in the society, would be appropriately dealt with according to the laws of Nigeria'.[22]

The Civil Disturbances Special Tribunal

The federal government convened a Civil Disturbances Special Tribunal to try the suspects. The defendants could not appeal to a civil court against its verdict, and only the Provisional Ruling Council could confirm or commute its sentences. On November 21, 1994 the chief justice of the federation, Mohammed Bello, swore in the three members of the tribunal. All the members had considerable legal experience. Its chairman, Justice Ibrahim Nadhi Auta,[23] was a Federal High Court judge in Lagos and a former attorney-general of Borno State. The other tribunal members were Justice Etowa Enyong Arikpo,[24] a High Court judge and former attorney-general of Cross River State, and Lt-Colonel Hameed Ibrahim Ali,[25] a serving military officer from the corps of military police, who had bachelor's and master's degrees in criminology.

Despite being detained for nine months, the accused were not brought before the tribunal until February 6, 1995, at the Rivers State House of Assembly complex. Armed soldiers were positioned inside at both ends of the courtroom, behind and facing the tribunal members. Family members and supporters of both the defendants and the deceased were also in attendance along with observers from the Nigerian Bar Association, human rights organisations, and international legal observers. Philip Umeadi led the prosecution team. He was the lawyer for the notorious Association for a Better Nigeria whose court antics in 1993 led to the annulment of the June 12, 1993 presidential election. Gani Fawehinmi led the defence legal team, assisted by several other lawyers including Femi Falana, Fatai Osho and Emmanuel Ukala. Ledum Mitee defended himself since he was a lawyer. The lawyer Bayo Fagduba watched the proceedings on behalf of Shell.

'No more'

Fawehinmi asked the tribunal to grant a two-week adjournment to allow him to prepare his case, since none of the defendants had been allowed to see their lawyers. When Umeadi opposed his motion, Fawehinmi drily observed that he was requesting two weeks to study a case which had taken Umeadi eight months to prepare. The tribunal granted Fawehinmi's request. After the adjournment, Gani addressed a crowd of Ogonis gathered outside the courtroom and told them: 'For several years, this country has lived on your sweat, on your tears, on your blood. Now, no more!' This led the crowd into loud chants of 'no more!' before they were dispersed by security forces.

This incident led to reinforced armed security at the tribunal. In February 1995 police stopped several cars carrying the defence lawyers outside the courtroom. The police insisted that the lawyers had to obtain accreditation from Okuntimo before being allowed into the courtroom. When Fawehinmi refused, police and soldiers tried to force him into a vehicle. In the ensuing melee, Fawehinmi's suit was ripped, and one of the security men slapped Falana when he protested against Fawehinmi's treatment. After much bickering and manhandling by security, the defence lawyers were permitted to enter the court house after a senior police officer, Assistant Commissioner of Police KZ Dudari, arrived and apologised to the lawyers. While defusing that particular conflict, Dudari found time to tell Fawehinmi in Hausa: '*Gani: Kai, Gani, mai surutu ne*' (Gani, you are a troublemaker).

The Case for the Prosecution

The thrust of the prosecution's case was that Saro-Wiwa had incited the mob to murder the victims whom he blamed for colluding with the government to prevent him from attending a rally. There were fifteen defendants. Saro-Wiwa, Mitee and Kiobel were charged with 'counselling and procuring' Kpuinen Bera and others to murder the victims. Two prosecution witnesses, Charles S Danwi and Nayone Akpa, swore statements in June 1994 alleging that Saro-Wiwa told his supporters to 'deal with' the 'vultures'. However, Danwi and Akpa later retracted their statements and claimed that they had been bribed to give false evidence against Saro-Wiwa.[26] Eleven other defendants were accused of being among the murderers that killed the Ogoni Four.

The Case for the Defence

The defence argued that the police officers who escorted Saro-Wiwa away from the rally had made no mention of his blaming the murder victims for his fate, and that even if Saro-Wiwa did, this did not amount to incitement to kill.

On several occasions prosecution witnesses made statements that were contradictory to those previously given to the police. When the defence lawyers sought to tender their previous statements, the tribunal refused to admit them. Witnesses Nayone Akpa and Charles S Danwi claimed they had been given inducements of money and government employment to give false evidence against Saro-Wiwa and MOSOP. They also alleged that they had been coached on what to say at the trial, and that seven other witnesses had also been similarly bribed.

The defendants and their lawyers also had to deal with harassment by the security forces. Oronto Douglas, an environmental lawyer in Saro-Wiwa's legal team, alleged that on June 26, 1994 he, the lawyer Uche Onyeagocha and Nicholas Ashton-Jones, a British representative of the environmental group Pro Natura, went to see the defendant Ledum Mitee. Lt-Colonel Okuntimo arrived while they were meeting, and flew into a rage, drawing his pistol and berating the security men for allowing the visitors to see Mitee. He kicked a police officer and ordered him to be detained in a cell. Okuntimo also ordered Douglas, Onyeagocha and Ashton-Jones to be flogged before driving them away in a jeep.

Mohammed Kobani was a key prosecution witness since he was present when the victims were murdered, and was a brother of one of the victims. He also appeared at the May 23 press conference at which Komo alleged that MOSOP was responsible for the murders. The defence sought to demonstrate inconsistencies between Kobani's account given at the May 23 press conference and in his written witness statement. When defence lawyers sought to present a video recording of the press conference, the tribunal refused to allow the defence to submit its own copy of the video tape. For its part, the Rivers State government claimed it could not produce a copy of the tape as it had either been erased or did not exist. Despite the claim, footage of the press conference had been broadcast by Channel 4 on UK national television.

This was the last straw that broke the camel's back. On June 22 the defence lawyers, with Saro-Wiwa's blessing, walked out in protest at the tribunal's biased conduct. They felt that their participation was giving legitimacy to a sham trial. From that moment on, Saro-Wiwa ceased to cooperate with the tribunal, ignored its proceedings, and busied himself reading newspapers and periodicals. Saro-Wiwa's mocking wit and humour did not endear him to the tribunal. When Justice Auta probed Saro-Wiwa on medical reports concerning his alleged psychiatric problems, Saro-Wiwa responded that he must be suffering mentally as he saw kangaroos every time he looked up at the judges. He detached himself from the proceedings and often had the demeanour of a bystander rather than a defendant in a trial where his life was at stake. He refused to cooperate with the replacement lawyers appointed for him by the tribunal. When the prosecution called witnesses, they testified without being cross-examined since there was no functioning defence team.

On October 31, 1995 the tribunal found Saro-Wiwa and eight other defendants guilty and sentenced them to death by hanging. Saro-Wiwa said he had been convicted before the trial even began and told the tribunal, 'There is no possibility whatsoever that either I or MOSOP could have planned any such action, and I will forever vow it no matter what any forum decides upon.'

Although there was no right of appeal from the tribunal's verdict, the sentences were subject to confirmation by the Provisional Ruling Council. Although Saro-Wiwa's brother Letam was a captain in the army, the convicted men's fate was bleak; sentenced to death with no right of appeal to civil courts, they could only be saved by the military regime against which they had campaigned.[27] The timing of the death sentences was potentially explosive. The verdict coincided with a Commonwealth Heads of Government meeting in Auckland, New Zealand, and Nigeria's human rights record had already antagonised the other member states.

The Commonwealth leaders pressed Nigeria to commute the death sentences, as did the US and EU. One notable figure who refused to join the public clamour for clemency was South African President Nelson Mandela. He was criticised for not being more vocal in pressuring Abacha. The death sentences also embarrassed the Commonwealth secretary-general, Emeka Anyaoku, who was a Nigerian. Unbeknown to the public, both Mandela and Anyaoku privately telephoned Abacha to appeal for clemency. Mandela's experience of negotiating with hard-line regimes had taught him that public hectoring was unlikely to bring about change, and he had faith that his charm and back-door mediation with Abacha would save the lives of the convicted men. When pressed by reporters on live television, Mandela refused to criticise Abacha directly.

Saro-Wiwa's son Ken Jr appeared on British television to raise international awareness of his father's impending fate. The wives of Kiobel and Kpuinen also sent appeals for clemency to Abacha. On November 9 Kiobel's wife Esther said that 'people's minds are already shaking, but mine is not. No matter how hard your heart is, God can touch it. They are not going to kill these men.'[28]

November 10, 1995—Port Harcourt

At 11.30 am on November 10, 1995, a black police van arrived at Bori Camp and took the convicted men to the Port Harcourt prison. They were simply told that they were being transferred. They had their legs chained and marched in single file into the prison records office. Their countenances suddenly changed when they saw a priest waiting for them inside the office. A prison official read out the death sentence to each man individually. They were then taken to cell block C, which was the holding area for convicts on death row. Some of the men remained stoic while others wept or screamed their innocence. Each man was placed in a separate holding cell, and they were taken out one by one to the gallows that had been erected inside a hut to the side of the prison courtyard.

There have been conflicting accounts of Saro-Wiwa's execution and last words. However, all of the accounts agree that his execution was botched. After the guards put a hood over his head and a noose around his neck, things did not go according to plan. When the executioner activated the trapdoor, the hanging mechanism would not work and the trapdoor did not open. The guards removed Saro-Wiwa from the hut, rechecked the mechanism, and tried a second time. Although the trapdoor opened, the mechanism malfunctioned a second time and the gallows did not drop Saro-Wiwa down far enough. A doctor who took his pulse confirmed that he was still alive. The guards picked Saro-Wiwa up and hanged him for a third time until he died. The eight other convicts were hanged after Saro-Wiwa.

After the executions, the corpses were removed from the federal prison in Port Harcourt, loaded onto trucks, covered by tarpaulin, and driven under heavily armed guard to the Port Harcourt Cemetery on Aggrey Road, less than a kilometre away from the prison—and close to Saro-Wiwa's office at 24 Aggrey Road. Many media outlets reported, and many Ogonis believed, that Komo personally attended and supervised the executions, and had them filmed, so that copies could be distributed to Provisional Ruling Council (PRC) members. Komo denied this. Contrary to press reports and popular belief, the condemned men were not buried in a mass grave, nor was acid poured on their bodies. Their bodies were buried in nine separate graves while police officer Hassan Abila supervised the process.

The fate of those convicted for the 1995 coup influenced the fate of the Ogoni Nine. The international community's lukewarm response to Abacha's clemency earlier in the year did not give Abacha any incentive to show further clemency. From Abacha's perspective, he had done what no other Nigerian ruler had ever done: spared the lives of convicted coup plotters. Rather than commending him and granting him diplomatic esteem for his unprecedented act of magnanimity, the international community instead continued to berate him pressed for the men to be released, refused to ease their diplomatic pressure and criticised everything he did. Abacha later complained to a senior US State Department official: 'I had to bend down to the ground and commute sentences after intervention by President Clinton ... John Major, Jimmy Carter and Bill Clinton all called. John Major called twice, but it was Clinton I wanted to please. I had to bend down. *I got no appreciation.*'[29]

The Provisional Ruling Council had met two days before the executions to discuss the sentences. Sparing the death sentence in the case of the coup plotters had drained the PRC's residual goodwill towards the international community. The PRC could not afford to look weak by commuting death sentences twice in one year. A memorandum summarising the PRC meeting noted that 'the government's decision on the [1995 coup] plotters had sent wrong signals to the generality of Nigerians and that the current case should be used to correct that wrong impression'. Abacha said that 'no sympathy should be shown' to the condemned men, and executing them 'would be a lesson for everybody'.[30]

The Ogoni Nine were executed on the very day that the Commonwealth Heads of Government meeting started. The decision to execute them in defiance of international appeals for clemency was deliberately timed to send a message to the Commonwealth and other international leaders that Nigeria was impervious to outside pressure. But the Nigerian government badly misread the mood of the international community. International leaders were outraged. The defiant manner and timing of the executions was like a contemptuous slap in the face especially of respected leaders like Mandela who had appealed for clemency. Even African countries that rarely criticised Nigeria were stung. Zimbabwean President Robert Mugabe said that he and other African leaders had 'tried to assist [Nigeria] as friends and brothers ... but apparently they are inexorably set on a path of self-destruction'. British Prime Minister John Major referred to the executions as 'judicial murder'. He recalled his country's high commissioner to Nigeria, Thorold Masefield, and suspended all military relations with Nigeria. Britain also banned the sale of military equipment to Nigeria, and extended its already existing visa ban on Nigerian government officials to include their family members. The US, South Africa, Russia and other European countries recalled their ambassadors from Nigeria. Nigeria was now an international pariah.

Mandela felt personally betrayed as he had put at risk his considerable reputation by not publicly criticising Nigeria after the verdict in the hope of preserving goodwill and influence with the country. He said, 'I have tried persuasive diplomacy to get Nigeria on track [but] with the latest development there is nothing I can do other than call for Nigeria's suspension [from the Commonwealth].'[31] At Mandela's behest, the Commonwealth suspended Nigeria from the organisation.

Open questions remained. A very large mob killed the Ogoni Four. The riotous nature of the murders probably involved scores or hundreds of potential murderers. Even if some of the murderers were apprehended, the vast majority of them escaped justice and are still at large. The agent provocateur who arguably did most to incite the crowd to violence—Timothy Ntoo—by alleging that the 'vultures' were meeting to 'share money', was not among the defendants even though several witnesses identified him by name and physical appearance. Given the absence or death of the principal witnesses, we will never know whether Saro-Wiwa incited the murderers. No forensic evidence linked any of the defendants to the crime scene and none of them confessed. Much of the evidence against them consisted of oral testimony by their enemies and rivals. Although we cannot establish with certainty what Saro-Wiwa said, the fact that the youths acted so rapidly and violently to something they thought he said (whether true or not) was a sure indication of the influence that he had on them. If Saro-Wiwa was not legally culpable for the murders, one may still ask whether he and other NYCOP members bear moral responsibility for creating an intense atmosphere of denunciation in which anyone who urged caution or dialogue with government authorities was vilified as a traitor.

Conclusion and Postscript

MOSOP's rhetoric of resource control and restitution resonated with other communities in the oil-producing areas and acted as a motivation for the formation of other protest groups in the Niger Delta. The intra-Ogoni wars led to the neighbouring Ijaw ethnic group's displacement of the Ogoni as the vanguard of those advocating control of resources in the Niger Delta. The murders and executions robbed Ogonis of their leadership. After the murders Komo said: 'the Ogoni are killing each other ... It is going to take Ogoni-land almost forever to produce the quality of people they have lost.'[32]

10

MURDER INC.

Although Abacha had always possessed 'a consuming phobia for security',[1] the manner in which Abiola, NADECO and the trade unions confronted him in 1994 intensified his security consciousness. After the exit of Alli and Madueke from government, and the civil unrest that Abiola's presidential declaration generated, Abacha began to rely more on the counsel of his security aides, and distanced himself from Diya and his civilian advisers. He had good reason to be wary: powerful opponents had converged against him.

'A country under siege by its own army'

Abacha's continual use of a military sledgehammer to attack pro-democracy activists had suppressed overt protests, but not the underlying bitterness. After the military crackdowns of 1994 drove most of NADECO's members into exile, the organisation and other opposition figures took their campaign abroad. They urged the US and EU to impose sanctions on the Nigerian government, and also launched and sponsored a radio station opposed to military rule called Radio Democrat.[2] Anti-government fugitives were frequent guests on the station. A *Newsnight* television documentary that aired on BBC2 in December 1994 gave the opposition a chance to let Abacha know exactly what they thought of him and his government. The documentary described Nigeria as 'a country under siege by its own army'.

'this terrorist organisation that calls itself a government'

The playright Wole Soyinka had been forced into exile after being followed and harassed by security agents, who also seized his passport. Soyinka, appearing on the *Newsnight* programme, referred to Abacha as 'this creature' and described his government as a 'terrorist organisation that calls itself a government'. The civil rights lawyer Gani Fawehinmi, who had filed several lawsuits against military governments and who proudly proclaimed that he had been arrested by the military more times than any other Nigerian, was obviously not on good terms with Abacha's government. On August 26, 1994, unknown gunmen attacked Fawehinmi's law chambers in Lagos and wounded two of his guards. The attackers screamed insults at the guards, who were northerners, and asked them (in Hausa) why they were disgracing themselves by working for a southerner. Fawehinmi did not hesitate to apportion blame for the attack. He posted a defiant statement at his chambers that read: 'Notice to Abacha. Your security forces visited us with bullets and created pools of human blood in our chambers premises today Friday August 26, 1994. Our reply We shall continue to resist your regime until your regime ends. And it will end disgracefully. Chief Gani Fawehinmi.'

'Nigeria is worse than a police state'

Even though the Abacha government had banned political parties, Fawehinmi defied the ban and launched the National Conscience Party on October 1, 1994. Security forces arrested him in Lagos the same day. After being released, Fawehinmi declared: 'Nigeria is worse than a police state. We are virtually in an undeclared martial law.' When reminded of the danger that his defiance posed to his safety, Fawehinmi replied, 'We will try. We may die. We hope others will follow.'[3]

Even members of the clergy joined in the chorus of condemnation. In 1994 the archbishop of the Anglican Church of Nigeria, Abiodun Adetiloye, wrote a letter to Abacha saying, 'I have prayed for you that God may grant you the grace and courage to quit when there is still some ovation left.'[4] The prolific Nigerian rumour mill was also awash with stories of alleged military coup plots against Abacha. As a result the intelligence agencies conducted surveillance on the military in addition to pro-democracy activists. The threat of a coup became such a serious problem that in 1995 the director of military intelligence, Brigadier-General Sabo, initiated a security awareness programme for army officers, which offered advice on how to respond to military coups.

With so many opponents and threats, Abacha responded in the way he knew best. Lacking charisma and popularity, he resorted to a military iron fist to elicit compliance and maintain control. Major-General Alli said: 'For Sani Abacha, security was a religion and Aso Rock [the presidential villa] his temple.'[5] Alli added that at the end of every meeting, Abacha would, 'without exception, caution on security'.[6] It is a measure of the effectiveness of his security that though Abacha had less support than any other military leader in Nigeria's history, he yet exercised more control than any of his predecessors.

Attrition among Abacha's personal staff was high. His first ADC was Lt-Colonel Abdul Malik Jubrin, who, like Abacha, was from Kano. Major Aminu succeeded Jubrin, but in turn departed and was succeeded by Lt-Colonel Muhammad Mustapha Abdallah from Yobe State. One officer always seemed to survive these culls. Major Hamza al-Mustapha was appointed by Abacha to the newly created position of chief security officer. Al-Mustapha was a military intelligence officer from Nguru in Yobe State in the north-east. His appointment gave him unprecedented security powers, access to Abacha, and control over his movements. Al-Mustapha became Abacha's de facto gatekeeper, with the ability to closet him away or grant access to him. Consequently, senior military officers, government ministers and officials, and hangers-on who wanted to see Abacha had to go through him.

Strike Force

In addition to the traditional government bodyguards from the Brigade of Guards, al-Mustapha reinforced Abacha's security by creating new units. In January 1995 he formed the Strike Force and Special Bodyguards.[7] These new forces were trained in Libya and North Korea, and operated autonomously outside the military chain of command. They were answerable to no one except al-Mustapha and Abacha. While members of the Brigade of Guards were drawn from army units and wore army uniforms, Strike Force members dressed in ominous black T-shirts and jeans, wore sunglasses, and were known for charging around Abuja at terrific speed in their SUVs. Their official responsibility was to guard Abacha and his family, and conduct counter-terrorism operations. They were fanatically loyal to al-Mustapha in a manner not seen in Nigeria since the time Joe Garba commanded the Brigade of Guards from 1966 to 1975. A former official was astonished by the thoroughness of the background checks that Abacha's agents conducted on him, and described them as 'proper security people'. He also told me that the Strike Force 'were willing to do anything for him [al-Mustapha].[8] Al-Mustapha and his men swore personal oaths of allegiance to Abacha, vowing to lay down their lives for him if necessary. A police officer, Suleiman Abba, acted as ADC for Abacha's wife Maryam. He later became inspector-general of the entire Nigerian police force.

Abacha also increased the power of the national security adviser, Ismaila Gwarzo. He transferred control of his presidential plane fleet from the air force to Gwarzo. Gwarzo was an archetypical intelligence officer, being quiet, inconspicuous and secretive. He was the first director-general of the State Security Service. He and al-Mustapha set up a strict security regime around Abacha. His travel routines and other schedules were closely guarded secrets and were often revised at the last possible moment, making it impossible for would-be saboteurs to get to him. He rarely travelled abroad, and when he did so he ventured only to nearby West African countries which he could travel to and return from within a few hours. His travels abroad were never announced in advance and even government ministers would not be aware that he had been away until after he returned. Sometimes senior officers arrived for scheduled meetings with Abacha and would discover that he had left the country. He would also leave and return at odd hours, often after midnight. When he travelled domestically, security agents closed the airspace and the roads he used one hour before he started and for thirty minutes after he passed. Entire neighbourhoods would be cordoned off prior to his arrival. The only officers who had frequent access to Abacha were al-Mustapha, Gwarzo, the commander of the Brigade of Guards, Yakubu Mu'azu, and the minister of the Federal Capital Territory, Lt-General Useni. Their unique access to Abacha, and their desire to ration and control others' access to him, simultaneously amplified their own power in the regime, and made them objects of resentment by other officers.

Abacha also deployed spiritual protection. He had marabouts, seers and sorcerers from Chad, Mauritania, Niger and Sudan who would advise him and warn him of impending threats.[9] He accommodated them in guest houses at the presidential villa and at the Sheraton Abuja Hotel. His closest spiritual adviser was the Sarkin Sasa—head of the Hausa community in Ibadan—Haruna Maiyasin Katsina.

In March 1994 senior security agencies asked Abacha for permission to arrest Babangida and the 'IBB boys'. Although Abacha declined to approve the arrests, the IBB boys, including former national security adviser Lt-General Aliyu Mohammed Gusau, were confined to their Local Government Areas and were barred from travelling abroad without permission.[10]

Ibrahim Abacha

Yet despite the omnipresent surveillance and constant emphasis on security, some events were beyond even Abacha's control. On January 17, 1996 a British-made Hawker-Siddeley private jet crashed near the Abacha family's home town of Kano. The plane was flying to Kano from Lagos and went down a few minutes before it was scheduled to land. All 14 passengers and crew died in the crash. The casualties included Abacha's oldest son, 28-year-old Ibrahim, and Bello Dangote, the younger brother of the wealthy businessman Aliko Dangote. Ibrahim was a popular member of the Abacha family, and his death devastated his mother, Maryam. The Abacha family went into deep mourning and sympathisers besieged the presidential villa and their family home in Kano. A previously unknown group calling itself the United Front for Nigeria's Liberation (UFNL) claimed responsibility for the crash. The UFNL released a statement saying that it 'carried out this patriotic attack against the enemies of the Nigerian people, and with it we are signalling an intensification of the campaign to remove this brutal dictatorship by every means possible'. However, investigators believed passenger over-loading and pilot error were more likely causes of the crash. The day after the plane crash, a bomb exploded at the Durbar Hotel in Kaduna, and on the day following that, another bomb exploded at the Aminu Kano International Airport in Kano. The Durbar Hotel was said to be owned by a company linked to the Abachas.

Alfred Rewane

The octogenarian Alfred Rewane was a wealthy businessman, veteran politician and key financier of NADECO. Although he was Itsekiri, he had been a financier of Awolowo's mainly Yoruba Action Group party in the 1960s.[11] As a young businessman in the 1960s, he was well known in elite Lagos circles for his flamboyance, wealth and lavish lifestyle. He was often spotted driving a Jaguar or other luxury car. With NADECO confronted by the seemingly limitless resources of the federal government, Rewane's wealth became critical to the group's existence and funding.

Rewane was scheduled to attend the AGM of Ovaltine Nigeria Limited, a company of which he was chairman, on Friday October 16 1995. Around 8 am that day, five men in a blue Peugeot 504 drove to his house at 100 Oduduwa Crescent in the Government Reservation Area of Ikeja, Lagos. The driver of the car told Rewane's gateman that he had an urgent message from

Rewane's home town of Sapele. The gateman opened the gate after spotting a sticker on the car's windscreen bearing the logo of Life Flour Mills, one of Rewane's companies. After passing the beautifully manicured lawns and hedges in Rewane's compound, they approached the one-storey building where Rewane lived with his family, and rang the doorbell. When a member of Rewane's staff answered the door, one of the visitors again said in Rewane's native Itsekiri language that he was bearing a message from his home town. The staff member led them inside. Once inside, one of the visitors drew a gun and locked Rewane's wife and domestic staff inside a room at gunpoint. The men then entered Rewane's bedroom and shot him in the chest sometime between 8.15 and 8.30. The intruders escaped and left Rewane's corpse lying in a pool of blood in his bedroom.

Kudirat Abiola

With her husband imprisoned, Abiola's senior wife, the 44-year-old Kudirat, became a prominent figure in the pro-democracy struggle. She often took part in demonstrations and denounced the government. In 1994 the US forced Haiti's military ruler, Lt-General Raoul Cédras, into exile after threatening to invade Haiti unless he and his military government resigned and ceded power back to the elected president, Jean-Bertrand Aristide, whom Cédras had overthrown in a military coup in 1991. Inspired by US strong-arm measures against Haiti's military government, Kudirat appealed to President Bill Clinton to do the same to Abacha's regime. She appeared in a BBC *Newsnight* documentary during which she said: 'What happened in Haiti, we want it here [in Nigeria].'

Around 9.30 am on Tuesday June 4 1996, Kudirat left her home in Lagos for an appointment at the Canadian High Commission in the company of her personal assistant, Mark Olufemi Adesina, and her driver, Dauda Atanda. Adesina sat in the front passenger seat beside Atanda, while Kudirat sat in the back. As Atanda manoeuvred Kudirat's white Mercedes-Benz on the Lagos–Ibadan Expressway past the Seven-Up Junction on Oregun Road in Ikeja, two Peugeots, one a 505 and the other a 504, approached them. One of the cars swerved twice in front of Kudirat's car, forcing Atanda to slow down. Several gunmen then opened fire with machine guns at close range. The hail of gunfire smashed the windshield and back window of Kudirat's car and forced it off the road. Adesina instinctively fell to the floor as shards of broken glass and spent ammunition rained down on top of him. Despite the bursts of gunfire,

Adesina survived. The car's other occupants were not so fortunate. The driver Atanda screamed hysterically after suffering bullet wounds to his mouth and shoulder. One of the bullets hit Kudirat's forehead and lodged in her brain. As she lay on the back seat bleeding, passers-by were at first too afraid to stop and help while the gunmen fled.

After a delay of several minutes, some soldiers and passers-by eventually came to her aid and put her in a Volkswagen minibus driven by a Good Samaritan. They took her to the Eko Hospital on Mobolaji Bank Anthony Way in Ikeja, Lagos. Medical personnel immediately took her into the hospital's operating theatre where doctors, including Abiola's personal physician, Dr Ore Falomo, examined her before calling a team of neurosurgeons from the Lagos University Teaching Hospital to operate and remove the bullet from her head. However, Kudirat died between 12.15 and 12.30 pm before they were able to extract the bullet. The government offered a $45,000 reward to anyone who could provide information leading to the arrest of the killers. After Kudirat's murder, Radio Democrat changed its name to Radio Kudirat in her memory.

The excesses of military rule ironically created as well as energised a large pro-democracy and human rights movement. The largely southern-based press became the voice of this movement. Independent anti-government magazines and newspapers such as *Tell, The News, The Sunday Magazine* and other tabloid-style publications emerged. Every week they published exposés of military corruption and military excesses, and made incessant calls for the military to leave power. In response the State Security Service constantly raided their offices, seized copies of their publications before they published critical articles, and arrested their editors. At various points the government issued decrees that banned *The Concord* (owned by Abiola), *The Guardian* and *The News* and stopped them from publishing. Such bans led to the phenomenon of 'guerrilla journalism'. The editors of *TheNews* ignored the decrees and continued writing and publishing from secret locations (without ever telling their readers that they were reading a banned publication), and also produced a new magazine known as *Tempo*. In 1995 a journalist at *TheNews*, James Bagauda Kaltho, mysteriously disappeared after writing an article about the alleged 1995 coup. Kaltho was never seen again. In 1998 the assistant commissioner of police, Hassan Zakari Biu, claimed that Kaltho had died in a bomb blast at the Durbar Hotel in Kaduna. The staff of banned publications wisely avoided working at their offices and instead wrote and held meetings in unusual locations such as churches or on the back seats of cars and taxis, where they could evade the State Security Service, who constantly hunted them.

Alex Ibru

The unexplained violence was not targeted exclusively at members of the opposition. Even those with close ties to the government were not safe.

As well as being the minister of internal affairs in the Abacha government, the wealthy businessman Alex Ibru also owned *The Guardian* newspaper. *The Guardian* placed its owner in a difficult position when it criticised the government of which he was part. When Abacha objected to *The Guardian*'s criticisms Ibru's stance was that he could not compromise the independence of his editorial board and did not control its written output. In August 1994 the government banned *The Guardian* from publishing for a year. Just two months after it reopened in 1995, there was an arson attack on its headquarters at Rutam House. Things got worse for Ibru after he left the government in 1995.

Around 6.30 pm on March 2, 1996, Ibru's driver, Solomon Oghenekume Okah, picked him up from the Federal Palace Hotel in Victoria Island, Lagos, in his Peugeot 504 to drive him home to Ikoyi. David Udi, a former police officer who worked as a security officer for Ibru, accompanied them and sat in the front passenger seat beside Okah, while Ibru sat in the back seat. While they were driving on the Falomo flyover, two vehicles (each with two male occupants) approached them. A man in one of the cars drew an AK-47 rifle and shot at Ibru's car from the driver's side. Some of the bullets hit Ibru's head and hand. He collapsed in the back seat of the car in a pool of blood. The driver Okah made a detour and took Ibru to the IMCC hospital in Victoria Island, which in turn referred him to St Nicholas Hospital in Lagos. Ibru survived but lost an eye and one of his fingers had to be amputated. He recovered after travelling abroad for further medical treatment and recuperation.

Olu Onagoruwa

Abiola had encouraged the attorney-general and minister of justice, Olu Onagoruwa, to join the Abacha government. Before long Onagoruwa found himself frozen out. He protested that even though he was the government's chief legal officer, the government had promulgated eight decrees without his knowledge or approval. Then in 1994 Onagoruwa approved the release of Turner Ogboru, who had been imprisoned for four years for being an alleged accomplice in the April 1990 coup financed by his brother Great Ogboru.[12]

'That man wanted to kill me!'

Abacha summoned Onagoruwa and scolded him for releasing Turner. Security agents re-arrested Turner and returned him to prison. When Onagoruwa explained that he had released Turner in compliance with a court order, Abacha retorted: 'That man wanted to kill me!'[13] On December 18, 1996 unknown gunmen broke into Onagoruwa's compound in Lagos, took his son Oluwatoyin, an employee of the National Intelligence Agency who was a lawyer like his father, and shot him dead after firing a gun at his face and back. Onagoruwa was devastated by his son's murder, and later had a stroke from which he never fully recovered. He died in 2017.

The violence against opposition figures continued into 1997. In January 1997 unknown gunmen trailed NADECO's leader Abraham Adesanya and sprayed his car with bullets. Remarkably, the 75-year-old Adesanya escaped unharmed. Unknown assailants also fire-bombed the houses of other opposition figures such as Bola Tinubu, Alani Akinrinade and Wole Soyinka. In 1996 and 1997 several bomb explosions rocked military convoys and installations in Lagos. One of the bombs in December 1996 targeted the convoy of the military administrator of Lagos State, Colonel Mohammed Marwa. On January 7, 1997 a bomb destroyed an army bus in the Surulere suburb of Lagos, killing two soldiers and wounding several others. The government blamed the bombings on NADECO and the opposition, and issued arrest warrants for Enahoro, Soyinka, Akinrinade and Olu Falae on charges of treason. NADECO denied involvement in the bombings and instead accused intelligence agencies of deliberately planting the bombs so that NADECO could be blamed and punished as a scapegoat. Few believed that the elderly pensioners of NADECO could pull off a bombing campaign. A member of an opposition group cryptically informed me that security agents 'were going after the wrong people'.[14] Nonetheless, Abiola's continued incarceration made NADECO desperate. They considered a daring plot to hire German mercenaries to rescue Abiola. Bola Tinubu and the publisher Dele Mumodu went so far as to meet with the mercenaries in west London, and consider their plans to storm Abiola's place of detention and free him. NADECO dropped the plan over concerns that Abiola might be harmed or killed during the rescue attempt.[15]

Shehu Yar'Adua

The mysterious episodes of violence and death were not limited to the streets. Even those in prison were not safe. Yar'Adua remained in prison after his death sentence for plotting a coup in 1995 was commuted to life imprisonment. During his time in jail Yar'Adua became a father figure to other inmates and took responsibility for their care and feeding. He promised the convicts that they would be released within a few years.

'You owe me your lives'

On October 15, 1995 Yar'Adua spoke to the other coup inmates at the Kirikiri Maximum Security Prison in Lagos. He told them: 'You all must be resilient and ensure that you do not succumb to illness or death throughout the remaining part of your ordeal. You owe me your lives.'[16] After Kudirat Abiola's murder, Yar'Adua became concerned for his family's safety and was alarmed when his wife Binta did not arrive for one of her scheduled prison visits to see him. He should have worried about his own safety as well.

In February 1997, a government doctor came to examine Yar'Adua and take blood samples from him. Yar'Adua complained: 'I was handcuffed with my hands behind my back and some doctor, apparently from Aso Rock, said he was going to take my blood. And even when I objected to my blood being taken with my hands tied behind my back, he said, "Oh, it doesn't matter." He could do it. That was when I began to suspect something.'[17]

Yar'Adua told his younger brother Umaru that the officer who used a syringe to draw his blood was the army doctor Lt-Colonel Ibrahim Yakasai, a gynaecologist and member of the Strike Force.[18] Yar'Adua became concerned that he had been poisoned and smuggled a sample of his blood out of prison for tests by a medical doctor in Victoria Island, Lagos. One of the tests revealed that Yar'Adua had been infected with HIV.[19] The doctor said that the strain of HIV he detected in Yar'Adua's blood was rare in Nigeria.

On November 26, 1997 Yar'Adua fell seriously ill and complained of a loss of appetite, fever and aches in his joints. He fainted after playing tennis inside the Abakaliki Prison in Ebonyi State to which he had been transferred. His brother Umaru visited him and was alarmed by his jaundiced appearance. Yar'Adua's liver had also become enlarged and sore. On December 1 the chief superintendent of prisons in Ebonyi State, Chris Obua, contacted the state's military administrator, Navy Commander Walter Feghabo, and requested permission to move Yar'Adua to Enugu for medical treatment. Feghabo replied that he had forwarded the request to the federal authorities in Abuja. As Obua and Feghabo awaited a reply from Abuja, Yar'Adua's condition deteriorated. He was sweating profusely and had suspected pneumonia and bronchitis. Abacha sent Lt-Colonel Yakasai to examine Yar'Adua again in the first week of December 1997. Yakasai again took blood samples from Yar'Adua and headed back to Abuja. On December 7 Yar'Adua's condition deteriorated even further. Overnight he repeatedly called out for his brother Umaru, and collapsed at 3 am in his bathroom. Obua once again contacted Feghabo to alert him to the seriousness of Yar'Adua's condition and said that he was slipping in and out of consciousness. Obua wrote: 'Your kind approval to this humble request to save life would be highly appreciated.'[20] On this occasion the federal government gave permission for Yar'Adua to be taken from prison to hospital by ambulance around 4 pm on December 8. Although hospital staff tried to save him, he died that day at the age of 54.

Although no autopsy was conducted on Yar'Adua, his prominence meant that some people would not let his death pass quietly. The inspector-general of police, Ibrahim Coomasie, who was also from Yar'Adua's home state of Katsina, informed Yar'Adua's family of his death, and travelled from Abuja to Katsina to receive Yar'Adua's body upon its arrival from Enugu. Coomasie also ordered the police's Criminal Investigation Department to investigate and report on the death. Somehow Yomi Edu, who was close to Yar'Adua's acolyte Atiku Abubakar, managed to smuggle out a sample of Yar'Adua's blood. The official cause of his death was listed as severe pneumonia, which can be the result of HIV. Yar'Adua's death was the tipping point in a murderous three years.

The murders, arson attacks and violent incidents of the period from 1994 to 1996 remained unsolved mysteries. Most people assumed (but dared not say out loud) that it was the work of pro-government agents who were intent on eliminating the opposition. The attacks bore all the hallmarks of assassination attempts. Despite all the victims being wealthy and well known, there was no attempt to rob them. The mission of the gunmen seems to have been solely to kill. The sophistication of the weapons used was also curious. The bullet that killed Kudirat was fired from a Belgian-made FN P90 sub-machine gun. The P90 is a high-calibre weapon that can fire up to 900 rounds per minute. It is normally utilised by special forces and counter-terrorist units. However, there were also several peculiarities about the violent episodes and murders that suggest that not all of them were the work of pro-Abacha agents alone. The bomb blasts were incoherent. They ranged from sophisticated remote-controlled bombs to crude explosives handled by attackers so careless or inexperienced that they prematurely detonated their bombs, killing themselves in the process. The haphazard nature of the bombings made it unlikely that they were the work of a single unified force with a coherent strategy.

The opposition at the time was more fragmented than the government and public realised. The government's singleminded approach tended to conflate all opposition under NADECO's umbrella. However, radical camps emerged within other opposition groups. Some members of groups like the Oodua People's Congress (OPC) and Wole Soyinka's National Liberation Council of Nigeria (NALICON) felt that armed resistance and sabotage, not radio stations and pleas to foreign governments, were the appropriate response to Abacha. Soyinka publicly admitted that he was considering armed struggle against the government.[21] Some younger elements among the opposition also regarded the older politicians in Afenifere and NADECO as part of the same corrupt elite they opposed. When I asked the OPC's secretary-general, Kayode Ogundamisi, whether pro-democracy activists were behind some of the bombings, he refused to reply. When I pressed him for more insight, the most he grudgingly told me was that the pro-democracy movement 'were involved in sabotaging the military', and that 'there were attempts to take it [pro-democracy agitation] beyond words'.

The violence had sources more complex and opaque than a simple binary confrontation between security forces and the opposition. An unintended consequence of Abacha's preoccupation with security was that it created a financial incentive for security agencies to exploit his paranoia with constant threat warnings that would justify an increase in security budgets. Some security agents deliberately intensified the atmosphere of mystery, paranoia and insecurity in the country in order to fortify their position. The then commissioner of police in Lagos State, Abubakar Tsav, said:

> When I was in police in Lagos as commissioner of police, there were these bomb blasts everywhere in Lagos and security agencies started saying it was NADECO that was doing it. In the end, we found out that it was security agents that were throwing bombs and they will go and tell ... Abacha that it was NADECO that was doing it. And Abacha would just give them money. That is how some of them became very rich.[22]

A veteran army officer who worked for Major-General Bamaiyi said that 'it was the cheapest way to get money from General Abacha in those days. They create imaginary climate of insecurity and the moment they tell Abacha about [a] possible security risk, he will release money to them.'[23]

Abacha's health problems and inaccessibility also limited his ability to rein in the excesses of his subordinates. This provided ample opportunity for them to appropriate and exercise power in his name. The security team's isolation of Abacha and their exploitation of his security consciousness were so successful that it is possible he never realised how unpopular he was in the south. It is an open question whether Abacha was aware of or approved the violence against opposition members. Abacha's deputy, Lt-General Diya, later said he was convinced that many events that occurred during Abacha's tenure 'probably happened without his knowledge'.[24] Whether or not Abacha ordered or approved of the violence, his Orwellian intelligence network and the murders, bombings and arson attacks under his watch terrified much of the population into silence or tacit acceptance of his rule. Abacha had become the most feared head of state in Nigeria's history.

11

THE WEEPING GENERALS

By 1997 the senior military consensus that brought Abacha to power had dissipated. However, given the known consequences of standing up to Abacha, no officer dared to openly voice dissent directly to Abacha or in the presence of other officers. Abacha had systematically picked off military rivals from the day he seized power. He had even sidelined two of the three officers who helped bring him to power four years earlier. Lt-General Aliyu Mohammed was antagonised into retirement after he disagreed with Abacha, and Colonel Gwadabe was serving a life sentence in prison after being convicted of plotting a coup against Abacha. Yet one of those three officers still clung on in the government by his fingernails.

'I will ask a sergeant to flog you publicly'

Although Diya escaped these purges, he did not have much power. He admitted that after the 1994 controversies with Abiola and NADECO in which he was active, he and his supporters 'lost out and we became less and less consulted on government issues'.[1] Diya also opposed calls for Abacha to become a civilian president, Abiola's continued detention, and Abacha's dismissal of Yoruba ministers and military officers. As Abacha became more reclusive due to ill health and security paranoia, his attendance at public functions became increasingly rare. Yet he seldom delegated Diya to deputise in his absence. Instead the minister of foreign affairs, Tom Ikimi, represented Abacha on foreign trips, while Abacha's wife Maryam, the chief of defence staff, Major-

General Abubakar, or the minister for the Federal Capital Territory, Lt-General Jeremiah Useni, did the same for domestic functions.

Diya's influence waned as both the inspector-general of police, Ibrahim Coomasie, and the secretary to the government of the federation, Aminu Saleh, refused to recognise his authority or seniority over them. When Diya declined to sign a detention order to arrest Abiola in 1994, the enabling decree that gave him this power was amended in under 24 hours without his being consulted, and Coomasie was empowered to independently approve detention orders without reference to Diya. Saleh also later vetoed a list of senior civil servants approved by Diya, modified it, got Abacha to approve a different list, then released it to the public. The usually mild-mannered Diya was so enraged that he threatened Saleh, 'If you do this next time, I will ask a sergeant to flog you publicly.'[2]

Smoke and Mirrors

Abacha's firm grip on power meant that a coup was the most realistic—albeit also the most risky—option for replacing him. The fate of Obasanjo, Yar'Adua, Alli, Madueke and other senior officers demonstrated the risks of opposing Abacha, and that no one, no matter how highly placed, was untouchable in Abacha's Nigeria. Even senior officers were cowed into playing a cat-and-mouse game of camouflaging their opposition to Abacha beneath euphemisms and innuendo. The former chief of army staff, Major-General Chris Alli, claimed that on several separate occasions senior officers approached him to complain obliquely about Abacha. Alli said that in the first quarter of 1994 the director of military intelligence, Brigadier-General Ahmed Abdullahi, jocularly suggested to him in a car that they should relieve Abacha of his position.[3] Alli claims that another such incident occurred in July 1994 while he travelled in a car with Major-General Tajudeen Olanrewaju en route to Maiduguri in the north-east. According to Alli, Olanrewaju complained about senior officers from the 'core north' and suggested that it would be easy to move troops against them and remove them. Alli simply nodded his head to demonstrate that he was listening, but did not say a word in response.[4] Alli was a wily former military intelligence officer and knew the rules and risks of the game. Careless chatter was dangerous and officers had been 'set up' and executed in previous coup plots after being baited into grumbling about the government or gossiping about a coup. Alli said: 'Whoever voiced the coup option met with my stony silence. It is extremely difficult to prove knowledge or intent without a recorded voice or third party corroboration. If a suggestion is carried on wire, unless your voice utters your response, the recording is worthless.'[5]

Alli also claimed that on three separate occasions Diya told him that Abacha should be overthrown. According to Alli, on the third occasion Diya suggested that they should draw Major-General Ishaya Bamaiyi into the plan since Bamaiyi was then commander of the strategic Lagos Garrison Command. During one of Bamaiyi's visits to Flagstaff House, the official residence of the chief of army staff, Alli cryptically told him, 'It would appear that the boys have hijacked the regime on a course not very clear to me.'[6] Bamaiyi wisely did not respond to the remark but merely stared back at Alli, who quickly changed the topic of conversation.

The Four Point Demand

However, some others were not as circumspect as Alli. In August 1997 senior officers including Diya, Bamaiyi, Major-General Patrick Aziza and the chief of defence intelligence, Air Vice-Marshal Idi Musa, began discussing a list of four demands that anonymous junior military officers had allegedly drafted and sent to their seniors for onward transmission to Abacha. The 'Four Point Demand', as the list became known, insisted that Abacha should renounce any plan to 'succeed himself' by becoming a civilian president, that the October 1998 handover date to civilian rule should not be postponed, that the original draft of the 1995 constitution should be promulgated, and that political prisoners should be released. Bamaiyi assured Diya that all GOCs except that of 1 Mechanised Infantry Division in Kaduna, Major-General Mukhtar (who was abroad), were aware of, and endorsed, the Four Point Demand. Diya said:

> I was convinced in my mind that the demands were legitimate and if addressed, would go a long way in ensuring peace and stability in the country. It would also prevent the extensive damage that would have been done to the image of the Nigerian Army, were the C-in-C [Abacha] to turn himself into a civilian president. It was a question of loyalty to General Abacha as a person or loyalty to my country, Nigeria! ...the distinction was very clear to me. The proposition of the junior officers was noble and legitimate. I chose loyalty to my fatherland and resolved to encourage the officers as much as possible.[7]

The senior officers decided to present the Four Point Demand to Abacha. After this decision some or all of them held several meetings in September, October and December 1997 at Diya's Abuja office. At one of their meetings

Diya noticed that Bamaiyi's 'chest was bulging out'.[8] In December 1997, Diya also introduced the Four Point Demand to the minister of works and housing, Major-General Abdulkarim Adisa, a Yoruba Muslim from Ilorin in Kwara State,[9] and the minister of communications, Major-General Tajudeen Olanrewaju, another Yoruba Muslim. Adisa and Olanrewaju were suspicious and hesitant about getting involved with the Four Point Demand. Both were close supporters of Abacha. Adisa had been one of the most vocal advocates of Abacha's self-succession. However, both men reluctantly acquiesced as they did not want to break Yoruba ethnic solidarity with Diya, but only after Diya reassured them that Bamaiyi had informed him that all the GOCs supported the Four Point Demand. Adisa may have been reassured when his friend, the director of military intelligence, Brigadier-General Ibrahim Sabo, joined the group of senior officers supporting the Four Point Demand. The GOC of 2 Mechanised Division in Ibadan, Major-General Bashir Magashi, also came on board.

The senior officers held further meetings at Olanrewaju's house at 5 Thompson Avenue, Ikoyi, in Lagos, and at Adisa's home.[10] The officers deliberated on how they would respond if Abacha rejected the Four Point Demand. Diya suggested an approach that was akin to an intervention. He said, 'I suggested to Bamaiyi that he and the GOCs should confront Abacha with the demands of the junior officers and ask him to address them or stand the risk of being removed. Bamaiyi and the GOCs agreed it was not a bad idea at all.'[11] The discussions had quickly escalated from discussing the Four Point Demand with Abacha to giving him an ultimatum, then ultimately to overthrowing him if he did not implement the demands. Adisa also recalled:

> I even asked General Diya who informed me of the four-point demand that what about if [Abacha] refused to consent to them. But, he told me that if he does not agree to them, he said we would force him to consent and to me, this is a coup against the government of General Abacha. Others may not call it a coup, but to my own understanding, it is a coup because it would involve the use of force.[12]

Compelling Abacha to accept anything would be an awesome challenge. However, Abacha made a move to talk to some of the conspirators before they were ready to talk to him. He invited Olanrewaju and Adisa for meetings at the presidential villa. Abacha asked both men whether they had any complaints about his leadership. Neither of them raised any objections. Adisa had planned to tell Abacha about the Four Point Demand but may have lost his nerve in the presence of his commander-in-chief. As Adisa prepared to leave after his meeting, Abacha asked him whether he had anything else he wished to disclose. Adisa departed without revealing anything but, as he reached the gate, he turned back and went to see Abacha again. Abacha asked him whether there was anything on his mind that he had forgotten to say. But Adisa left without disclosing anything of note.[13] There was now no turning back.

On December 13, Diya prepared to travel to Makurdi in Benue State for the funeral of the mother of Major-General Lawrence Onoja, a dashing and popular Idoma officer from the middle belt. However, Diya had a stomach upset and had to use the bathroom before boarding his plane at the Abuja airport. Diya's bathroom break delayed his flight. As he prepared to board the plane, a bomb exploded, and killed one of Abacha's bodyguards, Samaila Usman. Pieces of Usman's body were scattered around the airport car park. The bomb also seriously wounded two others. One of the wounded body-guards, Samaila Shuaibu, was taken to hospital but died a few days later.[14] The bomb blast would have killed Diya had he been on time. He later claimed that the explosion was an attempt to assassinate him. Yet the plan to confront Abacha continued.

'When the old man goes, you boys should not forget to maintain the hierarchy'

The group set December 20 as the date for their confrontation with Abacha. Bamaiyi and Magashi met Diya at his house on that day. Bamaiyi claimed that Diya gave Magashi a speech to read and rehearse in preparation for announcing Abacha's displacement. He claimed Diya suggested that Magashi should read the speech because he, like Abacha, was from Kano, and would be acceptable to the north.[15] However, Diya claimed that the speech was drafted in Olanrewaju's house in the presence of Bamaiyi and Aziza, and that the plan was that Bamaiyi would read the speech. Bamaiyi also averred that Diya reminded the group that 'General Abacha has a terminal illness' and that 'when the old man goes, you boys should not forget to maintain the hierarchy'—that is, they should not forget that Diya was Abacha's deputy and should succeed him as head of state.[16]

Overnight on December 20/21 armed soldiers were deployed at strategic locations though they were not told why. Diya stayed up late that night. He had guests in his house and played draughts late into the night with his long-time friend Abiodun Okunuga. Okunuga went to bed sometime between 1 and 2 on the morning of December 21. However, the night was still young. Al-Mustapha unexpectedly called Diya's residence on the presidential villa's intercom system. The call spooked Diya, who wondered why al-Mustapha was not already under arrest: which was to be the signal for the confrontation. When he heard al-Mustapha's voice, Diya panicked and dropped the receiver without saying anything. Al-Mustapha called Diya a second time but was instead transferred to the security gate at Diya's house. Al-Mustapha then decided to visit Diya in person. However, by the time he arrived, Diya had departed after a State Security Service operative named Isaiah Adebowale, who worked for Diya, persuaded him to leave immediately. Adebowale and Diya left together in the former's car and drove to his residence in the OAU quarters of Asokoro, Abuja. However, security officers somehow discovered Diya's destination, exchanged gunshots with the guards at Adebowale's house, entered the grounds, and led by Sergeant Ja'atu and a State Security Service operative named Abdulrahman, arrested Diya, who some say was hiding under a mattress.

Similar scenes took place elsewhere. Soldiers from the corps of military police besieged the houses of Diya's staff and friends such as his ADC, Major Kayode Keshinro; his special political adviser, Professor Olufemi Odekunle, a professor of criminology at Ahmadu Bello University in Zaria; Adisa; and Olanrewaju, and arrested them at gunpoint. Both Keshinro and Odekunle were badly beaten up and hit with gun butts as they were arrested. Something had gone wrong.

'We gave you a small opportunity to come and eat'

With security officers in Abuja and Lagos conducting arrests, al-Mustapha took the precaution of confining the Abacha family inside the presidential villa and barred any of them from leaving. The detainees were driven to the presidential villa, which, despite the late hour, was a beehive of activity. About forty to fifty members of the Strike Force were milling around in the courtyard in front of Abacha's office. The detainees were brought to the Strike Force and their commander, al-Mustapha. The atmosphere was hostile. When there is an attempt to overthrow a military government, everyone except the head of state becomes a suspect and soldiers are under extreme pressure to demonstrate whose side they are on. Aggression is likely in such circumstances. Odekunle claimed that as al-Mustapha fired questions at him, Strike Force members beat him and taunted him and other detainees. He said: 'Any time Mustapha was talking to me somebody would just come and give me a blow on the back saying, "CSO is talking to you and you are standing, kneel down!" Another one would come and say, "CSO is talking to you and you are kneeling down, stand up!" And he too would give a blow. Somebody told me later that he thought they were going to kick me to death the way they were raining blows on me with both hands and feet.'[17]

Odekunle also claimed that Abacha's ADC, Lt-Colonel Abdallah, told him, 'We gave you a small opportunity to come and eat and better your life a little bit and see what you have done.'[18] After being roughed up, some of the senior detainees were brought to various rooms inside the presidential villa where al-Mustapha interrogated them. Adisa was taken to a room he described as 'extra bright'.

However, Diya was the biggest fish arrested, and special arrangements were made for him. His captors took him to al-Mustapha's office where he met his co-conspirators Magashi, Musa, Bamaiyi and Sabo, before being given a one-on-one meeting with al-Mustapha himself. Al-Mustapha tried the 'good cop' routine and told Diya, 'If you want me to help you, I can help you talk to Oga[19] [Abacha] but I need all the facts.' Diya protested: 'You know you don't allow me to see Oga.' Diya's captors removed his handcuffs and leg chains and granted him an audience with Abacha. Diya and Abacha met in a room inside the presidential villa, and sat next to each other on large, comfortable, sand-coloured sofas, with Diya seated to the right of a relaxed Abacha, who was wearing slippers. A coffee table with white cups and jugs was positioned in front of the two men. An observer who did not know either man would have been tempted to think this was a social gathering between two long-time friends. After the audiences with al-Mustapha and Abacha, Diya and the other detainees were taken into custody and flown to Jos.

The following morning, the chief of defence staff, Major-General Abubakar, announced that the government had foiled a coup attempt. On January 3, 1998, he set up a Special Investigation Panel (SIP) of twelve military officers to investigate the alleged plot. The SIP's chairman was the commandant of the National War College, Major-General Chris Garuba, an Idoma artillery officer from Benue State in the middle belt. Garuba was a respected officer who was awarded the sword of honour for being the best cadet from his graduating class in 1970. He was also a former military governor of Bauchi State, and a former peacekeeping commander of the United Nations Verification Mission in Angola (UNAVEM). Lt-Colonel Joseph Akaagerger acted as the SIP's secretary.[20] The SIP was based at the Rukuba Cantonment in Jos. Investigators cast the net far and wide, and arrested at least sixty military personnel and civilians, including ancillary staff who worked with or were friendly with the key suspects. These included Diya's chief security officer, Major Fadipe, his military assistant, Colonel Emmanuel Shode, the former military administrator of Diya's home state of Ogun, Lt-Colonel Akintonde,[21] and the officer in charge of disbursements from the Petroleum Trust Fund (PTF), Major-General Edward Unimna (though the investigators did not bother the PTF chairman, Major-General Buhari).

The suspects were kept in grim conditions. They were initially driven to the State Security Service office in Abuja, then moved to Gado Nasko Barracks (also in Abuja), before being flown to Jos in January 1998 to face the SIP. During their detention they were handcuffed, had their legs chained, and were placed in small cells which they shared with around four or five other inmates. They were chained to the ground in their cells, and had to sleep on a bare, hard, concrete floor for the first few weeks of their incarceration. They were locked inside their cells all day and night, and were allowed out only for one hour a day between 7 am and 8 am to go to the toilet or to bathe. During their 'toilet breaks' they were ordered out one cell at a time, and were forbidden to speak to each other, or look to their left or right on their way to the toilet, lest they see or recognise detainees in neighbouring cells. Their toilet breaks were conducted in full view of a security guard who observed their every move. Detention conditions were so severe that they looked forward to their interrogation sessions with the SIP as it gave them an opportunity to leave their cells, walk and get fresh air, even though they were subjected to hostile accusations and questioning.

'If somebody told me Diya was staging a coup, I would go to sleep'

Many thought either that the coup story was a hoax or that, even if it was true, Diya, Adisa and Olanrewaju (despite being combatant officers) were incapable of pulling it off. Former President Babangida later casually dismissed Diya's ability to stage a coup by mockingly stating: 'If I were in office and somebody told me Diya was staging a coup, I would go to sleep. I would even go into a deeper slumber if I knew Diya was working with Olanrewaju and Adisa.'[22]

'Devil-inspired and mischievous elements'

After the 1995 coup controversy the government was anxious to demonstrate that the latest episode was not another 'phantom coup'. To counter accusations that the suspects were framed, and to mobilise public opinion against them, in January 1998 the government invited over a thousand traditional rulers, including Yoruba obas, journalists, military administrators and retired military officers to the Abuja Conference Centre for a special event. The director of military intelligence, Brigadier-General Sabo,[23] acted as the MC. As Sabo addressed the guests, he motioned for the lights to be turned off. Then a giant screen started playing a series of videos to the guests for the next three and a half hours. The general public had no knowledge of the videos' content. However, the reaction of those who watched them suggested that they contained something damning. After watching the videos, some Yoruba traditional leaders were so appalled and shocked that they condemned the coup suspects outright. These included traditional rulers from the same towns as some of the suspects, such as the *soun* of Ogbomosho (Akintonde's home town), Oba Oladunni Oyewumi Ajagungbade III, and the emir of Ilorin (Adisa's home town), Ibrahim Gambari. The *ewi* (traditional ruler) of Ado-Ekiti, capital of the newly created Ekiti State, Oba Rufus Adejugbe, said: 'From what we have heard from audio records and images of the preliminary investigations, we wish to condemn the dastardly act conceived and attempted by the plotters already arrested.'[24] The 87-year-old Oba Adeyinka Oyekan of Lagos declared: 'The dastardly act by the unpatriotic devil-inspired and mischievous elements is condemned in all its ramifications by the peace loving people of Lagos State.'[25] Other traditional rulers trooped to Abuja to pay homage to Abacha and express their relief that he had survived the coup attempt.

The Nigerian Bar Association (an association of Nigerian lawyers) issued a statement calling on the government to stop disseminating videos and other incriminating statements about the suspects, as it had the effect of portraying them as guilty before they had been tried.

The SIP submitted its report to Major-General Abubakar in late January 1998 and recommended that 26 of the suspects should be placed on trial. On February 10, the chief of defence administration, Rear-Admiral Festus Porbeni, announced that the government would create another Special Military Tribunal to try the suspects in Jos. It was the first time in Nigeria's history that a coup trial would ever take place outside Lagos. All the trials for the failed 1976, 1985, 1990 and 1995 coups had been in Lagos. The reasons for moving outside Lagos were obvious. Since most of the key defendants were from the south-west, holding a trial in that region, which already harboured massive grievances against the government, would not be prudent. Additionally, Abacha needed a credible person to head the tribunal at a time when he was still being criticised for the controversial 1995 coup trial that had imprisoned Obasanjo and Yar'Adua, and the 1995 tribunal that had sentenced Saro-Wiwa and other MOSOP members to death. Diya's seniority was a problem. In such trials officers are usually tried by a tribunal led by an officer of equal or senior rank. However, Diya was one of only three lieutenant-generals in the army. His only senior was Abacha, and his only rank contemporaries were Lt-Generals Useni, who was too close to Abacha to be considered neutral, and Haladu, who was suffering from ill health. Major-General Abdullahi Sarki Mukhtar, who had a degree in law, was the most qualified officer to lead the trial. However, he was a Muslim northerner, and was from the same state (Kano) as Abacha. The need to avoid the appearance of a regional or religious alliance with Abacha ruled him out.

Abacha chose Major-General Victor Malu, a Tiv Christian from Benue State in the middle belt, to lead the tribunal. The Tivs are one of the most heavily represented ethnic groups in the army's fighting units and have a reputation as warriors. Malu's appointment was astute. It demonstrated how much Abacha wanted to show the public that this coup plot was real, and that the trial verdict would be legitimate. Although he could be a blunt and controversial character, Malu was renowned for being forthright, straight to the point and fair-minded. He had returned to Nigeria only two months earlier from a successful tour of duty as the field commander of the Nigerian-led ECOMOG[26] military peacekeeping force in Liberia. His absence abroad made him one of the few senior officers not to have been personally exposed to the coup controversies. At a time when the Nigerian army's reputation had plummeted to an all-time low, Malu was one of the few officers with good local and international standing. Liberians and the international media praised his performance during the ECOMOG mission. *The Daily Telegraph* of London described him as 'a stocky quick-witted general [who] ... transformed a national disgrace into a rare public relations triumph for the ruling junta', and quoted a diplomat who said, 'I can only compare him to [US General] Norman Schwarzkopf or Gen. Patton.'[27] During the ECOMOG mission, Malu curbed bribery by driving up to military checkpoints disguised as a civilian and waving cash, and would then promptly arrest any soldier who accepted the bribe. He had replaced Major-General Bashir Magashi as the GOC of 2 Mechanised Division headquartered in Ibadan just a few days before being appointed to lead the tribunal (2 Division was coincidentally the army unit in which Malu started his army career). Malu had much in common with the SIP chairman, Garuba. Both men were from Benue State in the middle belt, although from different ethnic groups. Malu, Garuba and Rear-Admiral Porbeni were also members of the most famous military cadet cohort in Nigeria's history: the graduates of the third regular combatant course at the Nigerian Defence Academy. Malu also satisfied the requirement of ethnic and religious neutrality. Unlike Abacha, he was not a Muslim, and was from a different part of the country from Abacha and the Yoruba defendants.

Nonetheless, leading the tribunal placed Malu in a difficult personal position. Some of the defendants were his colleagues or friends. He was a good friend of Olanrewaju, and was also in the same Nigerian Defence Academy cadet intake as Adisa. He and Adisa had been close friends for thirty years. Now he faced the daunting prospect of potentially having to sentence his friends and colleagues to die. He said:

> This assignment affected me both personally and professionally. I knew some of the officers personally and instinctively empathised with them. In fact one of the suspects, Major-General Adisa, had been my coursemate and we had remained very close friends over the years. I also had frequent social and professional interactions with some of the officers. So much was on my mind. My reputation, professional integrity, and indeed my humanity were all on the line.[28]

The Trial: The State versus Diya and Others

The trial of 26 defendants for treason and related offences began on February 14, 1998 at the Rukuba Cantonment in Jos, Plateau State. Investigators later referred another four suspects for trial, thereby raising the total number of defendants to 30. The tribunal members and prosecution lawyers are listed in the accompanying table.

Several people involved in the investigation and trial had previous coup investigation experience on one side or another. Al-Mustapha, who had a background in military intelligence, was an interrogator during the 1990 coup trials. Duniya was a member of the defence legal team during the same trials.[29] A further little known irony, was that the defendants who were found not guilty during the initial 1990 coup trial were put on trial again and sentenced to death by two further special military tribunals. One of those tribunals was chaired by then Brigadier Tajudeen Olanrewaju. Diya had also chaired a coup tribunal that tried and jailed Major Akinloye Akinyemi in 1987. Both Olanrewaju and Diya were now defendants in the current coup trial.

Special Military Tribunal, 1998

Special Military Tribunal	Prosecution Lawyers
Major-General Malu (chairman)	Colonel Bitrus Duniya
Brigadier-General Ibrahim Karmashe (who, like Bamaiyi, was from Zuru in the far north-west)	Colonel ZO Shuaibu
	Lt-Colonels Dave Ike, DB Fatai, and UN Muku
Brigadier VI Ombu	Commander J Abu
Colonel SM Lemu	Squadron Leader I Shaffi
Colonel John Olu	Navy Lieutenant AC Akagun
Commodore SA Olukoya	Chief Superintendent of Police Libo Komimbo
Wing Commander Ahmed Muoya	
Lt-Colonel Yusuf Braimah (a University of London-educated lawyer, who acted as judge advocate)	

'That image still gives me chills'

Journalists were allowed to attend the tribunal's inaugural session, where they witnessed controversy on the first day. The defendants entered the courtroom in handcuffs and with their legs chained, wearing ill-fitting clothes and tattered footwear and slippers. Observers who had known them as wealthy, flamboyantly dressed and gregarious officers were shocked to see their despondent, haggard and terrified appearance. They sat down on long wooden benches in classroom style. Detention had not been kind to them. While detained, one of the defendants had threatened to commit suicide. Diya seemed to have aged during his two months in detention. He looked frail and elderly. The small patch of grey hair at the front of his head had expanded greatly and he suddenly appeared much older than his 53 years. Even Malu was shaken by the defendants' emaciated and fragile appearance.

> Though I had seen pictures of the coup suspects on television and newspapers, I had never seen them up close. I was moved to see army generals, and especially my coursemate and good friend, General Adisa, in shackles, helpless and visibly shaken. The images of generals in shackles, robbed of their integrity, remain etched in my memory. Till this day that image still gives me chills.[30]

Nonetheless, the defendants became optimistic when they learned that Malu would be the tribunal's chairman. His reputation and opening address gave them hope. Malu opened the trial by reading from a prepared text. He promised the defendants that they would get a fair trial, but also warned them that the tribunal would be firm. One of the defendants commented:

> this man is likely to do justice. When he delivered his opening remarks, it was like a ray of hope for me who had been in darkness since December when I was held—a flicker of light at the end of the tunnel ... And I was praying to God that that flicker of light would not go out because he said he would not allow trial by ambush. It appeared he was determined to give everybody a fair trial ...[31]

'You have never objected to this aspect of military law'

The defendants were given a list of 40 military lawyers from which they could choose a defence lawyer. They were permitted to choose others as long as they were serving military officers. Malu asked the defendants whether they had objections to the tribunal's composition. Adisa and Olanrewaju expressed reservations about whether military lawyers could zealously defend them without being themselves intimidated (a defence lawyer who had defended his client with too much enthusiasm during the 1995 coup trial was himself arrested and placed on trial). Malu told them, 'Well, you should have said this before now. You are in the system and you have never objected to this aspect of military law.'[32] The tribunal denied Adisa's request to be defended by a civilian lawyer. Olanrewaju pleaded for time to prepare his defence and for his glasses to be given back to him so that he could read his defence documents.

'The mastermind, planner, and executioner'

Despite being subdued, Diya managed to comport himself enough to make an extraordinary and well-publicised opening address that reverberated throughout the trial and affected public opinion. He accused Bamaiyi of being 'the mastermind, planner, and executioner of the coup' and added, 'This is a clear case of set-up. I am the target and it was organised right from the top. I am surprised that the chief of army staff, who is the mastermind, chief planner, and executioner of this incident is not here.' Diya's cryptic comments about being 'set up' set tongues wagging, and brought back incendiary memories of the 1995 'phantom coup'. Press coverage of his statement turned public opinion and speculation (at least in the south) even further against the trial and made it seem like an orchestrated attempt to eliminate Abacha's Yoruba ene-mies. Diya's comments about being set up, and the public furore it caused, angered the authorities. According to Diya, after the first day of the trial, Sergeant Rogers entered his cell at night and 'beat me until blood started coming out from my head'.[33] Rogers repeated the beating the following night as well. Major Mohammed also complained to the tribunal that someone entered his cell late at night and beat him up. Malu ordered that the beating should stop. The tribunal's security officer, Major Mumuni Bashiru, then warned the guards to stop beating the defendants. However, some of the defendants claimed that the soldiers who arrested them also looted or vandalised their houses, cars. and other property.

After being allowed to attend the opening day, journalists were banned from the tribunal's subsequent proceedings in the Rayfield Government Reservation Area of Jos. The defendants' optimism about Malu took a blow on the second day of the trial. Their hearts sank when Malu arrived wearing a badge with Abacha's image emblazoned on his uniform. Malu was unre-pentant. He later said, 'I feel very proud wearing the badge of Abacha. I will wear it again if I am given any.'[34] Malu was also a member of the Provisional Ruling Council, which had created the tribunal, and which was the only body that could confirm or commute the tribunal's verdict. Diya subse-quently complained:

> What manner of justice can anyone hope to receive from a military justice sys-tem where the complainant chooses the members of the tribunal and is at the same time the chief confirming authority of the findings and awards of the tri-bunal? Is it judicially acceptable that the president of a tribunal should at the same time be a member of the confirming authority?[35]

The Case for the Defence

For reasons that will become apparent later, I will first analyse the case for the defence. Although Diya had a degree in law, he asked the tribunal for permission to have Major-General Abdullahi Mukhtar defend him. The tribunal rejected his request and instead, Lt-Colonel Ahmadu represented Diya, who later claimed that he was allowed to discuss his case with his lawyer for only one hour per day and that the discussions had to take place in the presence of a security operative. Colonels RO Adekegba and Joseph Okanbor, Benjamin Muyiwa Badewole and Audu represented the other defendants alongside Ahmadu.

Diya claimed that he had been lured to join a bogus coup plot whose aim was to entrap and eliminate Yoruba army officers, himself included. He also testified that Bamaiyi, Aziza, Sabo and Musa entrapped him. He said that Bamaiyi approached him with the Four Point Demand, claiming it had already been endorsed by the senior army leadership. He pointed out that none of the key defendants such as he, Adisa and Olanrewaju commanded troops that they could use to stage a coup. They had no armed personnel other than a few bodyguards, who were insufficient to mobilise a coup. Diya also denied that he discussed a coup while travelling in a car with Aziza. He said he would not be naive enough to discuss such a plan in a car within earshot of his driver and orderly.

Some of Diya's denials were persuasive. It would indeed be strange if, while plotting a coup against Abacha, Diya decided to confide his plans to the director of military intelligence, whose job it is to stop coup plots, and to another officer, Aziza, who was known to be loyal to Abacha, and who only two years earlier had chaired a trial that convicted over forty people, including a former head of state, for plotting a coup. It also required a tremendous leap of courage (or stupidity) to storm the presidential villa to arrest Abacha and al-Mustapha given the heavily armed security presence there. Abacha had already been on the winning side in seven different coups. It would be utter madness to take on a veteran coup expert at his own game.

When conscripted to join an anti-government plot, military officers face a harrowing damned-if-you-do, damned-if-you-don't dilemma. If they join the plot and it fails, they risk being executed for treason. If they refuse to join the plot, they risk being slated for elimination by the coup plotters. Diya placed his chief security officer, Major Fadipe, in just such a dilemma when he informed him of the plot in December 1997. The proper course of action for Fadipe was to report the plot to his boss. However, how could he do so when his boss was part of the plot he was supposed to report? Unwilling or unable to defy Diya, Fadipe suggested that they should use chloroform to subdue al-Mustapha in order to avoid killing him. Fadipe did not want al-Mustapha to be harmed as the two had been colleagues and friends for over fifteen years. Bamaiyi put Fadipe in touch with his security officer, Captain Umar Bature, who would assist Fadipe in locating al-Mustapha and the commander of the Brigade of Guards, Brigadier-General Yakubu Mu'azu at the appropriate time. During their detention Fadipe spoke to Diya and suggested that they should both confess. However, Diya refused, and told Fadipe to confess if he wanted to die. Fadipe did exactly what Diya dared him to do. He testified that the coup had been planned, that he was part of it, and said that he wanted to tell the truth in order to unburden his conscience and save the lives of other soldiers who had simply obeyed orders without realising they were part of a coup plot.

The Case for the Prosecution

The accounts of the accusers and the accused did not differ much in fact. Both sides admitted to the existence of the Four Point Demand and that they were going to confront Abacha with it. The difference in their accounts related to who initiated the Four Point Demand, who decided to confront Abacha with it, and who presided over the series of meetings in furtherance of the plan.

Diya's insistence that he was set up convinced Malu to call some special witnesses to testify. Diya was stunned when his supposed co-conspirators, Bamaiyi, Aziza and Sabo, arrived at the tribunal not as defendants, but as prosecution witnesses. Bamaiyi was a blockbuster witness. He testified that during one of Diya's visits to the Lagos Garrison Command in September 1997, Diya began a controversial conversation in a car with Aziza as he was leaving. Although Aziza is an Urhobo, he spoke Yoruba fluently. During the conversation with Aziza, Diya allegedly accused Abacha of misrule and advocated his overthrow. Diya then allegedly told Aziza to speak to Bamaiyi about the coup, and also repeated the same complaints to Bamaiyi in a separate conversation at Diya's office in October 1997. During his conversation with Bamaiyi, Diya allegedly complained that Abacha had marginalised him, would not listen to advice, and that he (Diya) was taking the blame for Abacha's misrule. Additionally, Bamaiyi claimed that on December 1, 1997 Diya contributed $60,000 to fund the coup. The money was meant for onward transmission to the GOCs so they could pay the soldiers who would participate. Diya also allegedly contributed another 2 million naira (around 5,500 USD at the time of print, which he ordered Major Fadipe to give to the commanding officer of 3 Guards Battalion, Lt-Colonel Garba. Unbeknown to Diya, after his initial discussions with Bamaiyi, the latter immediately contacted Abacha's ADC, Lt-Colonel Abdallah, to book an appointment to see his commander-in-chief. He met and briefed Abacha on the plot. The wily Abacha told Bamaiyi to 'play along' with Diya, pretend he supported the plot, and keep him apprised of the plans.

According to Bamaiyi, Olanrewaju promised the group that he would recruit artillery officers Colonels Nathaniel Madza and Edwin Jando, both of whom were Tiv officers from Benue State. Madza then informed the chief of defence intelligence, Air Vice-Marshal Idi Musa, and as a result he was not detained or placed on trial. Unlike Madza, Jando allegedly did not report the approach from Olanrewaju and was placed on trial for concealment of treason (in his defence Jando claimed that Madza gave false testimony against him).

Adisa supposedly secured the cooperation of some of Abacha's bodyguards and also contacted Major Bilyaminu M Mohammed, an administrative officer in the presidency, who would procure other bodyguards at the presidential villa to assist. Bamaiyi also claimed that Diya introduced him to a retired Nigerian Telecommunications (NITEL) engineer named Adebola Adebanjo, who would disconnect the telephone system in Abuja on the day they were to confront Abacha. Bamaiyi averred that Diya kept Adebanjo in his house so that he would not leak the plan.

Bamaiyi further testified that the original plan was to arrest Abacha in Enugu during the opening of the 1997 chief of army staff annual training conference on Monday, December 8. However, that plan was shelved after Abacha failed to attend. The group therefore devised an alternative plan to arrest Abacha as he departed for the ECOWAS summit in Lomé, Togo, on December 17, 1993. Major-General Magashi was to coordinate the operation in Abuja using the 3 and 81 Guards Battalions, commanded by Lt-Colonels Garba and Ribah respectively. Abacha would be overthrown the minute he left the Abuja airport and the group would arrest al-Mustapha, the national security adviser, Ismaila Gwarzo, and the commander of the Brigade of Guards, Brigadier-General Yakubu Mu'azu, at the airport while they accompanied Abacha. They would then announce the change of government immediately afterwards. However, this plan also did not come to pass after Abacha cancelled his travel. According to Bamaiyi, they therefore devised a third plan to assassinate Abacha on Friday, December 12 on his way back from the mosque. However, this plan was dropped because of the high casualties that would ensue. Hence they devised a fourth plan to get Abacha after he attended a dinner at the Sheraton Hotel in Abuja on December 19, 1997. Bamaiyi claimed that Adisa had contacted Lt-Colonel Garba to provide soldiers to fire rocket-propelled grenades at Abacha's car on its way back from the hotel. However, Abacha did not attend the dinner as planned. Hence, according to Bamaiyi, the group was left with no choice other than to storm the presidential villa overnight on December 20/21 and arrest al-Mustapha and Mu'azu.

Aziza's testimony corroborated Bamaiyi's account. Aziza also testified that Diya invited him into a car during one of Diya's visits to Lagos and started discussing how to overthrow Abacha. The conversation alarmed Aziza and he reported it to Bamaiyi. Aziza also gave evidence against Olanrewaju. He alleged that on December 2, 1997 he met Olanrewaju and Bamaiyi at the former's house in Lagos. At that meeting Olanrewaju allegedly promised to contribute 1 million naira to the coup as a 'take-off grant'. Aziza and Bamaiyi presented the money they received from Olanrewaju to the tribunal as an evidence exhibit.

'He was fully briefed every inch of the way from the first moment to the last'

The prosecution played audio and video recordings of the defendants meeting in connection with the plot. The voices of Bamaiyi, Aziza and Sabo seemed more audible on the tapes than those of Diya, Adisa, Olanrewaju and the other defendants. The reason for the difference in audio quality soon became apparent. Diya finally discovered why Bamaiyi's chest was 'bulging out' during a number of their pre-arrest meetings. Bamaiyi, Sabo and some of the other officers had secretly worn hidden microphones underneath their clothes during their meetings. Abacha had instructed all of them to 'play along' and pretend they were planning a coup with Diya so as to discover the full extent of his intentions. They passed on the tapes to al-Mustapha, who transcribed the recordings for Abacha. Military intelligence technicians worked on the tapes to improve their audibility for the trial. Al-Mustapha also testified as a prosecution witness and later said that 'no coup ... has had the overwhelming exhibits like the coup of 1997'.

'You wear three faces'

To Diya's and the other defendants' horror, their supposed co-conspirators Bamaiyi, Aziza, Sabo and Musa had been passing on details of their discussions to Abacha, who was 'fully briefed every inch of the way from the first moment to the last'.[36] Diya was unaware that he had been under surveillance throughout their meetings. In the month prior to his arrest, security officials surreptitiously infiltrated Diya's bodyguards and swapped the traditional Brigade of Guards contingent that guarded him with soldiers from the Special Bodyguards unit commanded by al-Mustapha and State Security Service officers who disguised themselves as regular soldiers or Nigerian Mobile Police (MOPOL). Diya's personal security was infiltrated in order to monitor his movements and make his arrest easier. Some of these replacement guards tipped off al-Mustapha when Diya left his residence and tried to escape on the night the coup was supposed to take place. Diya was so horrified that his friends had turned against him, recorded incriminating evidence against him and generally (in his view) set him up that he confronted Bamaiyi with the accusation that 'you wear three faces, one for Abacha, one for me and one for yourself'.[37]

Additionally, investigators had used hidden cameras provided by the National Intelligence Agency to record the suspects being interrogated. After being arrested, the suspects were taken to specially wired rooms inside the presidential villa with hidden cameras and microphones that taped them meeting with and being questioned by Abacha and al-Mustapha. The prosecution played 17 dramatic audio and video tapes of these meetings and interrogations to the tribunal.

Scene 1: Abacha and Diya

This video showed Abacha and Diya meeting at the presidential villa the night Diya was arrested. The conversation was tense and emotional. Abacha asked Diya to tell him what had happened. Diya did not need much encouragement to open up, and explained that other senior generals had informed him that the army leadership had decided to change the government's leadership. When Abacha asked Diya why he agreed to join the other generals, Diya replied that he was afraid that if he refused to join, he would become targeted by the plot's ringleaders.

'You joined them to kill me, eh, Dipo?'

Abacha exclaimed to Diya: 'You that I relied on, you joined them to kill me eh, Dipo?' Diya then lost his composure, got down on his hands and knees, clasped his hands together in supplication, and, weeping, started to beg Abacha. After about a minute of kneeling, begging and crying, Diya went back to his seat. Abacha casually brought out some tissues and gave them to Diya to wipe his tears away.

Scene 2: Al-Mustapha and Adisa

'We in the army have no reputation left'

In this video, Adisa wept and pleaded with al-Mustapha to 'help us to beg Oga [Abacha] to forgive us ... You know if Oga forgives us I will campaign for Oga [to rule] for another five years.' Adisa was so desperate that he got on his knees to beg al-Mustapha to intercede on his behalf with Abacha. Al-Mustapha repeatedly told Adisa, 'Sir, calm down.' Adisa later showed no regret for begging a subordinate officer: 'I have no shame and I have no apology for what I did. I had to do what I did to save my life. In the army at that time … anything goes … A lieutenant can arrest a general.'[38]

It was these tapes that the government had played to the Yoruba traditional leaders and some chosen others a few months before the trial. The humiliating images of frightened senior generals kneeling before and begging a subordinate like al-Mustapha for mercy, and offering to support Abacha as a civilian president if he forgave them, had so disgusted the Yoruba traditional rulers that they condemned the defendants before the trial even began.

Diya later claimed that the videos had been heavily edited to show only incriminating comments. To demonstrate that they were filmed on different dates, then stitched together to form an incriminating whole, he pointed out that he was wearing different clothes in the tapes. Sabo admitted that Diya did wear different clothes in the tapes, but only because he was so terrified when told that he would be taken to see Abacha after his arrest that he soiled himself inside al-Mustapha's office and had to be given fresh clothing. Sabo and the other prosecution witnesses clearly enjoyed humiliating Diya.

'a coup within a coup'

However, some investigators were not impressed by Bamaiyi's appearance as a prosecution witness. Military intelligence personnel such as Sabo and Colonel Frank Omenka suspected that there was 'a coup within a coup'. They regarded Bamaiyi as a double agent who had played both the Diya and Abacha sides. According to their analysis, Diya agreed to participate after assurances from Bamaiyi that most GOCs and senior army commanders supported the plot. Then when Bamaiyi realised that his plot would leak or would fail, he decided to save himself by sacrificing Diya and reporting it to Abacha. They noted that, conveniently, there was no audio tape of Bamaiyi's first conversation with Diya about the plot. They were so convinced of Bamaiyi's involvement that Omenka even told Diya during his interrogations that Bamaiyi had set him up. Sabo urged Abacha to approve Bamaiyi's arrest and prosecution for involvement in the coup. The back-and-forth accusations may have caused even Abacha to start doubting some of what he had been told.

According to Diya, Abacha telephoned him one night in Jos, where he was detained, and offered to forgive Diya if he publicly apologised, pledged support for his self-succession bid, and testified against a very senior officer in the government. Diya asked for time to consider the offer, and discussed it with other detainees. But Diya feared that the offer was a trap and declined it.

Judgement Day

In view of the breathtaking revelations, and the fact that the SIP had referred four additional defendants for trial, the tribunal was unable to complete its work before its original deadline at the end of March. It took nearly another month to finalise the trials. The head-spinning accusations, counter-accusations and betrayals made the hearings opaque, and no one seemed to be sure exactly who had planned or said what. Who would the tribunal believe? The tribunal rendered its verdict on Tuesday, April 28, 1998. Olanrewaju pondered whether he would be condemned to die on his daughter's birthday. On their way back to Rukuba Cantonment in Jos for the judgment, a number of defendants prayed, and some reassured each other that they would survive the ordeal. Others claimed to have had dreams or visions of being freed. The less optimistic gave final instructions to their wives and families. Since outsiders would be readmitted to hear the verdicts, barbers trimmed the defendants' hair and shaved their beards to make them look slightly more presentable. Security teams also provided second-hand clothes to those who needed to replace their tattered garments. They were not handcuffed, but were still led inside the trial room chained to each other by their feet.

'Very soon, they would learn their fate and find out if they would live or die'

The atmosphere in the trial room was of stomach-turning fear and tension. Even Malu felt the pressure. He recalled:

> As I entered the room to deliver the judgment, I was overwhelmed by emotion. I was going to deliver a judgment that would forever change the fortunes, careers, and lives of my fellow comrades in arms and their families ... The room was quiet, and there was immense suspense, perhaps anxiety. A sense of fear and despair infused all of the accused persons ... The drama and theatre of the trials had vanished. All the parties knew that the hour of judgement had come. Very soon, they would learn their fate and find out if they would live or die ... Things would never be the same again for most, if not all of us.[39]

Prior to the verdict, the judge advocate, Lt-Colonel Braimah, summarised the evidence against each defendant and the critical issues of law to be considered. After Braimah's address, Malu decided to respond to Diya's claim that he had been set up. Malu knew that whatever verdict he rendered would be tainted unless he specifically addressed the claim. Malu said that the tribunal's job was not to find out who initiated the plot, but merely to ascertain whether the defendants had participated in that plot once it commenced. Thus he intriguingly left open the question of who initiated the coup attempt.

Malu told each defendant to stand up as he prepared to announce the verdicts. He methodically called each defendant by rank and name, then read out the charges and verdicts. Malu found 16 of the 30 defendants guilty of various offences. With the verdicts rendered, the defendants listened intently for their sentences to determine whether their next destination was further imprisonment or death. Malu announced that he had sentenced six defendants to death. In what was perhaps the cruellest compliment of all time, Malu said that the tribunal 'commends the candour and display of courage and integrity by Major O.O. Fadipe whose testimony assisted the tribunal in no small measure. We thank you most sincerely.' Despite Malu's admiration for Fadipe's testimony, he did not refrain from sentencing him to death for treason along with Diya, Adisa, Olanrewaju and Akiode. Adebanjo was the only civilian sentenced to death. All six defendants who received death sentences were Yoruba. Malu sentenced the others to terms of imprisonment ranging from two years to life.

'He will leave the army in disgrace'

Four years after Diya's long-time colleagues and cadet coursemates, Lt-General Aliyu Mohammed and Major-General Ishola Williams, predicted that he 'will leave the army in disgrace' and 'wasn't going to last long', the ominous warnings came true. Diya was heading for a firing squad.

Abacha had once again defeated his opponents, and seemed immovable.

12

FIVE LEPROUS FINGERS

Abacha's rule generated so many enemies that comfortable and inconspicuous retirement was unlikely for him. His incarceration of powerful rivals such as Obasanjo, Abiola, Yar'Adua and NADECO members meant that he could not realistically ride off into the sunset without spending the remainder of his life sleeping with one eye open. Leaving power would make him susceptible to investigation and prosecution for the hundreds of people imprisoned, tortured or killed under his watch. To that extent, he was trapped in power, and became the embodiment of the Sudanese proverb that 'Power is like a stick: put it down and someone else will pick it up and hit you on the head with it'.

Abacha's supporters had a potential solution for this problem. Although Abacha stated that military rule would end on October 1, 1998, he had not indicated that he himself would leave power on that date. Rumours about whether Abacha would 'succeed himself' by standing for election as a civilian president dominated political conversations. Some Nigerians and foreigners had good reasons to advocate Abacha's transmutation into an elected civilian president. Several of his political and security aides had become rich from their association with him and wanted to continue riding on his cash-stuffed coat-tails. Abacha was also an unofficial policeman in West Africa and was willing to commit Nigerian money and soldiers to fight ugly wars in Liberia and Sierra Leone in which the Americans and Europeans did not want to get involved.

'The most suitable leader for Nigeria'

In the absence of Abacha's confirmation or denial that he would transmute into a civilian president, exasperated senior officers and government officials played a deft game of guesswork, anxious to back the right horse. In 1997 the former minister of labour and productivity, Brigadier Samuel Ogbemudia, said:

> General Abacha has done very well. I stand to support that he becomes civilian head of state at the end of the transition next year. The result of Abacha's three years in office is quite impressive ... He has projected the dignity of Nigerians and of Africa as a whole.[1]

Prior to his conviction for coup plotting, the minister of works and housing, Major-General Adisa, had described Abacha as 'the most suitable leader for Nigeria'. However, military support for Abacha's transformation into a civilian president was not unanimous. In November 1997, the chief of army staff, Major-General Bamaiyi, described those campaigning for Abacha to continue in power as 'doubtful characters'. Bamaiyi said: 'It is the Nigerian people, not the Nigerian army who will decide who should be the next president of Nigeria.'[2] Bamaiyi's comments caused enough consternation in government circles for his press officer, Lt-Colonel Liman Adelugba, to issue a swift clarifying statement the next day to emphasise that 'there should be no doubt about the army's support for General Abacha if he chooses to run for the presidency'.[3]

However, Abacha had other backers. Several of his civilian and military associates egged him on, assuring him of his popularity and that only his strong leadership could hold an unwieldy country like Nigeria together. Apocryphal stories about his courage, supernatural powers and wisdom became rife. His aides did not allow him to discover the extent of local and international opposition to him. A US official claimed that Abacha was 'clustered with a few sycophantic aides who don't tell him any bad news'.[4] To create an Orwellian sense of his popularity and his omnipresence, his supporters released Abacha-branded soap, televisions, sandals and rice for sale at subsidised prices. Military officers also wore badges with Abacha's image on them to demonstrate their allegiance.

Mysterious youth groups also emerged to campaign for Abacha to extend his tenure. The National Committee of Youth Associations (NACYAN) published pro-Abacha advertisements in newspapers. They called for a 'Two Million Man March' on March 3–4, 1998, a 48-hour carnival during which there would be 'No school, no work, no sleep'. Daniel Kanu was the chairman of Youths Earnestly Ask for Abacha (YEAA). Kanu's father was the wealthy Igbo Catholic Knight and businessman, Sir Empire Nduka Kanu, who later became Nigeria's ambassador to Argentina. The younger Kanu was articulate and his 'mid-Atlantic' accent with American pronunciations revealed his secondary school and university education in the US (he grew up in Dallas). His prominent biceps and WWE wrestler physique suggested that he spent as much time in the gym as he did in the classroom. Kanu and YEAA threatened to go on a hunger strike and to make Nigeria 'ungovernable' if Abacha did not agree to continue in power. Kanu said: 'We will do whatever it takes to ensure Abacha continues.'[5]

Despite claiming to be autonomous, NACYAN and YEAA seemed suspiciously well funded. They had a budget of 500 million naira for the Two Million Man March, they managed to mobilise significant logistics, and they procured government cooperation at every turn. When a coalition of civil society groups called the United Action for Democracy (UAD), led by the lawyer Olisa Agbakoba,[6] organised anti-government demonstrations in Lagos, the Lagos State commissioner of police sternly reminded them that they did not have a permit for the demonstration. When the UAD proceeded with the demonstration anyway, the police fired tear gas at them, hit them with gun butts, broke up the demonstration, and arrested Agbakoba. When demonstrators objected to the heavy-handed treatment, the police responded by firing more tear gas at them. Yet when NACYAN planned a pro-government rally in Abuja, the police promptly issued them with a permit. The Federal Road Safety Corps also promised to facilitate their rally by keeping the roads clear. Civil servants were given time off work to enable them to attend the event. Despite a massive fuel shortage, the managing director of the Pipeline and Product Marketing Company Aminu Suleiman said that petrol stations would open until midnight to ensure free movement of persons during the rally. The government also made police bomb disposal and helicopter surveillance units available for the event.

'The children are calling'

The rally itself was part political procession, part carnival and featured pro-Abacha balloons and posters. Its organisers claimed that 3 million people attended though opposition estimates were only 100,000. Prominent actors, actresses and musicians attended and performed while the political elite was also present, including the national chairmen of the five political parties, and leading political figures like Arisekola Alao, Sam Mbakwe, Uche Chukwumerije, Maitama Sule and Evan Enwerem. At the rally Kanu read from a prepared script and described Abacha as 'the best head of state that this country has ever had. We want you to continue ... the children are calling. Please against all odds you must answer us.' Kanu also subsequently appeared in a CNN television interview. In a well-drilled performance he demonstrated in-depth knowledge of government policies and effortlessly reeled off statistics about the government's finances and economic achievements. He also took time to criticise Abacha's opponents such as Wole Soyinka, whom he referred to as 'a wife abuser'.

Five political parties were to contest the presidential election on August 1: the Congress for National Consensus (CNC), Democratic Party of Nigeria (DPN), Grassroots Democratic Movement (GDM),[7] National Centre Party of Nigeria (NCPN), and the United Nigeria Congress Party (UNCP). Between April 6 and 9, 1998, the parties held conventions to choose their presidential candidates. Only the GDM allowed nominees other than Abacha, namely the former inspector-general of police, Muhammadu Dikko 'MD' Yusuf, and Tunji Braithwaite. The government took an unusual interest in the GDM's convention. The GDM chairman, Gambo Lawan, was a close friend of Hamza al-Mustapha. Lawan and al-Mustapha flew together with members of the GDM's national executive committee in the presidential jet to the party's convention in Maiduguri.

'Five fingers of the leprous hand'

All five parties chose Abacha as their presidential candidate, even though he was not a member of any of them. Some of the parties amended their constitutions to make Abacha eligible. Braithwaite walked out of the GDM's convention in protest at the manipulation of the nomination process. A member of the UNCP claimed that the party was 'being run from the [presidential] Villa ... we could not agree on anything, except [if] the directive came from the Villa. [Lt-General] Jeremiah Useni was the anchor man.'[8] NADECO member Bola Ige contemptuously described the parties as 'five fingers of the leprous hand' and announced that he had 'started the Siddon Look Movement' (meaning that he was going to sit down and watch from the sidelines rather than participate in a political process he considered a sham). Rather than voting in a presidential election, it seemed that Nigerians would instead vote yes or no in a referendum for an Abacha presidency. In typical fashion, Abacha did not confirm or deny whether he would accept any party's nomination of him.

Yet Abacha was sensitive to the need to improve his image. With corruption an ever-present phenomenon in Nigerian public institutions, Abacha understood that he could obtain legitimacy by positioning himself as more financially responsible than past governments. Given that he was part of the corrupt Babangida government for eight years, he could not do that alone. Abacha had created the Petroleum Trust Fund (PTF) in 1994 to house excess oil revenue for disbursement on essential services such as roads, water and health projects. Abacha appointed former head of state Major-General Muhammadu Buhari as the chairman of the PTF. Despite being out of power for a decade, Buhari still retained a reputation for probity. One source informed me that before appointing Buhari, Abacha apologised to him and asked for his forgiveness for his role in the coup that overthrew him. Riding in the slipstream of Buhari's anti-corruption reputation would make Abacha appear serious about fighting corruption.

Reaction to the June 12 annulment and Abacha's rule was apathetic in the north until three events caused new opposition to emerge from surprising quarters. Firstly, in April 1996 Abacha deposed the sultan of Sokoto, Ibrahim Dasuki, then banished him into exile and confinement in Zing, Taraba State. Secondly, there was the imprisonment, then death, of Yar'Adua. The fact that Abacha had summarily deposed the spiritual leader of Nigeria's Muslims and confined him to house arrest, then brazenly sent a wealthy, powerful northern politician and retired general from a royal family to prison (and allowed him to die in murky circumstances), demonstrated to powerful northerners that not even they were safe from Abacha. Finally, Abacha's refusal to cede power also blocked the political ambitions of other northerners who aspired to leadership.

In April 1998, a group of 18 northern politicians calling themselves the 'G18' (Group of 18) wrote an open letter to Abacha in which they opposed his self-succession bid. Given the calibre of the G18, they could not be dismissed as rabble-rousers or southern sympathisers. The G18 included eminent northern leaders such as Adamu Ciroma, Solomon Lar, Sule Lamido, Balarabe Musa, Abubakar Rimi and Ahmed Joda.[9] The G18's public opposition to Abacha was significant and demonstrated that he could not take the north's support for granted. It also reassured the south that not all northerners supported Abacha. Shortly after the G18's letter, 14 politicians from the southeast under the leadership of former Vice-President Alex Ekwueme also issued a statement opposing Abacha's candidacy as a civilian president. The two groups coalesced to form the 'G34' (they also went by the name Institute of Civil Society). Opposition to Abacha from the northern and south-eastern wings of the G34 slightly eased the ethno-regional coloration of the crisis, which depicted it as a confrontation between the Muslim north and Yoruba south-west. It also demonstrated that NADECO were not the sole proprietors of the democracy struggle.

Nigeria's Western allies were initially unimpressed with rumours of Abacha's planned self-succession. In March 1998, President Bill Clinton visited six African countries, but skipped Nigeria. Abacha was unlikely to have been surprised. He had complained to a US congressman that 'Bill Clinton has done nothing but lead a campaign against me'.[10] Abacha's reign was an excellent demonstration of the international community's impotence where big money is at stake. Although they made token gestures of isolating Nigeria, their bark was far worse than their bite. Lots of strong words were thrown at Nigeria, but little real action was taken against it. Even though several Western countries had imposed arms embargoes on Nigeria, and placed a visa ban on members of the military and government and their families, the sanctions were applied haphazardly. One of Abacha's sons and Kingibe's wife were denied visas for Germany. However, former President Babangida travelled to Germany at the invitation of the construction company Julius Berger. Besides, Western hectoring of Nigeria merely pushed the country to deepen its relationship with China. Nigeria had to find new friends that did not kick up such a fuss about democracy, elections and human rights. Additionally, money talked. Some press reports claimed that Britain sold 150 Vickers tanks to the Nigerian army. The US already had oil embargoes against Libya, Iraq, Iran and Syria. Stopping oil imports from Nigeria would leave it even shorter of options. An American congressman declined to press for an oil embargo on Nigeria because if the Americans did so, the Nigerian oil market 'will be taken over by the British and the Germans'.[11] While the US and Europe conducted their on-again, off-again love affair with Nigeria, the pope visited Nigeria, met Abacha on May 21, 1998, and blessed him and his family. Before departing, the pope made a plea for justice, and for the dignity and rights of citizens to be respected, in a barely concealed reference to the government's tactics against the opposition. He also gave Abacha a list of 60 detainees he wanted to have released. As usual, Abacha did not promise or decline to release the detainees.

'Two cheers'

The international community's inconsistent approach to Abacha revealed that they needed him despite reviling him. Ironically, while Abacha delayed democracy in Nigeria, he was busy restoring it elsewhere. On May 25, 1997 Sierra Leone's army overthrew its elected president, Ahmed Tejan Kabbah, during a military coup and replaced him with Major Johnny Paul Koroma. In an announcement of ultimate irony and hypocrisy, military-ruled Nigeria condemned the coup, demanded the resignation of Koroma's junta, and the reinstallation of Kabbah. Nigeria also issued a 'jump or be pushed'[12] ultimatum to Koroma, threatening to use force to remove him unless he ceded power back to Kabbah. Nigeria lost patience with Koroma's unfulfilled promises to restore power to Kabbah and in February 1998 troops commanded by Colonel Maxwell Khobe launched an attack to overthrow Koroma. A BBC journalist who met Khobe described him as 'a true warrior'.[13] Nigerian navy ships blockaded the Sierra Leone capital of Freetown, while ground troops then invaded the country and sent Koroma's forces fleeing in an intense, one-week offensive. A smug Abacha travelled to Freetown to witness Kabbah's reinstatement on March 17, 1998. Western countries would not give Nigeria overt credit for restoring democracy to Sierra Leone. However, the British minister of state for Africa, Tony Lloyd, could not resist replying 'two cheers' when he was asked for his thoughts on Nigeria's ousting of Koroma's junta.[14] While Nigeria's military government was reviled domestically and by Western countries, it was viewed as a saviour in Sierra Leone. The victorious Colonel Khobe became a national hero in Sierra Leone, where he remained, and where he was appointed the country's chief of defence staff.[15] A street in Freetown was also named after him.

'I will soon make my decision known'

Despite the constant speculation, Abacha declined to confirm or deny whether he would contest the upcoming presidential election on August 1, whether he would release Abiola and other prisoners, and whether Diya and the other coup prisoners would be executed. He ignored speculation with the unflappable air of a man who had made a vow of silence. After nearly five years in power, Abacha had not granted a single interview to the Nigerian media. However, in May 1998, Abacha broke his silence. He agreed to an interview with *Jeune Afrique Economie* on his alleged self-succession plan. He was his usua_ enigmatic self and said: 'Power and authority belong to God and only he can decide the future with certainty but I do not, absolutely speaking, have the intention to perpetuate myself in power.' He added, 'I will soon make my decision known.'[16]

President Bill Clinton seemed worn out by Abacha's obduracy and indicated that he would accept Abacha continuing as Nigeria's president, so long as he retired from the military and stood for election as a civilian. Clinton said, 'There are many military leaders who have taken over chaotic situations in African countries, that have moved toward democracy, and that can happen in Nigeria ... If [Abacha] stands for election, we hope he will stand as a civilian.'[17] The 'leader of the free world' seemed to have grudgingly accepted the inevitability of an Abacha presidency. It was now up to Abacha.

The civilian opposition and military plotters had tried everything to topple Abacha, and failed. Neither strikes, protests, international condemnation, sanctions nor military coups could wrest power from Abacha's hands. With his domestic enemies subdued, and his foreign critics exhausted, everything was going Abacha's way. Then Heaven decided to stage a coup.

13

A COUP FROM HEAVEN

'Whenever there was a party worth attending anywhere in town, Abacha and Useni almost always showed up.'

No country does unpredictable cliff-hanging drama like Nigeria. Even by Nigerian standards the events of one month in mid-1998 were so extraordinary that no fiction writer could have conjured up anything so remarkable.

Sunday June 7 1998

The chairman of the Palestine Liberation Organisation, Yasser Arafat, made a brief stop in Nigeria during an international tour en route to Morocco. Abacha and Arafat met briefly at the Nnamdi Azikiwe International Airport in Abuja. After the meeting Arafat inspected a guard of honour mounted by the Brigade of Guards, then departed for Morocco. Abacha returned to the Aso Rock presidential villa on the evening of Sunday, June 7, 1998 between 5 and 6 pm.

After returning, Abacha as usual entertained guests late into the night, even though he was due to deliver a speech as the special guest of honour at a workshop the following day. The chief security officer, al-Mustapha, later commented that 'by 9 pm, the Head of State was bouncing and receiving visitors until much later'.[1] One of Abacha's VIP visitors was a prominent northern politician who still remains active in Nigerian politics. Another visitor was Abacha's good friend, the minister of the Federal Capital Territory,

Lt-General Useni. Abacha and Useni had been friends for over thirty years, from the time of their days as young army officers in the mid-1960s. The two men usually needed little excuse to party. A former military colleague of theirs referred to Useni as Abacha's 'inseparable companion' and described them as 'men who were perpetually on the lookout for "where it is happening"'.[2] Useni recalled: 'It is true that I always saw him [Abacha] in the evening … we had been long time friends. Sometimes I would wait up till 11 pm or 12 midnight so that he would have finished with all those people who would normally take their problems to him.'[3] Useni met Abacha around 10 pm and stayed with him in a guest house at the presidential villa until he left sometime between 3 and 3.30 am.

Monday June 8 1998

9 am—Monday morning

Staff members arrived for work on Monday morning but were turned away without explanation by unusually hostile and tense soldiers stationed at the entrances. Guests at a Federal Ministry of Information workshop on information management and national planning waited for Abacha to come to open the event. He was supposed to arrive at 9 am but by 11.30am there was no sign of him. The minister of information and culture, Ikeobasi Mokelu, apologised to the waiting guests at the International Conference Centre in Abuja, and assured them that Abacha would be there shortly.

Back at the presidential villa, al-Mustapha and the inspector-general of police, Ibrahim Coomasie, summoned PRC members for an urgent meeting with Abacha at 9 on Monday morning. No agenda or reason was given for the meeting. All PRC members except one were invited. Senior officers arrived from all around the country. The chief of defence staff, Major-General Abubakar, the chief of army staff, Major-General Bamaiyi, the chief of naval staff, Rear-Admiral Akhigbe, the chief of air staff, Air Vice Marshal Eduok, general officers commanding from the army, flag officers commanding from the navy, and air officers commanding from the air force, all turned up. Al-Mustapha also invited a few other strategically placed officers who were not PRC members, such as the director of military intelligence, Brigadier-General Sabo, and the commander of the Brigade of Guards, Brigadier-General Mu'azu. The military administrator of Lagos State, Colonel Mohammed Marwa, flew in from Lagos to attend after being tipped off that something unusual was happening at the presidential villa. Al-Mustapha and Coomasie also invited senior civilian officials such as the secretary to the government of the federation, Gidado Idris, the minister of power and steel, Bashir Dalhatu, and the chief justice of the federation, Mohammed Lawal Uwais. Idris had been a close friend of Abacha for several decades, going back to Abacha's days as a junior army officer in Kaduna. He was from a northern royal family and was a close aide to the late premier of the Northern Region, Ahmadu Bello. He was one of those that identified and recovered Bello's corpse after he was murdered in January 1966. Idris' wife Maryam was a friend of Maryam Babangida, wife of former head of state General Babangida, and the two women had studied together at the Federal Training Centre in Kaduna. Dalhatu had married Abacha's daughter Zainab in 1999.

11 am, presidential villa—Abuja

The assembled senior officials were kept waiting without explanation for over two hours. As their audience was with Abacha, none of them dared to complain aloud about the wait. Al-Mustapha finally appeared and told the most senior officers such as Abubakar and Bamaiyi that Abacha was waiting to see them in his living room. When they entered, they saw Abacha's wife Maryam and his son Mohammed, but there was no sign of Abacha himself. While they sat and waited for Abacha to meet them, Coomasie and the national security adviser, Ismaila Gwarzo, addressed them around 11 am and told them what had happened in the villa overnight.

Events overnight: 5 am—Monday, June 8, 1998

About two hours after Useni departed in the early hours of the morning, some of Abacha's guards noticed that he was feeling unwell. Around 5 am, they went to al-Mustapha's residence to inform him. The security-conscious al-Mustapha at first thought he was being lured out of his house in another coup attempt. Al-Mustapha recalled: 'At first, I thought it was a coup attempt. Immediately, I prepared myself fully for any eventuality.' He went to Abacha's guest house to see for himself. 'When I got to the bedside of the Head of State, he was already gasping.' He knelt beside Abacha's bed and called out to him several times. After receiving no response, al-Mustapha became concerned. 'Ordinarily, I could not just touch him. It was not allowed in our job. But under the situation on ground, I knelt close to him and shouted ... I again knocked at the stool beside the bed and shouted in the same manner, yet he did not respond.'[4]

Al-Mustapha phoned the chief State House physician, Professor Sadiq Suleiman Wali,[5] around 6 am, and told him to 'drop whatever you are doing'[6] and come to the villa immediately. He did not inform Dr Wali why he was being summoned at such an early hour. Wali was an experienced and esteemed medical doctor who served as the personal physician to five consecutive Nigerian heads of state. He was an alumnus of the famous Barewa College and attended the school at the same time as former head of state General Murtala Muhammed.

As Wali was getting ready to leave, he was surprised when security officers sent by al-Mustapha arrived at his residence to pick him up a few minutes after his phone call, rather than wait for him to make his own way to the villa. Wali was surprised again when the security officers entered the villa through a gate normally used only by Abacha. Wali suspected that a coup had taken place.

When Wali arrived, al-Mustapha ushered him into Abacha's living room. Wali saw Abacha lying unconscious on a couch. When he got closer he was shocked to see that Abacha was 'very seriously ill' and foaming at the mouth. Another doctor named Dr Maina had been attending to Abacha, and Dr Wali joined in the efforts to resuscitate him. He found that Abacha had only a 'very feeble' heartbeat and was 'almost dead'.[7] Wali administered injections to Abacha's chest and neck. After forty minutes of failed attempts to resuscitate Abacha, Wali turned to al-Mustapha and informed him that Abacha was dead. Al-Mustapha refused to give up and replied, 'Are you sure?' He asked whether there was another doctor they could call, or whether his life could be saved by taking him overseas for further medical treatment. When Dr Wali finally convinced al-Mustapha that nothing more could be done, the latter woke up Abacha's older brother, Abdulkadir, a major in the army, and Abacha's son Mohammed and broke the news of Abacha's death to them. Abdulkadir and Mohammed started weeping profusely. Al-Mustapha's wife Hafsat also burst into tears after her husband told her the news.

Al-Mustapha declined to inform the staff at the presidential villa that Abacha had died. One member of staff managed to find out when his boss telephoned him and sharply told him, '*Oga* has died. Keep your mouth shut!' before he abruptly put the phone down.

'They killed him'

Al-Mustapha called Gwarzo to the villa and conferred with him while Dr Wali and the medical team secured Abacha's corpse. Al-Mustapha also called

Coomasie, and sealed access to the villa so that no one could enter or leave.[8] Dr Wali suggested that a post-mortem should be conducted. Coomasie agreed as did Abacha's wife Maryam, who had been repeatedly exclaiming that 'they killed him'. Maryam then entered a room with her son Mohammed for a private discussion. When they re-emerged, Maryam changed her mind, and mother and son were adamant that there would be no post-mortem. Dr Wali instead took blood samples from Abacha's corpse and sent them to the UK for toxicology tests.

Senior officers were shocked when Coomasie finally told them that Abacha had died.[9] His corpse was laid on the floor in the villa, covered by a white sheet. Abubakar asked for, and was granted, permission to see Abacha's body and pray over it.

The situation had become dangerous. Nigeria was without a head or deputy head of state. The power vacuum could have led to a dangerous bloodbath if news of Abacha's death leaked prematurely to the wrong people. Some soldiers were looking for someone to blame for Abacha's death. In the tense atmosphere itchy trigger fingers could have exacted misplaced 'revenge' and worsened the situation. Abacha's brother Abdulkadir restrained the military hotheads who wanted to arrest senior officers whom they blamed for being complicit in Abacha's death. Al-Mustapha also telephoned former head of state General Babangida, who advised him of the need to avoid bloodshed or a power vacuum.

With Abacha dead, Abiola was back in contention to become head of state. However, threats were being made to Abiola's life. In the midst of the crisis al-Mustapha kept a cool head. He ordered Abiola's guards to relocate him from the Kado housing estate where he was being detained to Gado Nasko Barracks in Abuja. He also withdrew Abiola's usual guards, and replaced them with soldiers from the Brigade of Guards. Abiola was not told why he was being moved or why his guards were replaced.

Jos Prison, northern Nigeria

Strike Force member Sergeant Rogers and the comptroller-general of prisons, Ahmed Jarma, came to Jos prison where Diya and the other coup prisoners were detained, and told them that they were going to be transferred to Abuja. This was the second time in two weeks that soldiers had tried to relocate them. The first attempt, in the first week of June, was blocked by the GOC of 3 Armoured Division in Jos, Brigadier-General Peter Sha, who refused to allow them to be moved unless he received an order to that effect from Abacha. This time the prisoners feared the worst. A 'prison transfer' was a euphemism that guards had previously used to shield bad news from prisoners on death row just prior to their being led out to the execution ground. Just before being executed in 1986, those convicted of plotting a coup were also led out of their cells on the pretext that they were about to be transferred to another prison but were instead taken to the execution ground where they were shot by a firing squad with machine guns. In 1995, Saro-Wiwa and the other members of the Ogoni Nine had also been told that they were being transferred to another prison, but were instead executed shortly afterwards. Given these precedents, and the fact that they were led out of their cells in chains by heavily armed guards wearing black, Diya and the others feared that their final day had come.

Despite being told that they were going to Abuja, they were instead flown to Kano where they were handed over to Lieutenant Dagari. They were handcuffed, had their legs chained, and were ordered onto a Peugeot J5 bus. With his instantly recognisable shock of grey hair at the front of his head, Diya was told to sit on the floor so that passers-by would not notice him through the bus windows. The bus drove them to a private bungalow in Kano, where they were locked inside a room. While there, they overheard arguments between Sergeant Rogers and the other guards as to whether they should be executed. The bewildered prisoners had no idea of what was going on, and did not realise that al-Mustapha had ordered them to be relocated from Jos to various prisons around the country for their own safety.

'They all knew I was the closest to him.'

Meanwhile, back at the presidential villa, no one had bothered to inform or invite Lt-General Useni even though he was the most senior officer. Useni was at his office working, unaware of events at the villa. Abubakar then sent an oblique message to Useni, informing him that he was wanted for a meeting at the villa. When he arrived, the other officers told him that Abacha had died. After composing himself after his initial shock, Useni complained at the way news of his friend's death had been concealed from him. Smarting, he demanded to know, 'Why were all these people contacted before anybody called me to tell me? They all knew I was the closest to him.'[10]

1 pm—council chambers—presidential villa

The senior officers then convened an emergency meeting inside the council chambers. There were two key items on the agenda: arrangements for Abacha's funeral, and who would succeed him. By 5 pm the meeting was still continuing and no consensus had been reached. Disagreement arose over whether they should prioritise Abacha's burial arrangements or his succession. Brigadier-General Magashi, who like Abacha was from Kano, angrily interjected and demanded that they show respect to Abacha by finalising arrangements for his burial. Magashi argued that it was getting late in the day and they were running out of time to bury him on the same day in accordance with Islamic rites. The PRC deferred discussion of Abacha's successor until after he had been buried. Some officers wanted Abacha to be given a military burial with full military honours. However, his family objected and opted for a modest Islamic burial later that night.

'Where is the corpse?'

Around 6 pm Abacha's corpse, still wrapped in a white sheet, was loaded onto an ambulance, which headed for the Nnamdi Azikiwe airport in Abuja in a convoy of vehicles. Abacha's family and senior members of the government such as Abubakar, Bamaiyi and Marwa followed the ambulance. For Maryam and the other members of the Abacha family it would be a one-way journey. After nearly five years as residents of the presidential villa, they took their belongings with them, knowing that they would never be allowed to return. The members of the convoy prepared to board after Abacha's corpse was loaded onto the presidential plane, 001. Just before the plane took off Abubakar suddenly asked, 'Where is the corpse?' When he was told that it was inside the luggage hold, he ordered staff to bring it inside the main passenger compartment. The presidential plane flew straight to Abacha's home town of Kano. Three other planes followed and landed in quick succession. Al-Mustapha stayed behind to maintain vigilant watch in Abuja.

Kano—Monday evening

The chief imam of Kano, Sheik Idris Kuliya Alkali, prayed for Abacha at the Kano central mosque, and his body was taken to his family compound at number 8 Gidado Road in Kano for burial the same night. Among the chief mourners were former heads of state Buhari and Babangida and his wife Maryam, and Abacha's childhood friend, the multi-millionaire businessman Dan Kabo. Although security was tight, several thousand members of the public pushed past the security men at the gate and entered the compound.

Abacha's corpse was lowered into the ground around 10 pm. Over the next few days several sympathisers, including former head of state General Gowon and former chief of staff, Supreme Headquarters, Tunde Idiagbon, paid visits of condolence to Abacha's family at their home in Kano.

'He will go to the hottest part of hell'

Foreign media broke the news of Abacha's death before most Nigerians were aware that their head of state had died. Abacha had already been buried by the time most Nigerians knew that he was dead. Some members of the public refused to believe that Abacha had really died until some soldiers informed them in pidgin that 'Baba don quench'. Public reaction to Abacha's death, particularly in the south, was unsympathetic. Some elated Nigerians dubbed Abacha's death 'a coup from heaven'. The human rights lawyer Gani Fawehinmi said, 'We thank God that he has passed away. He was a thoroughly evil and wicked man. Everybody is jubilant. And I have no doubt in my mind that he will go to the hottest part of hell.'[11] A student in the southeast informed me that when she and her classmates heard during a lecture that Abacha had died, they broke out into spontaneous jubilation and ran out of their classroom to celebrate.

Back to Abuja—Monday night, Tuesday morning

Senior officers flew back to Abuja late at night immediately after the funeral. They landed around midnight and drove straight to the presidential villa to reconvene their meeting. They re-entered the council chambers and finally addressed the elephant in the room: who would succeed Abacha? The atmosphere was so tense and uncertain that some PRC members came into the council chambers clutching Bibles and Korans. There was no clear successor to Abacha. Ordinarily the chief of general staff, Lt-General Diya, would have succeeded Abacha. However, as he was on death row, he was out of contention. In Diya's absence there were three contenders to succeed Abacha.

Useni

The minister of the Federal Capital Territory, Lt-General Jerry Useni, was the most senior officer by rank and was the longest-serving general left in the army. He was a Christian of Tarok ethnicity from Langtang in Plateau State.

He belonged to the cadre of Tarok military officers from Langtang in the middle belt whom the Nigerian press nicknamed the 'Langtang Mafia'. Although Langtang is a small town, it produced an extraordinary number of senior military officers in the same generation. However, Useni had two 'strikes' against him. The Abacha family did not like him and considered him a bad social influence on Abacha. Useni's nickname of 'Jerry Boy' was more a reflection of his social habits than of his age. He and Abacha were well-known in the Nigerian army as party-goers. A former colleague of theirs recalled that in their younger days, 'Whenever there was a party worth attending anywhere in town, Abacha and Useni almost always showed up.'[12] Maryam Abacha in particular could not stand Useni and blamed him for encouraging her husband's late-night socialising.

'He was my closest friend for 30 years'

The second 'strike' against Useni was that the Abacha family, as well as some military officers, were suspicious of him as he was the last person to see Abacha alive.[13] When a government delegation later paid a visit of condolence to Maryam, she asked Coomasie to arrest Useni for complicity in her husband's death. The shocked Useni protested his innocence and retorted:

> I have worked for your husband to my own detriment in the last four and a half years. He knew that I supported and was committed to him 110%. No one has worked harder or committed himself more totally to him than me. I challenge anybody. He was my closest friend for 30 years. I am as grieved as, if not more than, even his family over his death.[14]

Some officers also wanted Useni to be arrested. As the most senior officer after Abacha, in their view he had a clear motive for Abacha's murder.

Abubakar

The chief of defence staff, Major-General Abdulsalam Abubakar, was different from Useni. He had wisely kept himself out of the Machiavellian coup plots on which his military colleagues had built their careers. However, he was junior to Useni by rank, and did not have the support of some senior army officers. He had other things in his favour, though. He was from the same home town (Minna) and ethnic group (Gwari) as the former head of state Babangida, and the two men were childhood friends who grew up in the same household. When Babangida's father died in 1955, followed shortly afterwards by his mother, the orphaned Babangida and his sister were sent to live with relatives in the same household as Abubakar. Afterwards Babangida and Abubakar became classmates at the Government College, Bida. The two men also owned neighbouring hilltop mansions in their home town of Minna.

Bamaiyi

The chief of army staff, Major-General Ishaya Bamaiyi, was the one from 'furthest north'. Although he hailed from Zuru in Kebbi State in far north-western Nigeria, he was, like Useni, a Christian from a minority but militarily prominent ethnic group, the Dakarkari.[15] The Dakarkari are known for their warrior culture and had produced a large number of senior military officers disproportionate to their numerical size. Unlike Useni and Abubakar, Bamaiyi commanded troops and thus could press his candidacy by force. Bamaiyi became prominent after assisting Abacha, then the chief of army staff, to foil a 1990 coup attempt to overthrow Babangida. Bamaiyi was at the time a member of the Lagos Garrison Command. His role in suppressing that coup marked him out as a rising star in the army and earned him a promotion to command the elite Brigade of Guards, which was responsible for protecting the head of state. His older brother, Musa, whom he closely resembled, was also a major-general in the army, and was the chairman of the National Drug Law Enforcement Agency. The Bamaiyi brothers joined the army on the same day in 1967, and sported elaborate handlebar moustaches, which were a trademark of officers who served in the Brigade of Guards. However, Bamaiyi was junior to both Useni and Abubakar. He was also tainted by allegations that he had framed Diya and other senior Yoruba officers in a coup plot. Other professional considerations and intra-military rivalries counted against Bamaiyi. He had many detractors among his military colleagues, some of whom considered him intellectually unfit to be chief of army staff, let alone head of state. That contempt may have been the product of an unofficial but powerful form of professional snobbery in the Nigerian army between the so-called 'regular' trained officers and those who enlisted by way of brief short service commission training courses. Bamaiyi fell into the latter category as he enlisted by way of a short service commission during the rush to attract soldiers for the civil war, and did not undergo the full four-year training programme of regular trained officers at the Nigerian Defence Academy.

There was another senior officer who should also have been in contention: Abacha's friend, the minister of industries, Lt-General Mohammed Balarabe

Haladu. Like Abacha, Haladu was also from Kano. However, Haladu was seriously ill.[16] The meeting remained deadlocked. With no clear candidate emerging, pieces of paper were distributed to the officers so they could nominate their choice for head of state in a 'ballot'. Although he had senior army officers backing him, Bamaiyi suddenly withdrew his candidacy and recommended that Abubakar should be appointed as the new head of state. At this stage it became a straight choice between Abubakar and Useni. The PRC was divided over whether to follow rank seniority (which would have favoured Useni) or military seniority (which favoured Abubakar). Useni's closeness to Abacha and unpopularity with the Abacha family counted against him. He admitted that 'the suspicion that I had a hand in his [Abacha's] death also played a role in the whole thing and that was why I was bypassed'.[17] In contrast Abubakar was considered a political outsider to the Abacha regime. He was even suspected by some to be Babangida's sympathiser or spy inside Abacha's government. Abubakar was not a polarising figure like Useni or Bamaiyi. He therefore became the best candidate since he was the titular head of the armed forces and the least closely identified with the unpopular policies of the Abacha regime. Useni acquiesced, stood up and saluted Abubakar. Either Bamaiyi or Useni recommended that Abubakar should be promoted to a four-star general with immediate effect.[18] Having been bypassed as head of state, Useni also lost his portfolio as minister of the Federal Capital Territory to (retired) Major-General Mamman Kontagora, who was a childhood friend of Babangida and Abubakar. Useni retired less than two months later.

The state-owned Nigerian Television Authority showed Chief Justice Uwais administering the oath of office to Abubakar as the new head of state just before 2 am on Tuesday June 9. He carried the Koran in a brown satchel slung over his left shoulder. After he finished reading the statement, photographers and reporters applauded as Abubakar, wearing an olive green military uniform but still with a major-general's epaulettes, turned to face and shake hands with the smiling Uwais, before saluting him. The secretary to the government of the federation, Gidado Idris, then set the commander-in-chief's chair underneath the Nigerian coat of arms, Abubakar sat down and signed the official register in front of the television cameras. His first act as head of state was to declare seven days of national mourning for Abacha during which flags would be flown at half-mast. He later extended the official mourning period to thirty days.

Abacha's death, Abubakar's resulting elevation and Diya's death sentence created multiple vacancies in the chain of command. There was no chief of general staff or chief of defence staff. Since Abubakar was a northern Muslim, the unofficial rule meant that a Christian from the south was required to be the new chief of general staff. Rear-Admiral Jubril Ayinla (navy) and Major-General Rufus Kupolati (army) were the most senior officers from the south. Although Ayinla was Yoruba, he was a Muslim. That ruled out Ayinla and he was instead appointed as the new chief of naval staff. Kupolati had spent considerable time abroad away from the Nigerian army in UN peacekeeping missions such as the ECOMOG mission in Liberia. As a result the chief of naval staff, Rear-Admiral Akhigbe, an Afenmai from Edo State in the south, was promoted to chief of general staff in early July. Abubakar promoted his good friend from the air force, Air Vice-Marshal al-Amin Daggash, a Shuwa Arab from the north-east, from his position as commandant of the Nigerian Defence Academy, to succeed him as chief of defence staff on July 13. Daggash's father, Musa Daggash, had been a senior civil servant in the 1970s.

In the first few days after Abacha's death, very few bothered to discuss or ascertain how he died. The public discourse was dominated by talk of what Abubakar would do, when the military would leave power, and whether Abiola would emerge from prison to claim his presidential mandate five years later. However, the only Nigerian industry that has never suffered a recession is its extremely productive rumour mill. Nigerians love a good conspiracy theory. Abacha's unpopularity meant that a heart attack was not a suitably grotesque form of death that would satisfy the public's and media's desire for him to be shamed even in death. Consequently, several lurid conspiracy theories of varying degrees of fantasy gained currency. The more conservative of these theories involved Abacha dying after eating a poisoned apple or dying after over-exerting himself with Indian prostitutes following a Viagra overdose.

'He was undergoing treatment for an ailment'

However, Abacha had pre-existing health issues. He had been ill and on medication for several years prior to his death.[19] Rumours about Abacha's ill health were so frequent that in September 1997 his chief press secretary, David Attah, responded by stating that Abacha was 'in sound health'. However, senior generals such as Bamaiyi and Diya later commented in passing about his health problems. After his death, Abacha's former minister of works and housing Major-General Abdulkarim Adisa, said, 'I believe too General Abacha wouldn't have lasted 1998 anyway because he was sick and was living on a very serious dose [of medication] .... He was undergoing treatment for an ail-

1. From left to right: Aliyu Mohammed Gusau, Malami Nasarawa, MD Jega, Mohammed Mayaki, and Bello Kaliel. Credit: Gusau Institute.

2. Former Vice-President Atiku Abubakar. Credit: Shehu Musa Yar'Adua Foundation.

3. Beko Ransome-Kuti. Credit: Independent Communication Network Limited.

4. From left to right: Brigadier-General David Mark, General Abdulsalam Abubakar, Lt-General Victor Malu. Credit: Terver Malu.

5. Gani Fawehinmi. Credit: Independent Communication Network Limited.

6. Left: Sheikh Abubakar Mahmud Gummi, second from left—General Sani Abacha. Right—Lt-General Aliyu Mohammed Gusau. Second from right—Admiral Murtala Nyako, Saudi Arabia, 1994. Credit: Gusau Institute.

7. Binta Yar'Adua. Credit: Shehu Musa Yar'Adua Foundation.

8. Ken Saro-Wiwa. Credit: Independent Communication Network Limited.

9. Kudirat Abiola. Credit: Independent Communication Network Limited.

10. Lt-General Aliyu Mohammed Gusau in 1990. Credit: Gusau Institute.

11. Lt-General Victor Malu. Credit: Terver Malu.

12. Major-General Abdulkarim Adisa (left) and then Brigadier-General Victor Malu (right). Credit: Terver Malu.

13. Major-Generals Abdulsalam Abubakar (left) and Victor Malu (right). Credit: Terver Malu.

14. Maryam Abacha. Credit: Independent Communication Network Limited.

15. Moshood Abiola. Credit: Independent Communication Network Limited.

16. Left to right: President Obasanjo, Fidel Castro, Lt-General Gusau, in Cuba in 1999. Credit: Gusau Institute.

17. At the U.S. Oval Office in 2001, far left: President Obasanjo, far right: U.S. President George W. Bush. Credit: Gusau Institute.

18. At the Nigerian presidential villa in 2002, right: Former U.S. President Bill Clinton, second from right: President Obasanjo, centre: Obasanjo's wife Stella. Credit: Gusau Institute.

19. Lt-General Oladipo Diya. Credit: Independent Communication Network Limited.

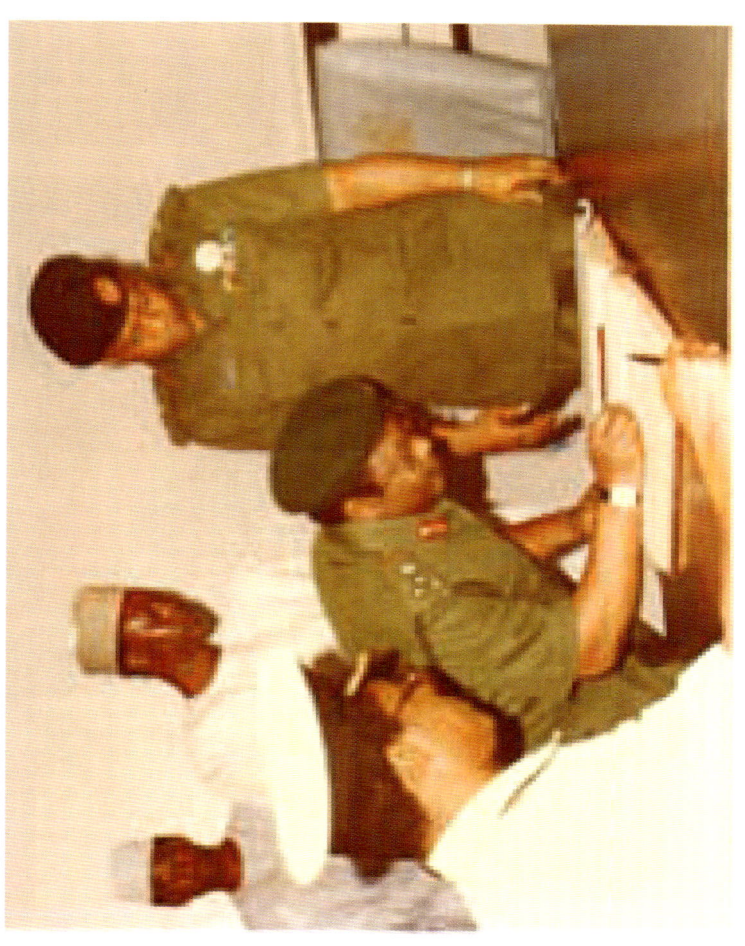

20. Left to right: Commodore Ebitu Ukiwe (seated in white uniform), Brigadier-General Gusau (signing register), and Major-General Ibrahim Babangida (standing to right in green uniform) in 1986. Credit: Gusau Institute.

21. Lt-General Jeremiah Useni. Credit: Independent Communication Network Limited.

22. Shehu Musa Yar'Adua and his family (1990): left to right: Tukur, Ibrahim, Asyia, Buhari, Shehu Yar'Adua, Murtala, Binta Yar'Adua, Maryam, Ahmed, Aminu. Credit: Shehu Musa Yar'Adua Foundation.

23. Pres dent Babangida (right) and Major-General Aliyu Mohammed Gusau in 1989. Credit: Gusau Institute.

24. Lt-Gereral Sani Abacha (middle, wearing sunglasses) – Abeokuta, July 18, 1990. Credit: Gusau Institute.

ment.'[20] Someone who saw Abacha the month he died recalled his surprise when Abacha became noticeably out of breath after climbing up a flight of stairs. However, for some reason the Nigerian public believed that a heart attack was not a plausible cause of death for an ill 54-year-old man with a penchant for late-night revelry and a work-hard, play-hard lifestyle, who had fought in a civil war, taken part in or suppressed seven coups, and survived several assassination attempts during a 32-year military career. Instead the Nigerian rumour mill believed he was far more likely to have died from a Viagra overdose or poisoned apples or at the hands of an assassin team of foreign prostitutes.

Al-Mustapha also denied these lurid claims by saying: 'I must reiterate that the issue of my boss dying on top of women was a great lie just as the insinuation that General Sani Abacha ate and died of poisoned apples was equally a wicked lie.'[21] Useni similarly dismissed reports of foul play in Abacha's death, saying: 'In my own view, he died a natural death and the reports are there. But, of course, some people just wanted to give the man a bad name; hence they were insinuating that he was a womaniser and the rest of it.'[22]

Abacha's widow Maryam was hurt by the public *Schadenfreude* over her husband's death and by the media's denigration of his memory. She claimed that her husband's government took decisions collectively and that those who supported such decisions had turned around to criticise his memory now that he was dead. She said: 'We have had to bear not only the painful loss of our dear father and husband, but also the often more agonising experience of seeing his name and legacy being subjected to the most malicious attack and bitter denigration ever visited on any former Nigerian head of state, dead or alive.'[23]

Abacha's death also affected sporting matters. He was a football fan and knew some of the Nigerian national football team's players personally. The national team's first match at the 1998 World Cup was against Spain. The Spaniards had been undefeated for 30 games and two years and were one of the favourites to win the World Cup. FIFA rejected Nigeria's request to hold a minute's silence in memory of Abacha before the start of the game. The Nigerian players instead wore black armbands in a pulsating game where they twice came back from behind to win dramatically 3–2 after a late goal by Sunday Oliseh.

From the civilian opposition's perspective (although they did not know it at the time), Abubakar was the least threatening general that could have succeeded Abacha. The political atmosphere relaxed as soon as Abubakar became head of state. In contrast to Abacha's quiet and intimidating persona,

Abubakar appeared warm and genial. Like Abacha, Abubakar also wore glasses. However, his were normal prescription glasses, and not the dark Mafia-style sunglasses that Abacha wore. Abubakar smiled, shook hands, and was willing to talk. The 56-year-old general was a member of perhaps the most famous class in Nigerian history: the 1962 graduating class of the Government College, Bida, fifteen of whom later joined the army. That 1962 class produced more army generals than any other in Nigeria's history. However, rather than join the army along with his classmates, Abubakar was one of the pioneer cadets who joined the Nigerian air force in 1963. He attended air force training in Germany before returning to Nigeria in 1966, and transferred to the army in 1967. He was a member of the second emergency commission set up in readiness for the Nigerian civil war, along with Bamaiyi and Chris Alli. He commanded the Nigerian battalion during the United Nations peacekeeping mission in Lebanon in 1979. Although Abubakar had never been a military governor or a minister, serving in the Nigerian army of the 1990s made it hard for an officer to stay clear of all controversy. He was a member of the 1990 Special Military Tribunal that sentenced dozens of officers to death after a failed coup attempt against his childhood friend Babangida. His wife Justice Fati Lami Abubakar was a High Court judge who later became the chief judge of Niger State, and his eldest daughter was a medical student. Becoming head of state was a spectacular change of fortune for Abubakar. He had been preparing for retirement just a few days earlier, as he was slated to be retired by Abacha just before he died.

However, he was under tremendous pressure and had to reconcile conflicting demands from within the military and from the opposition. Opposition groups demanded the release of Abiola and all other political prisoners, the military's immediate resignation from government, radical restructuring of the country, a national conference, and the inauguration of a new civilian government of national unity. How could all this be done in less than three months before the October 1 deadline for the military to hand power to civilians? The opposition also wanted him to conduct a major spring clean and throw all Abacha loyalists out of the government. Abubakar opted for minor dusting instead. He created enough distance between himself and Abacha's supporters to deflect criticisms that he was an Abacha clone, but also had the good sense not to create an intra-regime conflict with Abacha loyalists.

Abubakar astutely removed Abacha's security team. He redeployed al-Mustapha firstly to the Directorate of Military Intelligence, then subsequently as an intelligence officer at 82 Division in Enugu in the south-east. Abubakar appointed the more sedate Major Abdulrasheed Aliyu to succeed al-Mustapha as chief security officer. He also disbanded al-Mustapha's Korean- and Libyan-trained Strike Force, and removed the Brigade of Guards commander, Brigadier-General Mu'azu, and the national security adviser, Ismaila Gwarzo. Colonel Mohammed Mana and retired Major-General Abdullahi Mohammed replaced Mu'azu and Gwarzo, respectively.

'We have decided to free this nation and there is no going back'

On June 15, Abubakar ordered the release of nine people who had been detained by the Abacha regime. The most prominent among them was former head of state General Obasanjo. The government arranged for Obasanjo to be flown to Lagos aboard a presidential jet, from where he travelled to his home in Ota on June 17. Abubakar also ordered the release of the former sultan of Sokoto, Ibrahim Dasuki. Although Obasanjo and Dasuki were released and allowed to see their families, they were not permitted to move freely. Obasanjo was confined to his home at Ota and Dasuki was to stay in Kaduna, forbidden to go to his home state of Sokoto. Frank Ovie Kokori, one of the other released detainees,[24] made an emotional address after his release:

> First, let me thank the militant press ... Let me thank Chief Gani Fawehinmi, the Senior Advocate of Nigeria. God bless that man! [*bursts into tears*] ... we have decided to free this nation and there is no going back. The people will overcome. God just brought the incidents of these past few days to show Nigerians that nobody can play God ... I'm now a changed man after about four years in Bama prison.[25]

Abubakar appealed to members of NADECO and the opposition who had fled abroad to return home, promising them safe passage. When NADECO member Bola Tinubu returned to Nigeria, he too took time to thank those who had kept the struggle alive during his exile:

> I want to say a big 'thank you' to all journalists. Without you, without your steadfastness, your commitment to truth and justice, your tenacity, the struggle would have been nothing. We are back to strengthen that section of the press which stood for justice courageously. I salute the religious leaders, particularly the CAN (Christian Association of Nigeria)[26] with honourable men such as Reverend Sunday Mbang, Reverend Adetiloye and the rest of them. To have seen this nation go through struggle without loss of lives in their hundreds of thousands, without turning this Nigeria into Rwanda or Burundi, was due to their prayers, and their courageous support for justice and truth. We will con-

tinue to praise them and hold them in the highest esteem. The history of this country will not be complete without their names being written in gold.[27]

Although Abubakar took the credit, there is evidence that Abacha had already approved their release before he died. The statement that announced the release of prisoners acknowledged that in his October 1, 1997 (Independence Day) broadcast to the nation, Abacha had 'announced his intention to release some detainees. Although some detainees were released, the whole process could not be concluded before his sudden death.' The statement then went on to declare that the release of Obasanjo and the others was 'in furtherance' of Abacha's objectives. It is therefore possible that Abubakar was therefore merely implementing a measure that had already been approved by Abacha. If so, then Abubakar would be the second northern head of state to get credit for implementing the release of a famed Yoruba prisoner which had already been authorised by his predecessor just before he died. In mid-1966 the head of state, Major-General Aguiyi-Ironsi, ordered the release from prison of the detained leader of the opposition, Obafemi Awolowo. However, Aguiyi-Ironsi was assassinated before Awolowo could be freed. A few days later, Aguiyi-Ironsi's successor, Lt-Colonel Gowon, released Awolowo and got all the credit. No one realised that Awolowo's release had already been approved by Aguiyi-Ironsi.

Abubakar was off to a good start. However, one big problem remained: Abiola.

14

DIVINE INTERVENTION

'You and your entire family will always be considered by me and my whole family as friends, brothers and sisters. As I assured your late husband ... despite all he has done and will probably continue to do, I could never hate him. In my heart, my love for him never diminished because I know that Satan ... was the cause of the schism.'

Moshood Abiola

Even without Abacha, Nigeria remained in a terrible position. Abacha's rule had amplified Nigeria's internal sectarian cleavages and conflicts, increased intra-military tension, and created an internal siege mentality within Nigeria. Additionally, Nigeria was internationally isolated, treated as a pariah, and was mired in debt.

Yet Abacha's death provided an opportunity for Nigeria's frozen relations with the rest of the world to thaw. Military regimes and democratisation were on the international community's agenda. British Prime Minister Tony Blair spoke with Abubakar on June 24, reopened diplomatic contacts between Nigeria and the EU, and agreed to send his minister of state for Africa and human rights, Tony Lloyd, to meet Abubakar on June 26. Lloyd's visit was the first by a British minister to Nigeria for two years. The US also agreed to send senior diplomats to Nigeria.

Nigeria needed all the help it could get to extricate itself from the mess it was in. The message from foreign dignitaries was identical and repetitive: Abubakar should release Abiola, organise new elections, and hand over power to a democratically elected civilian government as soon as possible. With

Obasanjo and other detainees being freed, and exiles returning home, there seemed little justification for Abiola's continued detention. Even Babangida was critical. He said: 'I would not have jailed Chief Abiola ... I used to joke that if Abiola had come to me when I was in power and said, "I am the president", I would have said, "Sure but I am the head of state." ... Jailing Abiola was a bad move by Abacha.'[1]

Abubakar certainly wanted to release Abiola, but faced a problem. If after being released Abiola continued to insist on becoming president, he could destabilise the country and intensify animosity against the military. Additionally, those who had annulled Abiola's election victory and approved his arrest and detention were still in the military and the government. An Abiola presidency would provide an opportunity for Abiola to get his revenge. No right-thinking military officer would give Abiola a free pass into the presidential villa.

Local and international diplomats tried to find a way to get Abiola out of detention but away from the presidential villa. The UN secretary-general, Kofi Annan, met the minister of foreign affairs, Tom Ikimi, on June 22, 1998 in Annan's living room in New York. Annan agreed to support Abubakar's political transition programme if Abubakar released Abiola. Ikimi and the Nigerian government were so encouraged by Annan's potential support that they invited him to Nigeria on June 29 on board a plane provided by the Nigerian government. Nigeria was so high on the UN's agenda that Annan made an unscheduled four-day trip to Nigeria to meet Abubakar and Abiola. Annan and Abubakar had previously met briefly in January 1997 in Lomé, Togo, during a peace summit. On that first meeting, Annan observed that Abubakar had also served as a member of the UN peacekeeping force in Lebanon and he used their shared involvement in peacekeeping to break the ice with Abubakar. Annan had found Abubakar to be 'reasonable in his outlook and straight speaking, in contrast to the quiet, strange character of Abacha'.[2] When Annan met Abubakar again in 1998, he urged him to release Abiola. Abubakar agreed on condition that Abiola would withdraw his claim to the presidency.

Meanwhile, the detained and secluded Abiola was totally unaware of unfolding events or of the fuss that he was causing outside. He had not been allowed to see any member of his family for 32 months, since November 3, 1995. Abiola had been detained at a very inconspicuous house in the Kado housing estate in Abuja. To avoid attracting attention, the house had only a few guards at the gates. Abiola was kept in a room upstairs, with his exercise equipment downstairs. Apart from his doctor, Ore Falomo, Abiola rarely had guests. Despite his bleak situation he was usually jovial and often spoke to, and joked with, his guards. One of Abiola's police guards was assistant superintendent of police Theodore Bethnel Zadok. After Abacha's death, Abiola's detention conditions were eased. Abiola's guards moved him to Gado Nasko Barracks in Abuja. As local and international dignitaries began to make their way to see Abiola, they again moved him to the guest house of the secretary to the government, inside the complex in which the presidential villa is located.

'Two heads are better than one'

Abiola did not know why he was being moved until Sunday June 28 when the chief of army staff, Major-General Bamaiyi, and chief of air staff, Air Marshal Nsikak Eduok, met him at Aguda House, the official residence of the vice-president, inside the presidential compound. After exchanging pleasantries, Bamaiyi and Eduok informed Abiola that Abacha had died twenty days earlier.

Abiola contemplated the news in silence for several moments, then said a prayer for Abacha's soul. He then wrote a condolence letter to Abacha's widow Maryam, and forwarded it to Abubakar for review and approval before sending it. In the letter Abiola described Abacha as a 'friend and brother', and assured Maryam that:

> you and your entire family will always be considered by me and my whole family as friends, brothers and sisters. As I assured your late husband ... despite all he has done and will probably continue to do, I could never hate him. In my heart, my love for him never diminished because I know that Satan ... was the cause of the schism.

Abiola had in the past also written condolence letters to the Abachas from detention; when Abacha's sister died in November 1994, and when his son Ibrahim died in January 1996.

'What was Shehu doing in jail?'

Bamaiyi and Eduok also gave more shocking news to Abiola. They told him that his friend and former business partner, Yar'Adua, had died six months earlier. Abiola was stunned by the news, and repeatedly asked himself, 'What was Shehu doing in jail?' He also drafted a condolence letter to Yar'Adua's widow Binta.

The relaxation of Abiola's detention restrictions reinvigorated him. Over the next few days he wrote more letters to several other people including Abubakar, Akhigbe, Eduok and Bamaiyi. Although the letters' authenticity has not been confirmed or denied by the Abiola family, there is very strong evidence that they are genuine. Magazines published the letters verbatim, and Bamaiyi corroborated the authenticity of the letter that Abiola wrote to him.[3] Bamaiyi's autobiography published the letter in full and its text matches the verbatim text of the corresponding letter published by the magazines.[4]

Solitary confinement had not broken Abiola's spirit or dulled his senses. Despite his deprivations during the previous five years—winning a presidential election only to have the result voided, being threatened, arrested, detained, and taken to court, being prevented from seeing his family, having his wife murdered and his businesses closed—he remained defiant. Abiola was a proud man and he still retained his sense of self-importance. The following interactions demonstrated that he had not been cowed and still had immense self-respect, clarity of mind, and resolve.

'What happened to the Egyptian?'

While the US, UK, EU and UN continually urged an end to military rule, and a rapid transition to a democratically elected civilian government, they stopped short of insisting that the civilian government had to be led by Abiola.

On Tuesday, June 30 1998, Annan finally met with Abiola. Annan briefed Abiola on the efforts he had made to secure his release. Abiola thanked Annan. Annan's grey peppercorn beard, baritone voice and full head of white hair made him one of the most instantly recognisable people on the planet. However, after speaking to Abiola for thirty minutes, Annan was astonished when Abiola suddenly asked him, 'Who are you?' Abiola later recalled, 'For the first 30 minutes, I did not know who I was talking to.' When the embarrassed Annan identified himself as the UN secretary-general, Abiola asked, 'What happened to the Egyptian?'—a reference to Annan's predecessor, Dr Boutros Boutros-Ghali. During his detention Abiola had not been allowed to watch television or read newspapers, and was permitted to read only the Bible and the Koran. As a result he was not aware that a new UN secretary-general had been appointed eighteen months previously. Annan awkwardly informed Abiola that he had replaced Boutros-Ghali. For some strange reason, Abiola's captors had not thought it pertinent to inform him whom he was going to meet. They instead told him only that he was 'going to meet a very important man'. Although Annan observed that Abiola was alert and asked several questions, 'from the questions and the reactions it was obvious that his isolation—he was in solitary confinement—had been almost total'.[5]

During the meeting, Abiola laced the conversation, as was usual for him, with biblical and Koranic quotations. Annan informed Abiola that Abubakar had agreed to release him on condition that he withdrew his presidential claim. Annan explained to Abiola that no one in the international community would support his candidacy on the basis of a five-year-old mandate, since even had he been allowed to serve as president, his term of office would have expired.

After the meeting Annan claimed that 'Abiola said he would want to be released to get on with his life ... He told me, "I am not naïve enough to think I can come out and be president."'[6] Annan also added that Abiola 'was in very good health, he was alert. I found him in some ways more realistic than some of us outside.'[7] However, Abiola's prison notes indicate that he refused to give up his mandate. The most he was willing to offer was that he would not make a new declaration that he was president. Abiola said: 'I told him firmly that I can give no such an undertaking as requested because it will be worse than useless. My declaration was made in public at a mass rally at Epetedo, Lagos, before thousands of people despite the heavy downpour of that evening. It was made in clear terms, without any ambiguity.'[8]

Meeting with Commonwealth Secretary-General Emeka Anyaoku

The Commonwealth secretary-general, Emeka Anyaoku, held a similar meeting with Abiola, which Rear-Admiral Akhigbe also attended. Ironically the meeting between the compatriots was less successful than Abiola's meeting with the Ghanaian UN secretary-general. Anyaoku told Abiola that he had obtained legal advice indicating that his five-year-old mandate was no longer enforceable. Abiola rhetorically asked Anyaoku which country had ever solved its political problems through legal advice. When Anyaoku mentioned that he had met other prominent personalities like Shonekan, Abiola contemptuously added that such 'big men' did not have the support of the Nigerian masses and that Shonekan was so uncharismatic that he was incapable of winning a ward councillor election in his own Abeokuta Local Government Area. Abiola found the discussion with Anyaoku to be 'very narrow and unreal' and again refused to give a categorical commitment that he would stop claiming to be the rightful president.

By allowing Abiola to meet with diplomats, the government was trying either to show goodwill to Abiola or to use powerful figures to pressure him into retiring from politics. If the latter was their objective, then it was akin to a hostage negotiation with the hostage negotiating on his own behalf. Abiola himself concluded that even if he had agreed while in detention to refrain from claiming the presidency, once he was released such an agreement 'could not have a binding effect as it would be construed as given under duress to expedite my release from the iniquitous detention'.[9]

Nonetheless, after these meetings the government assured diplomats that Abiola's release was 'imminent'. After spending 1,473 days in detention, Abiola was finally on the verge of regaining his freedom. Rumours of Abiola's release excited his supporters in the south-west. Some of them maintained a vigil at the international airport in Lagos, and his family also expected his release at any point.

Sunday July 6 1998

Abiola's access to visitors improved in advance of his anticipated release. Abubakar also allowed two of Abiola's wives, Doyin and Adebisi, and his oldest daughter, Mrs Lola Edewor,[10] to visit him at Akinola Aguda House in Abuja on July 6, 1998. They met around 10.45 pm and stayed with him until around 1.30 the following morning. Doyin said, 'He was full of life ... chatting with his humour. He was delighted to see us.'[11] However, several things about Abiola's physical condition alarmed his visitors. He revealed that he had been suffering from bouts of malaria and diarrhoea for the previous six months, and he was limping after injuring his leg after a fall in the bath. Abiola's family also noticed that he went to the bathroom on five separate occasions during the time they spent with him. However, Abiola's police guard Theodore Zadok gave a contrasting account and said that Abiola was in 'a sound and healthy condition'.[12]

Monday July 7 1998

After meeting Abiola, his wives and daughter went to the Nnamdi Azikiwe airport in Abuja to fly back to Lagos. Before being allowed to board, a security officer stopped them and told them to immediately return to the presidential villa. The women were optimistic and assumed that the government had brought Abiola's release date forward so he could return to Lagos with his family. They went back to the villa in a state of excitement and anticipation. When they arrived, they were met by officials who instantly rose to their feet to welcome them. They wondered why they were being accorded that sort of respect. Clearly something major had occurred or was about to occur.

Meeting with the Americans

A senior American diplomatic delegation including US under-secretary for political affairs, Thomas Pickering, assistant secretary of state for Africa, Susan Rice, and the Pentagon's deputy commander-in-chief of European Command, General James Jamerson, had arrived in Nigeria on July 6. They met with Abubakar, Ikimi, the minister of finance, Anthony Ani, and the minister of aviation, Air Commodore Ita Udo-Imeh, the following morning. The Americans urged Abubakar to release Abiola, and asked for permission to see him.

Abubakar called his chief security officer, Major Abdulrasheed Aliyu, and ordered him to bring Abiola to meet the Americans at Akinola Aguda House. Aliyu and Zadok picked Abiola up from his detention base shortly after 12.30 pm and took him to Aguda House. As well as guarding Abiola, Zadok also had the unenviable task of tasting all of Abiola's food and drink before he touched it. Zadok observed, 'Before we all left the base, Chief MKO Abiola was in sound and healthy condition. He did not complain to me of any illness.'[13] When they arrived at Aguda House, Zadok received a radio message from the security comptroller telling him to go to the office of the chief of general staff, Vice-Admiral Akhigbe. Zadok led Abiola inside Aguda House and then left to see Akhigbe as instructed.

The meeting between Abiola, Pickering, Rice and the US ambassador to Nigeria, William Twaddell, started shortly after 1 pm. Abiola appeared to be in good spirits and shared jokes with the Americans. He was wearing one of his trademark flowing white *agbadas*, which one person who saw him that day described as 'beautiful'.[14] When the Americans asked him about his health, he replied that he felt good apart from some swelling in his legs. He recognised Pickering, who had been the US ambassador to Nigeria between 1981 and 1983, and greeted him warmly. Pickering recalled that Abiola 'looked robust and in good health ... was big and seemed not to have lost any serious amount of weight'.[15]

As Abiola chatted with the Americans, a steward came in with refreshments. Pickering and Twaddell drank coffee, while Rice drank tea, which she also served to Abiola. Since Zadok was away, he was not present to taste Abiola's tea before it was served to him. As the guests took their drinks, Abiola started coughing and 'became incoherent'[16] as he talked. He asked to be excused to go to the bathroom. When he returned he remained in discomfort, and asked for cough medicine and painkillers. He then started having hot and cold flushes. At first he complained of being cold, so the air conditioner was switched off. As his temperature began to rise, he removed his shirt and asked for the room to be ventilated. The windows were opened at his behest. The American delegation was surprised and realised that 'there was something truly wrong'[17] with Abiola when he (a Muslim) removed his shirt in the presence of a woman (Susan Rice) to whom he was not related. Abiola felt so unwell that he lay down on the ground, and Susan Rice asked for a physician to be called.

Major Aliyu called the Aso Rock doctor, Dr Wali, who arrived less than ten minutes later. For the second time in one month Dr Wali was summoned to the presidential villa to save the life of a severely ill VIP politician. Wali knew Abiola well. As well as being his patient, Abiola had also been a good friend of his since they met in the late 1960s at the Lagos University Teaching Hospital. Shortly afterwards, Zadok returned from his meeting with Akhigbe and was shocked to find Abiola ill and lying on the floor.

After examining Abiola, Dr Wali insisted that Abiola should be taken to hospital immediately. The medical team called and alerted the presidential clinic to get ready to receive an emergency patient. Given Abiola's rapidly deteriorating condition, Dr Wali did not want to wait for an ambulance. Instead they improvised, and Pickering and Twaddell helped Wali, Aliyu and Zadok to lift Abiola into Zadok's Peugeot which was parked outside. The medical and security teams then drove Abiola to the clinic inside the presidential compound, while the American diplomats followed them.

Wali performed cardiac massage on Abiola inside the car on the way to the clinic He observed that Abiola started to foam at the mouth, and displayed similar symptoms to those he saw in Abacha just before he died a month earlier.[18] The doctors took Abiola inside the clinic's emergency room and worked on Abiola while the Americans watched through a glass window.

Major Aliyu used his mobile phone to call and update Abubakar on what was happening. Abubakar was very worried by the news that Abiola had fallen ill, and asked Aliyu to contact Babagana Kingibe to bring Abiola's family to the clinic so they could witness the efforts being made to save his life. Akhigbe also came to the clinic but left without being allowed to see Abiola. The doctors worked on Abiola for an hour and a half, but to no avail. On the day that the official thirty days of mourning for Abacha expired, Abiola, too, died between 4.30 and 5 pm on July 7 1998. For the second time in one month, a Nigerian president (elect, on this occasion) had collapsed and died in the presidential compound.

'Oh my God! What can I tell his family?'

Dr Wali told State House officials to inform Abubakar and to announce Abiola's death immediately before the news leaked out. He also asked the American delegation to persuade the Nigerian government to conduct an autopsy on Abiola. From the hospital Major Aliyu phoned Abubakar again and informed him that Abiola had died. In response to the news Abubakar screamed, 'Oh my God! What can I tell his family?'[19]

Susan Rice offered to break the news to the family and to confirm the efforts that had been made to save his life. In the end, the unpleasant task of informing Abiola's family of his death was left to Dr Wali. By this time Abiola's senior wives, Doyin and Adebisi, and daughter Lola had returned to the presidential villa and were ushered into an inner room where Pickering, Rice, Akhigbe and Dr Wali were waiting for them.

'You have killed my father!'

Dr Wali spoke first and told the women that Abiola had developed chest pains. Lola interrupted him and shouted, 'Is he dead?' Dr Wali grimly replied 'yes'. Grief and hysteria filled the room. Lola kept screaming, 'You have killed my father! You have killed my father!' Adebisi slumped to the floor and wept, while Doyin charged at Akhigbe and was restrained by guards after trying to tear at his clothing. Pickering, Rice, Akhigbe and Wali tried to restrain and console them, but to no avail. Abiola's wives and daughter were adamant that the ubiquitous 'they' had killed Abiola. Pickering, Twaddell and Rice extended their stay and Abubakar asked them to speak to Abiola's family, who remained unconvinced by their denials of American involvement in his death. Conspiracy theories about alleged international complicity were given credence by the fact that he had died shortly after he refused to give in to demands by international diplomats to renounce his presidential mandate as a condition of his release. Abiola's US-based daughter Hafsat was adamant that her father was either assassinated or died from medical neglect.[20] She said, 'It was too convenient. All of a sudden at the eve of his release, he dies.'[21]

'A national tragedy'

Abubakar was shaken. Abiola's death was a baptism of fire for him only one month after he had become head of state. Abubakar later arrived looking 'really disturbed'[22] and spoke to Abiola's family, who demanded to see the corpse and for a team of international medical staff to conduct an autopsy on him. Abubakar took them to Aguda House, and showed them the room where Abiola collapsed. The teacups from his meeting with the Americans were still in the room.

Abubakar announced Abiola's death to the nation in a tense televised broadcast during which he described his passing 'on the brink of his release from detention' as a 'national tragedy'. Abubakar sounded like a man in distress when he admitted, 'I never envisaged that I will be faced with such momentous tragedies within the space of one month.' He became so worried by the danger, tension and deaths in the presidential villa that he sent some of his personal staff abroad for their own safety. Abubakar later telephoned a shocked Obasanjo to inform him that 'our man has died'.[23] He also dispatched Bamaiyi to lead a government delegation to visit and condole with the rest of Abiola's family in Lagos.

'We have to get the Hausas'

Reaction to Abiola's death in the south-west was swift and violent. Angry mobs took to the streets, lit bonfires, and accused the military government of murdering Abiola. Protesters set a market in Lagos ablaze, and clashed with police. Police fired tear gas to disperse rioters. Fifty-five people were killed and more than 400 were arrested during the rioting. Anti-northern and anti-Hausa sentiment among Yorubas ran high. A protester, Adaoye Phillips, said, 'We have to get the Hausas. They were made powerful by the white man, they run the military, they keep us from getting jobs, they killed Abiola, they have destroyed our country.'[24] Yoruba protesters attacked northern traders in Lagos during the rioting. A northern petty trader in Lagos, Ibrahim Abdullahi, whose shop was set on fire by Yoruba protesters, said, 'Kai, Yoruba people are wicked. I will go back to my state even to do less profitable business. No one can tell when these problems will end.'[25] The US issued its customary travel warning for its citizens to avoid all unnecessary travel to Nigeria.

Radio phone-in programmes conducted lively debates and interviews with opposition figures, and repeated tributes to Abiola. The chaos and defiant dissent, under a military dictatorship, was typical of the contradictions of

Nigeria. An article in the *Mail & Guardian* two days after Abiola died magnificently juxtaposed the contrasting narratives of Nigeria.[26] Reading or hearing the dissent in the print and broadcast media would convince any reader or listener that they lived in a lively democracy. But the deserted roads of Lagos would also make them think they were living in a Cold War-era autocracy. At the same time, the angry youths and area boys who patrolled the quiet streets wearing bright-coloured American branded clothing would make one feel as if one were in the midst of an inner-city gang war in the US.

Abubakar allowed an international team of doctors from Canada, the UK, US and Nigeria to conduct and witness Abiola's autopsy. The lead pathologist for the autopsy was the Canadian Dr James Young, who trained at the same medical school as Dr Wali. Young was an esteemed pathologist who served as the chief coroner of the Canadian province of Ontario. His extensive experience later included identifying victims of the '9/11' 2001 terrorist attacks in the US, and the 2002 terrorist bombings in the Indonesian island of Bali that killed over 200 people. The British doctor was Richard Shepherd, a leading forensic pathologist, and lecturer in forensic medicine at St George's Hospital in London. Shepherd had conducted or participated in several high-profile autopsies, including those of Princess Diana, the black teenager Stephen Lawrence who was stabbed to death by a racist gang in 1993, and sixteen young children who were killed by a gunman in the 'Hungerford massacre' in 1987.[27]

Dr Wali nominated two senior Nigerian pathologists from the north and south to represent the Nigerian Medical Association: respectively, Dr Abdulmumini Rafindadi of Ahmadu Bello University, and Dr Edward Attah, a fellow of the Royal College of Physicians of Canada, former provost of the College of Medical Sciences of the University of Calabar, and an Ibibio from Akwa-Ibom State. Wali himself represented the federal government. The government also allowed Abiola's personal doctor, Ore Falomo, and Abiola's son Kola (who had not seen his father since November 3, 1995) to attend the autopsy. Prior to Abiola's death, Falomo had not been allowed to see his patient for over a year. Security agents had limited Falomo's access to Abiola after suspecting that he leaked details of where Abiola was being detained.

The government wanted the autopsy to be conducted in Abuja, but Falomo insisted that it should be done in Lagos in the south-west, right at the door of Yorubaland. Given the tense situation in the country and the assumption in the south-west that Abiola had been assassinated, Falomo's proposal presented the government with a headache. If the government put its foot down and insisted on Abuja as the autopsy venue, they could have further antagonised Abiola's family, and the south-west by extension.

Eventually the government agreed to permit the autopsy to be conducted in Lagos, with secrecy akin to a military operation. The commissioner of police in Abuja informed the Nigerian doctors of their appointment. Given the incendiary atmosphere in the south-west, Abiola's body was kept in an Abuja mortuary. To avoid detection, the body was flown from Abuja late at night and taken straight to the hospital at the British High Commission in Lagos after midnight. These plans were so secret that only the military governor of Lagos State, Colonel Marwa, was informed of them.

'The examination was detailed and painstaking'

The autopsy team landed in Abuja on July 10 and travelled to Lagos in secret after midnight to avoid attracting attention. They were taken to a military facility before being brought to the autopsy venue. The autopsy commenced at 2 am in a medical facility that one of the participating doctors described as 'first rate'.[28] The same doctor said: 'The examination was detailed and painstaking.'[29] The coroners ostentatiously showed all normal and abnormal findings and tissues to those present, and recorded them as such in writing. The coroners also extracted fluid and tissue samples from Abiola's body and sent them to a forensic laboratory in Ontario, Canada, for toxicology tests.

The coroners found that 'evidence of serious and death-causing hypertensive and coronary artery diseases affecting the heart was obvious'. Abiola's arteries had narrowed, and his heart was thickened and enlarged.[30] All these were signs of heart disease and risk factors for a heart attack. Abiola also had a prior medical history of high blood pressure and diabetes. He also slept very little (sometimes only two or three hours per day) and had been confined in a room for several years without much mobility or chance for exercise outside.

After the autopsy was concluded, the team prepared to depart for the American Embassy, where they would discuss and review their findings. However, given that conspiracy theories about alleged American complicity in Abiola's death were already circulating, the president of the Nigerian Medical Association, Dr George Okpagu, intervened and suggested an alternative venue. Accordingly, the Nigerian doctors successfully insisted that the meeting should be relocated to a conference hall inside the building where the autopsy was conducted.

The autopsy team released their preliminary findings in July 1998 and concluded, 'In our opinion the mechanism of death is due to a rapid deterioration in a diseased heart. Our preliminary opinion is that death was due to natural causes as a result of his long-standing heart disease.'[31] On August 12, 1998, Dr Young addressed a press conference in the Canadian capital of Ottawa to give the final autopsy result. The conclusion was that Abiola had severe heart disease and listed a heart attack as the official cause of death. The toxicology report showed no foreign agents in his body other than anti-malaria drugs.

'Did you people see how them wicked us?'

On Saturday July 11 1998 more than twenty thousand mourners gathered in front of Abiola's compound in Lagos for his funeral, which had been delayed by the autopsy. Although Abiola's family wanted a solemn burial, the atmosphere resembled more a protest than a funeral. The compound was a boiling cauldron of noise, songs, wailing, raw emotion, and teeming humanity. Anger and bitterness flowed from the compound towards his presumed killers and the Nigerian state. Islamic incantations blared out from loudspeakers as an armoured personnel carrier and police officers stood guard at the compound's gate, while a police helicopter buzzed overhead in the sky. Several hundred students still managed to surge past the security and get into the compound, demanding that they too should be allowed to attend the funeral because Abiola 'does not belong only to the family. He also belongs to the people.' The mood turned near-riotous as they carried banners with 'Oduduwa' printed on them and chanted, 'Did you see how they suffer us? Did you people see how them wicked us?' Some departed only after members of Abiola's family appeared on the balcony and used microphones and megaphones to shout over the noise of the crowd and appeal for them to leave.

'Concubine!'

Abiola's senior surviving wife, Adebisi, sat on a red sofa inside their lavishly furnished home, as mourners approached and knelt out of respect to her. Another wife, Dupe, declared: 'The Bible says "each unto his own tent, O Israel", and that is how Nigeria will develop now that the regime has killed my husband. He was the essence of Nigerian unity. Now each tribe must have its own nation.'[32] Dupe managed to get in a few words before she was pressed out of the mourning area by supporters of another wife who shouted 'get out' and threw contemptuous taunts of 'Concubine!' at her. Her treatment was symptomatic of the sharp divides in Abiola's family. A scuffle broke out between rival factions of the family when some of Abiola's wives tried to sit in an area that had been reserved for his two senior wives, Adebisi and Doyin.

Abiola's body was wrapped in a white cloth, and laid on a red carpet inside his house while an imam recited Islamic prayers over the body. The crowd went wild when the body was brought out in a white coffin with gold trim to be lowered into the ground. They surged towards the grave to get one last look. The pallbearers almost had to fight their way through the crowd, which chanted angry slogans and kicked earth into the grave as the coffin was lowered into the ground. Abiola was buried underneath a tree in his compound, beside his beloved first wife, Simbiat, who died in London in 1992 after battling cancer.[33] This was the third funeral at Abiola's compound in six years. Two of Abiola's wives had already been buried in the compound: Kudirat in 1996 and Simbiat.

We will never know how Nigeria would have fared under an Abiola presidency. A reasonable perspective is that an Abiola presidency might have been very messy. Opposition to him in the army was intense. Various senior officers had vowed that 'Abiola will be President over my dead body', and that they would rather spill blood than allow Abiola to become president. Former head of state Babangida surmised that Abiola would have been a 'lousy president' and 'would not have lasted six months ... The military would have toppled him.'[34]

Abiola did not win the June 12, 1993 election because he was an anti-military firebrand. He did after all make his fortune in deals with the same military officers that voided his election victory and later detained him. He won the election and was adopted as an unlikely symbol of democracy by a public that was battered and exhausted after three decades of military rule and desperate to rid Nigeria of increasingly corrupt and authoritarian rule by any means. To the public, any candidate was better than the military.

Abiola had many weaknesses, which might have proved toxic had he become president. His first and foremost weakness was for female company. His appetite for women was such that not even his own family knew exactly how many wives and children he had. Educated estimates put the number of his wives and concubines somewhere between 25 and 40, and children anywhere between 60 and 120. An incident during a party for his 50th birthday illustrated some of the complications of his personal life. A young woman approached him while he was making a speech. In response to something the woman said to him he replied, 'No. I do not agree that the matter should be kept private.' He then turned to the stunned audience and told them, 'This lady says I am the father of her baby.' He asked the woman, 'Can you tell the audience where I slept with you?'[35] Perhaps Abiola was vulnerable to such accusations because rumours said that he deposited a million naira into a bank account for every child born to him. His doctor, Ore Falomo, claimed that some of his wives had children that were not biologically fathered by him:

> there are a lot of people Chief looks after who are not his children. Some of the children here are not even his ... Some women had children already before they got married to Chief, but they are bearing his name ... Chief has already let them bear his name.'[36]

Such a complicated personal life could have proved embarrassing and destabilising for a president in the public eye and would probably have occupied several column inches in gleeful tabloids.

Abiola also made serious tactical mistakes. He often sought alliances with those he should have shunned, and alienated those with whom he should have created alliances. The causal chain of events that led to the election annulment began with Abiola's choice of a vice-presidential running mate in May 1993. His party's political godfather, Shehu Musa Yar'Adua, wanted Abiola to choose Yar'Adua's protégé Atiku Abubakar as his running mate. Meanwhile, President Babangida warned Abiola to 'forget about the presidency' if he did not select labour union leader Paschal Bafyau as his vice-president. Abiola had the daunting task of choosing whom to offend: the president or his party's godfather. He ended up simultaneously offending the most powerful man in the country and the most powerful man in his party, when he selected the former intelligence officer Babagana Kingibe, who was not endorsed by either of them. An enraged Yar'Adua admitted, 'I wasn't going to have anything to do with Abiola after that, and I didn't hide it.'[37]

In the end the military leviathan that Abiola sponsored and supported turned on him and devoured him. Abacha and Abiola had three identical weaknesses: money, women and their (physical) hearts. Those three weaknesses combined to seal the fate of both men. The Abacha versus Abiola power struggle had held the entire country hostage for five years. Their deaths removed from the political scene the two key protagonists whose jostling for power had paralysed Nigerian politics for half a decade. Both men placed Nigeria in an inescapable political maze, with Abacha at one end and Abiola's status as the 'linear' undeclared president at the other end. Each man presented a different complicating factor. Abacha's desire to remain in power held democracy at bay, and Abiola's unrealised mandate meant that no other civilian could be a credible president so long as Abiola lived.

The manner in which both of them miraculously, suddenly and conveniently disappeared from the scene tied up all loose ends of the political crisis. With both of them out of the way Nigeria could finally make a fresh start and move on from the Abacha–Abiola logjam. The outcome was so miraculously convenient that Nigerians dubbed it 'divine intervention'. However, there are those who ascribe their death to sinister forces. Al-Mustapha bluntly declared that 'their deaths were organised, pure and simple!'[38]

'Only God can save this nation'

Abiola's death also posed another serious problem. If the military held elections and a northerner won, Yorubas would continue to feel cheated. Yoruba animosity against the north had become so intense that they would never accept a president other than a Yoruba—not even another southerner. The Abuja-based lawyer Olugenga Oku-Samuel said: 'The geographical expression called Nigeria has now reached a dead end with the death of Abiola. Only God can save this nation.'[39]

15

NIGERIA INC.

Perhaps no question in Nigeria makes its people disagree as much as that of the country's existence. There is no compelling emotional or ideological rationale for the country to exist. It came into being simply because a former British government desired it. It did not fight a war of national liberation like America, its citizens do not have a deep emotional or theological attachment to their country like Israel, nor is it united by a common language (like France) or religion (like Saudi Arabia). It is therefore perhaps unsurprising that existential questions about Nigeria are still being asked over a hundred years after the country's creation. Nigerians have constantly had to deal with the imposed reality of their country's existence and simultaneously debate and frame the parameters of that existence. All three regions of the country representing the three largest ethnic groups have advocated secession, threatened it or attempted it.

Military rule did not generate the controversies about Nigerian unity but certainly intensified them. In each region of the country military rule accumulated various ethnic, geographic and religious grievances, against other regions and against the Nigerian state. Southern animosity against the north increased during Abacha's rule: the south was demanding not just an end to military rule, but also a reconsideration of Nigerian unity.

The View from the Centre

Whether or not Nigerians admit it, the fate of their country is usually interwoven with the fate of its army. A united army usually means a united Nigeria.

The military has invested in Nigerian unity more than any other institution. It is no coincidence that Nigeria's civil war was preceded by the worst bout of intra-army violence in the country's history.

Perhaps no event has shaped national political thought and development as much as the civil war. The relief that greeted the end of the civil war in 1970, and the remarkably rapid military reconciliation following it, were mirrored in civil society. Fidelity to Nigerian unity ironically reached its zenith shortly after the civil war during which one region of the country seceded, a second region threatened to secede, a third sat on the fence, and only one of the four regions was firmly committed to national unity. After the war two forces coalesced to stitch the bonds of Nigerian unity more tightly together. The first force was money. The presence of large reserves of crude oil in the deep south created an economic incentive for Nigerian unity that placed advocates of Nigerian dissolution in the minority. Nigeria's earnings from crude oil exports increased by over 500% between 1970 and 1974. All regions were united in their desire to access the huge sums of money derived from crude oil exports during the 'oil boom' years of the 1970s. Military governments empowered the federal government as the repository of oil revenues and the distributor of those revenues to the states. The second force for unity was the military. The military's victory in the civil war, and the preservation of the Nigerian union, gave it legitimacy as a force for national unity.

After the war concluded in 1970, the federal leader, Major-General Gowon, insisted that Igbos should be treated as prodigal sons rather than defeated foes. Gowon declared a general amnesty for all combatants on both sides, and spoke in a Lincolnesque manner of 'healing the nation's wounds'. He also vowed that there would be 'no victor, no vanquished', and allowed some members of the defeated Biafran army to rejoin the federal army at the ranks they held before the war, declined to conduct war crimes trials, and refused to award medals to his own soldiers who fought the war. Commenting on the reconciliation that followed the war, the British journalist John de St Jorre observed that 'when history takes a longer view of Nigeria's war it will be shown that while the black man has little to teach us about making war he has a real contribution to offer in making peace'.[1/2]

The Four Commandments

Fresh from its victory in the civil war, the army first remoulded its broken officer corps, then set out to do the same to its country. Thereafter the military acted as an architect of national unity. Seven of Nigeria's eight military heads of state fought in the civil war, and so did most of the generals who became members of military governments over the next three decades. This civil war cadre saw themselves as guardians of Nigeria's unity. They acted as the board of directors of Nigeria Inc. Gowon, Obasanjo, Buhari, Babangida, Danjuma, Yar'Adua, Wushishi, Gusau—every time the Nigerian ship sailed into stormy waters, these civil war generals always seemed to be on hand to steer the ship back to port. They had a strong conviction of Nigerian unity and a particular vision of how the country should be structured. Since there was no emotional reason for Nigerian unity, the military imposed a manu-factured militarised brand of unity not based on consent or emotive reasons. They also implemented four measures that are akin to the Four Commandments of Nigerian unity. These were military federalism, multipli-cation of states, federal character, and uncompromising commitment to the corporate existence of the country.

The Federation

In its constitution and official documents, Nigeria is referred to as 'the federa-tion'. The country's statute books are referred to as 'Laws of the Federation'. Nigeria is the world's fifth-largest federation, after India, the US, Brazil and Russia. However it is a strange federation. It is not like the US whose states voluntarily formed a binding union and grew by the acquisition of additional states. In contrast, Nigeria's territorial evolution followed a path of territorial consolidation, then fragmentation into smaller and smaller territorial units during its century-long existence.

The land that would later become Nigeria originally had three territorial units: the Colony of Lagos, and the Protectorates of Northern and Southern Nigeria. British colonial authorities merged the colony of Lagos into the southern protectorate in 1906. They then merged the southern and northern protectorates to form Nigeria in 1914, then split the southern protectorate into the Western and Eastern Regions in 1939. The federal government increased the number of regions to four in 1963 when it created the Mid-Western Region from the Western Region.

Less than eighteen months after the military seized power, it rapidly increased the number of states to 12 in 1967. It further increased the number to 19 in 1975, 21 in 1987, 30 in 1991, and finally 36 in 1996. There was noth-ing unique about any of the states that the military created. The states were, and remain, 36 smaller replicas of the federal government. The constant multiplication of states has led one scholar to describe Nigeria as 'a biological cell which sub-divides and sub-divides again, creating more and more replicas of itself'.[3] In other federations substantial powers are usually delegated to regional governments, which enjoy substantial autonomy to manage their affairs independent of the federal government. In contrast, Nigeria's military governments implemented a peculiar version of federalism that strengthened the powers of the federal government and weakened those of the states. Instead of being conduits for the transmission of regional interests to the federal government, states became mere outlets for the implementation of federal policies in local areas, and pipelines for the distribution of money from the federal government to state level.

Federal military governments acquired for themselves the right to appoint and dismiss a state's governor at will, and to create, abolish and adjust the boundaries of any state in the country—even without the state's consent. Federal authorities could also declare a state of emergency in any state whether or not it consented. State power became emasculated and reduced to a simple 'power' to implement minor variations to delegated federal policies. Babangida's deputy and vice-president, Admiral Augustus Aikhomu, admitted: 'Federal measures tended to detract from the independence and autonomy of states even in areas where state and federal governments had concurrent powers. States tended to lose their distinct identities ... These developments lent strength to the impression of a unitary state of Nigeria instead of a federated union.'[4]

Two Words

Perhaps the most fundamental military contribution to Nigeria's unity can be encapsulated in two words. When the head of state General Murtala Muhammed inaugurated the Constitution Drafting Committee (CDC) in 1975, he expressed his government's desire to introduce a new political system that would ensure that future governments would 'reflect the federal character of the country'. Little did he know that his casual use of the phrase 'federal character' would set in motion a domino effect that would give birth to 'one of the largest affirmative action programs in the world'.[5] Federal character has been interpreted and implemented to mean that all states in the federation must have equal quota representation in state agencies, such as the government, civil service, military, police, and even universities and schools.

However, the multiple ethno-regional controversies of the years of military rule dissipated the tentative post-war consensus on national unity. The military innovations of national unity came under attack. Although the military's accumulation of powers for the central (federal) government had fulfilled its basic purpose of preventing the country from breaking apart, it also caused disunity and instability by generating intense life-or-death competition for control of the centre. Instead of demands to reinforce Nigeria's bonds of unity, the regions made new demands to loosen those bonds and accommodate regional interests. Even the innovation of federal character was not spared. Predictably the states with fewer educationally and professionally qualified people defended federal character, while states with too many educationally and professionally qualified people for the civil service criticised it for sacrificing merit and for elevating the mediocre for the sake of ethnic diversity. Predictably, that disagreement about the utility of federal character was divided on a north-south basis. Federal character's most severe critics claimed it created a situation in which 'the public service became a dumping ground for incompetent, ill-motivated servants from different parts of the country'.[6]

Military governments continued preaching the post-civil war gospel of national unity long after they needed to. After the 1970s the political conversation had turned away from whether the country should remain united, to a consideration of the form of unity under which the country should exist. Yet military governments continued to cling uncompromisingly to the indivisibility of the country as an article of faith, without addressing the shades of grey that had emerged around the issue of national unity. Military governments had always presented themselves as 'corrective' doctors administering therapeutic political medicine to Nigeria. However, by the 1990s the military doctor was still providing treatment to the civilian patient without the patient's consent, and also refused to discharge him.

The View from the South-west

By the time Abacha came to power in 1993, northern rulers had led Nigeria for 29 of Nigeria's 33 post-independence years. One of the two southern generals to rule in that time was assassinated by northern soldiers, and the other became head of state by default when the northern head of state was assassinated in 1976. No southerner had been head of state for nearly 15 years, and southerners complained bitterly about northern domination of the military and of politics. Yoruba grievances have been described in earlier chapters. The ethno-regional animosity caused by the annulment of the June 12, 1993 presidential election, and northern domination of the federal government, eroded Yoruba commitment to national unity. NADECO's leader, Abraham Adesanya, criticised 'the arrogant and reckless manner in which political power has for years been monopolised by a section of our country which is determined to hang on to power at all costs'.[7]

Yorubas had vacillated on the question of national unity during the prior four decades. In January 1954, during the constitutional conference leading to Nigeria's independence, the Action Group party perceived Nigeria as a contractual union that could be rescinded at will. It argued on behalf of the Western Region that the constitution should have a provision allowing any region of Nigeria to secede. During the crisis immediately preceding the civil war, Awolowo had threatened: 'If the Eastern Region is allowed by acts of omission or commission to secede from or opt out of Nigeria, then the Western Region and Lagos must also stay out of the Federation.'[8] Yet when the Eastern Region seceded, Yorubas supported the federal government and went into alliance with the north against the Eastern Region. That decision cost Yorubas valuable political capital in the Eastern Region.

The former chief of defence staff Lt-General Julius Akinrinade, a Yoruba, had been commander of the 6th Brigade during the civil war, and, as the general officer commanding 1 Mechanised Infantry Division in Kaduna in February 1976, he opposed a coup attempt to overthrow a northern Muslim head of state. Akinrinade joined NADECO, but was driven into exile and became a fugitive from the country he had once served. He had been called in for interrogation by the State Security Service, and his house was fire-bombed. He escaped from would-be assassins or captors by jumping over a wall. Akinrinade described the harassment he was subjected to as 'state terrorism'. Bristling at his treatment and the lack of support from Igbos, Akinrinade later said he regretted fighting against Igbos during the civil war.

In September 1997 Justice Akinola Aguda, a retired Yoruba judge who led the panel which recommended the relocation of Nigeria's federal capital from Lagos in the south to Abuja in the old Northern Region, expressed regret at the move. He said:

> Those of us who are still alive will continue to take the blame for recommending the relocation of the federal capital from Lagos to virgin land which we thought would be a blessing but has now turned out to be the tragedy of Abuja ... The whole concept of our unity and nationhood has been completely assassinated and buried.[9]

By the mid-1990s Yoruba political interests were being expressed at national level by two organisations: NADECO and Afenifere. These groups demanded four things: the release of Abiola, a government of national unity headed by Abiola, a sovereign national conference to deliberate on the country's future, and the restructuring of the Nigerian federation with a return to 'true federalism'. No one ever defined what true federalism meant, but it was generally presumed to be a synonym for devolution of power from the federal government to the regions, and for greater regional control and share of oil revenues. Abiola's death made things worse. Shortly after Abiola died, a 36-year-old Yoruba typewriter salesman named Yomi Segun said that Nigeria could only be run by three different governments, one for each of the Igbo, Yoruba and Hausa ethnic groups. He argued:

> We had a civil war about tribes and in those days we were with the Hausa ... nobody trusts politicians, nobody goes to vote. Even Abiola had dined with the military in his time. So all this talk of transition to democracy is a joke to us. Whose transition anyway? The military's? The rest of the world is playing their game by talking to the military who are all Hausas, or at least from the north. This is our problem and we need to sort it out. The Northerners are not our legitimate rulers.[10]

The View from the South-east

The Igbos are a paradox. They need Nigeria more than most of Nigeria's other ethnic groups. When other ethnic groups hesitated about maintaining a united Nigeria, they more than others championed the need to maintain the country's unity. Yet their loyalty to the Nigerian state is frequently doubted.

The January 15 1966 military coup, during which a group of young Igbo army majors overthrew the leaders of the northern-led government, transformed Igbos from national integrationists into national outcasts. Unfortunately for Igbos, the manner in which northerners were murdered during that coup coincided with, and reinforced, pre-existing northern stereotypes of Igbos as duplicitous and treacherous. The Igbo officer in charge of the prime minister's security, Major Okafor, was involved in the coup. An Igbo brigade major shot and killed the northern brigadier to whom he reported. Northern outrage at the murders was amplified by the fact that the killers attended a party with their victims on the night of the coup, then returned a few hours later to rouse their victims from sleep and shoot them in the middle of the night. Northerners interpreted the coup as an Igbo-led conspiracy to displace the northern-led government and impose 'Igbo domination' on Nigeria. Anti-

Igbo sentiment flared in the north, and northern mobs killed over thirty thousand Igbos in the north between May and October 1966. The Eastern Region was shocked as thousands of decapitated corpses and badly mutilated Igbo survivors arrived back from the north. Over a million Igbos fled the Northern Region and returned to their homeland in the Eastern Region in a rapid mass population transfer that stretched the Eastern Region to breaking point. A reporter who witnessed the carnage wrote:

> Nigerians have been sheltered from knowing the full magnitude of the disaster that has overtaken the Igbos in the northern region. The danger is that the truth will not be believed and so proper lessons learnt, once the horror is over. While the Hausas in each town and village in the north know what happened in their own localities, only the Igbos know the whole story ... hacked, slashed, mangled, stripped naked and robbed of all their possessions, the orphans, the widows, the traumatised. A woman, mute and dazed, arrived back in her village after travelling for five days with only a bowl in her lap. She held her child's head which was severed before her eyes. Another stepped off a refugee lorry, her face battered. By her side was a little boy, one of whose eyes had been gouged out, and her little girl who had severe scalp wounds. 'What', she kept on repeating, 'has happened to my baby?' It had been tied to her back before she was knocked to the ground. Men, women and children arrived with arms and legs broken, hands hacked off, mouths split open. Pregnant women were cut open and the unborn children killed ... after a fortnight, the scene in the eastern region continues to be reminiscent of the ingathering of exiles into Israel after the end of the last war. The parallel is not fanciful.[11]

These horrors eroded Igbo fidelity to Nigeria, and the Eastern Region seceded from Nigeria and declared itself a new independent country called the Republic of Biafra in 1967. The federal army forcibly reintegrated Igbos into Nigeria after the civil war. The extent and speed of reconciliation surprised even the Igbos.

After the war the word Biafra became taboo. The Bight of Biafra on Nigeria's southern Atlantic coast was renamed the Bight of Bonny. The Biafra light oil pumped from that area of the country was also named Bonny light. Given that more than 80% of Nigeria's population was born after the civil war, its memory became an intellectual curiosity rather than an immediate, pressing concern. The Igbos who fought the Biafran war are now dead, old, injured or too mentally scarred to fight a second war of independence. Yet Igbos continued to be viewed as potential separatists. Their stereotype as reluctant Nigerians is difficult to reconcile with their history. They were the ethnic group that most demonstrated national commitment in the pre-independence and early post-independence years. They and their leader, Nnamdi Azikiwe, were the first to develop a political party—the National Council of Nigerian Citizens—with pan-national ideals.

The small size as well as intense population density of the Igbo homeland in the south-east creates economic pressure for them to migrate to other parts of Nigeria. This perhaps explains why they are Nigeria's most prolific internal migrants. Millions of them reside across Nigeria in faraway cities outside the south-east such as Lagos, Abuja and even Kano in the far north despite the fact that they are frequently victims of pogroms or ethnic and other communal violence. Their frequent wandering to other parts of Nigeria evokes both admiration and irritation in equal measure from their host communities. The man who led the Biafran secession, Lt-Colonel Chukwuemeka Odumegwu-Ojukwu, said that Nigeria's problem was 'how to accommodate these Igbos who don't stay in their area but wander around everywhere. That is why it was easy to think that the answer was to kill them off and prevent them from ever coming back.'[12]

Defeat in the civil war and exclusion from Nigeria's economic and political elite generated a cynical self-reliance that led to Igbos becoming Nigeria's most well-known micro-entrepreneurs. While Muslim northerners dominated politics, westerners the judiciary, and middle-belters the military, Igbo traders can be found in every far-flung corner of Nigeria. They can also take credit for one of the most prominent developments in Nigerian video entertainment. Igbos from the town of Onitsha 'spawned a vibrant if somewhat bizarre film industry, with their torrid tales of witchcraft and romantic adventure becoming increasingly popular'.[13]

Yet a feeling of being betrayed by fellow southerners persisted long in Igbo memory. They never forgave the Yorubas or the minority ethnic groups of the Eastern Region for joining the northern-led federal army to fight against them instead of helping form a united southern front against the north. When the June 12, 1993 election was annulled, Igbos wanted nothing to do with the new national crisis. Many Igbos wept little when a military-appointed tribunal sentenced Ken Saro-Wiwa to death by hanging. They remembered that Saro-Wiwa had joined forces with the northern-led military that killed over a million Igbos. Igbos sat on the fence and watched the Yorubas' and south-east minorities' grievances with a stoic 'I told you so' *Schadenfreude*. To Igbos, the chickens had come home to roost, and it was poetic justice that the northern military establishment with whom Yorubas and minorities colluded to gang up against Igbos during the civil war, had now turned against them.

Yet Igbos also had other major concerns apart from settling old scores. They were chastened by their defeat and suffering during the civil war and were no longer the economically and politically dominant group they had been in the 1960s. Even though Igbos are among the three most populous ethnic groups in Nigeria, they spent four decades in the wilderness after their secessionist attempt was suppressed. Many Igbos feel that successive governments deliberately punished them for seceding by excluding them from Nigeria's economic and political mainstream. They can recite from memory historical injustices against them with ease. Igbo resentment about being cheated and excluded is so strong that I may receive protest petitions if I do not devote as much text in this book to their grievances as I do to those of Nigeria's other regions.

After the war many Igbos lost their life savings after the federal finance minister changed the currency, resulting in their money being rendered worthless. They were allowed to exchange up to a maximum of 20 Nigerian pounds of the new currency. The finance minister who spearheaded these measures was Obafemi Awolowo. In 1972 the government embarked upon an indigenisation programme to transfer foreign businesses to Nigerian ownership. Northerners and westerners with close links to the federal government and disposable cash bought in and got rich. The wealth of many prominent Nigerian generals and families originates from this indigenisation programme. Igbos had neither close links to the federal government nor disposable cash, and were still reeling from the poverty that descended on them after the war. Thus they were excluded from the indigenisation bonanza.

Military officers from south-eastern Nigeria made up two-thirds of the officer corps at independence in 1960. Seven years later the Igbo presence in the army had been almost totally eliminated by the combined forces of pogroms and the civil war. Although a few Igbo officers were reabsorbed at the end of the war, their pre-war ranks were frozen and they fell behind in seniority to their colleagues from other regions. Igbo officers were also distrusted, kept away from senior command positions, and regarded as a potential fifth column in the army. After the first coup in 1966, it took another 21 years for an Igbo officer to be appointed as a general officer commanding one of the army's divisions. Even then, the officer in question, Major-General Ike Nwachukwu,[14] was half Fulani. Six years after Nwachukwu's promotion, Abacha appointed the first Igbo military service chief in 27 years, Rear-Admiral Allison Madueke, who in 1993 became the first ever Igbo chief of naval staff, but fired him nine months later. Over thirty years after the war started, no Igbo had become president, minister of defence, inspector-general of police or chief of defence, army, naval or air staff, the traditional positions of influence in Nigeria. Ojukwu said that Nigeria confined Igbos 'in a glass cage beneath a glass ceiling'.[15]

Over thirty years after the first attempt at Igbo secession, separatist agitation returned to the south-east. Demographics played a role in Biafra's resurgence. Young Igbos born after the civil war became the most zealous advocates of Biafra. A middle-aged Igbo woman sarcastically remarked to me: 'even their mothers had not been born when Biafra was declared'. This younger generation absorbed bitterness from their grandparents' tales of suffering during the war but, having not personally experienced it, do not carry their ancestors' fear of a relapse into conflict and suffering. Yet not everyone shares the young generation's zeal for Biafra. A retired Igbo man drily told me, 'Don't mind them' (referring to the youths) and added that he did not support renewed calls for Biafra because he did not want to be associated with 'extremist' groups. The older Igbo generation does not want separation from Nigeria, but instead inclusion in its economic and political mainstream. Mature Igbos know that another Biafran secession would once again be disastrous for Igbos. For a new Biafran nation to succeed, it would likely have to become a heavily militarised Igbo state, with inchoate borders, and would be extremely vulnerable to external invasion and internal insurrection. It would either have to incorporate minority ethnic groups in south-east Nigeria by force or allow them to opt out. If it chooses the former option, it would be viewed as an occupying force, and if it chooses the latter, it would be landlocked and deprived of the great oil wealth that lies in the Niger Delta. A landlocked country surrounded by resentful neighbours, with no coastal access and no oil wealth, would be doomed to fail. This is what happened the previous time the Igbos tried secession.

'God should remove it from their mind'

A septuagenarian Igbo man who fought for Biafra during the civil war (and who was shot and left for dead before being rescued by the Red Cross) sighed heavily before telling me, 'They [Biafra supporters] have not thought this through ... One month is not enough time to describe everything that happened last time' when the south-east seceded. He concluded by emotionally telling me: 'If anyone even dreams of Biafra again, God should remove it from their mind.'

The View from the North

Northerners were thoroughly fed up with southerners blaming them for Nigeria's problems. Given their military and political leadership, northerners became a convenient southern scapegoat for Nigeria's problems. Southern grievances tended to get more air time because most of Nigeria's print news media is located in the south, and they incessantly repeated a mantra about northern political domination of Nigeria and its unwillingness to share power with the south. The north did not possess the range of media houses to respond in kind.

Contrary to southern perception of them as the biggest beneficiaries of Nigeria's existence, most northerners had gained little from their region's political leadership. From the northern perspective, Nigeria's wealth was concentrated in the south, while the north (which was more than twice as large as the south, and had a larger population as well) suffered from poverty and was threatened by encroaching desertification. Decades of northern-led governments had not improved living conditions in the north. Although an elite with contacts with the government, emirs and senior military officers flourished, the working-class northerners (so-called *Talakawa*) continued to suffer. The vast majority of the north's non-elite population were engaged in subsistence farming or low-level agriculture.

While the south resented political domination by the north, the north feared economic domination by the south. The economic and educational disparity between the north and south was (and remains) enormous. Three years before independence, nearly 90% of Nigerian secondary school students were southerners. At Independence in 1960, only 5% of Nigeria's secondary schools were located in the north. These educational disparities had tremendous effects on the north's economic potential and ability to produce a modern professional workforce that could compete with the south. Although many Muslim northerners were educated and literate in Arabic and Hausa thanks to Koranic education, jobs in the civil service and large corporations were given to those who attended English-language secondary schools and universities, not to those who were educated only in Koranic studies.

The former governor of Kaduna State, Balarabe Musa, said in 1994:

> The domination of political power by the north has not bridged the gap in development which exists between the north and south since independence in 1960 ... The gap between the north and the south in all aspects of development that concerns the masses of the people which existed in 1960 remains and has even widened in areas like education and health care.[16]

The geographic dispersal of economic and educational opportunities was starkly polarised. In 1993, the three southern states of Anambra, Delta and Edo had more students enrolled in universities than all 16 northern states combined. Less than 15% of lawyers called to the Nigerian Bar in that year were northerners. Over 80% of students enrolled at Nigerian universities in the 2000/2001 academic year were southerners. The former military governor of Kaduna State, Colonel Abubakar Umar, claimed that eight out of ten beggars on Nigerian streets were northerners. Medical experts also claimed that the north accounted for 80% of all leprosy cases and 90% of all cases of river blindness.[17] Owing to the intensely controversial nature of inter-ethnic and inter-regional relations in Nigeria, mentioning such statistics in public is almost taboo and can rarely be done without accusations of bias.

The north's economic and educational vulnerability to the south initially made it insular and sceptical about Nigerian unity. The former premier of the Northern Region, Ahmadu Bello, referred to Nigeria's creation as 'the mistake of 1914', and said that southern political leadership of Nigeria would 'be utterly disastrous'.[18] Bello reasoned that if the apparently fair-minded British had failed to develop the north during colonial rule, then it would be naive for the north to expect hostile and unsympathetic southern politicians to bring about that development:

> If the British Administration had failed to give us the even development that we deserved and for which we craved so much—and they were on the whole a very fair administration—what had we to hope from an African Administration, probably in the hands of a hostile party. The answer to our minds was, quite simply, just nothing, beyond a little window dressing.[19]

The north successfully delayed Nigerian independence until 1960, against the wishes of the south. Thereafter northern leaders remained hesitant about forging closer links with the south, and kept secession as an emergency exit route. The 1950 Ibadan constitutional conference proposed that the Northern, Eastern and Western regions would have 45%, 33% and 33% of seats (respectively) in the federal parliament. In response the emir of Zaria, a member of the Northern Region's delegation, threatened that 'unless the Northern Region was allotted 50 per cent of the seats in the Central Legislature, it would ask for separation from the rest of Nigeria on the arrangements existing before 1914'.[20] The north again seriously considered secession after the July 29 1966 northern soldiers' counter-coup led by Lt-Colonel Murtala Muhammed. The initial intention was not to seize control of the government, but instead to take the Northern Region out of

Nigeria. They were dissuaded only after northern civil servants in Lagos convinced them that secession would be disastrous for the north, and would leave it landlocked and impoverished, without access to a sea outlet in the south.

The north's distance from the southern coastline and its dependence on oil revenues from the south led to a northern reassessment and pragmatic acceptance of Nigerian unity. The prospect of being landlocked with no access to the sea or oil revenues has made it the region with the most to lose if Nigeria breaks up. While accepting Nigeria's unity, many northerners feared cultural, economic and social pressure from the south, and that political leadership by southerners would disadvantage the north even further. To southerners, the north had an unnecessary (almost obsessive) preoccupation with maintaining political leadership of Nigeria. While southerners accused northerners of treating political leadership as their 'birthright', for many northern elites political leadership was the only way to insulate the north from the threat of southern economic domination. As the prominent northern leader Maitama Sule[21] said: 'Everyone has a gift from God. The Northerners are endowed by God with leadership qualities. The Yoruba man knows how to earn a living and has diplomatic qualities. The Igbo man is gifted in trade, commerce, and technological innovation. God so created us equally with purpose and different gifts.'[22]

The View from Elsewhere

After the violent suppression of their agitation for resource control, and the execution of Ken Saro-Wiwa and eight other MOSOP members, the oil-producing minority areas of the Niger Delta became increasingly mutinous and aggrieved. Anti-military and anti-northern hostility was high in the Niger Delta. Northern political leaders had historically espoused a 'one north, one people, one destiny' narrative. Yet, as the north continued to be split into more and more states, new forms of micro identity and competition were generated. Minority ethnic groups in the middle belt such as the Tiv, Igala, Idoma and Jukun were separated from the Hausa and Fulani in new states that allowed them to express increasingly localised forms of identity. Middle-belt Christian minorities began to reject the 'one north' narrative which, in their view, tended to give prominence to the Hausa and Fulani. They complained of marginalisation and of being treated as second-class citizens in their own communities. They wanted 'to be rid of Hausa-Fulani domination.'[23] Religion also emerged as an unpredictable cleavage that disrupted the north's cohesion. Ethnic differences tended to become exaggerated when accompanied by religious differences too, as was the case between the Hausa, Fulani and middle-belters. It is pertinent that some of the most stringent opposition to northern proposals for the implementation of sharia law came from Christian middle-belters.

The Niger Delta and middle-belt grievances found an armed outlet during the April 1990 coup attempt against the Babangida government, which the plotters described as 'a well conceived, planned and executed revolution for the marginalised, oppressed and enslaved peoples of the middle belt and the south with a view to freeing ourselves and children yet unborn from eternal slavery and colonisation by a clique of this country'. Although coup plotters usually denounce the status quo, the April 1990 coup speech by Major Orkar was distinguished by the ferocity of its angry rhetoric against the north. Orkar said:

> Our history is replete with numerous and uncontrollable instances of callous and insensitive dominatory, repressive intrigues by those who think it is their birth right to dominate till eternity the political and economic privileges of this great country to the exclusion of the people of the Middle Belt and the south. They have almost succeeded in subjugating the Middle Belt and making them voiceless and now extending same to the south. It is our unflinching belief that this quest for domination, oppression and marginalisation is against the wish of God and therefore must be resisted with all vehemence ... even though they contribute very little economically to the well being of Nigeria, they have over the years served and presided over the supposedly national wealth derived in the main from the Middle Belt and the Southern part of this country, while the people from these parts of the country have been completely deprived from benefiting from the resources given to them by God.

Orkar's most stunning announcement was the coup plotters' expulsion of the far north states of Bauchi, Borno, Katsina, Kano and Sokoto from Nigeria. Citizens of the five states were suspended from any offices they held in the south or middle belt, and those living in the middle belt or south were required to repatriate to the north within one week but would be 'allowed to return and join the Federal Republic of Nigeria when the stipulated conditions are met'. Similarly, citizens of southern or middle-belt origin living in the excised states were required to return to their states of origin until the mutineers' conditions were met. Although troops led by General Abacha foiled the coup, its shock waves reverberated around Nigeria and pushed taboo issues about "northern domination" of Nigeria to the top of southern political discourse. Southern support for the coup evinced the heartfelt but unstated desire by some southerners to be rid of the north. After the coup southern criticism of the north became more frequent and vociferous.

The narrative of Nigerian unity had come full circle and reverted to the immediate pre-war 1967 position in some respects. Just as in 1967, the north was the most enthusiastic about national unity and maintaining the status quo, while the south was lukewarm about continued unity, and demanded major national restructuring as a condition of continued southern participation in Nigeria, or else it would secede.

The Constitutional Conference

In this maelstrom of inter-regional acrimony, southerners demanded that Abacha should convene a 'Sovereign National Conference' to deliberate on, and resolve, these contentious issues of national coexistence. In his maiden broadcast on November 17, 1993 Abacha had promised to convene 'a constitutional conference with full constituent powers ... to determine the future constitutional structure of Nigeria'. Members of the opposition assumed that 'full constituent powers' meant that the conference's decisions would be binding on the government and could not be altered. The attorney-general, Olu Onagoruwa, confirmed this perspective when he said that 'the government has taken a decision on that long ago that the decision of the constitutional conference is not subject to anybody's ratification. This is why the conference is sovereign and nobody is above it.'[24] The decree that created the conference empowered it to 'propose a new constitution which *shall* be promulgated into law by the PRC'.[25] However, the secretary to the government of the federation, Aminu Saleh, contradicted Onagoruwa by saying that the conference 'would be limited only to gathering the views of Nigerians which the government would study before coming out with a tentative political framework'.[26]

While southerners wanted the conference's recommendations to be binding, northerners were reluctant to hold such a conference at all, and feared that it would lead to Nigeria's dissolution or restructuring in a manner that would reduce or terminate northern access to oil revenues or political power. The former minister of transport, Umaru Dikko, complained: 'Despite a series of warnings and advice by the northern elders in which I sent representatives that Abacha should look for an alternative way of solving Nigeria's political stalemate, he has turned deaf ears and gone ahead in setting the constitutional conference in motion ... No man becomes a hero by selling his father's house to buy a land.'[27]

Suddenly the government started backtracking on its earlier commitments. It bowed to southern demands to hold the conference, but reassured the north by diluting the conference's powers and making them subject to ratification by the PRC. On June 27 1994 Abacha inaugurated a National Constitutional Conference. Major-General Chris Alli claimed that the enabling decree for the conference was promulgated without debate by the PRC, and that Abacha reduced the event from a sovereign national conference to a constitutional conference without referral to or debate by the PRC.[28]

Yet the conference's powers were unclear even to its members. When asked whether their decisions would be binding, a conference member told television reporters that the government had assured them that it was 'not likely' to overrule their decisions.

When the conference commenced, Yorubas refused to let the Abiola issue go away quietly. On Tuesday, July 19, 1994, the Yoruba *oba*, Dr Adedapo Tejuoso, delivered a speech, recommending that the issue of the annulled June 12 1993 election should be revisited, and that Abiola should be released. When he rhetorically asked what offence Abiola had committed that others present at the conference had not also committed, northern delegates began heckling him and shouted him down, so much so that nobody could hear what he said. Yoruba delegates were utterly appalled at the disrespect their *oba* was subjected to and walked out en masse from the hall in protest. The conference's proceedings were halted while moderate northern and Igbo leaders pleaded for the Yorubas to return. Prominent delegates from other parts of the country such as Shehu Yar'Adua, Alex Ekwueme, Sam Mbakwe and Olusola Saraki interceded and convinced the Yorubas to come back.[29]

The *oba* returned to the conference hall first, and the other Yoruba delegates followed behind him. After he sat down, each Yoruba delegate approached and knelt before him, before proceeding to their seats. It was a captivating show of solidarity by the Yoruba delegates. The *oba* completed his aborted speech and complained that he would not have been subjected to such derogatory treatment had he been a northerner.

One of the conference's most noteworthy recommendations was to split the country into six geo-political zones (see Map 1). The six zones separated the three largest ethnic groups of Hausa–Fulani, Yoruba and Igbo from each other by demarcating them in the north-west, south-west and south-east zones respectively. Crucially, the zones also separated the big three from the other minorities, thereby ending the three regional tyrannies of Yoruba, Igbo and Hausa–Fulani dominance over minority ethnic groups in the south-west, south-east and north respectively. The zones also corresponded approximately to historical geo-cultural locales. The north-west zone was composed mostly of Hausa–Fulani-speaking areas that were part of the Sokoto Caliphate. The north-east zone included areas that were part of the Kanem–Bornu Empire of the Kanuri-speaking people. The north-central zone was the most diverse and consisted of numerous ethnic groups in Nigeria's 'middle belt'. The south-south zone was inhabited by minority ethnic groups in the deep south, including the oil-producing Niger Delta.

Zone	States in Zone	Main Indigenous Ethnic Groups	Main Religions
North-west	Jigawa, Kaduna, Kano, Katsina, Kebbi, Sokoto, Zamfara	Hausa, Fulani	Islam and Christianity
North-east	Adamawa, Bauchi, Borno, Gombe, Taraba, Yobe	Bachama, Bura, Fulani, Jukun, Kanuri, Shuwa Arab	Islam and Christianity
North-Central	Benue, Kogi, Kwara, Nasarawa, Niger, Plateau	Angas, Birom, Ebira, Gwari, Idoma, Igala, Nupe, Tiv, Yoruba	Christianity and Islam
South-east	Abia, Anambra, Ebonyi, Enugu, Imo	Igbo	Christianity
South-South	Akwa Ibom, Bayelsa, Cross River, Delta, Edo, Rivers	Annang, Edo, Efik, Esan, Ibibio, Igbo, Ijaw, Itsekiri, Ogoni, Urhobo	Christianity
South-west	Ekiti, Lagos, Ogun, Ondo, Osun, Oyo	Yoruba	Christianity and Islam

The conference also made other notable recommendations such as:

- The rotation of the presidency on an alternating north-south basis;
- The rotation of each state's governor, deputy governor, and speaker of the House of Assembly among the three senatorial districts in the state;
- A modified presidential system that would have three vice-presidents;
- A single five-year term of office for the president and all state governors;

- The distribution of the offices of the president, vice-presidents, Senate president, and speaker of the House of Representatives (all of whom would hold their positions for a single term of five years) among the six geo-political zones;
- The introduction of proportional representation, such that any political party that gained at least 10% of seats in the National Assembly or 10% of electoral votes would be entitled to ministerial appointment in the federal cabinet;
- The creation of the Federal Character Commission to enforce the constitution's federal character provisions.

Delegates from the far north fiercely resisted the southern proposal for a rotational presidency. The usual northern–southern conflict on the issue was resolved by two prominent developments. Firstly, middle-belt delegates supported the south's call for a rotating presidency, thereby discrediting the 'one north' narrative which often presents the north as a political monolith. Secondly, delegates from the far north successfully passed a motion for the creation of a Federal Character Commission to monitor and enforce federal character. This was a classic Nigerian compromise. The south got the rotating presidency it wanted, while the north had the promise of a Federal Character Commission which it could use as a shield to protect itself and ensure that it would not be denied economic, educational and government appointments if and when the presidency rotated to the south. The conference also anticipated that a zone could have its 'turn' in power interrupted by the death, impeachment or resignation of the president. In such a scenario, one of the vice-presidents was to come from the same zone as the president whose term was not completed, and he or she would complete that president's term of office.

The conference completed its proceedings in exactly one year and submitted a draft constitution containing these provisions to Abacha on July 27 1995. It was the eighth constitution in Nigeria's history,[30] but the first to incorporate institutionalised ethno-geographic power-sharing provisions. Abacha amended some of the power-sharing provisions in the draft constitution. Rather than alternating the presidency on a north-south basis, the rotation would be between the six geo-political zones. Also, he replaced the system of a president and three vice-presidents with that of a president, a vice-president, a prime minister and a deputy prime minister, each of whom would be from, and would rotate between, different geo-political zones. Finally the rotation of political positions would last for a transitional period of thirty years. Nigeria now had the basis for a constitution with elaborate power-sharing provisions unlike anything the country had ever seen before.

'Sometimes you think the whole world is going to end'

On October 1, 1995 Abacha announced that he would cede power to an elected civilian president on October 1, 1998, at which time the draft 1995 constitution would take effect. Of course, things did not go according to plan. Abacha's sudden death in June 1998, followed by Abiola's death exactly one month later, intensified the country's problems. Many Nigerians jocularly compare their country's unity to an unhappy marriage. The squabbling Nigerian couple constantly fight and periodically go for marriage counselling, but they never break up. In 1998, Nigeria was finally on the brink of a divorce. It stood at the precipice of another massive sectarian conflict. The board of directors of Nigeria Inc. faced a seemingly unsolvable crisis. If they got things wrong, they might trigger a second civil war or a volcanic destabilisation of the country. However, one member of the board remained optimistic. Babangida said: 'I believe in what Obasanjo used to say, "God is a Nigerian." ... Sometimes you think the whole world is going to end. But no matter the turbulence, no matter the bumps, you realise there's always a way out.'[31]

16

END OF THE ROAD

By 1998 both civilians and soldiers were fed up with military rule. For the first time in Nigeria's history the pressure for democratisation from within the military matched the external pressure from civil society groups. There was a realisation within the military that military rule was not only ruinous to Nigerian society, but was also corroding the military itself. Ten military coups during nearly thirty years of military rule, a civil war, and constant involvement in political controversies infected the military with corruption, indiscipline, inefficiency and ethno-regional rivalry. The military became plagued by the same societal ills that military rule was supposed to cure.

The perks, power and wealth of military political office-holders incentivised many officers to campaign to be posted out of the military to political positions to serve as military governors or ministers. This constant scrambling for political opportunities severely degraded the military's efficiency and professionalism. It also affected the type of person that applied to join the military. The military became viewed in large segments of society as a ladder for political and social elevation, and a shortcut to power and rapid wealth. Many cadets enlisted in order to position themselves for an eventual political career. For several years, veteran senior officers had been warning that military rule was propelling the military towards self-destruction. As far back as 1986, the former chief of naval staff, Vice-Admiral Akin Aduwo, sent a letter to President Babangida which lamented:

> I have been highly privileged to see very clearly from within the establishment what great damage the incursion of the Armed Forces into the administrative

politics of the country has done to the very foundation of the otherwise proud military institution. It is regrettable to find that young Nigerians now join the armed forces not solely to fight bravely as soldiers, sailors and airmen in defence of their fatherland, but with the wish to one day be in the ruling class as military governor, ministers, chief of staff or head of state. No more is there the professional ambition to one day rise to become a gallant general, seasoned, toughened and proved worthy on the battlefield, or an admiral soaked in saltwater, or an air marshal dazed by the blue sky.[1]

Aduwo also warned Babangida: 'Unless we have a depoliticized Armed Forces, we could never have a stable country.' After the June 12, 1993 election annulment, the military became acutely aware of the extent of public disgust with them. Civilian hostility to the military became so severe that many soldiers stopped wearing their uniforms on their way to and from work. They would instead leave home in civilian clothes, change into uniform at work, then change back into civilian clothes prior to their journey home.[2]

The constant coups and claims of officers plotting against each other created an excruciating level of distrust and paranoia in the military. The former quartermaster-general Major-General Rabiu Aliyu informed me that the army's 'coup mania' caused severe friction and compounded the military's problems. Officers constantly plotted against each other and against the regime in power. Officers were also reluctant to engage in too much casual conversation with their colleagues, not knowing which were acting as informants or wearing hidden recording devices. Major-General Malu later recalled: 'Security operatives had infiltrated every unit and watched superior officers very closely.'[3] The merciless executions that followed the failed Dimka (1976), Vatsa (1986) and Orkar (1990) coups were demonstrations that the military was not safe from itself, and had to create an example by killing its own men in order to deter future coups. Over a hundred soldiers were executed for involvement in these three plots. Their execution weakened the military by eliminating some of its most skilled officers.

The clamour in southern civil society for an end to northern-led military rule became mirrored by southern military officers' complaints about northern and Islamic domination of the military. Northern over-representation in the military and intelligence agencies caused most southerners to view the army as a northern army of occupation and an instrument of northern political will. At the time of Abacha's death, the chief of defence staff, chief of army staff, inspector-general of police, national security adviser, director of military intelligence, director-general of the National Intelligence Agency, commander of the Brigade of Guards, chief security officer, and commandant of the

Nigerian Defence Academy—most of the positions of power and influence—were all northern Muslims. Additionally the minister of the Federal Capital Territory, chief of defence intelligence, and commandants of the National War College and Command and Staff College were also northerners, albeit they were Christians. After almost forty years of independence, Nigeria was yet to have a southern minister of defence, and it had been nearly twenty years since it had last had a southern chief of army staff.[4]

'We had overstayed our welcome'

The military was chastened by the realisation that it had brought itself and its country to ruin. After being released from prison in 1998, one of General Obasanjo's first statements was: 'The military has to find a way to get out of power. They could face a massive civilian uprising if they fail.'[5] Intra-military squabbling, coups and involvement in politics had weakened and demoralised the military. It was a shadow of its former self and had run out of excuses to govern Nigeria. It accused civilian politicians of being corrupt, but included officers who had become inexplicably wealthy almost overnight after participating in government. It also accused politicians of generating crises, but the military had itself plunged the country into civil war and several near-death experiences. It claimed to be more cohesive and disciplined than civilians, but several coup plots had exposed that it was just as venal and divided as civil society. As Major-General Aliyu informed me: 'Every right-thinking officer knew we had overstayed our welcome and had reached the end of the road.' It was time to go.

17

POWER SHIFT

'The south-east wants it. The south-west wants it. The minorities want it. The north cannot resist it.'

Adamu Ciroma

The deaths of Abacha and Abiola did not remove north–south antipathy. The north's and south's mutual hysteria and paranoia had reached its highest point since the end of the civil war. By 1998 northern leaders had ruled Nigeria for 35 of its 38 post-independence years. Southern faith in Nigeria was at an all-time low, and southern resentment against the north was at an all-time high. The demands for the validation of the June 12, 1993 election results evolved into a southern demand for a political 'power shift' to the south. Southerners were convinced that the north would never relinquish political power or allow a southern president to emerge. The former director-general of the Centre for Democratic Studies, Omo Omoruyi, said:

> The question that everyone needs to ask is why an Okonkwo [a typical Igbo name] cannot be president of Nigeria or why a man from Calabar or Delta and Yoruba region cannot be president? This is the issue that must be resolved if there is going to be peace in Nigeria.[1]

Although most southerners wanted Nigeria's next president to be a southerner, the clamour in the south-west for 'power shift' was most acute. The south-west would not accept any president other than a Yoruba as legitimate. However, power shift was difficult to sell to the north. A northern-led military government had little incentive to cede power to a southern civilian. Several prominent northern intellectuals attacked power shift at a Vision Trust Foundation conference at Arewa House in October 1998. The former president of the Academic Staff Union of Universities, Professor Attahiru Jega, agreed with the idea of power shift but 'not to the south or south-west, but in the sense of devolution of developmental and fiscal responsibilities'. The principal manager of the United Bank of Africa's credit risk management division, Sanusi Lamido Sanusi, criticised power shift because it 'is divisive as it stresses differences between peoples; its consequences are unpredictable and unmanageable'. He said that the north would support a southern presidential candidate, but only as the product of campaigning and normal political horse-trading—not by blackmail or constitutional fiat. The conference participants issued a communiqué rejecting power rotation and the zoning of political offices because 'we view it as undemocratic and a recipe for promoting divisiveness and political instability'.[2]

Despite the intellectuals' rejection of the notion, multiple trends converged to convince the Islamic north that power shift was the least damaging of the threats to them on the horizon. During the Abacha-organised constitutional conference a few years earlier, delegates from the Christian middle belt broke ranks with those from the Islamic far north, and supported the south's demands for the zoning and rotation of political posts. This divergence shattered the myth of one indivisible hegemonic northern bloc. Additionally, the south-west's demands for power shift had become so persistent and deeply entrenched that to publicly oppose it was to risk becoming a political outcast. Southern hostility towards the north meant that no northern political candidate stood a realistic chance of gaining significant votes from the southern electorate.

'The north cannot resist it'

To make matters worse, southern political groups were making conflicting and irreconcilable demands on the military that it could not realistically satisfy. How could Abubakar organise elections, restructure the country, devolve power to the regions, reform the military, and abdicate power to a civilian government of national unity in only three months before the October 1, 1998 deadline for the military to leave power?

Veteran northern power-brokers understood that blocking the shift of political leadership to the south would intensify southern demands for more fundamental restructuring of Nigeria and a dilution of northern military influence. Power shift was the one concession the north could make without risking more serious social tumult or the prospect of a northern president struggling to govern without cooperation from the south. The former governor of Kaduna State, Balarabe Musa, said: 'Northerners have held all the big political posts that matter in this country since 1960 and they cannot hope to dominate forever. It is time for them to renegotiate their interests.'[3] Almost forty years after the late premier of the Northern Region, Ahmadu Bello, had described the prospect of southern political leadership of Nigeria as 'utterly disastrous,'[4] a moment of political reckoning finally arrived for the north. The only way for it to guarantee national unity was to cede political leadership to the south. Adamu Ciroma, a Kanuri Muslim from the north who had served three different northern-led governments[5] as governor of the Central Bank of Nigeria, minister of trade and industry, and minister of agriculture, said of power shift: 'The south-east wants it. The south-west wants it. The minorities want it. The north cannot resist it.'[6]

Agreeing to power shift in principle was far more difficult than implementing it. As logical as the demand was, it was difficult to achieve without the military government further tarnishing its reputation by rigging the next election in favour of a southerner, or without enacting laws that would discriminate in favour of, or against, entire regions of the country. Additionally, how could power shift be enacted without stoking northern and military fears that power would fall into the hands of a southerner who would marginalise the north or extract a retributive pound of flesh from the military? To get out of the political mess it was in, Nigeria needed an ingenious solution. Historically, there had been a severe lack of leadership succession planning in Nigerian politics. The country had a series of accidental heads of state who had leadership thrust upon them after coups or assassinations. For a change, political elites tried to facilitate a planned change of leadership by means of an orchestrated strategy. In 1998 the board of directors of Nigeria Inc. conjured another political magic trick.

The Role of Babangida

After five years away from the public limelight, former President Babangida suddenly broke his silence. He was one of the first people that al-Mustapha phoned to ask for advice after Abacha's death. Although Babangida respectfully described Abacha as a 'great leader' at his funeral, one month later he was less charitable. In an illuminating interview with *The Guardian* of London shortly after Abiola's death, he described Abacha as 'a man who could not give you an articulate position on anything'.[7] He was unlikely to have been displeased when his childhood friend and school classmate Abubakar succeeded Abacha. He gave Abubakar credit by acknowledging that 'Abubakar is trying to unwind all the belligerence of Abacha'.

He also gave a very detailed outline of how the transition to civilian rule should unfold. He rejected the October 1, 1998 handover date by saying, 'There is nothing sacrosanct about October 1. There have been calls for a national government of unity and reconciliation ... For me if we are asking for democracy, this is not the way forward. The international community has a better idea—elections.' In his view the transition process should be extended and could be completed in 'six to nine months'. He also recommended that the five political parties created under the Abacha regime should be discarded ('we all know why they were created and that reason no longer exists'). Intriguingly he had a very clear idea of the sort of civilian president that would be acceptable to the military. Babangida said the next president would need to 'have an excellent understanding of our political history and be able to speak for all Nigerians. He would be commander-in-chief of the army so he would have to have an understanding of the military—so we could do business with him.'[8] Rather conveniently, everything turned out exactly as Babangida envisaged.

Abubakar addressed the nation on July 20, 1998 to announce the dissolution of all five political parties, and that the October 1, 1998 handover date had been postponed to May 29, 1999. All these decisions sounded like the reading of a script from Babangida.

Party Formation

After the dissolution of the Abacha-era parties, several new political associations emerged. Most of them had two core issues to contend with: which other groups should they align with, and which part of the country should their presidential candidate be from? These thorny issues caused new alliances to be formed and old ones to be broken. Abubakar's dissolution of the 'five fingers of the leprous hand' left the G34 as the most prominent political 'party in waiting' to contest the next elections. It already had the nucleus of an embryonic political party. The G34's credentials had also been enhanced by its public opposition to Abacha. It entered into a political alliance with Afenifere, which saw itself as the heir apparent to the presidential throne and inheritor of Awolowo's and Abiola's political legacies. The Yoruba lawyer Bola Ige was a member of both the G34 and Afenifere. He prompted the G34's northern faction to write a letter of protest to Abacha in 1998 by challenging them to demonstrate that not all northerners supported Abacha. However, Afenifere broke away from the G34 after different factions supported Ige and Olu Falae, a 60-year-old Yoruba economist who had a master's degree from Yale University, and who had formerly served as secretary to the government of the federation, and minister of finance under Babangida.

The All People's Party (APP)

The political affiliation of certain APP members led some cynical Nigerians to nickname it the 'Abacha People's Party'. Afenifere joined the APP but then aborted its alliance in protest after finding 'itself in the midst of many discredited people, who have sneaked into the leadership of the proposed party through the back door'.[9] The murky circumstances of Abiola's death and the widespread belief in Yorubaland that northerners murdered him were not matters that Afenifere was likely to quickly forgive or forget. They refused to stay in alliance with those they held responsible for Abiola's incarceration and death.

The Alliance for Democracy (AD)

Unable or unwilling to work with the G34 or the APP, Afenifere decided to go it alone. On the eve of the Independent National Electoral Commission (INEC) deadline for the registration of political parties, Afenifere formed the Alliance for Democracy (AD) party on September 7, 1998. The AD's hurried formation meant that it did not have time to launch nationwide and fulfil constitutional and electoral requirements for national spread. However, given the dark mood in the south-west, INEC dared not deny it registration. INEC turned a blind eye to the AD's lack of national spread and registered it even though it was an ethno-regional party with a narrow power base and popularity in the Yoruba south-west. The AD's existence as a blatant vehicle for Yoruba interests simultaneously increased its popularity in the south-west, but restricted its appeal in the rest of the country. Afenifere's problems increased after it surprisingly chose Olu Falae, rather than Bola Ige, whom many regarded as Awolowo's heir, to be the AD's presidential candidate. The controversial choice of Falae over Ige split loyalties within Afenifere and ceded political momentum to the G34 group.[10]

The People's Democratic Party (PDP)

The G34 forged alliances with other groups to form a new political party called the People's Democratic Party (PDP) on August 31, 1998. The PDP was a coalition of divergent interests rather than a grouping with a common ideology. It was a hybrid formed by three main political factions: the G34, other veteran politicians from the 1979–83 democratic era, and members of Yar'Adua's People's Democratic Movement (PDM). The G34 faction included former Vice-President Ekwueme, Solomon Lar, Sunday Awoniyi, Adamu Ciroma, Abubakar Rimi and Sule Lamido. The veteran political group included the former governor of Bendel State, Samuel Ogbemudia, and the former chairman of the National Party of Nigeria, Tony Anenih. Yar'Adua's PDM group included Atiku Abubakar, Chuba Okadigbo, Lawan Keita, Yomi Edu, Dapo Sarumi and Sunday Afolabi.

Although Abubakar's government refused to promulgate the draft constitution that emerged from Abacha's constitutional conference, the political parties implemented the ethnic and regional power-sharing provisions of the abandoned constitution anyway. The NPN veterans in the PDP went back into their political locker and revived two power-sharing devices they had previously used during their tenure in government between 1979 and 1983. These two devices were called zoning and rotation. Zoning was the sharing of political posts between incumbents from different geographic regions of the country, and rotation meant that the region to which each post was allocated would be swapped at predetermined moments in the electoral cycle.

The Trojan Horse

The PDP zoned its presidential nomination to the south. Once power shift was accepted across the political spectrum, Afenifere's priority should have been to ensure that it hitched a ride with the political horse that was galloping fastest towards the presidential villa. Instead it failed to back the right horse. Afenifere's refusal to join forces with the PDP was a tactical mistake that denied it the opportunity to determine which Yoruba would be Nigeria's next president. Its exit from the PDP left the PDP's door ajar for a fourth Trojan Horse faction to enter and conquer the party. The military had a vested interest in interfering with the process by which its successor would be determined. It sought a reliable political movement it could invest in. Afenifere's circular trot across the political dance floor with the G34, APP and finally the AD made it appear indecisive and unpredictable. In contrast, the PDP was experienced and organised. Its members were political heavyweights with years of experience in elections and government.

The military and the PDP understood that power shift was the only game in town. They also understood that there were far more important issues at stake than the ethnicity of the next president. The south-west and south-east were making (in the north's and the military's view) dangerously radical demands for a restructuring of the country. The most visible southern presidential aspirants—Bola Ige and Olu Falae from the south-west and Alex Ekwueme from the south-east—were the type of politicians that would keep agitating for such restructuring if they became president. Northerners had nervously noted that during the Abacha-organised constitutional conference, Ekwueme was the architect of the six geo-political zones in the country, and had also advocated devolution of power to the regions as well as military restructuring. The extent of northern apprehension about separatist sentiment in the south was revealed when a group of northern PDP members led by Professor Jibril Aminu met individually with the southern PDP presidential aspirants and asked them to sign an undertaking not to act against northern interests and to reserve certain cabinet positions for the north.[11]

If the military ignored the south's reformist demands, there was a substantial risk that the incoming civilian government would simply invoke radical new constitutional amendments as soon as the military departed from power. Additionally, the military had several skeletons in their cupboard—or, more accurately, they had an entire cemetery of bodies that they did not want their civilian successors to exhume. Given the atmosphere of hostility against them, the military government dared not raise the topic of whether the incoming civilian government would be compelled to grant them amnesty from prosecution for the corruption and human rights abuses of the Abacha era. Nonetheless power shift had to come with strings attached. The military needed to ensure that the next occupant of the presidential villa would be someone they could trust to contain the escalating separatist demands across the country, cure the military's coup addiction, and protect the military from ridicule and persecution. He would also have to be, in Babangida's words, someone they 'could do business with'. The military already had someone in mind.

'God and Nigeria need you'

Babangida had visited Obasanjo in his ancestral home town of Abeokuta just over a week after the latter was released from prison in mid-1998. Babangida

223

disclosed nothing about what he discussed with Obasanjo except to say when he arrived: 'I have come to see my big brother.' After their meeting finished, and as Babangida prepared to enter his car before departing, he suddenly turned to Obasanjo and told him, 'God and Nigeria need you.'[12]

After Babangida's visit, two curious trends emerged. Firstly, flattering articles about Obasanjo appeared in the international media. *The Times of London* published an article with the headline 'Yoruba general is best hope to avert civil war'.[13] The article claimed that 'he is probably the only man with the credibility and charisma to hold the country together'. Additionally, northern politicians from the Northern Elders Forum (such as Lawan Keita) and the PDM (such as Sunday Awoniyi) visited Obasanjo at his farm in Ota to encourage him to stand for election as president. Wealthy retired generals such as former chiefs of army staff Lt-Generals Danjuma, Wushishi and Aliyu Mohammed donated millions of naira to Obasanjo's election campaign. Two of these three generals were linked to Babangida. Wushishi and Babangida were schoolmates (along with the head of state Abubakar) at Government College, Bida, and Mohammed had served as Babangida's national security adviser. Danjuma threatened to go into exile if Obasanjo was not elected president. The generals' involvement made the transition akin to a bargain between serving and retired military elites, rather than an electoral competition between rival civilian political parties. The alliance between Obasanjo and the generals (such as Babangida), whom he had formerly criticised, was one of convenience. The generals needed a reliable southern hand to which to pass the baton of leadership, and Obasanjo needed campaign money from Babangida and his rich military friends. Babangida said: 'He [Obasanjo] had a vision for this country and he pursued it religiously. I think he is a patriot. The country will be safe in his hands.'[14]

Presidential Nominees

The PDP held a convention between February 13 and 15 1999 to choose its presidential candidate. Former Vice-President Alex Ekwueme was Obasanjo's main rival for the PDP presidential nomination. Ekwueme was far more erudite and gentlemanly than Obasanjo, and ran a slick campaign. Senior PDP member Bamanga Tukur, a northerner from Adamawa State, was impressed by Ekwueme's polished style and compared him to the driver of a Rolls Royce. However, Tukur argued that 'Nigeria needs a truck driver', not someone able to drive a Rolls Royce.[15] In the cut-throat world of 20th-century Nigerian politics, sophisticated marketing campaigns did not mean much. Money talked instead. The PDP's presidential primaries became a microcosm of the electoral malpractices that plague Nigerian politics. Everything and everyone was for sale. Each candidate's supporters used tremendous sums of money to bribe delegates to vote for their favoured candidate. *Africa Confidential* alleged that the 'going rate' for buying a delegate's vote was 150,000–200,000 naira (over US$7,000 at the then official exchange rate).[16] The efficacy of such bribery was unknown since the vote was by secret ballot. Nothing stopped delegates from collecting money from a candidate's supporters (or from those of all candidates) and then voting for the opposing candidate. The governor-elect of Adamawa State, Atiku Abubakar, a protégé of the late Shehu Yar'Adua, and the other 18 PDP governors-elect were also influential in mobilising votes for Obasanjo by promising appointments and influence in a future PDP government, and by threatening to withhold such benefits from those who did not vote for him. Obasanjo won the PDP's nomination after 67% of PDP delegates supported him. He chose Abubakar as his vice-presidential running mate.

The PDP's wealth and military backing made it clear to the AD and APP that neither of them could defeat the PDP alone. The AD and APP therefore decided to field Olu Falae as their joint presidential candidate. This was not in itself a problem, except that the APP already had a presidential candidate, Ogbonnaya Onu, an Igbo. Only one day after he had been declared the APP's candidate, Onu was forced to stand down in favour of Falae in acrimonious circumstances. The former director-general of the National Security Organisation, Umaru Shinkafi, was Falae's vice-presidential running mate. The decision by all three parties to field Yoruba presidential candidates constituted a paradigmatic event. For the first time in Nigeria's history, all political parties reached consensus on the ethnicity of the next president. It also meant that each side in the upcoming election had rejected Igbo candidates in favour of a Yoruba.

Obasanjo held a fundraising dinner at the Nicon Noga Hilton Hotel in Abuja on February 22, 1999. The largest donation to Obasanjo was 120 million naira (nearly US$6 million) from the Fulani businessman Aliko Dangote. His donation was more than a quarter of the total of 400 million naira raised at the event. Other notable civilian donors included Atiku Abubakar and his friends (80 million naira) and Bukola Saraki (2.5 million naira). Saraki's donation was surprising because his father Olusola was the main financier of the rival APP.

The military's endorsement of Obasanjo was matched by the disdain shown for him in his native Yorubaland and much of the south. His close relationships with northern military officers led many southerners to view him as a puppet of the northern military establishment. The former administrator of the mainly Igbo East Central State, Ukpabi Anthony Asika, said: 'When he [Obasanjo] was head of state, he was a passive one ... he was more or less in fear all through his tenure trying to satisfy the North whose interest he was representing.'[17] Obasanjo had committed multiple political sins that could lead to ostracisation in Yorubaland. He always seemed to take positions that were counter to the mainstream Yoruba political trends. In 1994, when secessionist sentiment was high in the south-west, he had said that he 'would be more diminished as a citizen of Oduduwa Republic than as a citizen of Nigeria'. He had criticised both Awolowo and Abiola, he was suspected of not doing enough to oppose the June 12 election annulment (although in his defence he claimed that he 'spent nearly two hours trying to convince General Babangida to de-annul' the election), and many Yorubas believed that Babangida's decision to form the Interim National Government, instead of ceding power to Abiola, was Obasanjo's idea. Obasanjo was the first Nigerian military leader to voluntarily cede power to a democratically elected president when his government oversaw elections and abdicated power to President Shehu Shagari, a Muslim Fulani from the north, in 1979 after a disputed election. However, Awolowo's supporters claimed that Shagari had not fulfilled the constitutional requirement to win at least 25% of the votes cast in at least two-thirds of the states. Since Nigeria's then 19 states were not divisible into exact thirds, exactly what constituted two-thirds became a contentious issue. A controversial Supreme Court ruling allowed Shagari to become president even though he had secured the requisite number of votes in only 12 states. Yorubas blamed Obasanjo for allowing Shagari to become president despite the mathematical anomaly.

Obasanjo's unpopularity among his own people threatened to derail the military's plans. The PDP had decided that its presidential candidates had to demonstrate their popularity by 'delivering' their state and Local Government Area to the PDP during the December 1998 local government elections. Although the PDP won about 60% of the local government votes nationwide, it suffered an embarrassing loss in the south-west. Obasanjo was booed by his fellow Yorubas on the local election campaign trail. The AD won in his home state of Ogun and in his home town of Abeokuta. As a test of Obasanjo's popularity, the election was a disaster. However, the PDP conveniently ignored its earlier decision about candidates having to deliver their states and still allowed Obasanjo to run as its presidential candidate.

February 27, 1999

On Saturday, February 27, 1999, Nigeria held only its third presidential election in twenty years. Ideological election campaigning had been almost absent. All energies were focused on the more important tasks of winning at all costs and mobilising ethno-regional votes. The head of state, General Abubakar, arrived 'late' at his local polling station after voter registration had closed. INEC officials told him he had come too late to vote. Abubakar's late arrival may have been an orchestrated public charade to avoid showing favouritism to either candidate.

According to the INEC, approximately 30 million of the almost 58 million registered voters cast their votes at 110,000 polling stations across the country. In a politically cynical country fed up with politics after almost forty years of misrule by civilians and soldiers, this was a curiously high turnout. Although the election was peaceful, election monitors witnessed several electoral malpractices such as ballot-box stuffing, vote inflation, and alleged thumb-printing of ballot papers by party agents and INEC officials. An election monitoring team led by Obasanjo's friend, former US President Jimmy Carter, wrote a letter to the INEC chairman, Justice Ephraim Akpata, noting the suspicious 'wide disparity between the number of voters observed at the polling stations and the final result that has been reported from many states'.[18] Some states in the oil-producing Niger Delta reported improbable voter turnouts of over 100%. Bayelsa State, with an alleged voter turnout of 123%, somehow managed to record more votes than the number of registered voters in the state. The official results showed that Obasanjo had been elected president after having won 62.8% of the votes cast. The fact that all parties participated in electoral malpractices convinced many observers that the parties' rigging cancelled each other out, and that the overall result was probably authentic, even if the actual number of votes for Obasanjo and Falae were inflated. Nonetheless Falae dismissed the results as 'a farce and a charade' and threatened to challenge them in court. He was dissuaded from doing so amid concerns that protracted litigation would give the military an excuse to postpone or abort the transition to civilian rule. The exhaustion with military rule and relief that an election had taken place at all allowed concerns about the legitimacy of the election result to be brushed under the carpet.

The PDP's victory was not due to a refined political ideology or to capturing the public's imagination. It won because it had more money, and was better organised and more adept than other parties at slicing up and sharing political power and shoehorning divergent ethnic and regional interest groups into the party. Although its presidential candidate was a Yoruba Christian, its vice-president was a Fulani Muslim from the north, the party's chairman (Solomon Lar) was a Tarok Christian from the middle belt, and the party selected a Christian Igbo (Evan Enwerem) a Senate president. Thus it managed to integrate all major geo-ethnic blocs into positions of influence within the political hierarchy. In contrast, the Afenifere–Awoist group yet again failed to capture power for the same reasons as their Action Group and UPN predecessors. They failed to realise that popularity in Yorubaland was not enough to rule nationwide. By failing to capitalise on the political consensus regarding power shift, and the willingness of other ethno-regional groups to make concessions to the Yoruba, the Awoists squandered a tremendous opportunity to be at the forefront of national politics. Instead, their refusal to compromise and coexist with political rivals once again relegated them to the ranks of the opposition as a regional party.

A peaceful transition was threatened when on May 17 Yorubas attacked northerners in Lagos after a rumour that Obasanjo had been assassinated by northerners. Peace was restored after Obasanjo appeared on national television to confirm that he was alive and appealed for calm. Yoruba violence on behalf of a man they despised, did not vote for and did not want to become president was an excellent demonstration of the bizarre contradictions in south-western Nigeria.

Democracy Day—May 29, 1999

Eagle Square was specially constructed in Abuja to serve as the official site for the launch of Nigeria's new democratic era. It was arguably the most significant democratic event in Africa since Mandela's inauguration as South Africa's president five years earlier. Twenty-five current and former heads of state from around the world attended Obasanjo's inauguration ceremony. Current heads of state included Nelson Mandela of South Africa, Jerry Rawlings of Ghana, Robert Mugabe of Zimbabwe, Yoweri Museveni of Uganda, Daniel arap Moi of Kenya, Ahmad Tejan Kabbah of Sierra Leone, Laurent Kabila of the Democratic Republic of Congo, and Yahya Jammeh of Gambia. Former heads of state in attendance included former German Chancellor Helmut Schmidt and former Tanzanian President Dr Julius Nyerere. The other dignitaries included Prince Charles of the United Kingdom and Jesse Jackson from the US (which ended sanctions on Nigeria the day before the election). Nigeria's five surviving former heads of state also attended. The crowd reaction to each dignitary provided an impromptu test of their popularity. Mandela received the loudest cheers. In a portent of future conflicts between their respective countries, Nigerian officials had to intervene to prevent a fight between the bodyguards of Uganda's Museveni and Congo's Kabila.

The inauguration ceremony included prayers, dancing and music. A troop of schoolchildren also participated in the jamboree. Police and military units mounted parades under the command of Lt-Colonel Mohammed Garba. The air force also conducted an aerial display using its Alpha jets and the home-made Nigerian 'air beetle'. The Alpha jets flew overhead and left patriotic trails of smoke in the sky in the national colours of green and white.

'You are permitted to march off the parade'

Vice-President Atiku Abubakar, who was wearing a flowing white agbada, was sworn in before Obasanjo.[19] Obasanjo, who was also wearing a white agbada, took his oath of office on the Bible. General Abubakar then presented Obasanjo with a bound copy of the 1999 constitution, along with the insignia of office, the national flag, and the green, red and blue defence flag. The two men then embraced. To symbolise Obasanjo's position as the new commander-in-chief, the parade commander, Lt-Colonel Garba, asked him (not Abubakar) for permission to leave the parade ground. Obasanjo responded, 'You can march off the colours and you are permitted to march off the parade.' Obasanjo then entered the state box to greet and speak to visiting dignitaries, where he spent most time chatting and exchanging jokes with Mandela. Afterwards Obasanjo and Abubakar climbed into an open-top Mercedes SUV and took a drive together across Eagle Square. It was an extraordinary reversal of fortunes. The military general who had ceded power to civilians twenty years earlier returned to accept power back as a civilian from his former military colleagues. An added irony was that the commander of the military handover parade at which Obasanjo ceded power to civilians in 1979 had been one Lt-Colonel Abdulsalam Abubakar.

Among the former Nigerian leaders in attendance there was great irony in their juxtaposition. Former President Shagari sat next to Buhari, who led the military government that overthrew Shagari, then arrested and detained him for two years. Sitting nearby was Babangida, who had in turn led the military government that overthrew Buhari, then arrested and detained him. One wonders how the former military rulers Buhari, Gowon and Babangida felt as they watched the ceremony and saw the esteem granted to their former colleagues, which was denied to them.

Nigeria survived a breathtaking eleven months during which there were three heads of state, two leaders collapsed and died inside the presidential villa, and Obasanjo completed the prison-to-president journey that is frequent for African heads of state. To some extent the 1999 return to civilian rule was similar to Nigeria's independence in 1960. Those who had campaigned for independence and democracy did not inherit the spoils. Most of the human rights groups, lawyers, civil society campaigners, students and south-western political groups that had been arrested, imprisoned or driven into exile were fenced off from the political process, while civilian and military political elites shared the spoils of their struggle.

Nonetheless, Nigeria's political elites have not been given sufficient credit for their dexterity at striking creative bargains for getting Nigeria out of its constant political dead-ends. For all their venality and corruption, Nigerian elites are grand masters at finding political solutions.

18

UNCLE SEGE

By mid-1999 Nigerians were being treated to the unusual experience of having an elected head of state for only the second time in over thirty years. They were unsure whether to call him 'general' or 'president'. When journalists fidgeted over the appropriate appellation by which to address him, Obasanjo jocularly told them they could call him 'Uncle Sege'[1]—his nickname among family and close friends. 1999 was not a good time to be Nigeria's president. The country's economic indicators had plummeted in the twenty years between Obasanjo's first stint in office and his return to power. During those years Nigerians became poorer, gross domestic product per capita dropped from $800 to $300,[2] and the national debt more than trebled, rising from US$9 billion to $34 billion. When Obasanjo was military head of state, the naira was stronger than the US dollar and exchanged at a rate of one naira to $2. By 1999 one US dollar was worth 100 naira on the black market. Even though Nigeria was a member of OPEC and the world's eighth largest producer of oil, the country had been suffering from fuel shortages for five years. Its oil refineries were deliberately allowed to fall into disrepair so that the few with import licences could make a huge profit by importing refined oil and selling it on the black market at twice the going rate to desperate motorists in a country that produced two million barrels of oil per day. Obasanjo had the daunting responsibility of tackling these challenges.

Most southerners expected Obasanjo to be a northern patsy. No one took seriously his promises to fight corruption and that there would be 'no sacred cows'. However, his swift actions upon becoming president shocked both his southern detractors and northern supporters. He revoked oil contracts awarded by the departed military government, which had allegedly been given to their members and friends, and also appointed a committee led by the respected industrialist Christopher Kolade to investigate large extra-budgetary expenditures of over $3 billion by the Abubakar government in its final months in power.

Armed Instability in the Democratic Era

Although the power shift provided an escape route out of the June 12 crisis, it did not resolve lingering ethno-regional and religious controversies or other malignant effects of military rule. Military rule had used force to crudely suppress separatist agitations. However, the military's exit from power provided an outlet for these pent-up frustrations to erupt. The return to democracy coincided with outbursts of communal violence and the rise of several ethno-regional protest groups and vigilantes such as the Oodua People's Congress in the south-west, the Movement for the Actualisation of the Sovereign State of Biafra (MASSOB) and Indigenous People of Biafra (IPOB) in the south-east, Egbesu Boys, and Movement for the Emancipation of the Niger Delta (MEND) in the oil-producing Niger Delta. These groups challenged the Nigerian state and demanded major alterations to its structure. The Arewa People's Congress in the north provided counter-narratives to these southern groups.

While the military can be blamed for failed policies under its political leadership, it was also a victim of the weakness of other state security forces. Nigeria does not have enough police officers for its large population. Over a third of the police are deployed to guard VIPs, leaving the remaining force to bear the disproportionate burden of protecting the rest of the population. The police are also intensely disliked and distrusted in many communities for their corruption and excessive use of force. Their inability to contain crime waves and multiple communal outbursts resulted in the government continually deploying military units to reinforce or replace police formations across the country. As a result the military had spent much of the past twenty years engaged in internal security operations to deal with terrorists, armed robbers, kidnappers, and ethnic, religious and other communal riots. These military deployments used force to retroactively tackle expressions of socio-economic and political disaffection, without addressing their root causes.

Many senior military officers opposed the routinised deployment of soldiers for internal security operations. The chief of army staff, Lt-General

Victor Malu, stated that he had 'always believed, and still believe, that soldiers should not be involved in basic law enforcement duties' because 'the army has neither the training nor the disposition for such assignments.'[3] However, the security situation around the country made military deployment unavoidable. Two such deployments were to prove Malu right.

By the time Nigeria returned to democracy in 1999, local dissatisfaction with oil companies in the oil-producing Niger Delta was on the verge of morphing into an insurgency. Two hundred people were killed in Warri during Obasanjo's first week in office.[4] On November 4 and 5, 1999, tension boiled over and local youths killed a dozen police officers at Odi in Bayelsa State. Obasanjo gave the Bayelsa State governor two weeks to find the killers or risk the declaration of a state of emergency in his state. After the deadline passed without the killers being apprehended, Obasanjo sent the military into Odi to find and arrest the killers. During a five-day operation between November 20 and 24, 1999, soldiers destroyed large parts of Odi and killed scores of civilians after using heavy weapons including artillery and mortar bombs. A serving officer admitted that 'by the time the soldiers left, only a church, a community center, and a bank were left standing ... Everything else was destroyed.'[5]

Rather than show contrition for the attacks, Malu, who coordinated the operation, defiantly and without remorse defended the military's actions in Odi by stating, 'We are not police officers. If you fire from a building I will dislodge you from your comfort zone by taking down the building. This is exactly what happened at Odi.'[6] Malu's reaction to military excesses changed when he became a victim of them. In October 2001, Tiv militiamen in Benue State in central Nigeria abducted and killed 19 soldiers in the town of Zaki-Biam. In retaliation the soldiers' colleagues returned to the town on a revenge mission. The soldiers destroyed at least seven villages and towns, burned markets, fired shells at buildings, displaced tens of thousands of people from their homes, and rounded up and shot dead more than 200 civilians. The fact that the soldiers attacked and destroyed Malu's house, where his wife and uncle had been staying, demonstrated the extent of the army's impunity.

The greatest threat to Obasanjo in confronting and resolving the massive challenges before him was his former constituency: the military. Military support for civilian rule was not unanimous. The coup specialists in the military usually prowled around civilian governments like lions stalking prey. This faction had been responsible for past coups and were waiting for Obasanjo to make a mistake that would justify a return to military rule. To such officers, Obasanjo's presidency was not a permanent return to democracy, but instead merely a temporary swing on the carousel of the military–civilian exchange of power. Lt-Colonel Martin Igwe said: 'A lot of young officers are now not professionally oriented. They want political appointment because that is where the action is. That is where the money is ... I think the Army has a long way to go.'[7]

'As a retired officer, my heart bleeds'

During his inaugural presidential speech in May 1999, Obasanjo mourned what had become of the military:

> The incursion of the military into government has been a disaster for our country. The *esprit de corps* among military personnel has been destroyed. Professionalism has been lost. Most youths go into the military now not to pursue a noble career but with the sole intention of taking part in coups and to be appointed as military administrators of states and chairmen of task forces. As a retired officer, my heart bleeds to see the degradation in the proficiency of the military. A great deal of re-orientation has to be undertaken and a redefinition of roles, retraining, and re-education will have to be done to ensure that the military submits to civil authority and regains its pride, professionalism, and tradition.

Shortly after coming to office, Obasanjo inaugurated a Presidential Policy Advisory Committee (PPAC) to advise him on policy and government appointments. The PPAC included a subcommittee on the military which was led by the former chief of army staff during the first Obasanjo regime, Lt-General Danjuma. Danjuma had already bluntly warned a group of army officers: 'There should be a massive purge of the armed forces and if that does not happen the army is going to destroy Nigeria.'[8] This subcommittee requested from the military secretary (army), Major-General Thaddeus Ashei, a list of all serving officers who had held political appointments during the years of military rule. Because of the confidentiality of the project, Ashei's office at Bonny Camp in Lagos was off limits to non-essential staff for two weeks. The purpose of the list soon became apparent. On June 17, 1999 Obasanjo compulsorily retired 93 officers who had been members of prior military governments. Their retirement stunned both the military and the public. Both were astonished that he reacted so swiftly and severely against his former institution. The retired officers included Major-General Aziza, who chaired the coup tribunal that convicted Obasanjo and Shehu Yar'Adua in 1995; Air Vice-Marshal Idi Musa, the former head of the Defence Intelligence Agency who was accused of framing Diya and others during the 1997 coup plot; Colonel Komo, who was instrumental in events leading to the arrest and detention of Ken Saro-Wiwa; and the popular former military administrator of Lagos State, Brigadier-General Marwa. Officers who held political appointments had previously been objects of awe and envy in the military. Obasanjo's spokesman Doyin Okupe signalled that this was about to change by vowing that henceforth 'the ultimate reward for participating or benefiting from coups will be premature or forced retirement from service'.[9] Since the majority of officers in military governments had been northerners, more northerners than southerners were retired. This led to grumblings from northerners that the retirement exercise discriminated against them.

However, the process of subordinating the military to civilian authority was not seamless. During several years of military rule, the military had become unaccustomed to civilian oversight and control. Malu typified this residual resistance, and continually challenged defence policies initiated by the Obasanjo government. A prominent example was the objection of Malu and other senior officers to Obasanjo's decision to appoint the American company Military Professional Resources International (MPRI) to provide training and advice on security sector reform. Malu's public criticism and obstruction of MPRI and other government-initiated defence policies became so persistent that the US ambassador to Nigeria, Howard Jeter, complained that dealing with the Nigerian military 'felt like the removal of several teeth without novocaine'.[10] Obasanjo finally tired of Malu's intransigence and summarily retired him in April 2001 along with the chief of air staff, Air Marshal Isaac Alfa, and the chief of naval staff, Vice-Admiral Victor Ombu. Although Malu was the target, Alfa and Ombu were also sacrificed to give diplomatic and ethno-regional cover for Malu's retirement. The officers Obasanjo selected to replace them (shown in the accompanying table) demonstrated that the northern and Muslim grip on the military's leadership was loosening. Three of the four service chiefs were Christians and all but one were from minority ethnic groups.

After these compulsory retirements, overt military challenges to civilian political authority decreased. However, the intensity of opposition to the modest reforms initiated by the Obasanjo government demonstrated that the military was still influential enough to slow down and restrict the scope of military reform. Additionally, dialogue on military reform was not broadened to address long-standing deficiencies in the military and institutional vices inherited from the era of military rule. The retirement of politicised officers achieved its short-term objective of preventing a relapse to military rule, but could not by itself reverse decades of institutional damage to and neglect of the military. By the year 2000, 75% of the army's equipment was either damaged or unusable.[11]

Senior military leadership, May 2001

Position	Name	Prior Position	Regional Origin	Ethnicity	Religion
Chief of Defence Staff	Vice-Admiral Ibrahim Ogohi	No change	North-Central (Kogi State)	Igala	Muslim
Chief of Army Staff	Major-General Alexander Ogomudia	GOC, 1 Mechanised Division, Kaduna	South-South (Delta State)	Isoko	Christian
Chief of Naval Staff	Rear-Admiral Samuel Afolayan	Flag Officer Commanding, Western Naval Command	North-Central (Kwara State)	Yoruba	Christian
Chief of Air Staff	Air Marshal Jonah Wuyep	Air Officer Commanding, Operations—Air Force Headquarters	North-Central (Plateau State)	Tarok	Christian

The poor state of military equipment and its maintenance was exposed on January 27, 2002 when over a thousand people were killed after military ammunition stored at the Ikeja Cantonment in Lagos exploded. Intermittent blasts continued overnight and rained down exploding projectiles across a five-kilometre radius onto nearby civilian neighbourhoods. Terrified residents fled in panic, fearing that the military was staging a violent coup. Those not killed by the blasts drowned in a lagoon while trying to escape in the dark. Even though the explosions were later shown to have been caused by negligence and poor maintenance and storage, neither the Ministry of Defence nor the military high command issued an apology. The military also failed to explain why a large quantity of high-grade explosives was stored so close to a heavily populated civilian neighbourhood. No soldiers were prosecuted for the explosions, or for the excesses at Odi and Zaki-Biam.

Obasanjo was caught between the conflicting demands of a military and political establishment that expected protection from him and the victims of military excesses who demanded justice. Yet he recognised the need for national healing after so many years of acrimony, injustice and misrule. In June 1999 he inaugurated a Human Rights Violations Investigations Commission (HRVIC) chaired by a retired Supreme Court judge, Justice Chukwudifu Oputa. The commission was colloquially known as the 'Oputa panel' and was empowered to investigate human rights abuses that occurred during the military-rule years. The panel had eight members, four from each of the north and south. The members included Elizabeth Pam, widow of Lt-Colonel James Pam, who was murdered during Nigeria's first military coup in January 1966. Many criticised the panel for being toothless, as it had no power to order arrests or prosecutions, to grant amnesty, or to award compensation. Former heads of state Generals Buhari, Babangida and Abubakar ignored the panel's requests to appear before it to testify about alleged human rights abuses during their tenure. Yet the panel still turned into riveting drama. Its proceedings were televised live as it toured the country and sat in Abuja, Enugu, Kano, Lagos and Port Harcourt to collect evidence and hear witness testimony. It received over 10,000 petitions regarding various alleged abuses and had 320 witnesses appear before it. Obasanjo was the only head of state who testified to the panel. He appeared as both accuser and accused. He said that he was framed and unjustly imprisoned for plotting a coup against Abacha in 1995. Obasanjo also had to defend himself from accusations by the family of Afro-beat musician Fela Anikulapo-Kuti that he ordered a military raid on Kuti's compound in 1977 during which soldiers burned the place, raped women inside, and caused the death of Kuti's 77-year-old mother Funmilayo after a soldier pushed her through an upstairs window. Fela was so outraged by his mother's death that he carried a coffin to Dodan Barracks, then the headquarters of Nigeria's military government, in protest, and also released a song called 'Coffin for Head of State' which criticised Obasanjo and his then deputy, Yar'Adua.

'We in the army have no reputation left'

The panel summoned former powerful and untouchable generals such as Bamaiyi, Malu, Sabo and Olanrewaju, and intelligence agents, and uncovered shocking evidence of assassinations, corruption, secret underground torture chambers, false imprisonment, and other abuses by intelligence and security agencies during military rule. *Newswatch* claimed that 80% of petitions concerned events that had occurred under Abacha's reign.[12] Ironically, two members of Abacha's government, Diya and Adisa, also petitioned the panel about abuses they had suffered. At a time when sympathy for the military was at an all-time low, their petitions elicited public scorn and derision, instead of sympathy. They failed to realise that the military itself was on trial. The manner in which feared generals turned on each other, traded blame and insults, and exposed state secrets to a captivated national television audience thoroughly disgraced the military, and destroyed its moral authority. Adisa admitted that 'we in the army have no reputation left'.[13]

Abacha's death left his family and former aides vulnerable. On 18 November 1998, the then chief of defence staff, Air Marshal Daggash, had convened a Special Investigation Panel (SIP) to investigate miscellaneous offences including an alleged coup plot against the Abubakar government. The SIP began its work on November 20, and took testimony from 15 witnesses, including James Ibori, a civilian fixer for Abacha who later became the elected governor of Delta State. The SIP raided al-Mustapha's house and found firearms, ammunition, night-vision binoculars, bullet-proof vests, classified video and audio tapes, and a document in al-Mustapha's handwriting entitled 'State of the Nation' which contained notes about Nigeria's political condition. These items were not enough to prosecute al-Mustapha for plotting a coup but the raid signalled to him that he was now a marked man.

On July 20, 1999 the State Security Service arrested a Strike Force member, Sergeant Barnabas Jabila. As Strike Force members were addressed by *noms de guerre* rather than their real names, the 29-year-old Jabila was known as Rogers. He was a Marghi from Borno State in the north-east.[14] Rogers's shocking confessions during interrogation ripped open the veil that had concealed the unexplained murders of the Abacha era. He disclosed that he had been part of a secret assassination squad that murdered Abacha's opponents. According to Rogers, the assassination squad carried out several murders and attempted murders on al-Mustapha's orders. He claimed that in 1996 al-Mustapha told him to travel with the chief superintendent of police, Rabo Lawal, who was the commander of the mobile police unit at the presidential villa, and 11 other Strike Force members to Lagos to meet Bamaiyi and the commanding officer of 26 Battalion at Bonny Camp, Lt-Colonel Jibril Bala Yakubu.[15] According to Rogers, Bamaiyi and Yakubu gave them instructions to assassinate Kudirat Abiola, Alex Ibru, Abraham Adesanya, Bola Ige and Olusegun Osoba, and to burn down the *Guardian's* headquarters at Rutam House. Yakubu allegedly organised a rehearsal of the operations for Rogers and his men.

Rogers admitted that he murdered Kudirat on al-Mustapha's orders, and claimed that to avoid having the weapons and ammunition used for the assassinations traced to their official duty weapons, Yakubu and the Lagos State commissioner of police, James Danbaba, gave them ammunition, AK-47 rifles and other guns recovered from armed robbers and Nigerian soldiers who served in the ECOMOG peacekeeping missions in Liberia and Sierra Leone. Rogers also claimed that Lateef Sofolahan, a Yoruba Muslim employee of the Abiola household who spoke fluent Hausa and who worked on Abiola's presidential election campaign in 1993, acted as their informant. Sofolahan allegedly identified the houses and offices of their victims, including Kudirat and Ibru, and provided them with information about Kudirat's routine. Rogers also confessed to being among the assailants who shot Ibru, along with Corporal Sani Garba and Sergeant Samaila Shuaibu, who died in a mysterious bomb blast in 1997, and to being behind the arson attack on the *Guardian's* headquarters. According to Rogers, al-Mustapha paid money to him, Danbaba and the others for their roles in the murders and violence. Security agents arrested al-Mustapha on October 24, 1999 and found arms, ammunition and large sums of money during a raid on his house in Kano.

Testimony from Sofolahan and other witnesses corroborated Rogers. In October 1999, security agents also arrested Abacha's 32-year-old son Mohammed after his driver, Mohammed Abdul ('Katako'), testified that he had ordered him to drive the killers during their assassination runs, gave each of them $10,000, and told them to flee from Nigeria and avoid testifying about the murders. Katako claimed that Rabo Lawal threatened him and warned him that he and his family would be killed if he told anyone what he knew about Kudirat's murder. In November 1999, the assistant commissioner of police Nuhu Ribadu[16] filed murder charges against the suspects in Lagos and their trial began on Tuesday, November 23, 1999. Prosecutors charged Mohammed Abacha with 37 different offences including being an accessory to murder and for several counts of embezzlement and money-laundering. The lead prosecution lawyer was the attorney-general of Lagos State, Professor Yemi Osinbajo.[17] Mohammed Abacha was tried for the murder of Kudirat Abiola alongside Sofolahan. Bamaiyi, Yakubu and Danbaba were tried for the attempted murder of Ibru. Al-Mustapha and Rabo Lawal were defendants in both murder cases.

As the trials proceeded, the regional and religious origins of the defendants created difficulties for Obasanjo. Most of those being tried for crimes committed under Abacha were Muslim northerners (although Danbaba was a Christian of Bille ethnicity from Adamawa State). To some northerners, the prosecutions thus appeared like a witch-hunt by the new Christian president from the south. Additionally, support for Obasanjo had started to dissipate in the north and underwent an ironic reversal. His southern detractors, who originally viewed him as a northern puppet, became his most ardent supporters while the powerful northerners, who had almost forced him on a reluctant south, regretted the support they gave him. Several prominent northerners withdrew their support for Obasanjo, and the Abacha family mobilised their vast resources to conscript powerful northerners to campaign for Mohammed's release. Additionally, several northern senators initiated impeachment proceedings against Obasanjo. With political vultures circling overhead and opposition from the north increasing, Obasanjo approved a deal to release Mohammed in September 2002, pursuant to which Mohammed agreed to repay $1.5 billion to the government, and he was allowed to keep another $300 million, which he argued was acquired by the Abacha family from legitimate businesses. The government provided a plane from the presidential fleet to fly Mohammed home to Kano. His mother Maryam shed tears of joy when she saw her son.

The other suspects were in and of court for the next decade. The case against Bamaiyi collapsed when key prosecution witnesses changed their testimony or said that the State Security Service promised them gifts in exchange for their evidence, and coached them on what to say. Rogers claimed that the government paid his wife a monthly stipend, and that the government officials who met and briefed him included the federal attorney-general, Bola Ige, the attorney-general of Lagos State, Yemi Osinbajo, the Lagos State director of public prosecutions, Fola Arthur-Worrey, and the director-general of the State Security Service, Colonel Kayode Are (retired). In April 2008, the Lagos State High Court acquitted and released Bamaiyi, and in January 2012 it sentenced al-Mustapha and Sofolahan to death by hanging for their role in Kudirat's murder. However, in July 2013 the Lagos State Court of Appeal quashed their convictions, revoked the death sentences, and released them. All the other defendants tried for the murders of Rewane[18] and Kudirat, and attempted murder of Ibru, have also been freed. No other suspects have been tried or convicted in their place.

19

PEOPLE OF THE BOOK

Nigeria is the only country in the world with its population equally split between Christians and Muslims. It is experiencing its third religious revolution in three successive centuries. The first was a Muslim jihad in the north in the 19th century, the second was the mass Christianisation of the south in the 20th century, and the third is a contemporary revival in both Islam and Christianity in the 21st century. Although rivalry between Christians and Muslims grabs the headlines, Nigeria's Christians and Muslims are not monolithic groups in united opposition against each other. Both religions have diversified in response to the fast-changing modern society around them. The real story is about the upstart reformist movements in both religions that challenge the established religious order. These movements have generated divisions within each of the two religions as much as they have generated competition between them.

The religious politics of modern Nigeria cannot be divorced from its colonial history. A complex series of political and social events interspersed hundreds of years apart are responsible for the modern-day religious character of Nigeria. Traditional religions, war, colonialism and changing economic fortunes combined to create the volatile mix that is modern religion in Nigeria.

In the Beginning

The religious changes that occurred in Africa in the 19th and 20th centuries were among the most rapid and remarkable mass religious conversions in the history of humankind. They were possible for several reasons. Spirituality existed before the arrival of Islam and Christianity. Belief in the supernatural cuts across many strata of African life. In African cosmology nothing happens by chance. The fluctuating daily fortunes of human beings were not attributed to concepts such as luck or coincidence. Rather, various deities and spirits were often given the credit (or the blame) for blessings and ills such as plentiful farm yields, droughts, marriages, births, infertility, sickness, and unsuccessful business deals. Daily life for many Nigerians involved worship and sacrifice to maintain good relations with benevolent spirits that could confer blessings, and to placate evil spirits that could bring misfortune.

Commander of the Believers

Islam was the first Abrahamic religion to arrive in Nigeria. It was brought to Nigeria's north-eastern frontier (in the modern-day Borno area) in the 11th and 12th centuries by traders and migrants, then spread westwards across the north into north-western Nigeria.

Islam's subsequent advancement was propagated by revolution and war. Perhaps the most seismic event ever to occur in northern Nigeria was the holy war waged in the 19th century by a Fulani cleric, Usman Dan Fodio. Dan Fodio criticised the Islamic practices of the Hausa states of northern Nigeria, accusing them of idolatry and of contaminating Islam with animist rituals. In 1804 he led a jihad to purify Islam, and conquered the pre-existing Hausa states. He established a massive confederation of emirates that stretched as far as Mali at its western end, traversed Nigeria, and extended into Cameroon at its eastern end. The jihad established a vast royal and Islamic empire known as the Sokoto Caliphate. Its capital was the city of Sokoto in Nigeria's far north-west. Dan Fodio took the title of Amir-al Mu'minin[1] (Commander of the Believers), the spiritual leader of Nigeria's Muslims.

The southward advance of Dan Fodio's jihad was halted not by a superior military power, but rather by two ecological forces that even his army could not overcome. The dense forests of the south proved impenetrable for the horses of Dan Fodio's cavalrymen, and the tsetse fly lurking in those forests menaced their horses with sickness. Hence, the jihad stopped in northern Yorubaland and was unable to penetrate further south. Remnants of the empire that Dan Fodio established still exist over two hundred years following his death in 1817. His descendants have succeeded him in occupying the position of sultan of Sokoto during the two hundred years since his death, and as emirs in northern cities such as Gwandu, Kano and Zaria.

Christianisation

In the south prior to the 20th century, most people worshipped traditional deities and practised animist belief systems. Nigeria's colonisation by Britain generated not only political change, but also religious change. The combined work of European missionaries and emancipated slaves brought mass Christian conversion to the south in the 20th century. This conversion simultaneously caused a religious revolution in the south, and in the north it insulated Islam from Christian encroachment. During the colonial era, British and northern authorities restricted the activities of Christian missionaries in Muslim areas of the north. This created a geographic segregation that led to the 'Muslim north' and 'Christian south' narrative common in Nigeria. The geographic containment of Christianity and Islam could not last forever. The two religions crept slowly towards each other from opposite directions. Christianity entered via Nigeria's southern coastal areas, while Islam entered via the north. They would eventually meet each other.

The coexistence of Christianity and Islam in Yorubaland is testimony to this. The Yoruba are peculiar for being one of the few ethnic groups in Nigeria that are split equally between Christians and Muslims. Yorubas have a religious flexibility and tolerance not found anywhere else in Nigeria. They may be Nigeria's religious saving grace. An evangelical Christian Yoruba woman I interviewed casually remarked to me, 'My mother is an Alhaja'—a Muslim woman who has made a holy pilgrimage to Mecca. After saying this, she casually changed the subject and started discussing other matters as if born-again Christians with devout Muslim mothers were not a noteworthy occurrence requiring further comment. It is common to find Yoruba families where husband, wife and their children practise different religions. Some Yorubas (whether Christian or Muslim) often invoke Bible and Koranic passages in the same conversation or have converted back and forth between the two religions. The sister of General Obasanjo, a born-again Christian, is a Muslim. The former military governor of Ondo State, Navy Commodore Bode George, a Yoruba Christian, said:

> Let me now tell you what we have in the south-west. My immediate elder sister is a Muslim. She was born a Christian, [and] she married a Muslim from Lagos State ... She is today an Alhaja ... She was brought up a Christian; she will sing all the songs. But you see, her husband and her children, they are Muslims ... I am a Christian. I have another younger brother who married a Muslim from Lagos State. She is now so converted that she preaches the Bible. But all her

family in the area are still Muslims. So to us, it's nothing. There is hardly any Yoruba family you will go [to where] you won't find a Muslim or a Christian.[2]

'There is only one God and there are so many paths to the top of the hill'

It is pertinent that Yorubas were on both sides of the sharia controversies in 1978 and 1988, and that a Yoruba, Simeon Adebo, chaired the subcommittee that proposed the compromise that resolved both conflicts. One scholar noted: 'again and again in my research in Yorubaland I found exceptional religious toleration.'[3] The typical Yoruba attitude to religion is encapsulated in an anecdote by Abiola regarding a conversation he and his father had about Christianity. Abiola said his father asked him, 'Is their [Christian] God different from our God?' When Abiola replied, 'It's the same God', his father told him, 'There is only one God and there are so many paths to the top of the hill. Our paths are different from theirs but we will all meet at the top of the hill. That is our belief.'[4]

Unfortunately, the religious tolerance in Yorubaland is not ubiquitous throughout Nigeria. Although the north is geographically larger than the south the south is more densely populated. As southern migrants moved to the north in search of new economic opportunities, they took their religion with them. Christian migrants to the north opened new churches and evangelised for new converts, including in areas where Christianity had not been previously practised. This created a competitive religious atmosphere with fervent proselytising by both sides. The fact that southern Christian migrants tended to live in the *Sabon Gari* ('strangers' quarters' or 'new town') on the outskirts of northern towns created a physical as well as spiritual separation between Christians and Muslims. Additionally, areas of the north that rejected Dan Fodio's jihad adopted Christianity as a symbol of resistance. Some members and pastors of Pentecostal churches regarded Islam as a rival to be confronted and defeated rather than as a sister religion. Christians also engaged in activities (such as drinking alcohol and eating pork) which were forbidden to Muslims, and which antagonised them. Conversely, some Muslim areas resisted the presence of Christians and sometimes burned churches or attacked Christians.

Although Islam recognises and accords respect to Christians as *Ahl al-Kitab* (Arabic for 'People of the Book'), flashpoints tend to occur in arenas where the two religions have to compulsorily coexist. Politics is such an arena. Three events in close proximity in the late 1970s accelerated the pace of religious radicalisation. These were the military's planned transition to democracy, the Iranian revolution, and the tremendous wealth that flowed from the oil boom.

Nigeria's religious diversity makes it impossible for adherents of one religion to govern without adherents of the other. A significant political test case for religious coexistence between the two Abrahamic faiths occurred in the late 1970s as Nigeria's military government led by General Obasanjo prepared to return the country to democratic rule. While a Constituent Assembly deliberated on a new Nigerian constitution in 1978, controversy erupted when Muslim members of the Assembly proposed that the new constitution should create a federal sharia (Islamic law) court of appeal. Christians vehemently opposed the proposal and argued that a sharia court of appeal would eliminate Nigeria's secular status, and would Islamicise the country. Both sides made outlandish statements. Alhaji Abdul Mashi of Kaduna State said that denying sharia 'is like passing a Bill in parliament ... suspending all Christians in this country from attending Sunday worship'.[5] Some Christian Assembly members retaliated against the sharia proposal by advocating the creation of a federal ecclesiastical court of appeal (even though no lower Christian courts existed).

Unusually, the sharia controversy could not be couched in pure north–south terms as sharia opponents and supporters could be found in both the north and south. Sharia supporters included Yoruba Muslims from the south such as Moshood Abiola and Dr Abdul Lateef Adegbite, while some of its most uncompromising opponents included northern Christians such as Solomon Lar and Joseph Tarka. The pro- and anti-sharia arguments became so incendiary that 92 Muslim Assembly members (including future President Shehu Shagari) walked out in protest on April 6, 1978. The Rev. Joseph Agbowuro of Ondo State lamented that the chairman of the Constitution Drafting Committee had 'spent 45% of his time on the explosive issue of sharia which unfortunately has engulfed this nation'.[6] With no end to the deadlock in sight, on April 19, 1978 Obasanjo intervened and removed the sharia issue from the list of review topics before the Assembly. A 16-member subcommittee chaired by Simeon Adebo proposed a successful compromise that enlarged the jurisdiction of the existing Federal Court of Appeal by empowering it to hear sharia cases. Rather than create a special sharia court of appeal at federal level, this ensured that three or more judges of the Federal Court of Appeal who were versed in Islamic law (but who did not have to be Muslims) could adjudicate in sharia cases.

The sharia animosity re-emerged the next time a military government prepared another constitution for an incoming civilian government. In 1988

Babangida's government appointed another Constituent Assembly to design a new constitution. Muslims once again advocated the establishment of a federal sharia court of appeal, and Christians predictably opposed them with equal vigour. The emotional outbursts from both sides once again increased the religious temperature to boiling point. The Assembly's embattled chairman, Justice Aniagolu, revealed that 'Of all the clauses of the Constitution Review Committee Report, none was viewed with as much awe or was as acrimonious, or was as potentially dangerous, or was as emotionally charged, or was pursued with as much relentless fervour, or had the capacity of destroying Nigeria as Clause 6 [on sharia law]'.[7]

The sharia issue threatened to tear the Assembly apart and deadlocked it for two months until the chief of general staff, Vice-Admiral Augustus Aikhomu, removed the emotionally explosive issue from its deliberations on November 28, 1988. Babangida refused to allow the Assembly to discuss sharia any further since 'the issue had already been settled by the 1979 constitution. That is the bottom line.'[8] As in 1978, sharia was retained only in civil law matters where all the parties are Muslims. Individual states were free to decide whether or not to create sharia courts within their states, but such courts could not hear cases involving Christians without their consent. This compromise postponed the sharia controversy but did not resolve it. Not all Muslims accepted this compromise. Some reformist Muslims continued to agitate for the expansion of sharia jurisdiction or an Islamic state, and were appalled at the possibility of non-Muslim judges adjudicating in sharia cases.

Unlike its two previous religious revolutions, Nigeria's third religious revolution was not caused by war or foreign invaders. The 1970s oil boom, corruption, crime, and the economic and political hardships of the 1980s and 1990s concentrated wealth in a tiny elite. While some could access that wealth, and defend themselves against economic hardships by exploiting ethnic, family and geographic networks, others could do so only by means of religion. Daily life became intensely religious. Public and private events almost always begin and end with prayers, and social conversations are often laced with religious vocabulary such as 'Insha Allah' (God willing) or 'by the grace of God'.

Pentecostalism

In a country where the government failed to provide its citizenry with necessities such as good roads, regular electricity and security, and in which fraud and injustice were rampant, people increasingly turned to religion and miracles for salvation from the excesses of daily life and disappointment with the government. As a result the country became intensely religious. In the 1953 census 68% of the population identified as either Christian or Muslim.[9] By 2012, 98% of the population identified as either Christian or Muslim.[10] New Christian Pentecostal churches emerged across the south and provided an outlet for those disillusioned by the moral decay in society and who sought an immediate remedy for everyday economic hardships. The emergence of these new churches has been one of the most remarkable social changes in Nigeria's recent history. Nigerian Pentecostal churches are ingenious at integrating secular concerns and interests within a religious system. Pentecostalism's message that intense fasting, prayer and worship can bring immediate wealth, miracles, healing and other blessings impressed many Nigerians in an era of economic hardship. Christians joined Pentecostal churches not only to earn entrance to heaven, but also to solve immediate daily problems related to health, relationships and wealth. The colourful, eye-catching effervescence of Pentecostal church services, which at times resemble music concerts more than religious services, with music, singing, dancing and constant applause, made established Catholic and Protestant churches appear stolid and dull. Christians left established churches to flock to these new Pentecostal churches in great numbers.

The Pentecostals took advantage of a depressed economic environment by buying the warehouses of companies that went out of business, and converting them into vast mega-churches. Their voracious demand for new land on which to build new churches inflated property prices in Abuja. The new churches raised vast amounts of money by constantly reminding their congregations about the biblical requirement of tithing.

Pastors became celebrities and alternative authority figures with their own television channels, massive budgets of several millions (supplemented by the giving of alms and tithes by their congregation), luxury bullet-proof cars, and even private jets. The corporate-sounding brand names of Nigerian Pentecostal churches, such as 'Winners Chapel', 'House on the Rock', 'Household of God' and 'Christ Assembly', and the celebrity profile of their pastors, such as Temitope B. Joshua, David Oyedepo, Chris Oyakhilome and Tunde Bakare, gave Pentecostal Christianity a high social visibility. The ostentatious affluence, charisma, designer suits and glamour of Pentecostal pastors made them economic role models for their congregations. In a country where people became rich (legitimately or by corrupt means) seemingly overnight, gaining wealth appeared to be the product of miraculous intervention.

Pentecostal churches seemed to offer miracles on demand. The rise of new charismatic churches that preach the 'prosperity gospel' coincided with the intensification of a rapacious thirst for money and materialism in Nigerian society. Father Matthew Hassan Kukah claimed that Pentecostal pastors could tell their congregations:

> You are the way you are because you've sinned. And if you repent and you become like me, God is going to bless you. So that found resonance. You know, in a country like Nigeria where you have over 20 years of military rule, people didn't have any other platform for contestation. There was increasing poverty. It's still persistent. And that brand of religion did manage to answer certain questions.[11]

Enoch Adeboye is the general overseer of the largest evangelical church in Nigeria, the Redeemed Christian Church of God, which has 14,000 churches and 6 million members in Nigeria alone. When an Al Jazeera television reporter asked Adeboye why it was necessary for him to own a private jet, he drly replied: 'When you have to oversee churches in 160 nations, you can't do that on a bicycle.'[12] Redeemed (as Adeboye's church is known) has the astonishingly ambitious goal of establishing a church within 5 minutes' walk of every person in developing countries, and within 10 minutes' drive of every person in developed countries. Such ambitions and the confidence and economic power that churches wield made Pentecostal Christians more assertive in contests for political power in a way that would have been unthinkable in the 1970s and 1980s. Some pastors have become so powerful and prominent that they have access to the highest levels of government. Adeboye was a spiritual mentor to President Obasanjo, and Obasanjo sought his counsel and prayers before contesting the 1999 presidential election. While born-again Christian revivalism flourished in the south, the north also experienced a religious revival.

Muslim Diversification

Nigeria has the fifth-largest Muslim population in the world.[13] However, Nigerian Muslims are not a homogeneous religious group. Like Christianity, Islam also splintered into different denominations.

Rivalry between different Muslim denominations contributed to the decision of the former premier of the Northern Region, Ahmadu Bello, to establish Jama'atu Nasril Islam (Association for the Victory of Islam) in 1963 as an umbrella group for Nigerian Muslims. One of the group's key members was a brilliant and revered Islamic scholar from Gummi village in Sokoto State called Sheikh Abubakar Mahmud Gummi. He devoted his life to the propagation of Islam. He served as the grand khadi (chief Islamic law judge) of the Northern Region from 1962 to 1967, and as religious affairs adviser to Bello. Gummi had been a childhood classmate of Shehu Shagari, who later became Nigeria's president (1979–83), and of the radical grassroots northern politician Aminu Kano. Gummi's fluency in Arabic allowed him to act as Bello's translator with King Saud when they travelled to Mecca together for the hajj in 1955. He also translated the Koran from Arabic to Hausa, thus disseminating the Koran more widely among Nigeria's Hausa-speaking population. Gummi's work and writing had an enormous influence on the development of religion in the north, and indirectly contributed to the subsequent fragmentation among Muslims.

Some 90–95% of Nigeria's Muslims are Sunnis, while the remainder belong to the minority Shia branch of Islam. Before Nigerian independence, Sufism was the dominant branch of Sunni Islam in the north. Many Sufis belonged to one of two prominent Sufi *tariqas* (brotherhoods or 'pathways'). These were the Qadiriyya (to which Usman Dan Fodio and many members of the northern elite belonged) and Tijaniyya. Although these Sufi brotherhoods were rivals, Gummi's followers criticised both of them, rejected many of their practices, and accused them of introducing innovations into Islam. On February 8, 1978 one of Gummi's students, Ismaila Idris, a Fulani former army imam, founded a reformist Islamic group named *Izalat al-Bida' wa Iqamat al-Sunnah* (Association for the Removal of Innovation and the Reinstatement of the Prophet's Tradition) in Jos, Plateau State.[14] The group is commonly known as Izala.[15] Izala historically received funding from Saudi Arabia. They are 'anti-innovation legalists'[16] who seek to purify Islam by promoting a back-to-basics version of Islam grounded on strict, literal interpretations of the Koran. Many of Gummi's other students also joined Izala.

Religious development in the north was also influenced by events in the global Muslim community. The moral decay in Nigerian society and the 1979 Iranian revolution inspired Muslim youths in Nigeria to believe that Islam could be similarly deployed in Nigeria to bring about radical political and social change. Reformist Muslim organisations increased in popularity in the north. Another prominent group is the Iranian-funded Shia Islamic Movement of Nigeria (IMN) led by Sheikh Ibrahim Zakzaky. Zakzaky's ancestors were from Mauritania. His great-grandfather had migrated to Nigeria in order to join Dan Fodio's jihad in the 19th century. IMN models itself on the Lebanese Shia group Hizballah[17] (the Party of God). In addition to the Sufi brotherhoods, the Salafists and Shiites, other fringe sects with idiosyncratic interpretations of Islam emerged. Muslim intra-religious rivalry intensified and autonomous mosques and sects multiplied.

Maitatsine

In the early 1980s northern Nigeria was traumatised by the violent uprising of an Islamic sect led by a Cameroonian preacher, Mohammed Marwa. The 53-year-old Marwa was a slightly built man from Marwa in Cameroon who migrated to Nigeria in 1945. His aggressive preaching and confrontations with Nigerian authorities led to his imprisonment in 1962 and deportation to Cameroon in 1966. He returned to Nigeria in the 1970s in violation of his deportation order and was arrested, then spent time in and out of prison several times throughout the 1970s. Marwa considered himself a prophet, and espoused ideas that were part religion, part sorcery. He declared that those who wore wristwatches, rode bicycles, drove cars, read books other than the Koran, or sent their children for Western education were infidels. Locals nicknamed him Maitatsine (a Hausa phrase meaning 'the one who curses') owing to his habit of exclaiming 'Wanda bata yarda ba Allah ta Tchine' (May Allah curse the one who disagrees with his version). Although many Muslims considered Maitatsine to be a heretic, he was able to attract followers from the fringes of society. Maitatsine's followers condemned other Muslims who did not belong to the sect, as infidels. They often walked great distances to demonstrate that vehicles were unnecessary. The sect carried weapons in public, prevented children from going to school, constantly clashed with the police, and constructed housing on land they did not own after expelling the owners. Some sect members who had previously served in the security forces provided military training to their comrades. Some also believed that Maitatsine was a mystic who invested them with magical powers to withstand bullets.

Maitatsine and two thousand of his devoted followers barricaded themselves into an enclave at 271 Kofar Wambai in the Yan Awaki area of Kano. Maitatsine's compound seems to have been chosen with the possibility in mind of a raid by security forces. It was separated from surrounding areas by a stream, and was located in an elevated area that allowed sect members to see those approaching from a distance. The sect was sufficiently feared for the police to order its officers to avoid the Kano neighbourhood where they were located, and the National Security Organisation informed its agents that it was too dangerous to conduct undercover surveillance there.

When police tried to arrest some of the sect's members on December 18, 1980, they lashed out, and attacked and killed police officers with bows, arrows, swords, daggers, dane guns and clubs. They then spread out into other parts of Kano and unleashed a ten-day orgy of violence during which they burned markets, schools, cinemas, cars and houses, and overwhelmed the police.

On December 28, President Shagari deployed the army to subdue the sect. When Shagari asked the officer leading the operation to minimise casualties, the officer bluntly declined to give such an assurance since he would not be able to restrain soldiers from inflicting casualties on those who had killed their colleagues.[18] Soldiers from 146 Infantry Battalion commanded by Major Haliru Akilu and 202 Armoured Battalion brutally suppressed the sect in bloody fashion.[19] They deployed tanks and fired artillery in heavily populated areas to subdue Maitatsine and his sect. Over five thousand people (including Maitatsine) died in the violence. The police recovered Maitatsine's corpse and cremated it in order to prevent his followers from turning his grave into a shrine. The sect fought so tenaciously that the commander of the operation, Colonel Yohanna Kure, said: 'I pray that Nigerians would be able to fight for this nation in the same manner as the fanatics fought in the event of an attack on Nigeria.'[20]

Despite the iron fist that suppressed the revolt, surviving members of Maitatsine's sect fled and caused subsequent disturbances in other northern cities such as Jos, Kaduna in the central part of the north, and Yola in the north-east. Their violence erupted sporadically for the next five years although on a smaller scale than the initial Kano explosion.

A government-appointed judicial commission that investigated the violence concluded: 'Because of the very wide gap between the rich and the poor in our society ... they [Maitatsine's sect] were more than prepared to rise against the society at the slightest opportunity.' The commission also advised: 'This regrettable social situation in our society ought to be remedied immediately [or] else it will continue to provide the required recruitment potential for disenchanted men ... to rebel against the society.'[21] The government did not heed the commission's warning. Economic inequality increased in the decades following Maitatsine's uprising, eventually allowing an even more malevolent form of religious extremism to emerge.

Religion in Post-Military Nigeria

When Nigeria returned to democracy in 1999, religion once again became a federal political issue. For the first time in twenty years Nigeria had a Christian president in Obasanjo. The presence of a born-again Christian president seemed strange in a country that had had Muslim heads of state for twenty consecutive years. Although the presidential villa contained a mosque it did not have a church. Obasanjo built a chapel inside the presidential villa. He was welcomed to office with unprecedented religious controversy.

In 2000 the governor of Zamfara State in Nigeria's north-west, Ahmed Yerima, extended the application of sharia to criminal law. Prior to then sharia applied only to civil law matters like divorce and inheritance. The extension of sharia to criminal law prescribed punishments such as stoning for adultery, amputation for theft, and flogging for drinking alcohol. Sharia also forbade bars to serve alcohol and segregated public transport by gender.

Political Sharia

However, many Christians opposed sharia, arguing that it violated Nigeria's constitution, which forbade states to adopt any religion as an official religion, and outlawed inhuman or degrading treatment. Although Christians argued that Nigeria is a secular state, the constitution's preamble states that Nigeria is one nation 'under God'. Sharia had a nebulous status as Nigeria's legal system is a cocktail of English common law, native law and customs, and religious edicts. In contrast to other countries that separate religion and the state, much debate in Nigeria concerns the extent to which the state should aid citizens in the practice of their religion. The government sponsors religious pilgrimages and has Christian and Muslim prayers by pastors and imams at official government events. Rather than seeing it as secular, there are two alternative interpretations of Nigeria's constitution: that it seeks to preserve Nigeria's multi-religious character, and that it seeks to ensure that no one religion is given preferential treatment over another. Arguably the government is entitled to engage in any religious activity so long as it does not adopt any official religion.

Nonetheless, Christians were undeterred in their opposition to sharia. The Catholic archbishop of Lagos and former president of the Christian Association of Nigeria, Dr Anthony Okogie, said that 'the imposition of sharia law, if allowed to see the light of day will breed religious intolerance and spark off violent reaction'.[22] In emotional outbursts, some governors of southern states threatened to declare Christianity the official religion of their states. Christians asked why Muslims did not implement sharia during the twenty consecutive years in which Nigeria had Muslim leaders, but suddenly managed to implement it less than a year after a Christian became president. Some

Christians also claimed that sharia was a political plot to destabilise the newly elected Christian president. Obasanjo's identity as a born-again Christian president ironically made sharia more likely to flourish and more difficult to stop. Sharia's expansion had been held at bay by previous Muslim leaders such as Babangida and Abacha who could suppress sharia agitation without being accused of pursuing a Christian agenda. Christians would conversely have interpreted the implementation of sharia by a Muslim president as evidence of pro-Muslim bias. Although Christians urged President Obasanjo to take an unequivocal stand and to declare sharia unconstitutional, it was difficult for a Christian president to do so. To resist sharia forcefully would have provoked a religious backlash from Muslims. The newly elected Obasanjo could not afford a confrontation with the Muslim north, which had assisted him to become president. Obasanjo sidestepped sharia by casually dismissing it as 'political sharia that will come and go'. Dr Bala Usman (a Muslim) of Ahmadu Bello University accused politicians of using sharia to restore their lost credibility: 'People have been imbued with the notion that *Sharia* is the answer to their frustration with life. These politicians want to use *Sharia* as a cover because the upper class in the north has come to the end of the line.'[23]

Whether or not it was politically motivated, sharia unleashed social forces that the northern political elite could not stop or control. Many Muslims hoped sharia would lead to a moral revival, and would be an effective antidote to crime. The northern 'street' also adopted the quest for sharia. In 1999 more than a hundred thousand people demonstrated in favour of sharia in Zamfara State, and there were similar demonstrations in other northern cities such as Kano and Minna. Sharia's momentum and popularity meant that Muslims who opposed it had to tread carefully lest they be labelled insincere or undevout. Sharia's irresistible tide swept across the north, as eleven other northern states followed Zamfara's example and also introduced sharia (see Map 3).[24] This placed a third of Nigeria's 36 states under sharia. Although the federal attorney-general, Kanu Agabi (also a Christian), sent a letter to the governors of sharia states to advise them that sharia was unconstitutional, federal authorities did not go further in opposing sharia.

Sharia could be easily implemented in states where most residents were Muslims. However, it proved explosive in states where Muslims and Christians were equally represented such as Kaduna. Kaduna State is a microcosm of Nigeria, and is split virtually equally between the mostly Muslim north and mostly Christian south of the state. When the Kaduna State government announced plans to introduce sharia, the state became the proxy battleground for an issue that was emotionally contentious across the entire country.

'I've never seen a slaughter of human beings like this'

In early 2000, Muslim youths in Kaduna held pro-sharia demonstrations for five successive days, and Christian youths carrying placards with slogans such as 'sharia is not Y2K compliant' held counter-demonstrations. When the two groups ran into each other, the outcome was predictably deadly. Muslim youths attacked and burned cars, churches, shops and businesses owned by Christians, while Christian youths did the same to those of Muslims. Corpses piled up in the streets after two to five thousand people were killed in the violence. A BBC correspondent said, 'I've seen enough. I've never seen a slaughter of human beings like this.'[25] Mortuary attendants at the Ahmadu Bello Teaching Hospital were overwhelmed by the number of corpses arriving, and stopped taking any more.

'There are times when you have to do the unthinkable'

As headless and mutilated corpses of Igbos killed in the north arrived back in the south-east, it evoked memories of the pogroms that had preceded the civil war. The mood among Igbos turned vengeful. The former Biafran leader Chukwuemeka Ojukwu warned: 'If we [Igbos] are attacked again, we will strike back. There are times when you have to do the unthinkable. We want Nigeria, and believe she can make progress. But Nigeria has to accommodate us as absolute equals.'[26] Igbos conducted reprisal attacks on northern Muslims in the south-east. A burned-out mosque in the commercial town of Aba bore a telling one-word graffito: 'Biafra'.

Yet Muslims and Christians also took great risks to protect each other. A middle-aged Igbo trader told me that she hid Hausas inside her compound and stoically replied 'no' when gangs of Igbo youths passed her home and asked her if any Hausas were inside. Another Igbo woman told me that she feared the worst when one of her northern colleagues (whom she affectionately called 'Mallam')[27] disappeared from work. She and her colleagues were so delighted when he emerged from hiding a month later that they held a party in his honour to celebrate his survival.

The year 2002 exposed the complications of sharia to an international audience. On March 22, 2002 a sharia court in the north-western state of Katsina sentenced a 31-year-old woman, Amina Lawal, to death by stoning for the crime of adultery after she gave birth out of wedlock. Her lawyers appealed against the ruling, and argued that she became pregnant after being raped. Ms Lawal's case gripped national and international news, and became entwined with the Miss World contest, which was scheduled to be staged in Nigeria after the previous edition was won by the Nigerian Agbani Darego, the first black woman ever to win the title of Miss World.

Miss World

The Miss World contestants fell into a religious, political and cultural maelstrom when they arrived in Abuja. Campaigners protesting against the death sentence on Ms Lawal urged the contestants to boycott the event. They were also unsettled by fierce criticism from Muslim youths and clerics who condemned the competition, which was scheduled during the Muslim holy month of Ramadan. Muslim outrage amplified after a Christian female journalist from southern Nigeria, Isioma Daniel, published an article in *This Day* newspaper on November 16, 2002 which made light of Muslim objections to the contest. Her article suggested that the contestants were so beautiful that the Prophet himself might have married one of them. Ms Daniel fled overseas after Zamfara State issued a fatwa calling for her death. On November 20, 2002 angry Muslim youths attacked and burned down *This Day*'s Kaduna office. More than 200 people were killed and another 500 injured during rioting between Muslim and Christian youths. Muslim mobs attacked and murdered the parents of the subsequent Chelsea and Nigerian footballer, Victor Moses, in their home. His father Austin was the pastor of a church in Kaduna. An uncle of Victor Moses, then aged 11, hid him with sympathisers who eventually smuggled him abroad to England. Despite the contestants being protected by armed guards, the Miss World organisers relocated the contest to London.

Sharia presented an extreme challenge to inter-regional and intra-regional cohesion. While liberal Muslims tried to find a way for sharia to coexist with the constitution, conservative Islamic scholars like Zakzaky ironically condemned its implementation under a secular state and constitution. Sharia increased the prominence of dissident Islamic groups and caused them to intersect with national politics. While such groups pressed for a more stringent implementation of sharia, they also splintered. Izala had fragmented into different rival factions. One of Izala's renowned scholars was Sheikh Ja'afar Mahmud Adam. He had a young protégé of Kanuri ethnicity named Mohammed Yusuf.

Yusuf was born in 1970 and his father was from Jakusko in the northeastern state of Yobe. Adam and Yusuf preached at the Alhaji Muhammadu Ndimi Mosque in the city of Maiduguri in north-east Nigeria.[28] Yusuf was a charismatic orator who was venerated by the young people of the mosque. Ideological differences caused Yusuf to leave Izala sometime between 2000 and 2002, and Izala distanced itself from him. Adam and Yusuf would also later become estranged when Adam opposed Yusuf's radical preaching.

Dawah[29]

Yusuf drew ideological inspiration from the Islamic scholar Ibn Taymiyyah, who died in 1328 while imprisoned in Damascus. Taymiyyah is regarded by many as a prominent figure in the emergence of Salafism, which espouses a literal and puritanical interpretation of the Koran and Islamic traditions. Salafists believe that the Koran and the teachings of the Prophet are clear, inerrant, and require no contextual reinterpretations or modifications. They seek to cleanse Islam of outside influences, and to return to a purist form of Islam practised by the Prophet and early Islamic patriarchs (the Salafs).

Like Maitatsine before him, Yusuf rejected several elements of Western culture and education which he believed had contaminated Islam, such as mixed gender schools, the teaching of evolution, and the use of a national flag, coat of arms, and a ceremonial mace to conduct business in Nigeria's National Assembly. The use of such emblems in his view constituted fetish worship. Yusuf's simple but logical premise that Nigeria's leaders were responsible for the corruption, immorality and injustice in society resonated with disenchanted young people. He could thank the corrupt incompetence of successive Nigerian governments for his popularity. Ahmad Salkida, a journalist who knew Yusuf, said that his group 'was founded on ideology, but poor governance was the catalyst for it to spread'.[30]

Yusufiyya

Yusuf's sermons were popular. Recorded audio and video tapes of them were available for purchase on CD and DVD, and were disseminated widely in north-eastern Nigeria as well as Cameroon, Chad and Niger. He appeared many times on radio and television during which he debated esoteric Islamic concepts with other Muslims. His followers were fanatically devoted to him and were sometimes called 'Yusufiyya' (followers of Yusuf) in view of their cult-like reverence for him. The group also called themselves *Ahl al-Sunna wal Jama'a* (Followers of the Prophet's Teachings). Yusuf garnered loyalty and created a communal spirit by providing micro-finance, loans and economic assistance to his followers.

Outsiders erroneously reduced the group's objective to the sole aim of eliminating Western education. Rejection of Western education was part (but not all) of Yusufiyya's ideology. Yusuf's hostility to Western education was caused by a combination of issues that were the product of local Nigerian history and the influence of Middle Eastern Islamic discourse. There had been a long-standing scepticism towards Western education in some Muslim areas of northern Nigeria because of its association with the Christian missionaries and European colonisers who brought it to Nigeria. There were two contending forms of *Ilimi* (education) in the north. These were *Ilimin boko* (Western education) and *Ilimin Islamiyya* (Koranic education). Many Muslim northerners prefer Koranic education to Western education and have resisted government campaigns to increase school enrolment in the north. Some considered *Ilimin boko* to be inauthentic and inferior to *Ilimin Islamiyya*. The fact that *Ilimin boko* was taught in a strange language (English) and was brought by European colonisers and missionaries who converted their neighbours to Christianity intensified the impression of *Ilimin boko* as an alien and untrustworthy medium of instruction. The complex etymology of the word 'boko' in northern Nigeria further demonstrated what many northerners really thought of *Ilimin boko*. In Hausa 'boko' refers not only to Western education, but to Western culture in general. The word is also used to refer to something that is fake or fraudulent.

Thus Yusuf did not introduce a new concept but, rather, resurrected a pre-existing historical prejudice against Western education. If, as according to Yusuf's narrative, Nigeria's Western educated leaders were responsible for the ills of society, it was easy to identify their acquisition of Western education as the cause of their straying from a righteous path.

However, the Yusufiyya were not the uneducated and backward reactionaries of external stereotypes. Some of them had attended university, and spoke English fluently, including their female members. A number of them resigned from their clerical or government jobs, dropped out of university, or tore up their degree certificates to join Yusuf. A University of Maiduguri graduate informed me that one of the Yusufiyya was a former staff member at the university. Although the Yusufiyya were regarded as eccentric and puritanical, they were not violent in the beginning or a danger to national security. Yusuf's brother-in-law Baba Kuru Fugu said: 'Yusuf did not start as a violent or radical man, he was just a Mallam preaching against injustice and corruption in the society.'[31] However, the sect's contempt for the government, and its uncompromising rejection of any knowledge or structure not based on Islam, inevitably put them on a collision course with state authorities. Yusuf's radical preaching attracted the attention of the State Security Service, who called him in for questioning many times, but released him after each interrogation. His followers gave him a hero's welcome every time he returned.

He was somehow more feared than Yusuf'

Yusufiyya's ideology became increasingly militant as more radical members joined the group. Mamman Nur, a Shuwa Arab born and raised in Maiduguri who later became a senior member of Yusuf's group, introduced Yusuf to another young man who had a similar background. The new inductee was, like Yusuf, from the Kanuri ethnic group, and was also born in a remote village in Yobe State near Nigeria's north-eastern border with Niger. Nur and the new member had met while pursuing Islamic studies at the Borno State College of Legal and Islamic Studies. The new member seemed even more devoted and severe than Yusuf. One of Yusuf's friends recalled: '[he] was always studying and writing, and was more devoted and modest than anyone else. He would only wear cheap clothes and did not accept even to drive a car, preferring a motorbike ... he was somehow more feared than Yusuf.'[32]

Although the new member went by the name Dar-al Tawhid ('abode of monotheism'), his real first name was Abubakar. He was originally from Shekau village in Yobe State. When he was a young boy, Abubakar's father sent him to study with a mallam (a Koranic studies teacher). His parents never visited him throughout his eleven years with the teacher. The mallam's son Baba Fanani recalled that Abubakar was 'the most troublesome of all of his students'[33] and that 'he was arguing with the mallam all the time'.[34] The mallam became alarmed by Abubakar's radicalism and aggression and expelled him. Abubakar moved to the Mafoni area of Maiduguri in 1990, and became an itinerant street preacher. He supported himself financially by selling perfume bottles in a market. He also preached and told anyone who would listen that the government had failed them. Nuhu Mohammed (who studied under him) described him as 'very harsh as a teacher' and recalled that 'nobody wanted to argue with him'.[35]

Yusuf also later met one Mohammed Alli, who, some accounts claim, fought alongside the mujahideen in Afghanistan and was radicalised by jihadi literature which he encountered in Saudi Arabia. Alli convinced Yusuf that Muslims could not serve of live under a secular government or constitution as they were not based on the Koran. Yusuf later said: 'Our call refuses employment under the government which does not rule by what Allah has revealed such as the French law, the American law, the British law or any other constitution or system that goes against the teachings of Islam and negates the Qur'an and Sunnah.'[36]

In 2002, an offshoot of between one to two hundred Yusufiyya declared the Nigerian state to be irredeemably corrupt and decadent. In early 2003 they decided to emulate the Prophet by embarking upon a *hijra* (migration) away from secular society,[37] and moved to a remote village in northern Yobe State called Kanamma, where they could establish their own society in accordance with Islamic law. Yusuf was not among this Hijra group (he was abroad in Saudi Arabia at the time) and some accounts claim that it was led by Mohammed Alli, and others that it was led by Mola Umar and a former University of Maiduguri student, Aminu Tashen-Ilimi.[38] Like Maitatsine before them, the Hijra group seem to have deliberately selected a location that was remote, defensible and difficult for outsiders to access. Their camp in Kanamma was forested, between two bodies of water, and protected by trenches and sandbags.

Nigerian Taliban

US diplomatic cables described the Hijra group as 'mostly urban, comparatively well off Nigerians who had moved to a commune-like village to set up their own isolated society'. They included 'individuals from wealthy Islamic families in Borno State' and unemployed university students. They lived a spartan life, devoted themselves to praying, fasting and their own interpretation of Islam, and isolated themselves from the rest of the community. Locals nicknamed the group the 'Taliban' after the Afghanistan Taliban. A professor in Maiduguri, Abdulmumin Sa'ad, tersely observed that the group was on an 'idealistic outing in Yobe State'[39] and warned that it and other groups could easily become violent and adopt extremist ideology or foreign ties. The professor and his colleagues noted an increase in religiously inspired sects on Nigerian university campuses, and warned that 'radical groups will likely emerge and youth may look to Islamic extremism to strike back at economic and political injustice'.[40]

Things turned sour in 2003 after the Taliban got into a dispute with locals about fishing rights. Local leaders asked the Taliban to leave, and called the police. In December 2003 the police intervened and destroyed the Taliban's camp and arrested several of its members. The Taliban retaliated by attacking the police station in Kanamma and seizing several guns and ammunition. They also attacked other police stations in Yobe State before security forces finally suppressed them in the Yobe State capital of Damaturu. This clash with the police marked the first step in the weaponisation of the group. At this stage, the Taliban directed most of their violence not against Christians, but against fellow Muslims whom they regarded as apostates or who acted as agents of the corrupt Nigerian state. In early 2004 the Taliban took their weapons into Borno State and also battled the police there. Scores of men wearing red bandanas, carrying a flag with an Islamic inscription, and chanting 'Allahu Akbar!' attacked police stations in Bama and Gwoza in Borno State. During their raids they also kidnapped some locals whom they tried to conscript and forced to dig trenches around their camp.

Taliban members who survived these clashes then returned to Maiduguri and rejoined Mohammed Yusuf's group. They built a new mosque there called the Ibn Taimiyyah Masjid[41] on land owned by Yusuf's father-in-law, Baba Fugu Mohammed. Although the Yusufiyya had shunned the government and politics, their popularity with youths made them attractive to politicians. They warmed to governorship candidate Ali Modu Sheriff, who was then a senator, when Sheriff promised to fully implement sharia law in Borno State if he was elected governor of the state during the 2003 election campaign. Yusuf returned from Saudi Arabia after Sheriff won the governorship. The Yusufiyya's prominence grew after Sheriff appointed a Yusuffiya member, Buji Foi, as Borno State's commissioner for religious affairs. *Africa Confidential* also claimed that Yusufiyya received further patronage[42] from the Borno State government, and that the government released some Yusufiyya members from prison, including Abubakar Adam Kambar, who had been imprisoned for armed robbery.[43] However, Borno State was not monolithically Muslim and contained several Christian communities. Yusuf and the Yusufiyya became disaffected when Sheriff did not implement sharia with the stringency they expected. Sheriff limited sharia mainly to civil law issues and declined to permit its most severe punishments such as amputation and stoning. In response, Foi left the government in protest,[44] Yusuf and the Yusufiyya turned on Sheriff, accused him of apostasy, and began preaching hostile utterances against the Borno State government. This estrangement with the government marked a symbolic point of no return for the Yusufiyya.

Chillingly, a US diplomatic cable in February 2004 warned that the Yusufiyya 'sect could easily turn to terrorism, or be used as a tool by international terrorist groups'.[45] Five years after this cable was transmitted, Yusuf, his father-in-law, Foi and several hundred Yusufiyya lay dead. The subsequent events that turned north-eastern Nigeria into a war zone are well known and do not require repetition here. The aim of this chapter has been to illuminate the multiple political and social processes that rapidly transformed the Yusuffiya from a proselytising sect into a transnational insurgent organisation that presented severe security challenges to four West African countries simultaneously. Nigeria has bred a form of extremism that does not have a one size fits all solution. Despite years of military assaults, there is no end in sight to Nigeria's insurgency. The often-repeated mantra is that economic development is the antidote to extremism. Nigeria's former chief of defence staff General Martin Luther Agwai said: 'You can never solve any of these problems with military solutions ... It is a political issue; it is a social issue; it is an economic issue, and until these issues are addressed, the military can never give you a solution.'[46] However, socio-economic measures will take years or decades to have an effect. Since neither the socio-economic carrot nor the military stick can resolve Nigeria's security problems in the short term, religious extremism may have become part of Nigeria's long-term fabric.

Nigeria may have six geo-political zones, but it also has three religious zones. The south-west is split evenly between Christians and Muslims who live alongside each other in the same neighbourhoods, houses and even bedrooms. Mosques and churches are built close to each other, yet religious violence there is rare. The remainder of the south is overwhelmingly Christian and sometimes gives the impression of having more church denominations than it has towns. Yet religious violence there is also rare. That leaves one area with an uncomfortable, taboo question hanging over it. Why is it that the vast majority of religious violence in Nigeria occurs in the north? Nigeria will soon have to ditch political correctness and answer this question.

20

BACK TO THE FUTURE

The major events of the decade chronicled in this book revolved largely around the complex interaction between five men (two of whom are named in the book title). Their relationship is a microcosm of the interconnected nature of Nigerian political elites. At the start of 1993 Nigeria was led by Babangida. The man who headed the military government after him, Abacha, had been his close friend and colleague for three decades. Thereafter Nigeria experienced five years of political paralysis due to a power struggle between two men, Abacha and Abiola, who had also been friends with each other, and with Babangida. We will never know what (if any) bargain Abacha and Abiola struck about sharing or taking turns in power, because neither is alive to defend or account for himself. After Abacha and Abiola died, a fourth man, Abubakar, who also happened to be a friend of both of them, as well as a childhood classmate of Babangida, ascended to power. The decade concluded with the accession to power of Obasanjo, who was a childhood classmate of Abiola, and the political, military and professional boss of Babangida, Abacha and Abubakar.

Abiola and Obasanjo had similar lives and backgrounds. They were from the same town, the same ethnic group, spoke the same languages, attended the same school, built their economic and political careers through relationships with northern-led military governments, were imprisoned by the same military regime, and were elected president of Nigeria. Yet only one of them emerged from imprisonment alive and got to rule. Abiola was in the right place but at the wrong time. Had he become president in 1993, he would almost certainly have been overthrown or assassinated by a northern general before long.

Obasanjo seemed to possess 'street smarts' and survival skills. He was politically astute enough to dine with and befriend foreign presidents and monarchs, and present himself to them as a pragmatic general. Yet domestically he was also rugged enough not to be intimidated by the military. Only a strong-willed and stubborn retired general like him could have subordinated the military to civilian control and weaned it off its coup addiction. Perhaps his greatest legacy to Nigeria was his use of carrots and sticks to weed out politically ambitious military officers, and browbeat the military into accepting that military coups should be consigned to the past.

Yet the cessation of military rule did not allow the military to escape the consequences of what it had done while in government. Military rule generated long-term conflicts with consequences that are still being contested two decades after the military left government. As a result the military has spent considerable time fighting insurgencies and emergencies that stemmed from problems it created or was unable to resolve while in power. The military continues to influence politics, daily security, and national defence priorities. Two of the four presidents since 1999 were former military heads of state, and military officers from past military governments have also served as Senate president, state governors, and House of Representatives members.[1] All of Nigeria's heads of state to date were born during the colonial era. Some of them have been steering events in Nigeria since 1966. Now wealthy grandfathers, they still wield enormous influence. The board of directors of Nigeria Inc. have held their board positions for over fifty years. They will not be around forever. It will be fascinating to see what becomes of Nigeria when a new, younger board of directors born in the post-independence era inevitably emerges.

Nigeria's story has not only been about its elites. Nigerians often treated elected civilian leaders and military dictators as two rival lovers courting them. When civilians are in power, Nigerians often nostalgically recall the supposed discipline and stability of military rule. Yet when suffering under military dictatorship, they campaigned for democracy as a utopian salvation. Being in Nigeria sometimes feels like being on a frightening rollercoaster ride. While on the ride one will scream in terror and want the ride to end. However, once it ends, one wants to get back on and experience the adrenaline rush again. Along with their adrenaline addiction, many Nigerians harbour a Messiah complex that their country is potentially a great one, if only power would fall into the hands of a visionary leader. Gani Fawehinmi said:

country has never produced a leader whose basic interest is the welfare of the people, a leader strong enough, resolute enough to usher in a progressive Nigeria ... We need a leader strong like Mao Zedong, resolute like John Kennedy, ruthless like Fidel Castro. We need a leader like J.J. Rawlings in Ghana who has the ruthlessness of principle ... People must be killed! They must pay with their lives, and the ill-gotten gains should be taken from their children.[2]

Nigerians often fantasise about this sort of take-no-prisoners revolution. There are two problems with it that they often overlook. Firstly, it has already been tried (in January 1966) and its net effect was a civil war, more than a million corpses, and nearly thirty years of military rule. Secondly, there is a reason why Nigeria has never had a nationally accepted heroic, 'father of the nation' figure such as Atatürk, Ben-Gurion, de Gaulle, Gandhi, Nasser or George Washington. Less than sixty years after its independence Nigeria is still too young and, more importantly, too diverse to have developed a national ethos that can weave a heroic legend of national liberation or history around one individual. Change in Nigeria is unlikely to come from a single visionary leader. It is more likely to emerge incrementally as the various rivalries in the country act as unwitting catalysts for change.

'Restructuring' is currently the most significant political buzzword in Nigeria. The demands for restructuring Nigeria's political and resource-sharing systems have traditionally been championed in the south but resisted in the north. Power shift was a Faustian bargain that addressed the clamour for a southern president, but deferred fundamental issues of national restructuring. The military played an ace card that once again gave Nigerian unity a stay of execution. Power shift was introduced as a temporary measure to get Nigeria out of a political logjam. However, its core concepts set precedents that led to zoning and rotation becoming the accepted methods of political succession in Nigerian politics. The ongoing rotation of the presidency between the north and south is a direct outcome and consequence of the 1999 power shift. However, the north may also have unwittingly provided the biggest boost to the south's restructuring agenda. The sharia controversy added a twist to the federal political calculus. By introducing sharia, the north, which resisted structural changes to Nigeria during the military rule years, has ironically kept the flames of regional autonomy and federal restructuring alive on the national agenda. The dual legal systems practised by some northern states may have provided a template from which southern states may similarly press their own demands for customisation in their states and differentiation from the rest of the federation.

Nigeria has been governed by elected civilian governments since 1999. Nigerians once placed their faith in their military as a political saviour. The five brutal years from 1993 to 1998 were akin to bitter medicine that Nigerians had to drink before being cured of their Stockholm syndrome regarding their military. Perhaps the military's greatest contribution to Nigeria's democracy was to rule long and badly enough to thoroughly ruin its reputation, and disabuse the public from considering it as an alternative government to civilians.

The past is not static. The way it is remembered and narrated changes over time. It flexes to reshape supposed facts and illuminate blind spots. The history in this book is based on the information available today. I have contributed my own part to collecting as many pieces of the Nigerian jigsaw as I can. Future researchers may find other missing pieces and one day piece them together with mine to complete the Nigerian historical jigsaw.

APPENDIX 1

TIMELINE OF KEY EVENTS, 1993–2003

Date	Event
June 12, 1993	Nigeria holds its first presidential election in 10 years. The presidential candidates are Bashir Tofa of the NRC and Moshood Abiola of the SDP.
June 23, 1993	As election results show Abiola (a multi-billionaire businessman and friend of the military president, General Babangida) heading to a comprehensive victory, the military government suddenly annuls the election results and suspends the National Electoral Commission. Street protests and violence follow.
August 3, 1993	Abiola travels abroad to seek international support for the validation of his election victory.
August 27, 1993	Babangida 'steps aside', resigns, and transfers power to an Interim National Government (ING) led by Ernest Shonekan.
October 25, 1993	Movement for the Advancement of Democracy hijacks a Nigeria Airways plane in protest at the June 12 election annulment.
November 10, 1993	Lagos State High Court declares the ING to be illegal.
November 17, 1993	Shonekan resigns and is replaced by the secretary for defence, General Sani Abacha. Abacha dissolves the ING and military rule recommences.

May 15, 1994	A group of veteran politicians form the National Democratic Coalition (NADECO) to press for the validation of the June 12, 1993 election result. NADECO gives the military government an ultimatum to resign by the end of May.
June 11, 1994	Abiola declares himself president at Epetedo in Lagos, then goes into hiding. Police declare Abiola a fugitive and issue a warrant for his arrest.
June 23, 1994	Abiola emerges from hiding and the police arrest him on charges of treason.
June 27, 1994	Abacha inaugurates a National Constitutional Conference to design a new constitution for Nigeria.
July 5, 1994	National Union of Petroleum and Natural Gas Workers (NUPENG) and Petroleum and Natural Gas Senior Staff Association (PENGASSAN) begin a strike to protest against Abiola's detention and to campaign for the validation of the annulled election results.
August 5, 1994	Abuja High Court grants bail to Abiola, but Abiola rejects bail conditions and remains in detention.
August 17, 1994	Abacha cracks down on striking workers and dissolves executive councils of NUPENG, PENGASSAN and the Nigerian Labour Congress, and bans the *Punch*, *Concord* (owned by Abiola) and *Guardian* newspapers from publishing.
December 6, 1994	Constitutional conference passes a motion calling on the military government to resign no later than January 1, 1996.
December 1994	Constitutional conference adjourned.
March 7, 1995	Director of defence information, Brigadier-General Fred Chijuka, denies rumours that several military officers have been arrested for coup plotting.
March 10, 1995	Chief of defence staff, Major-General Abdulsalam Abubakar, confirms that the government had detected and foiled a coup plot to overthrow the government and that some officers have been arrested.
March 1995	Former head of state General Obasanjo and his former deputy, Major-General Shehu Musa Yar'Adua, arrested as suspects in alleged coup plot.

April 1995	Constitutional Conference resumes and revokes its earlier motion for the military to resign no later than January 1, 1996, and on April 25, 1995 passes a new, unanimous motion allowing the military to determine how long it would remain in power.
June 5, 1995	Special Military Tribunal led by Brigadier-General Patrick Aziza commences trial of Obasanjo, Yar'Adua and other coup suspects.
June 27, 1995	The Constitutional Conference presents its final report to the government, including a recommendation for Nigeria to be split into six geo-political zones and to adopt a rotational presidency.
July 14, 1995	Government announces that several people have been convicted of treason and sentenced to death or imprisonment. Yar'Adua is sentenced to death, and Obasanjo is sentenced to life imprisonment. World leaders including Presidents Mandela, Clinton, Mugabe and Rawlings appeal for clemency.
October 1, 1995	Abacha commutes death sentences on coup convicts to imprisonment.
October 31, 1995	Civil Disturbances Special Tribunal sentences Ken Saro-Wiwa and eight other Ogoni activists to death by hanging for their alleged role in the murder of four other Ogonis.
November 10, 1995	Saro-Wiwa and eight others are executed by hanging in Port Harcourt. Nigeria is suspended from the Commonwealth.
January 17, 1996	Abacha's son Ibrahim Abacha is killed in a plane crash, along with Bello Dangote, the younger brother of the wealthy businessman Aliko Dangote. A total of 14 people on board the plane die in the crash.
February 2, 1996	Unknown gunmen shoot and seriously wound former minister of internal affairs, Alex Ibru, in Lagos during an assassination attempt. Ibru survives but loses an eye and a finger.
April 20, 1996	Abacha deposes the sultan of Sokoto, Ibrahim Dasuki, and exiles him to Zing, in Taraba State.
June 4, 1996	Unknown gunmen shoot and kill Abiola's wife Kudirat in Lagos.

October 1, 1996	Government announces the creation of six new states: Bayelsa, Ebonyi, Ekiti, Gombe, Nasarawa and Zamfara. This increases the number of states in Nigeria from 30 to 36.
November 14, 1996	A car bomb explodes at the Murtala Mohammed International Airport in Lagos and kills three people including the chief security officer of the Federal Airport Authority (FAA), Dr Shola Omasola.
December 16, 1996	The military administrator of Lagos State, Colonel Mohammed Marwa, survives a bomb explosion that targeted his convoy.
December 12, 1997	Government announces that it has foiled a coup plot to overthrow Abacha and arrested suspects including Abacha's deputy, Lt-General Oladipo Diya.
February 14, 1998	Special Military Tribunal led by Major-General Victor Malu commences trial of Diya and 25 other suspects for allegedly plotting to overthrow Abacha.
March 3–4, 1998	Daniel Kanu and Youths Earnestly Ask for Abacha organisation hold a 'million-man march' in Abuja to support Abacha's transmutation from military to civilian head of state.
April 16–20, 1998	All five registered parties adopt Abacha as their sole 'consensus candidate' for the presidential elections scheduled for August 1.
April 28, 1998	Special Military Tribunal sentences six people (including Diya, former minister of works and housing, Major-General Abdulkarim Adisa, and the former minister of communications, Major-General Tajudeen Olanrewaju) to death by firing squad for treason after convicting them of plotting a coup to overthrow Abacha.
May 1, 1998	The civil rights group United Action for Democracy (UAD) organises protests in Lagos against the political parties' adoption of Abacha as sole presidential candidate.
May 7, 1998	A coalition of eminent northern and southern politicians calling themselves the 'G34' sends a letter to Abacha, urging him to reject the parties' nomination of him as their sole presidential candidate.

June 8, 1998	Abacha dies of a heart attack. He is buried in his home town of Kano later the same day. The chief of defence staff, Major-General Abdulsalam Abubakar, succeeds Abacha as head of state.
June 15, 1998	Government approves the release of several prominent detainees including Obasanjo, former sultan of Sokoto Ibrahim Dasuki, Beko Ransome-Kuti, Bola Ige, Chris Anyanwu, Frank Ovie Kokori.
July 7, 1998	Abiola dies of a heart attack while meeting with an American government delegation. His death comes exactly one month after Abacha died.
July 9, 1998	Government commutes death sentences passed on Diya and other coup convicts, and reduces their sentences to imprisonment.
February 27, 1999	Nigerian holds first presidential election since the annulled June 12, 1993 election. Obasanjo of the PDP is elected president after defeating Olu Falae (joint candidate of the AD and APP).
March 4, 1999	Government releases prisoners convicted of involvement in the 1995 and 1997 coups.
March 23, 1999	Government releases eight prisoners convicted of involvement in the 1990 coup.
May 29, 1999	Former military head of state General Olusegun Obasanjo is sworn in as Nigeria's first democratically elected president in 15 years.
June 17, 1999	Obasanjo compulsorily retires 93 military officers who were members of prior military governments.
November 4 and 5, 1999	Local youths kill 12 police officers at Odi in Bayelsa State.
November 20–24, 1999	Military raid on Odi to find and arrest those who killed police officers earlier in the month. Soldiers destroy large parts of Odi and kill scores of civilians after using heavy weapons including artillery and mortar bombs.
January 27, 2000	Zamfara State in northwestern Nigeria adopts sharia law.
January–June 2000	11 other states in the north also adopt sharia law (Bauchi, Borno, Gombe, Jigawa, Kaduna, Kano, Katsina, Kebbi, Niger, Sokoto and Yobe States).

February 2000	Muslims in Kaduna State hold pro-sharia demonstrations, and Christians hold counter-demonstrations to protest against plans to introduce sharia in the religiously mixed state which is split between Christians and Muslims.
February–May 2000	Between 2,000 and 5,000 people are killed in violence between Muslims and Christians. Kaduna State government declares a 24-hour curfew, and the federal government orders the army to stop the violence.
October 12, 2001	Mutilated corpses of 19 soldiers are found in Zaki-Biam in Benue State.
October 22, 2001	Punitive military raids on Zaki-Biam in retaliation for the murder of 19 soldiers. Over 200 civilians are killed.
March 22, 2002	A sharia court in the north-western state of Katsina sentences 31-year-old Amina Lawal to death by stoning for the crime of adultery after she gave birth out of wedlock.
November 20–23, 2002	More than 200 people are killed and another 500 injured during rioting between Muslims opposed to the holding of the Miss World contest in Nigeria and Christian youths. The event's organisers relocate it to England over security concerns for the contestants.
Early 2003	Followers of Islamic cleric Mohammed Yusuf embark on a *hijra* (migration) away from secular society, and move to a remote village in northern Yobe State called Kanamma where they can establish their own society in accordance with Islamic law. Locals nickname the group the 'Taliban'.
April 19, 2003	Obasanjo is re-elected as president for a second and final term of office.
December 2003–early 2004	'Taliban' group clashes with police in Kanamma and Damaturu in Yobe State and in Bama and Gwoza in Borno State. Police arrest several members. The Taliban retaliate by attacking police stations, and seizing police weapons and ammunition.

APPENDIX 2

NIGERIA'S LAST MILITARY GOVERNMENT

	Provisional Ruling Council, 1999				
Name	*Position*	*Religion*	*Ethnicity*	*State of Origin*
1. General Abdulsalam Abubakar	Head of State and Commander in Chief of the Nigerian Armed Forces	Muslim	Gwari	Niger
2. Vice-Admiral Okhai Mike Akhigbe	Chief of General Staff	Christian	Afemai	Edo
3. Air Marshal al-Amin Daggash	Chief of Defence Staff	Muslim	Shuwa Arab	Borno
4. Lt-General Ishaya Rizi Bamaiyi	Chief of Army Staff	Christian	Dakarkari	Kebbi
5. Vice-Admiral Jubril Ayinla	Chief of Naval Staff	Muslim	Yoruba	Lagos
6. Air Marshal Nsikak Eduok	Chief of Air Staff	Christian	Ibibio	Akwa Ibom
7. Ibrahim Coomasie	Inspector-General of Police	Muslim	Fulani	Katsina

8. Lt-General Rufus Kupolati	Commandant, Task Force on Armed Forces/ Police and Petroleum Trust Fund	Christian	Yoruba	Kogi
9. Major-General Godwin Abbe	Commandant, National War College, Abuja	Christian	Edo	Edo
10. Major-General John Mark Inienger	Commandant, Command and Staff College, Jaji	Christian	Tiv[1]	Benue
11. Major-General Bashir Salihi Magashi	Commandant, Nigerian Defence Academy, Kaduna	Muslim	Fulani	Kano
12. Major-General Suleiman Said	Commandant, Training and Doctrine Command (TRADOC)	Muslim	N/A	N/A
13. Air Vice-Marshal Idi Musa	Chief of Defence Intelligence	Christian	N/A	Jigawa
14. Major-General Abdullahi Sarki Mukhtar	GOC, 1 Mechanised Infantry Division—Kaduna	Muslim	Fulani	Kano
15. Major-General Peter Gyang Sha	GOC, 2 Mechanised Division—Ibadan	Christian	Birom	Plateau
16. Major-General Ekpo Archibong	GOC, 3 Armoured Division—Jos	Christian	Efik	Cross River
17. Major-General Oladayo Popoola	GOC, 82 Division—Enugu	Christian	Yoruba	Oyo

18.	Major-General Samuel Victor Leo Malu	GOC, Lagos Garrison Command	Christian	Tiv	Benue
19.	Rear-Admiral Ibrahim Ogohi	Flag Officer Commanding, Western Naval Command	Muslim	Igala	Kogi
20.	Rear-Admiral Taiwo Odedina	Flag Officer Commanding, Eastern Naval Command	Christian	Yoruba	N/A
21.	Rear-Admiral Peter Ebhaleme	Flag Officer Commanding, Naval Training Command	Christian	Esan	Edo
22.	Air Vice-Marshal Isaac Mohammed Alfa	Air Officer Commanding, Training Command	Muslim	Igala	Kogi
23.	Air Vice-Marshal Emmanuel Edem	Air Officer Commanding, Tactical Command	Christian	Efik	Cross River
24.	Air Vice-Marshal Mohammed Ndatsu Umaru	Air Officer Commanding, Logistics Command	Muslim	Nupe	Niger
25.	Major-General Yunana Nom	Chief of Training, Operations and Plans at Defence Headquarters	Christian	Kataf	Kaduna
26.	Major-General Idris Garba	Chief of Operations, Army Headquarters	Muslim	Nupe	Niger
27.	Rear-Admiral Victor Ombu	Chief of Operations, Naval Headquarters	Christian	Ijaw	Bayelsa

28.	Commodore Emmanuel Acholonu	Director of Planning at Naval Headquarters	Christian	Igbo	Imo
29.	Group Captain Ikechukwu Nnamani	Air Force Headquarters	Christian	Igbo	N/A
30.	Musiliu Smith	Assistant Inspector General of Police, Zonal Headquarters, Kano	Muslim	Yoruba	Lagos

APPENDIX 3

COUP SENTENCES

1995 Coup Trial—Sentences

	Name	Charge	Original Sentence	Commuted Sentence
1.	General Olusegun Obasanjo	Concealment of treason	Life imprisonment	15 years' imprisonment
2.	Major-General Shehu Musa Yar'Adua	Conspiracy to commit treason, concealment of treason, illegal possession of a firearm, and theft	Death	Life imprisonment
3.	Colonel Gabriel Ajayi	Conspiracy to commit treason, and concealment of treason	Death	25 years' imprisonment
4.	Colonel Ralph Sixtus Babatunde Bello-Fadile	Conspiracy to commit treason, and concealment of treason	Death	Life imprisonment
5.	Colonel Olu Craig	Other offences	Retired	N/A
6.	Colonel Roland N Emokpae	Conspiracy to commit treason, and concealment of treason	Death	25 years' imprisonment
7.	Colonel Lawan Gwadabe	Conspiracy to commit treason, and concealment of treason	Death	Life imprisonment

8. Colonel Olusegun Oloruntoba	Conspiracy to commit treason, and concealment of treason	Death	Life imprisonment
9. Colonel Emmanuel I Ndubueze	Conspiracy to commit treason, and concealment of treason	Death	25 years' imprisonment
10. Lt-Colonel MA Ajayi	Conspiracy to commit treason, and concealment of treason	Death	25 years' imprisonment
11. Lt-Colonel Olumuyiwa Bamgbose	Other offences	6 months' imprisonment	N/A
12. Lt-Colonel Kefas Happy Bulus	Conspiracy to commit treason, and concealment of treason	Death	25 years' imprisonment
13. Lt-Colonel Lawrence Fabiyi	Accessory after the fact of treason	15 years' imprisonment	N/A
14. Lt-Colonel Martin Azuka Igwe	Conspiracy to commit treason, and concealment of treason	Death	25 years' imprisonment
15. Lt-Colonel Chidi Izuorgu	Other offences	6 months' imprisonment	N/A
16. Lt-Colonel SB Mapaiyeda	Concealment of treason	12 months' imprisonment	N/A
17. Lt-Colonel OE Nyong	Other offences	6 months' imprisonment	N/A
18. Lt-Colonel RD Obiki	Concealment of treason	15 years' imprisonment	N/A

	Offence	Sentence	Sentence
19. Lt-Colonel SE Oyewole	Conspiracy to commit treason, and concealment of treason	Death	25 years' imprisonment
20. Lt-Colonel D Usman	Other offences	Retired	N/A
21. Major Akinloye Akinyemi (retired)	Conspiracy to commit treason, and concealment of treason	Death	Life imprisonment
22. Major IO Edeh	Other offences	6 months' imprisonment	N/A
23. Major EO Obalisa	Conspiracy to commit treason, and concealment of treason	Death	25 years' imprisonment
24. Captain AA Ogunsuyi	Accessory after the fact of treason	2 years' imprisonment	N/A
25. Lieutenant A Olowokere	Conspiracy to commit treason, and concealment of treason	Death	25 years' imprisonment
26. Second Lieutenant Richard Emonvhe	Accessory after the fact of treason	Life imprisonment	15 years' imprisonment
27. Sergeant Patrick Usikpeko[1]	Accessory after the fact of treason	15 years' imprisonment	N/A
28. Corporal Ogbinowa	Other offences	6 months' imprisonment	N/A
29. Lance Corporal Joseph Onwe	Other offences	6 months' imprisonment	N/A
30. Navy Captain MA Ibrahim[2]	Other offences	Life imprisonment	15 years' imprisonment
31. Quinette Lewis Alagoa*	Concealment of treason	6 months' imprisonment	N/A

32. Kunle Ajibade*	Accessory after the fact of treason	Life imprisonment	15 years' imprisonment
33. Christine Anyanwu*	Accessory after the fact of treason	Life imprisonment	15 years' imprisonment
34. Moses Ayegba*	Accessory after the fact of treason	Life imprisonment	15 years' imprisonment
35. Julius Badejo*	Other offences	15 years' imprisonment	N/A
36. Rebecca Ikpe*	Accessory after the fact of treason	Life imprisonment	15 years' imprisonment
37. Dr Beko Ransome-Kuti*	Accessory after the fact of treason	Life imprisonment	15 years' imprisonment
38. Sanusi Mato*	Accessory after the fact of treason	15 years imprisonment	N/A
39. George Mbah*	Accessory after the fact of treason	Life imprisonment	15 years' imprisonment
40. Felix Ndamaigida*	Accessory after the fact of treason	15 years imprisonment	N/A
41. Ben Charles-Obi*	Accessory after the fact of treason	Life imprisonment	15 years imprisonment
42. Mathew Popoola*	Other offences	15 years imprisonment	N/A
43. Shehu Sani*	Accessory after the fact of treason, and operating an illegal organisation	Life imprisonment	15 years imprisonment
44. Colonel J. Isa	Conspiracy to commit treason, and concealment of treason	Acquitted	N/A
45. Ms Titilayo Ajanaku[3]*	Unknown charges	Acquitted	N/A
46. Adisa Akinloye[4]*	Unknown charges	Acquitted	N/A

47.	Yinka Johnson*	Unknown charges	Acquitted	N/A
48.	Abba Muazu*	Unknown charges	Acquitted	N/A
49.	Akin Ogunnola[5]*	Unknown charges	Acquitted	N/A
50.	Folorunsho Sangoleye*	Unknown charges	Acquitted	N/A
51.	JO Soremi*	Unknown charges	Acquitted	N/A

*Civilian

1997 Coup Trial—Sentences

	Name	Offence	Sentence
1.	Lt-General Oladipo Diya	Treason, and conspiracy to commit treason	Death
2.	Major-General Abdulkarim Adisa	Treason, and conspiracy to commit treason	Death
3.	Major-General Tajudeen Olanrewaju	Treason, and conspiracy to commit treason	Death
4.	Colonel Yakubu Bako	Illegal importation of firearms and receiving gratification	18 years' and 5 years' concurrent imprisonment
5.	Colonel Edwin Jando	Concealment of treason	Life imprisonment
6.	Lt-Colonel Olu Akiode[6]	Treason, and conspiracy to commit treason	Death

#	Name	Charges	Sentence
7.	Lt-Colonel Ibrahim Yakasai	Conspiracy to commit theft	28 years imprisonment
8.	Major Oluwaseun Fadipe	Treason, and conspiracy to commit treason	Death
9.	Major Bilyaminu M Mohammed[7]	Treason, conspiracy to commit treason, breach of trust, conspiracy to commit breach of trust, drafting false documents	20 years' imprisonment
10.	Lance Corporal Galadima Tanko	Theft	2 years imprisonment
11.	Adebola Adebanjo*	Treason, and conspiracy to commit treason	Death
12.	Isaiah Adebowale*	Accessory after the fact of treason	Life imprisonment
13.	Ojeniyi Ademola*	Theft	2 years' imprisonment
14.	Muktar Maidabino*	Conspiracy to commit theft, and receiving stolen property	5 years' imprisonment
15.	Niran Malaolu*[8]	Concealment of treason	Life imprisonment
16.	Sola Soile*	Treason, and conspiracy to commit treason	Life imprisonment
17.	Colonel Daniel Akintonde	Unknown charges	Acquitted
18.	Colonel Emmanuel Shoda	Unknown charges	Acquitted
19.	Major KA Yusuf Isiaku[9]	Unknown charges	Acquitted
20.	Warrant Officer Coker Oladosun	Unknown charges	Acquitted
21.	Staff Sergeant Moses Eni	Accessory after the fact of treason	Acquitted
22.	Corporal Eddie Egbunu	Treason, and conspiracy to commit treason	Acquitted

23. Corporal Ibrahim Kontagora	Treason, and conspiracy to commit treason	Acquitted
24. Lt-Commander DA Soetan[10]	Theft	Acquitted
25. Deputy Superintendent of Police Bawa Macindo	Accessory after the fact of treason	Acquitted
26. Owatimehin Abimbola*	Unknown charges	Acquitted
27. Musa Adede*	Accessory after the fact of treason	Acquitted
28. Ojeniyi Ademola*	Theft	Acquitted
29. Ms Halima Bawa*	Receiving stolen property	Acquitted
30. Iliyasu Mohammed*	Accessory after the fact of treason	Acquitted
31. Professor Femi Odekunle*	Unknown charges	Acquitted
32. Ibrahim Musa Ogar*	Unknown charges	Acquitted
33. Yomi Tokoya*	Sedition	Acquitted

*Civilian

APPENDIX 4

Military Officers Retired by President Obasanjo In 1999

Rank and Name	Former Position
1. Major-General Leo Ajiborisha[1]	Military Governor of Osun State
2. Major-General Samuel Omlago Ango	Sole-Administrator of the Nigeria Customs Service
3. Major-General Patrick Aziza	Minister of Commerce and Tourism
4. Major-General Idris Garba	Military Governor of Benue and Kano States, and Minister of Works and Housing
5. Major-General Joshua Madaki	Military Governor of Plateau State
6. Major-General Bashir Salihi Magashi	Military Governor of Sokoto State
7. Major-General Abdul-One Mohammed	Military Governor of Borno State
8. Major-General Garba Ali Mohammed	Military Governor of Niger State
9. Major-General Abdullahi Sarki Mukhtar	Military Governor of Kaduna and Katsina States
10. Brigadier-General Yusuf Abubakar	Sole Administrator of the Federal Housing Authority
11. Brigadier-General Sule Ahman	Military Administrator of Enugu State

12. Brigadier-General Ibrahim Aliyu — Military Administrator of Jigawa State

13. Brigadier-General Bassey Asuquo — Military Administrator of Delta State

14. Brigadier-General Ernest Attah — Military Administrator of Anambra State

15. Brigadier-General Salihu Tunde Bello — Military Administrator of Kebbi State

16. Brigadier-General Samaila Bature Chamah — Military Administrator of Katsina and Kebbi States

17. Brigadier-General Cletus Komena Emein — Military Administrator of Niger State

18. Brigadier-General Lawal Ja'afaru Isah — Military Administrator of Kaduna State

19. Brigadier-General Aliyu Kama — Military Governor of Plateau State

20. Brigadier-General Fidelis Makka — Military Governor of Benue State

21. Brigadier-General Mohammed Buba Marwa — Military Administrator of Lagos State

22. Brigadier-General Yakubu Mu'azu — Military Administrator of Sokoto State

23. Brigadier-General Dominic Oneya — Military Administrator of Benue State

24. Brigadier-General Olagunsoye Oyinlola — Military Administrator of Lagos State

25. Brigadier-General John Yeri — Military Governor of Edo State

26. Colonel Bzigu Afakirya — Military Administrator of Kogi State

27. Colonel Usman Ahmed — Military Administrator of Kaduna State

28. Colonel Daniel Akintonde — Military Administrator of Osun State

29. Colonel Hameed Ali — Military Administrator of Kaduna State

30. Colonel Anthony Amebo — Military Administrator of Kogi State

31. Colonel Theophilus Bamigboye — Military Administrator of Osun State

32. Colonel John Dungs — Military Administrator of Delta State
33. Colonel Moses Fasanya — Military Administrator of Ondo State
34. Colonel Dauda Musa Komo — Military Administrator of Rivers State
35. Colonel Aminu Kontagora — Military Administrator of Kano State
36. Colonel Mohammed Mana — Military Administrator of Plateau State
37. Colonel Musa Mohammed — Military Administrator of Yobe State
38. Colonel Anthony Obi — Military Administrator of Abia State
39. Colonel Peter Ogar — Military Administrator of Kwara State
40. Colonel Aina Joseph Owoniyi — Military Administrator of Taraba State
41. Colonel Habibu Idris Shuaibu — Military Administrator of Niger State
42. Colonel Musa Shehu — Military Administrator of Plateau State
43. Colonel Ahmed Usman — Military Administrator of Oyo State
44. Colonel Jibril Bala Yakubu — Military Administrator of Zamfara State
45. Colonel Tanko Zubairu — Military Administrator of Imo State
46. Lt-Colonel Joseph Akaagerger — Military Administrator of Katsina State
47. Lt-Colonel Mohammed Bawa — Military Administrator of Gombe State
48. Lt. Colonel Ahmadu Garba Hussaini — Military Administrator of Adamawa State
49. Lt-Colonel Abubakar Maimalari[2] — Military Administrator of Jigawa State
50. Lt-Colonel Bawa Mande — Military Administrator of Nasarawa State

51. Lt-Colonel Paul Obi — Military Administrator of Bayelsa State
52. Lt. Colonel Mohammed Abdulsalam Onuka — Military Administrator of Edo State
53. Lt-Colonel Abdulrasheed Shekoni — Military Administrator of Jigawa and Kwara States
54. Rear-Admiral Afolabi Afolahan — Military Administrator of Taraba State
55. Rear-Admiral Oladehinde Joseph — Military Governor of Ogun State
56. Rear-Admiral Sunday Olukoya — Military Administrator of Ondo State
57. Rear-Admiral Adetoye Sode — Military Governor of Oyo State
58. Commodore Emmanuel Acholonu — Military Governor of Katsina State
59. Commodore James Aneke — Military Administrator of Imo State
60. Commodore Temi Ejoor — Military Governor of Abia and Enugu States
61. Commodore Amadi Ikwechegh — Military Governor of Imo State
62. Commodore Anthony Oguguo — Military Governor of Imo State
63. Commodore Kayode Olofinmoyin — Military Administrator of Ogun State
64. Navy Captain Adedurotimi Adeusi — Military Administrator of Akwa Ibom State
65. Navy Captain Adewunmi Agbaje — Military Administrator of Enugu State
66. Navy Captain Walter Feghabo — Military Administrator of Delta State
67. Navy Captain Joe Kalu-Igboamah — Military Administrator of Adamawa State
68. Navy Captain Omoniyi Olubolade — Military Administrator of Bayelsa State
69. Navy Captain Anthony Onyearugbulem — Military Administrator of Edo and Ondo States
70. Navy Captain Christopher Osondu — Military Administrator of Cross River State
71. Navy Captain Rasheed Raji — Military Administrator of Bauchi and Sokoto States

72. Navy Captain Anthony Udofia — Military Administrator of Osun State

73. Navy Captain Atanda Yusuf — Military Administrator of Ekiti State

74. Air Vice Mashal Gregory Agboneni — Military Governor of Adamawa and Cross River States

75. Air Vice-Marshal Frank Ajobena[3] — Military Administrator of Abia State

76. Air Commodore Ibrahim Dada — Military Administrator of Borno State

77. Air Commodore Peter Gana — Managing Director of Nigeria Airways

78. Air Commodore Baba Iyam — Military Administrator of Edo and Kwara States

79. Air Commodore Ibrahim Kefas — Military Administrator of Delta State

80. Air Commodore Ndong Essiet Nkanga — Military Governor of Akwa Ibom State

81. Air Commodore Abubakar Salihu — Military Governor of Adamawa State

82. Group Captain John Ebiye — Military Administrator of Akwa Ibom State

83. Group Captain Sam Ewang — Military Administrator of Ogun and Rivers States

84. Group Captain Rufai Garba — Military Administrator of Sokoto State

85. Group Captain Lawal Haruna — Military Administrator of Rivers State

86. Group Captain John Ben-Kalio — Military Administrator of Yobe State

87. Group Captain Joe Orji — Military Administrator of Gombe State

88. Wing Commander Adamu Mshelia — Military Administrator of Bauchi State

89. Wing Commander EU Ukaegbu — Military Administrator of Anambra State

90. Assistant Inspector General of Police Dabo Aliyu — Military Administrator of Yobe State

91. Assistant Inspector General of   Military Administrator of Ebonyi
    Police Simeon Oduoye   and Niger States
92. Assistant Inspector General of   Military Administrator of Oyo
    Police Amen Oyakhire   and Taraba States
93. Commissioner of Police Mustapha   Military Administrator of
    Ismail   Adamawa State

NOTES

1. CHILDREN OF ODUDUWA

1. The title of a book on the Babangida years edited by Larry Diamond, Anthony Kirk-Greene and Oyeyele Oyediran.
2. Author's interview with former OPC secretary-general Kayode Ogundamisi.
3. Awofeso, 1990, p. 286.
4. Awofeso, 1990, p. 285.
5. Awofeso, 1990, p. 286.
6. Faruk, 2006, p. 363.
7. Awofeso, 1990, p. 287.
8. Awofeso, 1990, p. 287.
9. *Washington Post*, August 17, 1980.
10. *Tribune*, May 9, 2008.
11. Minutes of Afenifere Central Working Committee, quoted in Adebanwi, 2014, p. 131.

2. STEPPING ASIDE

1. *Daily Trust*, February 16, 2014.
2. Yar'Adua, 2004, p. 225.
3. *Daily Trust*, February 16, 2014.
4. Nwabueze, 1994, p. 8.
5. General Sani Abacha and Air Vice-Marshal Nura Imam.
6. Nwabueze, 1994, p. 76.

3. 82 DAYS

1. *New York Times*, August 27, 1993.
2. Such as Decree 2 of 1984: State Security (Detention of Persons) Decree, Decree 29 of 1993: Treason and Treasonable Offences Decree, Decree 35 of 1993: Offensive

Publications (Proscription) Decree, Decree 48 of 1993: Newspapers etc. (Proscription and Prohibition from Circulation) Decree.

3. Nwabueze, 1994, p. 60.

4. Author's interview with Major-General Williams.

5. *Daily Trust*, February 16, 2014.

6. Agbese, 2007, p. 58.

7. Economic Community of West African States Monitoring Group.

8. Ministerial titles were changed to 'secretary' in the ING.

9. *Tell*, September 20, 1993.

10. *Newswatch*, April 11 1994: 'The Abacha Coup: Our Original Plan'.

11. The others retired were Brigadier-Generals Anthony Ukpo, Ahmed Daku, SL Teidi, Colonels Abdulmumuni Aminu, Yohana Madaki, AN Sabo, Lt-Colonels JE Nyiam, I Nnonah, Major AM Mohammed and Captain Suleiman.

12. *Newswatch*, November 29, 1993.

13. *Newswatch*, November 29, 1993.

14. Alli, 2002, p. 292.

15. *Newswatch*, April 11, 1994.

16. *Newswatch*, November 29, 1993.

17. *Newswatch*, November 29, 1993.

18. Yar'Adua, 2004, p. 231.

19. *Newswatch*, November 29, 1993.

20. *Newswatch*, June 20, 1994, p. 18.

21. *Tell*, June 13, 1994.

22. Omoruyi, 1999, p. 248.

23. Some reports claim that the gendarmes fired shots and one person was killed.

24. Constitution of the Federal Republic of Nigeria (Suspension and Modification Repeal) Decree 59 of 1993.

25. Interim National Government (Basic Constitutional Provisions) Decree 1993.

26. Akinsanya retired in 2006.

27. Abiola, 1998, p. 15.

28. *TheNews*, October 18, 1998.

29. Ibid.

30. The reference to Dogonyaro may be an error, as Dogonyaro retired nearly two months prior to Akinsanya's ruling.

31. Interview with Bola Tinubu in *TheNews*, October 18, 1998.

32. Orji, 2003, p. 130.

33. *Newswatch*, November 29, 1993.

34. Abubakar retired in 2017 after 35 years of service at the NTA.

35. Akinjide and Elias, 1988, p. 114.

36. Alli, 2002, p. 220.

4. THE KHALIFA

1. Bode Oluwo.
2. Babatope, 2000, p. 105.
3. Fayemi, 2005, p. 74.
4. Author's interview with Major-General Williams.
5. Alli, 2002, p. 295.
6. His father is an Ebira from Koton-Karfi, and his mother is Oworo (a group linked to the Yorubas) from Kogi State.
7. *Vanguard*, November 27, 2016.
8. *Christian Science Monitor*, December 3, 1993.
9. *Tell*, December 6, 1993, p. 16.
10. *Newswatch*, April 25, 1994.
11. Omoruiyi, 1999.
12. *This Day*, January 14, 2001.
13. Kirk-Greene in UK *Independent*, June 10, 1998.
14. Straight Talk with Kadaria, https://www.youtube.com/watch?v=h-vWxrspj8U& feature=youtu.be&a (accessed October 14, 2017).
15. Currently the emir of Zuru.
16. Bello's son Abubakar is currently the governor of Niger State.
17. Former head of state General Murtala Muhammed is also an alumnus of Rumfa College.
18. Their sons were Ibrahim, Mohammed, Sadiq, Abba, Abdullahi, Mahmud, and Mustapha (who is the youngest and was born after Abacha became head of state), and their daughters are Zainab, Rakiya, and Gumsu.
19. Author's interview with Lieutenant Aloysius Akpuaka.
20. Maier, 2000, p. 62.
21. Those close to Abacha and within Nigeria knew exactly what he was doing at the guest house. His alleged activities at the guest house are outside the scope of this book.
22. Maier, 2000, p. 67.
23. Personal communication with a Nigerian soldier.
24. Omoruyi, 1999, p. 165.

5. HE SAID SHE SAID

1. *Guardian*, Saturday, April 3, 2004.
2. *Tell*, June 13, 1994.
3. Text of letter from Kingibe to Abiola, extracts in *Tell* magazine, September 26, 1994.
4. Ajasin, 2003, p. 500.
5. *Guardian*, Saturday, April 3, 2004.

6. Onagoruwa, 2006, p. 16.
7. Alli, 2002, p. 296.
8. Ajasin, 2003, p. 500.
9. Ihonvbere, 1996, p. 205.
10. *Newswatch*, May 9, 1994.
11. Alli, 2002, p. 285.
12. Author's interview with Major Aloysius Akpuaka.
13. Mark's younger brother was also an army officer and an instructor at the Command and Staff College in Jaji.
14. *Newswatch*, April 11 1994.
15. *Newswatch*, March 14 1994.
16. *Newswatch*, April 25 1994, p. 15.
17. *Newswatch*, May 9 1994.

6. CONFRONTATION

1. *TheNews*, October 18, 1998.
2. His 70th birthday was only two months away when NADECO was formed.
3. *Newswatch*, June 20 1994, p. 11.
4. *Newswatch*, June 13 1994.
5. *Newswatch*, June 6 1994, p. 15.
6. *Newswatch*, June 13 1994.
7. *Newswatch*, June 13 1994.
8. *Newswatch*, June 20 1994, p. 11.
9. Newswatch June 13 1994.
10. *Newswatch*, June 29 1994.
11. *Newswatch*, June 29 1994, p. 18.
12. *Newswatch*, June 6 1994.
13. *Newswatch*, June 29 1994, p. 12.
14. Text of address by Diya during his meeting with traditional rulers and elders on June 8, 1994. *Tell* magazine, June 20, 1994.
15. *The News*, March 9 1999.

7. ENOUGH IS ENOUGH

1. *PM News*, March 4 2002.
2. Ajasin, 2003, p. 503.
3. 'The Drama of Abiola's Death', *This Day*, July 5 2008.
4. Armed robbers shot and seriously wounded Oyenuga in the face and stomach in 1998 (in Onikoyi Street in Surulere, Lagos). Oyenuga survived after spending several months in hospital and surgery which left his face badly scarred.
5. *PM News*, March 2002.

6. *Tempo*, June 20 1996.
7. The NLC vacillated and periodically joined, then withdrew from the strike.
8. Onagoruwa, 2006, p. 88.
9. *Daily Post*, August 5 2017.
10. Abiola's wife Hamidat Doyinsola Abiola was the managing director of the newspaper.
11. The former sultan of Sokoto, Alhaji Ibrahim Dasuki, was Uwais's father-in-law.
12. *This Day*, June 6 2006.
13. Onagoruwa, 2006, p. 94.
14. Yar'Adua, 2004, p. 227.
15. *The Sun*, Monday, July 12 2004.
16. *PM News*, April 3 2012.
17. *The News*, March 9 1999.
18. Onagoruwa, 2006, p. 178.

8. THE 'PHANTOM COUP'

1. District leader of Katsina.
2. Yar'Adua, 2004, p. 36.
3. Yar'Adua, 2004, p. 92.
4. *Guardian*, February 17 2008.
5. Interview with Binta Yar'Adua in *Tell* Magazine, July 3, 2000, pp. 14–17.
6. *Newswatch*, March 14 1994.
7. *Newswatch*, May 9 1994.
8. Alli, 2002, p. 332.
9. Shagari, 2001, p. 459.
10. Shagari, 2001, p. 453.
11. Ikoku, 1985, p. 4.
12. *Pointblanknews*, January 25 2008.
13. *Newswatch*, 29, 1–13, 1998.
14. Colonel Nathaniel N Madza and Brigadier-General Momoh Lawani Yesufu were also members of the SIP.
15. He also later became the field commander of the Nigerian-led ECOMOG peacekeeping force in Liberia, and in 2006 became the *orodje* (king) of Okpe Kingdom in his native Delta State.
16. Comments by Mujakperuo during the HRVIC in 2000. Reported in *Newswatch*, December 4, 2000.
17. *Tell*, June 28 1999.
18. *Tell*, June 28 1999.
19. Ajayi, 2010, p. 103.
20. *This Day*, April 1 2001.
21. Nyiam and Ogboru were still wanted for their roles in the 1990 coup.

22. Charles-Obi died in 2014.
23. She died on Wednesday January 30th 2008 (aged 47).
24. Idehenre was speaking at the HRVIC. Excerpts reproduced in *The Guardian*, September 11, 2001.
25. Address delivered on Tuesday August 1 1995 at a reception organised for state representatives at the National Constitutional Conference. Quoted in *The News*, August 21, 1995, p. 15.
26. *Tell*, June 29, 1998.
27. Obasanjo, 2015, e-book location 7846.
28. Panafrican News Agency, November 21, 2000. He was speaking at the HRVIC.

9. THE OGONI THIRTEEN

1. The death sentence was later commuted when Boro was released from prison and agreed to fight for Nigeria during the civil war.
2. The leaders of the Eleme clan (incuding its traditional ruler Ngei O Ngei) declined to sign the Bill of Rights. The Eleme have at times sought to maintain a distinct identity separate from the Ogoni.
3. Kobani's son Kenneth served as the minister of state for industry, trade and investment in the cabinet of President Jonathan. He later became secretary to the Rivers State government in June 2015.
4. Timothy Naakuu Paul Birabi. He was a member of the Eastern Region House of Representatives and had a Moses-like reputation as an Ogoni leader.
5. The son of TN Paul Birabi, the Ogoni hero.
6. Lt-General Mohammed is sometimes referred to as Aliyu Mohammed Gusau (Gusau is his home town) as a way of distinguishing him from the other Aliyu Mohammed who served in the government at the same time.
7. This seemed to be a reaction to MOSOP's complaint that Shell was treating Ogonis and conduting oil exploration in a destructive manner that it did not carry out elsewhere.
8. *Newswatch*, November 28 1999.
9. *The Week*, November 27 1995, p. 12.
10. Maier, 2000, p. 103.
11. Letter from Saro-Wiwa to Kobani dated December 15, 1994. Quoted in Kukah, 2011, pp. 129–30.
12. Maier, 2000, p. 103.
13. 'Wasting operation' was a veiled euphemism for killing.
14. Reproduced in Maier, 2000, p. 107.
15. Maier, 2000, p. 106.
16. The Ogoni have different dialects.
17. The fact that the bodies were burned led the victims' families to claim that they were 'cooked and eaten' by the mob.

18. Newswatch, June 6, 1994.
19. Badey, Saro-Wiwa and Kobani were alumni of the University of Ibadan.
20. *Newswatch*, June 6, 1994, p. 24.
21. Several other Zuru officers had served in military regimes—including Ishaya Bamaiyi and his brother Major-General Musa Bamaiyi (former chairman of the NDLEA), Major-Generals Sani Sami (now the emir of Zuru), Mohammed Magoro and Tanko Ayuba.
22. Komo's wife Helen had paid a condolence visit to Albert Badey's widow.
23. Auta became chief judge of the Federal High Court in 2011.
24. Arikpo later became chief justice of Rivers State. He later described the trial as one of the worst experiences of his life. He died in July 2007.
25. In August 2015, President Buhari appointed Ali as the comptroller-general of the Nigerian Customs Service.
26. Kpuinen Bera, Fogbara Afa, Saturday Dobee, Monday Dowin, Felix Nwate, Nordu Eawo, Paul Levura, Daniel Joseph Kpante, Michael Vizor, Daniel Gbokoo, Albert Kagbara.
27. Letam Wiwa was chief security officer to former chief of army staff Major-General Chris Alli.
28. *The Week*, November 27, 1995.
29. *Washington Post*, January 25, 1996.
30. Memorandum of Provisional Ruling Council meeting, November 8 1995. Excerpts reproduced in *Premium Times*, December 12 2012.
31. Kolawole, 2004, p. 156.
32. *Newswatch*, June 6, 1994, p. 25.

10. MURDER INC.

1. Alli, 2002, p. 337.
2. Formerly known as Radio Freedom.
3. BBC Newsnight, December 1994.
4. *Newswatch*, June 20, 1994.
5. Alli, 2002, p. 346.
6. Alli, 2002, p. 337.
7. The Strike Force was formed in January 1995 and began operations in May 1995. It is not clear whether the Special Bodyguards were formed and became operational at the same time.
8. Personal communication with a former Nigerian government employee.
9. *Newswatch*, July 13 1998.
10. Alli, 2002 p. 355.
11. He was also a member of the Action Group delegation at the 1957 constitutional conference in London which preceded Nigeria's independence.

12. The Babangida government had pardoned 11 soldiers detained for involvement in the 1990 coup, but security agents continued to detain them until 1994.
13. Onagoruwa, 2006, p. 178. The April 1990 coup plotters tried to kill Abacha.
14. Author's interview with former OPC secretary-general Kayode Ogundamisi, 2018.
15. *This Day*, July 18, 2008.
16. Ajayi, 2010, p. 119.
17. Yar'Adua, 2004, pp. 282–3.
18. Yar'Adua, 2004, p. 283.
19. Ibid.
20. Yar'Adua, 2004, p. 294.
21. Soyinka, 2006, p. 428.
22. Realnewsmagazine.net, July 17, 2015, http://realnewsmagazine.net/featured/dss-is-hiding-suicide-bombers-tsav/ (accessed April 23 2018).
23. *Vanguard*, January 24, 2001. Although the article did not name the officer, it mentioned that he joined the army in 1968, fought the civil war and served as the chief military information officer of the ECOMOG peacekeeping mission from 1992 to 1993.
24. *This Day*, December 9 2000.

11. THE WEEPING GENERALS

1. *The News*, March 8, 1999.
2. Babatope, 2000, page 14.
3. Alli, 2002, p. 357.
4. Alli, 2002, p. 358.
5. Alli, 2002, p. 357.
6. Alli, 2002, p. 358.
7. *The News*, March 8, 1999.
8. *Vanguard*, December 13, 2000.
9. Adisa also has Fulani ancestry.
10. It is not clear which of Adisa's houses this meeting took place in.
11. *The News*, March 8, 1999.
12. *Vanguard*, December 13, 2000.
13. Bamaiyi, 2014, p. 50.
14. A member of the Strike Force later testified that Shuaibu was involved in the attempted murder of Alex Ibru in 1996.
15. *This Day*, December 15 2000.
16. *This Day*, December 15 2000.
17. *Tell*, August 31 1998.
18. *Tell*, August 31 1998.
19. A Yoruba phrase which is used in Nigeria to refer to the 'Boss'. Its literal translation is 'the Big One'.

20. Akaagerger was a Tiv and a former military governor of Katsina State. He was later elected a senator for the Benue North senatorial zone (2004–7). Other SIP members included Brigadier-General Yusuf Abubakar, Navy Commodore Adeyemi Ambrose Afolayan, and Group Captain Abdulrahman Suleiman.

21. Shode, Keshinro and Akintonde were released after being interrogated.

22. *PM News*, November 6 1998.

23. Sabo had a son in the NDA who had sickle cell anemia and later died. He also had another son who was a student at the Nigerian Military School.

24. *West Africa*, January 12–18, 1998, p. 21.

25. *The News*, January 12 1998.

26. Economic Community of West African States Monitoring Group.

27. *Daily Telegraph*, July 29, 1997.

28. Malu, 2013, page 55.

29. He later became a major-general and commander of the Nigerian Army Ordnance Corps. He died in a plane crash on September 17, 2006. Two other members of the tribunal (Lemu and Braimah) died in the same plane crash.

30. Malu, 2013, pp. 57–8.

31. Professor Odekunle, in *Tell*, August 31, 1998.

32. *Tell*, August 31, 1998.

33. *The News*, 8 March 1999.

34. Malu was speaking at the HRVIC in 2000.

35. *The News*, March 8 1999

36. *The News*, December 21, 2000.

37. *The News*, March 8 1999.

38. *Vanguard*, December 14 2000.

39. Malu, 2013, p. 60.

12. FIVE LEPROUS FINGERS

1. *West Africa*, February 17–23 1997, pp. 267–8.

2. *Africa Confidential*, November 7 1997.

3. *Economist*, January 8 1998.

4. *Washington Post*, January 25 1996.

5. *West Africa*, March 15–29, 1998.

6. Agbakoba helped establish Nigeria's first human rights group in October 1987, when he and other young lawyers founded the Civil Liberties Organisation.

7. James Ibori (who later became governor of Delta State) was also a member of the GDM.

8. Okwesilieze Nwodo in *Vanguard*, July 25 2009.

9. Ciroma was a former governor of the Central Bank of Nigeria and also a former secretary of the National Party of Nigeria; Lar was the former governor of Plateau

State; Lamido was a former member of the People's Redemption Party; Musa was a former governor of Kaduna State; Rimi was a former governor of Kano State; and Joda was a respected former civil servant. Other members of the G18 included retired Colonel Abubakar Dangiwa Umar, Dr Suleiman Kumo and Dr Usman Bugaje.

10. *Washington Post*, January 25 1996.
11. *Newswatch*, December 19 1994.
12. *Africa Confidential*, February 6 1998.
13. Mark Doyle, 'Farewell to the General', BBC, May 1 2000, http://news.bbc.co.uk/2/hi/programmes/from_our_own_correspondent/732491.stm.
14. *Africa Confidential*, special report, April 1998.
15. Khobe was wounded during the Sierra Leone mission but survived until he died from an illness in 2000.
16. Reproduced in *Newswatch*, July 13 1998.
17. Inter Press News Agency, http://www.ipsnews.net/1998/03/politics-us-clinton-opens-door-to-nigerias-abacha/ (accessed August 10, 2018).

13. A COUP FROM HEAVEN

1. *Daily Post*, June 19 2017.
2. Soluade, 2013, e-book location 944.
3. *Vanguard*, April 3 2010.
4. Pulse News, September 6, 2017, https://www.pulse.ng/news/local/what-you-probably-do-not-know-about-gen-abacha-id7266371.html (accessed August 22, 2018).
5. Wali was from a prominent family. Both of his parents were Islamic scholars. One of his brothers (Brigadier Abbas Wali) was a senior army officer and former adjutant-general of the Nigerian army.
6. Author's interview with Dr Wali.
7. Author's interview with Dr Wali.
8. Some sources claim that al-Mustapha ordered the arrest of some of Abacha's domestic staff as suspects in his death.
9. Sources differ on whether it was Coomasie or Gwarzo that informed the senior officers that Abacha had died. Bamaiyi said it was Coomasie, while Gidado Idris claims it was Gwarzo.
10. *Vanguard*, April 3 2010.
11. *Tell*, 25, June 22 1998.
12. Soluade, 2013, e-book location 2988.
13. Two years later, Useni admitted being the last person to see Abacha alive, but then tragicomically qualified his comment by abruptly delaring: 'but that doesn't mean I killed him!'

14. *Newswatch*, July 13 1998.
15. Also known as Lelna.
16. Haladu died a few weeks after Abacha.
17. *Vanguard*, April 3 2010.
18. Bamaiyi claims that he made this recommendation while Gidado Idris claims that it was Useni.
19. A reliable source informed me that, contrary to press rumours, these illnesses did not include cirrhosis of the liver.
20. *Vanguard*, December 16, 2000.
21. *Daily Post*, June 19, 2017.
22. *Sunday Trust*, Sunday, August 23, 2009
23. *Tell*, June 7, 1999.
24. The other released detainees were Christine Anyanwu, Beko Ransome-Kuti, Bola Ige (NADECO), Olabiyi Durojaiye (NADECO), Frank Ovie Kokori (NUPENG), Milton Dabibi (PENGASSAN leader), and Uwen Udoh (a labour union activist).
25. *Tell*, June 29, 1998.
26. Tinubu is a Muslim but still recognised the contribution of Christian associations.
27. *The Nation*, June 12, 2018.

14. DIVINE INTERVENTION

1. *Guardian*, July 17 1998.
2. Annan, 2012, p. 162.
3. Bamaiyi, 2014, pp. 77–9.
4. Texts of the Abiola letters were also tendered during the HRVIC in 2000.
5. Press conference of Annan, July 7 1998, http://www.un.org/press/en/1998/19980708.sgsm6634.html.
6. *Guardian*, July 3 1998.
7. *The Times*, July 3 1998.
8. Text from Abiola's detention diary. Quoted in *Tell*, July 20 1998.
9. Letter from Abiola to Rear-Admiral Akhigbe, June 1998.
10. Edewor later became a senator in Lagos State.
11. *Tell*, July 29 1998, p. 17.
12. Zadok's testimony at the Oputa Panel in 2001.
13. Zadok's testimony at the Oputa Panel in 2001.
14. Author's interview with Dr Wali.
15. Interview with Ambassador Pickering, BBC World Service, *Witness*, July 10 2015.
16. BBC World Service, *Witness*, July 10 2015.
17. BBC World Service, *Witness*, July 10 2015.
18. Author's interview with Dr Wali.

19. Zadok's testimony at the Oputa Panel in 2001.
20. Hafsat lived in Washington DC.
21. *The Times of London*, Thursday, July 9 1998.
22. Author's interview with Dr Wali.
23. Obasanjo, 2015, vol. 2, e-book location 110.
24. *Mail & Guardian*, July 9 1998.
25. *Tell*, July 20 1998.
26. *Mail & Guardian*, July 9 1998.
27. He also conducted autopsies on victims of the 1989 *Marchioness* boat disaster in England and on Rachel Nickell—a woman who was murdered in front of her infant son on Wimbledon Common in London in July 1992.
28. *Vanguard*, April 21 2017.
29. *Vanguard*, April 21 2017.
30. Author's interview with Dr Wali.
31. *The Times of London*, July 13 1998.
32. *Guardian*, Friday, July 10 1998.
33. Abiola was so close to the government that president Babangida attended Simbiat's funeral.
34. Maier, 2000, p. 72.
35. *West Africa*, July 6–26 1998, p. 585.
36. Dr Falomo in *Tempo*, June 20 1996.
37. Yar'Adua, 2004, p. 217.
38. Mustapha was speaking at his court trial in 2011.
39. *Tell*, July 20 1998.

15. NIGERIA INC.

1. St Jorre was an embedded reporter in Nigeria during the war and reported on it contemporaneously. He later admitted that he was also an undercover agent for MI6.
2. St Jorre, 1972, p. 407.
3. Dent, 1995, p. 129.
4. Aikhomu, quoted in Akindele, 2007, pp. 63–4.
5. Kendhammer, 2015, p. 158.
6. *Guardian* (Lagos), Monday, January 2, 2006.
7. *New African*, October 1998.
8. Kirk-Greene, 1971, vol. 1, p. 415.
9. *New African*, 35, November 1997.
10. *Mail & Guardian*, July 9 1998.
11. Colin Legum, in *Observer*, October 16 1966.
12. Maier, 2000, pp. 284–5.

13. *Financial Times*, Nigeria country report, 2000.
14. He was also the first Igbo to be promoted to major-general in 21 years.
15. Maier, 2000, p. 284.
16. *Tell*, November 14 1994.
17. Ibid.
18. Bello, 1962, p. 229.
19. Bello, 1962, p. 111.
20. *Proceedings of the General Conference on Review of the Constitution*, January 1950, p. 218.
21. Sule was the former minister of mines and power, and secretary to former Northern Region premier Ahmadu Bello.
22. *Tell*, November 14 1994.
23. *West Africa*, February 14–20, 1994.
24. *Newswatch*, May 9 1994.
25. Section 2(b), Decree 3 of 1994.
26. *Newswatch*, May 9 1994.
27. *West Africa*, February 14–20 1994.
28. Alli, 2002, p. 333.
29. Saraki has mixed Fulani and Yoruba ancestry.
30. The previous constitutions were the Clifford Constitution (1922), Richards Constitution (1946), Macpherson Constitution (1951), Lyttleton Constitution (1954), and the post-independence constitutions of 1963, 1979 and 1989.
31. Maier, 2000, p. 74.

16. END OF THE ROAD

1. Excerpts from a memorandum sent by Vice-Admiral Aduwo to Babangida dated May 1, 1986. Quoted in *Tell* magazine, June 27 1994, pp. 14–15.
2. Alli, 2002, p. 286.
3. Malu, 2013, pp. 53–4.
4. Air Vice-Marshal Idi Musa, and Major-Generals Chris Garuba and John Mark Inienger.
5. *The Times of London*, July 3, 1998.

17. POWER SHIFT

1. *Tell*, July 20 1998.
2. *The News*, October 26 1998.
3. *Tell*, June 28 1999.
4. Bello, 1962, p. 229.
5. Shagari, Babangida and Abacha.
6. *New African*, October 1998.

7. *Guardian*, July 17 1998.

8. Ibid.

9. Ironically one of the discredited people they objected to was a Yoruba politician, Lamidi Adedibu.

10. Afenifere's flirtation with the three main political groups, and Ige's background as a lawyer and sojourns through the three political groups, created the widespread impression that Ige drafted the constitution of all three parties (however, PDP members Sunday Awoniyi and Major-General David Jemibewon (retired) denied this).

11. Obasanjo, 2015, e-book location 663.

12. Obasanjo, 2015, e-book location 102.

13. *The Times of London*, July 7 1998.

14. *PM News*, November 6 1998.

15. Maier, 2000, p. 30.

16. *Africa Confidential*, February 19 1999.

17. *Tempo*, November 19 1998.

18. Carter Center, *Observing the 1998–99 Nigeria Elections*, p. 12.

19. A long, flowing and wide traditional garment.

18. UNCLE SEGE

1. Sege being a nickame for 'Segun', which is itself an abbrevation of his first name, Olusegun.

2. World Bank, https://data.worldbank.org/indicator/NY.GDP.PCAP.CD?locations=NG (accessed July 12, 2018).

3. Malu, 2013, p. 109.

4. *Africa Confidential*, June 11 1999.

5. Agbola, 2013, p. 20.

6. Malu, 2013, p. 109.

7. *Tell*, June 28 1999.

8. Momoh, 2000, p. 393.

9. *African Recorder*, 38, p. 56.

10. Novocaine is a painkiller.

11. *Africa Confidential*, October 13 2000.

12. *Newswatch*, November 6 2000.

13. *Vanguard*, December 14 2000.

14. Rogers is from Askira–Uba Local Government Area, an area whose residents include the Chibok, who came to global prominence in 2014 after several hundred schoolgirls were kidnapped by insurgents.

15. Yakubu later became the military administrator of Zamfara State.

16. Ribadu later became chairman of the Economic and Financial Crimes Commission (Nigeria's anti-corruption body).

17. Osinbajo is currently Nigeria's vice-president.
18. Three of Rewane's employees, Lucky Igbinovia, Elvis Irenuma and Effong Elemi Edu, were tried for his murder but the Lagos State High Court acquitted them in 2011. Five other defendants (Sylvester Iyasele, Saturday Egbeide, Ola Obanuso, Akeem Ali and Sunday Obanobi) died in prison while awaiting trial.

19. PEOPLE OF THE BOOK

1. The Hausa translation of this Arabic phrase is *Sarkin Musulmi* (King of the Muslims).
2. *Weekly Trust*, August 2, 2003.
3. Laitin, 1982, p. 427.
4. Afoweso, 1990, p. 286.
5. Laitin, 1982, pp. 417–18.
6. Laitin, 1982, p. 416.
7. *West Africa*, February 14–20 1994, p. 254.
8. *West Africa*, 1 2–18 December 1988.
9. Nigerian censuses no longer collect data regarding religious affiliation.
10. Pew Center, 2012.
11. Council for Foreign Relations, 2007.
12. Al Jazeera, April 13, 2013, https://www.youtube.com/watch?v=Cyjr2B5B8r8 (accessed January 7, 2018)
13. Only Indonesia, Pakistan, India and Bangladesh have more Muslims than Nigeria.
14. Gummi's stature loomed so large that even today many Nigerian Muslims errone-ously believe that he founded *Izala*.
15. Arabic for 'removing'.
16. Paden, 2002, p. 2.
17. Sometimes also transliterated as Hezbollah or Hizbullah.
18. Shagari, 2001, p. 324.
19. Akilu later became the director of military intelligence and a key member of Babangida's government.
20. Falola, 1998, p. 150.
21. Justice N Aniagolu (chairman), *Report of Tribunal of Inquiry on Kano Disturbances*.
22. *TheNews*, February 29, 2000.
23. Maier, 2000, p. 179.
24. The twelve northern states that adopted sharia are Bauchi, Borno, Gombe, Jigawa, Kaduna, Kano, Katsina, Kebbi, Niger, Sokoto, Yobe and Zamfara.
25. *TheNews*, February 29 2000.
26. *Financial Times*, 2000, Nigeria country report.
27. Teacher.
28. The deputy governor of Borno State also worshipped at this mosque.

29. The call to Islam—a form of proselytising.
30. *Financial Times*, May 22 2012.
31. http://www.nigerianbestforum.com/index.php?topic=40392.0;wap (accessed August 10,2018).
32. *Financial Times*, May 22 2012.
33. *New York Times*, May 14 2014.
34. Ibid.
35. Ibid.
36. Mohammed, 2014, p. 16.
37. They were trying to emulate the Prophet's migration to Medina.
38. Another account in the *New York Times* claims that Abubakar from Shekau village was one of the leaders of the Hijra group.
39. US Diplomatic cable, February 2004. Wikileaks: https://wikileaks.org/plusd/cables/04ABUJA183_a.html.
40. US Diplomatic cable, February 2004. Wikileaks: https://wikileaks.org/plusd/cables/04ABUJA183_a.html.
41. Named after the 12th-century Islamic scholar from whom they drew ideological inspiration.
42. The International Crisis Group (ICG) claims that the Borno State government donated 50 motorcycles to Yusufiyya, which they used to set up a motorcycle taxi business. ICG, 2014.
43. *Africa Confidential*, November 30, 2012.
44. Sheriff claims he terminated Foi's appointment, and some other accounts claim that Foi resigned in protest.
45. US Diplomatic cable, February 2004. Wikileaks: https://wikileaks.org/plusd/cables/04ABUJA183_a.html.
46. *Daily Independent*, May 24 2014.

20. BACK TO THE FUTURE

1. Including retired Admiral Murtala Nyako, Air Commodore Jonah Jang and Colonel Olagunsoye Oyinlola.
2. Watson and Barber, 2000, p. 66.

APPENDIX 2: NIGERIA'S LAST MILITARY GOVERNMENT

1. His father was Tiv and his mother was from Obudu in Cross River State.

APPENDIX 3: COUP SENTENCES

1. Died in prison. Was convicted of permitting others to meet with Gwadabe during his detention.
2. Ibrahim was a member of the SIP. He was arrested, tried, and convicted of being an accessory to treason after allegedly holding private conversations with Gwadabe.

3. A former local government chairman in Ogun State.
4. The 78-year-old former national chairman of the NPN.
5. A university lecturer.
6. Former military assistant to Olanrewaju.
7. Administrative officer at the presidency.
8. Editor of the *Diet* newspaper.
9. Former commanding officer, artillery depot, Abuja.
10. Staff officer (finance) to Diya.

APPENDIX 4: MILITARY OFFICERS RETIRED BY PRESIDENT OBASANJO IN 1999

1. He also served as Principal Staff Officer to General Abubakar.
2. The son of Brigadier Zakariya Maimalari, who was killed during Nigeria's first military coup in January 1966.
3. An Urhobo from a royal family. When Major-General Mujakperuo was crowned as the *orodje* of Okpe Kingdom in 2004, Ajobena unsuccessfully filed a court action to claim the throne from him.

BIBLIOGRAPHY

Abiola, Moshood Kashimawo Olawale. *Abiola Lives On! Quotable Quotes of M.K.O. Abiola (1937–1998)*. Pars Communications, Lagos, 1998.

Adebanwi, Wale. *Yoruba Elites and Ethnic Politics in Nigeria: Obafemi Awolowo and Corporate Agency*. Cambridge University Press, New York, 2014.

Agbese, Dan. *Newswatch Conversation with IBB*. Newswatch Books, Lagos, 2007.

Agbola, Colonel J.O. *Control of Large-Scale Civil Conflicts in Democratic Nigeria*. US Army War College, Carlisle Barracks, Pennsylvania, 17013, 2013.

Ajasin, Michael Adekunle. *Memoirs and Memories*. Ajasin Foundation, Lagos, 2003.

Ajayi, Gabriel. *End of the Road: The Travails of an Infantry Officer*. Sumob, Osogbo, 2010.

Akindele, R.A. *Federalism under General Babangida's Administration in Nigeria*. Malthouse Monographs on Africa, 2007, Numbers 1–3.

Akinjide, Richard, and Elias, Taslim. *Africa and the Development of International Law*. Martinus Nijhoff Publishers, Leiden, 1988.

Alli, Chris. *The Federal Republic of Nigeria Army: The Siege of a Nation*. Malthouse Press, Lagos, 2002.

Annan, Kofi. *Interventions: A Life in War and Peace*, Penguin, New York, 2012.

Awofeso, Abimbola. *MKO Abiola: To Make Whole Again*. Update Communications, Lagos, 1990.

Babatope, Ebenezer. *The Abacha Years: What Went Wrong?* Ebino Topsy, Lagos, 2000.

Bamaiyi, Ishaya. *Vindication of a General*. Daybis Limited, Ibadan, 2014.

Bello, Alhaji Sir Ahmadu. *My Life*. Cambridge University Press, Cambridge, 1962.

Carter Center. *Observing the 1998–99 Nigeria Elections*, https://www.cartercenter. org/documents/1152.pdf (accessed July 18, 2018)

Council for Foreign Relations. *Symposium on Religious Conflict in Nigeria: Contemporary Religious Dynamics in Nigeria, May 8, 2007*, https://www.cfr.org/ event/religious-conflict-nigeria-contemporary-religious-dynamics-nigeria-session-2 (accessed August 22, 2018)

BIBLIOGRAPHY

Dent, Martin. 'Ethnicity and Territorial Politics in Nigeria', in Smith, Graham (ed.), *Federalism: The Multiethnic Challenge*, Longman, London, 1995.

Falola, Toyin. *Violence in Nigeria: The Crisis of Religious Politics and Secular Ideologies*. University of Rochester Press, Rochester, New York, 1998.

Faruk, Usman. *From Farm House to Government House: Path of Destiny, Responsibility*. Amana Publishers, Zaria, 2006.

Fayemi, Kayode. *Out of the Shadows: Exile and the Struggle for Freedom and Democracy in Nigeria*. Centre for Democracy and Development, 2005.

Ihonvbere, Julius. 'Are Things Falling Apart? The Military and the Crisis of Democratisation in Nigeria'. *Journal of Modern African Studies*, 34, 2, June 1996, pp. 193–225.

Ikoku, Samuel Gomsu. *Nigeria's Fourth Coup d'Etat*. Fourth Dimension Publishers, Enugu, 1985.

International Crisis Group. *Curbing Violence in Nigeria (II): The Boko Haram Insurgency*. Africa Report No. 216, April 3, 2014.

Kendhammer, Brandon. 'Getting Our Piece of the National Cake: Consociational Power Sharing and Neopatrimonialism in Nigeria'. *Nationalism and Ethnic Politics*, 21, 2015, pp. 143–165.

Kirk-Greene, Anthony Hamilton Millard. *Crisis and Conflict in Nigeria: A Documentary Sourcebook* (volume 1). Oxford University Press, London, 1971.

Kirk-Greene, Anthony, Diamond, Larry, and Oyediran, Oyeleye. *Transition without End: Nigerian Politics and Civil Society under Babangida*. Lynne Rienner Publishers, Boulder, CO, 1997.

Kolawole, Dipo. *Nigeria's Foreign Policy since Independence: Trends, Phases and Changes*. Julius and Julius, Lagos, 2004.

Kukah, Matthew Hassan. *Witness to Justice: An Insider's Account of Nigeria's Truth Commission*. Bookcraft, Ibadan, 2011.

Laitin, David. 'The Sharia Debate and the Origins of Nigeria's Second Republic'. *Journal of Modern African Studies*, 20, 3, September 1982, pp. 411–430.

Maier, Karl. *This House Has Fallen: Midnight in Nigeria*. Public Affairs Books, New York. 2000.

Malu, Terver, and Oko, Okechukwu. *In the Name of Victor: Confronting Errors with the Truth*. AuthorHouse, Bloomington, 2013.

Mazrui, Ali A. *The Africans: A Triple Heritage*. BBC Publications, London, 1986.

Mohammed, Kyari. 'The Message and Methods of Boko Haram', in de Montclos, Marc-Antoine Pérouse (ed.), *Boko Haram: Islamism, Politics, Security and the State in Nigeria*. West African Politics and Society Series, 2, Leiden and Ibada: Africa Studies Centre and Institut Français de Recherche en Afrique, 2014, pp. 9–32.

Nwabueze, Ben. *Nigeria 93: The Political Crisis and Solutions*. Spectrum Books, Ibadan, 1994.

Obasanjo, O. *My Watch*. Amazon Kindle eBook, 2015.

BIBLIOGRAPHY

Omoruyi, Omo. *The Tale of June 12: The Betrayal of the Democratic Rights of Nigerians*. Press Alliance Network, London, 1999.

Onagoruwa, Olu. *A Rebel in General Abacha's Government*. Inspired Communication, Lagos, 2006.

Orji, Ogbonnaya. *Inside Aso Rock*. Spectrum Books, Ibadan, 2003.

Paden, J.N. 'Islam and Democratic Federalism in Nigeria'. *CSIS Africa Notes*, 8, March 2002, https://csis-prod.s3.amazonaws.com/s3fs-public/legacy_files/files/media/csis/pubs/anotes_0203.pdf (accessed July 18, 2018).

Pew Center. Religious Composition by Country, http://assets.pewresearch.org/wp-content/uploads/sites/11/2012/12/globalReligion-tables.pdf (accessed August 24, 2018).

Shagari, Shehu. *Beckoned to Serve*. Heinemann Educational Books, Ibadan, 2001.

Soluade, Babatunde. *Truth and Consequences*. Createspace, 2013 (Amazon Kindle e-book), 2014.

Soyinka, Wole. *You Must Set Forth at Dawn: A Memoir*. Random House, New York, 2006.

St Jorre, John de. *The Brothers' War: Biafra and Nigeria*. Houghton Mifflin, London, 1972

Watson, Patrick, and Barber, Benjamin. *The Struggle For Democracy*. Key Porter Books, Toronto, Canada, 2000.

Yar'Adua, Shehu Musa. *Yar'Adua: A Life of Service*. Shehu Musa Yar'Adua Foundation, Abuja, 2004.

Newspapers and Periodicals

Africa Confidential
African Guardian
African Recorder
Christian Science Monitor
Comet, The
Daily Independent
Daily Post
Daily Telegraph (London)
Daily Trust
Economist, The
Financial Times
Guardian, The (Lagos)
Guardian, The (London)
Mail & Guardian
Nation, The
New African

BIBLIOGRAPHY

New York Times
News, The
Newswatch
Observer
PM News
Pointblanknews.com
Premium Times
Sun, The
Sunday Trust
Tell
This Day
Tribune
Vanguard
Washington Post
Week, The
Weekly Trust
West Africa

INDEX

INDEX

INDEX